W9-AEW-677

The Savior Generals

BY THE SAME AUTHOR

The End of Sparta: A Novel
The Father of Us All
Warfare and Agriculture in Classical Greece
The Western Way of War
Hoplites (editor)
The Other Greeks
Fields Without Dreams
Who Killed Homer? (with John Heath)
The Wars of the Ancient Greeks
The Soul of Battle
The Land Was Everything
Bonfire of the Humanities (with John Heath and Bruce Thornton)
An Autumn of War
Carnage and Culture
Between War and Peace
Mexifornia
Ripples of Battle
A War like No Other
The Immigration Solution (with Heather MacDonald and Steven Malanga)
Makers of Ancient Strategy (editor)

The Savior Generals

How Five Great Commanders Saved Wars That Were Lost—from Ancient Greece to Iraq

VICTOR DAVIS HANSON

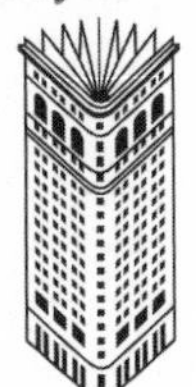

BLOOMSBURY PRESS
NEW YORK • LONDON • SYDNEY • NEW DELHI

Published by Bloomsbury Press, New York

All papers used by Bloomsbury Press are natural, recyclable products made from wood grown in well-managed forests. The manufacturing processes conform to the environmental regulations of the country of origin.

LIBRARY OF CONGRESS CATALOGING-IN-PUBLICATION DATA

Hanson, Victor Davis.
The savior generals : how five great commanders saved wars that were lost, from ancient Greece to Iraq / Victor Davis Hanson.—1st ed.
pages cm
Includes bibliographical references.
ISBN 978-1-60819-163-5
1. Generals—Biography. 2. Command of troops—History. 3. Themistocles, ca. 524-ca. 459 B.C.—Military leadership. 4. Belisarius, ca. 505-565—Military leadership. 5. Sherman, William T. (William Tecumseh), 1820-1891—Military leadership. 6. Ridgway, Matthew B. (Matthew Bunker), 1895-1993—Military leadership. 7. Petraeus, David Howell—Military leadership. I. Title.

UB200.H36 2013
355.0092'2—dc23

First Edition 2013

1 3 5 7 9 10 8 6 4 2

Typeset by Westchester Book Group
Printed and bound in the U.S.A. by Thomson-Shore, Inc. Dexter, Michigan

To Pauline, William, and Susannah
Servata fides cineri

Contents

Prologue: Saving Lost Wars

What Wins Wars?

How are wars won or lost? Through sheer luck? Surprise? Morale? Material resources? Or does the outcome of conflict hinge on the advantages of superior manpower? Are more brilliant strategic planning and tactical protocol the keys to success? Then again, do armies win through lethal cutting-edge technology—more accurate bombs, deadlier shells, and longer-range missiles? And do all these criteria shift and turn and hinge on how we define war—as conventional, asymmetrical, counterinsurgent, terrorist, or the like?

All these considerations in varying degrees have always determined military success. Hernán Cortés's destruction of the Aztec Empire (1519–21) was predicated largely on possessing better arms. The vastly outnumbered but well-led Spanish conquistadors had access to harquebuses, artillery, steel swords, metal breastplates and helmets, horses, and crossbows, while the Aztecs did not. Spanish technological monopoly allowed a few hundred mounted knights to help enlist indigenous allies and end an empire of millions in roughly two years.

The industrial might of the United States often ensured that American forces in the distant Pacific during the Second World War simply had far more food, weapons, medical care, and military infrastructure than did the imperial Japanese in their own environs. Nazi Germany's

Wehrmacht was usually outnumbered through much of 1944–45; nevertheless, its superior machine guns, artillery, and armor allowed spirited Germans to continue fighting when most other armies would have given up, in the face of terrible strategic decision making, supply shortages, an immoral cause, and superior enemy numbers.

Generals Still Matter

Yet on rare occasions, generals and the leadership of single individuals can still matter more than these seemingly larger inanimate forces. There are more than nine hundred admirals and generals in the U.S. military. They are not often considered to be in a position, under the protocols of postmodern conflict, to alter radically the course of battlefield action—especially given the role of twenty-first-century technology. Yet among them are a few rare military geniuses and inspired leaders who, when the planets line up, can still, by their own genius or lack of it, themselves either win or lose wars. Winston Churchill was not altogether wrong when he said of Admiral John Jellicoe's command of the British Grand Fleet in the First World War that he "was the only man on either side who could lose the war in an afternoon."

So often we forget the power of individuals in the anonymous age of high technology and massive bureaucracies. Today, machines and regulations seem to lessen the influence of humans. They lull us into thinking that events transpire organically, almost without human agency. Yet frequently the fate of millions, both on the battlefield and to the rear, has always hinged on the abilities of just a few rare men of genius. In somewhat similar fashion, the emergence of corporations like Apple or Microsoft was predicated on the singularity of a Steve Jobs or a Bill Gates. The success of either company would be hard to envision without the genius of a single man.

Take away Hernán Cortés, and for all their gunpowder and Spanish steel, the conquistadors would probably not have defeated the Aztecs when they did. The American Third Army's summer sprint across France seems unlikely without George Patton as its commander. The war in Europe might have been won without Patton at the head of the Third Army, but in a manner that would have been far more costly and lengthy. France had sufficient armor, artillery, and manpower to stop the German offensive through the Ardennes in May 1940; what the reeling French military tragically lacked was any sort of inspired or skilled leadership to translate its advantages into salvation—in other words, a George Patton, Erwin Rommel, or Charles de Gaulle in charge of ground forces. Any German general other than Rommel would probably never have reached El Alamein; British generals other than Montgomery in late 1942 would probably never have pushed him back so decisively. Had a gifted American General Creighton Abrams commanded much earlier in Vietnam in 1965, and had an equally talented North Vietnamese General Giap never commanded Communist forces at all, the war—despite its myriad political, moral, cultural, and technological contours—might have turned out quite differently.

For those historians who appreciate human agency, it is common to attribute such overarching powers of military leadership to history's great captains of the battlefield. The genius of an Alexander the Great, Julius Caesar, or Napoleon Bonaparte could decide the fate of thousands of soldiers on both sides of the battle line. Pity the Persian who lined up opposite Alexander's outnumbered troops at Gaugamela, or the Gaul who was besieged by Caesar at Alesia; had the former just faced a Parmenio or the latter a Pompey or Crassus, the overwhelming numbers of his kindred by his side might have saved him. Sometimes we grant such importance of command to sober and judicious organizers. Marcus Agrippa, Dwight D. Eisenhower, John J. Pershing, Alfred von Schlieffen, and Isoroku Yamamoto so mastered the planning of war and the mustering of forces at the general staff level that their insight and knowledge seemed to predetermine the course of upcoming battle. Even brilliant military bureaucrats at home such as George Marshall or Samuel Pepys on occasion ensured that forces at the distant front were likely to win battles before they started.

An industry of military history also exists to chart how and why some generals proved great, and most mediocre. Usually singular imagination, daring, charisma, speaking ability, instinct, calm, learning, physical robustness, relative youth, and an organizational mind are cited as the common gifts that, from Alexander to Napoleon, ensure success. Books on the untold secrets of the "Great Generals" appear each year—as do their antitheses, the aggregate lessons for modern leaders to be gleaned from the military disasters, errors, and follies of abject incompetents. We assume that there is an identifiable profile of both successful and disastrous military leadership across time and space. And such patterns can be studied, copied, and perhaps put to good use by those less naturally talented, from education to business. Rarely, however, do we read about saved, rather than won or lost, wars—or generals who in extremis rescued rather than started or finished a war. Perhaps we neglect saviors who rescue unwise interventions better written off as over and quickly forgotten; or we feel that they are mere relief pitchers of sorts, who can only preserve, but not claim credit for, the eventual successful efforts begun by their worn-out predecessors.

Yet often the best generals do not plan wars or assume control on the eve of the first battle, when instead the better-connected marshals of the peacetime bureaucracy exercise high-profile command. Instead, the savior generals prove to be a subset of history's great captains. Such men emerge far later from the lower echelons when wars are almost lost. They arise only because their superiors are desperate and turn to the unlikely, to whom, in normal circumstances, they otherwise probably would not. These eleventh-hour landscapes of battle, when most at home and officers in the field have given up on a war as irrevocably stalemated or lost, draw in a different sort of commander. Prewar education, reputation, influence, and rank matter little when the enemy is gaining ground and very few know how to turn him back.

These "firemen" are asked to extinguish the conflagration that others, of typically superior rank and prestige, have ignited. Their moment signals a crisis of national confidence, when the general public of a consensual society may already have favored retreat or even lost hope in their cause. William Tecumseh Sherman outside Atlanta in summer 1864, Matthew Ridgway retreating from Seoul in winter 1951, and David Petraeus trying to save Anbar Province in Iraq in early 2007, for all their assertions of calm and confidence, privately knew that only results would win back public support. In some sense, winning against impossible odds—when most others cannot or would not try—is the only mark of a great general.

Ulysses S. Grant certainly was felt to be such a figure by spring 1864, after he had come eastward to assume direct command of Union forces in Virginia that had been bled white since 1861. Yet by late summer 1864, all the Union dreams of ending the Civil War that year under Grant had been nearly wrecked, with the near destruction of the Army of the Potomac in a series of horrific battles in Virginia. The disasters of summer 1864 led not only to doubts about the reelection of Abraham Lincoln, but also to some initial worry over the president's renomination by his own party. Then yet again, thanks in part to William Tecumseh Sherman and the capture of Atlanta, the Union cause recovered, and both Grant and Lincoln were given a reprieve. It proved hard for the Northern public to give up completely on their unpopular president and the general responsible for the nightmare of Cold Harbor, when suddenly Atlanta fell and a huge Union army in the west was free to go where it pleased in the Confederate rear.

Unlike Alexander the Great, Epaminondas the Theban in 371 B.C. had not inherited a great army from his father, much less any blueprint of invasion. Rather, he marched his agrarian hoplites—classical Greek heavily armed and armored infantrymen who fought in the phalanx—to the battlefield at Leuktra when an invading Spartan army was only an hour's march from his capital, and outnumbering his shaky Theban army three to two. When defeat seemed inevitable, Epaminondas did the impossible by crushing the Spartans in battle, routing the invading army, killing their king—and in time was marching on the enemy capital to the south to free the Messenian helots from their Spartan serfdom and to end Sparta as a major Greek power.

The Suspect Few

Resentment and its twin, envy, arise through the higher echelon of the officer corps at the selection of an outsider such as William Tecumseh Sherman or Epaminondas the Theban to salvage the battlefield. After all, a change in command is inherently a harsh verdict on all those invested in everything that preceded it. The outward qualities in a military leader necessary to galvanize dispirited troops and resurrect national will—greater knowledge and insight, outspokenness, self-promotion, individualism, eccentricity—sometimes incite suspicion and engender spite. General George McClellan, and the succession of generals who followed him, felt that the successes of Sherman and Grant by early 1865 were predicated on unacknowledged lessons learned from the preceding generals' earlier failures.

Savior generals were often suspect outsiders well before their appointments. During their command, even spectacular recovery could be attributed to luck or the inevitable ebb and flow of the battlefield—or to the previous underappreciated efforts of their failed predecessors. Even after their successes, most saviors did not enjoy the commensurate acclaim and tranquillity that the moment of their military brilliance otherwise might have ensured. Heroes like Themistocles, Scipio, or Belisarius—and in the modern age, a Philippe Pétain or a Grant—died either in poverty, obscurity, or self-induced disgrace. Today mention William Tecumseh Sherman a near century and a half after he went into Georgia, and many are as likely to equate burning plantations with terrorism as appreciate a grand strategy to minimize loss of American life, both Union and Confederate. Mavericks of real genius such as George Patton and Curtis LeMay often ended up as buffoonish caricatures of their brilliant selves. When David Petraeus left Iraq, his real problems began rather than ended—continual stalemate in Afghanistan, controversy at the CIA over the killing of an American ambassador and three other Americans in Libya, and sudden resignation from the CIA amid rumor, innuendo, and scandal—the full consequences of which were not known when this book went to press. National laurels and a quiet retirement did not meet a triumphant Matthew Ridgway when he returned from Korea. Instead, forced retirement and endless controversies marked the next four decades of Ridgway's long life. The ascendance of a savior general is brief, the moment of his glory passing.

Lost Wars Won

The following case histories, from antiquity to the present, are admittedly somewhat arbitrary and varied. Sometimes generals turned defeat into victory in a matter of months, as in the case of Matthew Ridgway; at other times, they achieved success only after many decades of fighting, as the career of Belisarius attests. In many ways, George Washington, U. S. Grant, Curtis LeMay, George Patton, or Chester Nimitz could be seen as savior generals just as impressive. As an American, I have shorted the military tradition of other Western consensual societies—the brilliant recoveries engineered by Generals Kitchener, Slim, and Montgomery—and omitted non-Western savior generals altogether. Between antiquity and the modern age, Hernán Cortés, Don Juan of Austria, and the Duke of Marlborough won unlikely battles that turned around entire conflicts. Nor have I included, from the ancient world, the Spartans Gylippus or Lysander, the Theban Epaminondas, or the Roman Sertorius, who all inherited unfavorable military circumstances and were able to find, if only for a time, victory amid defeat. Considerations of space limited my selections, but the five generals in this book also seem to me to have inherited unprecedented failure that made their triumphs singularly spectacular.

Here I emphasize permanent recoveries (Athens, Byzantium, the Union, and South Korea were saved when most thought they would not be); rather than brief reprieves in the manner that Alcibiades for a time revived the Athenian navy, or Rommel for over two years turned a strategic backwater in North Africa into a major front. The verdict is still out on the survival of a constitutional Iraq.

There is another obvious bias in the choice of biographies: I more or less have favored generals of consensual societies over their opponents. There were Chinese Communist generals whose eleventh-hour planning stopped MacArthur at the Yalu. Most military analysts had expected the ultimately successful General Vo Nguyen Giap to lose the Vietnam War; few thought Marshal Zhukov could save Leningrad or even Stalingrad. Yet I am not so interested in such careers that are inseparable from authoritarian societies. Field Marshals Heinz Guderian, Erich von Manstein, and Walter Model ("Hitler's Fireman") were great recovery artists who, against all odds and on more than one occasion, saved Hitler from himself, but their causes ultimately were better lost than won. After all, the very notion of "savior" is embedded within some sense of a moral universe that should be saved. And "savior generals" would be paradoxes should we profile captains who advanced totalitarianism and saved tyranny from the forces of reform and liberation.

The following episodes are also meant to be representative of a military profile that can by analogy elucidate hundreds of other careers throughout history and likewise serve as some sort of guide to the future, rather than an attempt to be comprehensive and systematic. In short, there are history's great generals, and then among them are its far fewer savior generals who did the improbable and often changed history for the better.

CHAPTER ONE

Athens Is Burning

Themistocles at Salamis—September 480 B.C.

Athens Aflame (*September 480 B.C.*)

The "Violet-crowned" Athens of legend was in flames. It no longer existed as a Greek city. How, the Athenians lamented, could their vibrant democracy simply end like this—emptied of its citizens, occupied by the Persian king Xerxes, and now torched? How had the centuries-old polis of Theseus and Solon, with its majestic Acropolis, now in just a few September days been overwhelmed by tens of thousands of Persian marauders—enemies that the Athenians had slaughtered just ten years earlier at Marathon?

News had come suddenly this late summer to the once hopeful Athenians that the last-ditch Hellenic defense, eighty-five miles away at the pass of Thermopylae—the final gateway from the north into Greece—had evaporated. A Spartan king was dead. There were no Greek land forces left to block the rapid advance of the more than a quarter million Persian sailors and infantry southward into central Greece. The Greek fleet at Artemisium was fleeing southward to Athens and the Peloponnese. Far more numerous Persian warships followed in hot pursuit. Nearly all of the northern Greek city-states, including the important nearby city of Thebes, had joined the enemy. Now the residents of a defenseless Athens—on a desperate motion in the assembly of their firebrand admiral Themistocles—faced only bad and worse choices, and scrambled in panic to abandon their centuries-old city to King Xerxes.

Desperate Athenians rowed in boats over to the nearby islands or the northern coast of the Peloponnese. Anyone who stayed behind in the lost city would meet the fate of the Spartans and Thespians at Thermopylae—killed to the last man. It was as if the great Athenian infantry victory at Marathon that turned back the first Persian invasion a decade earlier had never occurred—like the French who lost their country in May 1940 to the Germans despite the valor of Verdun a generation earlier. All of Greece was to be the westernmost satrapy of an angry Xerxes' ascendant Persia that now for the first time incorporated European land into its empire. Athens—and everything north of it—was already Persian. The war seemed, for practical purposes, almost over, with only some mopping up of the crippled and squabbling Greek fleet at Salamis.

The ensuing mass flight of Athenians was a landmark moment in the history of Greece. Centuries later, the Roman-era biographer Plutarch, who in his own times could not conceive of Asians in Europe rather than Europeans controlling Asia, summed up the Athenian panic and the decision to forgo a last glorious land battle with the brief obituary: "The whole city of Athens had gone out to sea." But what exactly did that mean? Could a Greek polis—traditionally defined concretely by its locale, monuments, and landed patrimony—survive in name only without a home? Many Greeks could not conceive of handing over their shrines and tombs of their ancestors to the enemy without even a fight. That is, until the popular leader Themistocles had convinced them all that they had no choice but to leave. Only that way would the gods fight on the Athenian side and eventually give them victory and what was left of their charred city back.[1]

Soon almost all the fighting-age resident males—perhaps as many as thirty thousand to forty thousand Athenian citizens—had abandoned the city to man its fleet of triremes off Salamis. More than a quarter million elderly, women, and children had sought safety outside Attica, one of the largest transfers of population in the ancient world. In their haste, the despondent Athenians abandoned some of the ill and aged in the city or left them to their own devices out in the Attic countryside. Meanwhile, well over a hundred thousand Athenian civilians would crowd across the bay from the city to the rocky island of Salamis. They were gambling that their own seamen, along with still unconquered Greek allies from the Peloponnese, could wreck the Persian fleet before they all starved—and before the onset of autumn.[2]

There was little help from anywhere. None of the dwindling number of surviving but terrified large Greek states to the south—Argos, Corinth, Sparta—on the other side of the Isthmus of Corinth wished to send a relief force to its likely destruction on the Attic plain. The Greeks of Asia Minor were on the side of Xerxes, those in southern Italy and Sicily too distant to offer help—had they been willing. Apparently the remaining free Greeks to the south would write the Athenians off as an extinct race as they looked to their own defenses, or found some sort of accommodation with Persians. Most were still terrified by the news that King Xerxes' Persians, hot after the Greeks retreating from Thermopylae, had arrived in Attica to level Athens and demonstrate a similar fate waiting for other city-states to the south. The Persian king was becoming legendary, a force that could not be stopped by man or god; and in fact Xerxes was the first Asian invader to reach this far south into Europe in the long history of the Greeks—and he would be the last to do so in force until the Ottoman Turks entered Athens in 1458, nearly two millennia later.

Inside the empty city, the occupying Persians began the laborious task of destroying the stone shrines and temples and torching homes. They quickly finished off a few Athenian holdouts still barricaded on the Acropolis. Meanwhile Xerxes drew up his fleet nearby at the Athenian harbor of Phaleron. The Persians' war to annex Greece was now in a sense almost over. There was only the Megarid and the Peloponnese to the south left to occupy and the easy task of mopping up the retreating Greek ships and refugees trapped on Salamis.

The king himself ostentatiously perched his throne on Mount Aigaleos outside the city. He was eager to watch the final destruction below of what remained of the Greek fleet in the straits of Salamis, if the retreating Greeks could even be shamed into rowing out. Surely Xerxes' firing of Athens should have been an insult to all the Greeks, one that might incite some sort of last gasp of resistance. Or perhaps the humiliated Athenians, like most of the other disheartened Greeks up north, would simply just give up and wisely join the winners. If he could not cut off the head of another Spartan king, as he had done weeks earlier to Leonidas at Thermopylae, perhaps Xerxes could at least impale a Greek admiral or two.

For six months, Xerxes had enjoyed momentum and glory, like all of history's grand invaders. Their huge spring and summer expeditions at first rolled out with little resistance—always admiring their own magnitude, never worrying much about the unseen and surely inferior enemy to come. The legions that joined Napoleon's invasion force in summer 1812 sang as they headed out for Czarist Russia, hardly imagining that most would die there. The imperial German army that nearly surrounded Paris in August and September 1914 had no thought of a Verdun on the horizon. Hitler's Wehrmacht that plowed through the Soviet Union in June 1941 with thoughts of storming the Kremlin by August lost not only the theater, but the war as well. Amid such grand ambitions, few commanders wonder how to feed such hordes as supply lines lengthen, the enemy stiffens, the army loses men to attrition and the requirements of their occupations, the terrain changes, and the fair weather of summer descends into a crueler autumn and winter in a far distant hostile country.

Likewise, few in Xerxes' horde that crossed the Hellespont in April imagined what a distant September would bring. One side or the other inevitably would suffer enormous losses that would shake the foundation of their societies for decades after, given the magnitude of forces and the logistical challenges in play. Xerxes had transported tens of thousands of sailors and infantry nearly five hundred miles from his western capital at Sardis into southern Europe. He had successfully crossed from Asia Minor to Europe by constructing at Abydos an enormously expensive cabled pontoon bridge over the Hellespont—all on the gamble of being able to feed his forces in part from conquered or allied territory. His army and navy were not merely bent on punishing the Greeks in battle, but rather on absorbing the Greek people into the Persian Empire. What was left of the collective Greek defense rested upon fewer than 370 ships from little more than twenty city-states, about half the size of Xerxes' imperial fleet in the bay of Phaleron a few miles distant. Most of the assembled Greek admirals were already distraught at the idea of being blockaded by the Persians in the small harbors around Salamis. Nearly all commanders were resigned to retreat even further, fifty miles southward to the Isthmus at Corinth to join the last Greek resistance on land. Indeed, ten thousand Peloponnesians were frantically working there on a cross-isthmus wall as the Greeks bickered at Salamis. The historian Herodotus—who was a boy of four or five when Xerxes invaded—believed from his informants that many in the Greek alliance had already decided on a withdrawal from the proposed battle. France in 1940 or Kuwait in 1990 had at least kept their defeated peoples inside their occupied cities. But the conquered city of Athens was both taken over by the enemy and also emptied of its own residents. Unlike other defeated Greek city-states that "Medized" (became like Persians) and were governed by Persian overlords, the Athenians who fought at Salamis faced a different, existential choice: either win or cease to exist as a people.[3]

At the final meeting of the allied generals before the battle to discuss the collective defense of what was left of Greece, one Greek delegate bellowed that the Athenian Themistocles simply had no legitimacy. After all, the admiral no longer had a city to represent—a charge similar to that often leveled later in the Second World War against General Charles de Gaulle and his orphaned "free" French forces based in London. The Peloponnesian and island allies saw little point in fighting for an abandoned city. The overall allied fleet commander, the exasperated Spartan Eurybiades, in a furious debate with Themistocles, next threatened to physically strike some sense into the stubborn, cityless admiral. No matter: Themistocles supposedly screamed back, "Strike—but listen!"[4]

Eurybiades, who had far fewer ships under his own command, heard out the desperate Themistocles. He was well aware that the Athenian infantry generals who had won the battle of Marathon a decade earlier—Miltiades, Callimachus, Aristides—were either dead, exiled, or without the expertise to conduct naval operations. Likewise, his pessimistic Spartan antagonist also knew that three earlier efforts to stop the Persians to the north had all failed. Why should Salamis end any differently?

In fairness to the Spartan, Eurybiades' reluctance to join Themistocles in fighting here had a certain logic. King Leonidas had been killed at Thermopylae just a few days earlier. No more than twenty-two city-states remained to fight at Salamis, out of a near one thousand Greek poleis that had been free a few months earlier. Moreover, the Greek fleet depended largely on the contributions of just three key powers, the city-states Aegina, Corinth, and Athens. Their ships made up well over half the armada. It seemed wiser for those admirals to retreat back to the Isthmus at Corinth and not to waste precious triremes far from home in defense of a lost city.

Worse still for the coalition, the sea powers Corinth and Aegina were historical rivals—and yet both in turn were enemies of the Athenians. The Greeks may have claimed that they were united by a common language, religion, and culture, the Persians divided by dozens of tongues and races; but Xerxes presided over a coercive empire whose obedient subjects understood the wages of dissent, while the Greek generals rep-

The so-called Themistocles Herm is a Roman stone copy of a lost Greek bronze sculpture. Unlike most idealized classical statuary, the bust captures Themistocles more as a general than a near-god (presently in the Ostia Museum, Ostia, Italy). Photo courtesy of the Ostia Museum.

resented dozens of autonomous and bickering political entities who faced no punishment should they quit the alliance and go home. Even in their moment of crisis, these free spirits seemed to have hated each other almost as much as they did the Persians, who had thousands of subservient Ionian Greeks in their service and had shown singular brilliance in bringing such a huge force from Asia and battering away the Greek resistance at Tempe, Thermopylae, and Artemisium while peeling off more city-states to their own side than were left with the resistance. Indeed, until Salamis, Xerxes had conducted one of the most successful invasions in history.

The salvation of Athenian civilization rested solely on the vision of a single firebrand, one who was widely despised, often considered a half-breed foreigner, an uncouth commoner as well, who had previously failed twice up north at Tempe and Artemisium to stop Xerxes' advance.

How well Themistocles argued to the Greek admirals determined whether tens of thousands would live, die, or become permanent refugees or slaves in the next few days. Themistocles had earlier gone up and down the shores of Salamis rallying the terrified Athenians, and he kept assuring Eurybiades and the demoralized Greeks that they must fight at Salamis to save Hellenic civilization and could assuredly win. He pointed out that the Greeks could do more than just repel the enemy armada and reclaim the Greek mainland. By defeating the Persian navy, they could trap Xerxes' land forces and then bring the war back home to Persian shores. Yet to the Peloponnesians, who were about ready to sail away from Salamis, this vision of the stateless Themistocles seemed unhinged—or perhaps typical of a lowborn scoundrel who throve in the shouting matches of Athenian democracy but otherwise had no clue how to stop an enemy fleet three times the size of their own.

But was Themistocles wrong? He alone of the generals amid the panic fathomed enemy weaknesses that were numerous. He might have failed to save his city from burning, but he still had confidence he could save what was left of Athens from the Persians. Hundreds of thousands of Xerxes' army were far from home. The year was waning. And they were getting farther each day from the supply bases in Asia Minor and northern Greece—even as the army was forced to leave ever more garrisons to the rear to ensure conquered Greeks stayed conquered. The tipping point, when the overreaching attackers could be attacked, would be right here at Salamis.

Yet the general, and admiral of the fleet, was no wild-eyed blowhard. In his midforties, Themistocles had already fought at Marathon (490), conducted a successful retreat from the failed defense line at Tempe (480), battled the larger enemy fleet to a draw at Artemisium, and this year marshaled the largest Athenian fleet in the city's history. In the last decade, he knew enough of war with Persians to have good cause for his confidence that logistics favored the Greeks.

Nearly a hundred supply ships had to arrive daily just to feed the Persian horde—given that the summer's grain crops of Attica, and those of most of Greece, were long ago harvested. The Persian fleet was without permanent safe harbors as the autumn storm season loomed and already had suffered terribly from the gales at Artemisium. In late September, rowing on the Aegean began to turn unpredictable. Rough seas were a greater danger to the Persians than to Greek triremes that still had home ports down the coast. Moreover, most of the king's contingents were not

Persian. Those subject states—many of them Greek-speaking—for all their present obedience, still hated the Persian king as much as they did the free Greeks of the mainland. The Persian navy proved even more motley than the polyglot imperial army.[5]

Most of Xerxes' army also had been camped out on campaign for months. For all its pretense of being an imperial expeditionary force, the various allies would be squabbling more the farther they were from home, while the remaining Greeks grew more desperate for unity the more their homeland shrank in size. So far from joining the general despondency, Themistocles was supremely confident in the Greeks' chances at Salamis. Few others shared his optimism, perhaps because a Spartan king had just fallen in battle at Thermopylae, partly because unlike Themistocles they still had homes to retreat to for a while longer.

Themistocles was soon to be proved right: The Spartan supreme commander Eurybiades did not realize it, but the Persian fleet had, except for a sortie to nearby Megara, already reached its furthest penetration into Europe. Logistics, morale, and numbers had already conspired against Xerxes—even as he boasted of his conquest of Greece. Yet right now in late September 480, few could see it: "We Athenians have given up, it is true, our houses and city walls," Themistocles declared to the wavering generals, "because we did not choose to become enslaved for the sake of things that have no life or soul. But what we still possess is the greatest city in all Greece—our two hundred warships that are ready now to defend you—if you are still willing to be saved by them."

Themistocles talked of Greeks being "saved," not merely "defended," as if a victory at Salamis would be a turning point after which Xerxes could not win. Note further that Themistocles was making a novel argument to his fellow Greeks: A city-state was people, not just a place or buildings. His "free" Athenians with their two hundred ships were very much a polis still, even if the Acropolis was blackened with fire. As long as there were thousands of scattered but free-spirited Athenians willing to fight for their liberty, so Themistocles argued, there was most certainly still an Athens.[6]

What swung the argument to make a stand at Salamis was not just the logic of Themistocles, but also unexpected help from his former rival, the conservative statesman Aristides, who advised the other Greek generals to fight. The latter's reputation for sobriety reassured the Greeks that the Persians really were in their ships and poised for attack—and they believed the prior messages from Themistocles himself that they had better attack before the Greeks got away. Time had run out. Only three choices were left—fight, flee, or surrender.[7]

The Marathon Moment (*August 490 B.C.*)

What brought the squabbling Greeks to Salamis was a decadelong Persian effort to destroy Hellenic freedom—and the efforts of Athenians to stop Darius and his son, Xerxes.

The original east/west rivalry ostensibly started over the breakaway attempt of the subjugated Greek city-states on the coast of Asia Minor that had begun in earnest in 499–498—nearly twenty years before the invasion of Xerxes. By 493, after the failure of the Asiatic Greeks to end Persian occupation and win their freedom from King Darius, the emboldened Persians quickly sought to settle accounts and punish the Athenians. The latter had sent ships and hoplites to their rebellious Ionian cousins across the Aegean. Apparently they had hoped in vain thereby to preempt Persian aggrandizement abroad before it reached their own shores.

Despite an initial failure in northern Greece (492), Darius, father of Xerxes, began his payback in earnest in 490. The king dispatched his generals Datis and Artaphernes with a second expeditionary force of some twenty-five or thirty thousand sailors and infantry. They headed on a beeline path across the sea to the Greek mainland. After easily conquering the island of Naxos, the Persians took the key city of Eretria on the large nearby island of Euboea. Next, sometime in mid-August 490, they landed on the nearby eastern coast of Attica itself—at the plain of Marathon, just twenty-six miles from Athens.

There, in a set-piece infantry battle, the outnumbered but more heavily armed phalanx of the Athenians and their allies, the Plataeans, won a crushing victory over the lighter-clad Persians. The invaders had foolishly advanced into the enclosed plain of Marathon without much, if any, cavalry support. Despite numeric superiority, the Persians were trapped by the Athenians' double envelopment. Although the Athenian and Plataean defenders may have been outnumbered three to one, and had to weaken their center to envelop the larger Persian wings, the combined Greek forces nonetheless managed to kill more than 6,400 of the enemy—at a loss of only 192 dead. Heavy armor—and the discipline, solidarity, and columnar tactics of Greeks fighting for their own soil—

had smashed apart the more loosely deployed, lighter-clad Asian invaders and explained the one-sided slaughter.

Most Greeks, especially the conveniently late-arriving Spartans, who had stayed away from the battle, still could not quite fathom how just two Greek city-states had turned back an invasion by the enormous Persian Empire. Athenian spearmen had ensured the land victory and then immediately made a miraculous march to circumvent an amphibious landing. Amid the general euphoria, Sparta, the preeminent land power in Greece, was nowhere to be found.[8]

Themistocles himself had fought at Marathon. Indeed, he had been elected a magistrate, or archon, of the young democracy three years before the battle (493), allowing him a preeminent position in establishing Athenian foreign policy. But credit for the victory properly belonged to the more conservative Miltiades, commander in chief of the Greek infantry generals on the day of the fighting. Before the Greeks ran out to battle, Miltiades drew up the risky but winning strategy of weakening the Greek center to draw in and envelop on the wings the charging Persian mass—achieving the elusive dream of a double envelopment by a numerically weaker force. That moment of victory was immortalized later in a vast painting on the monumental Stoa Poikile at the north end of the Athenian Agora. The playwright Aeschylus' brother died in this glorious Marathon moment. Aeschylus himself chose to record his own service at the battle—not his fame as a dramatist—in his own epitaph.

A national myth quickly arose that an entire Persian invasion had been thwarted by a single glorious battle won by better men in bronze. The Athenians were determined never to forget who had won the battle—and how. For each Athenian or Plataean infantryman who fell, thirty-three Persians perished. Both the infantry victory and the subsequent famous twenty-six-mile march to beat the Persian fleet back to Athens were immortalized as proof of the nobility of traditional agrarian Athenian hoplites, and the proper way for landowning citizens to defend their city. No walls or ships were needed to save Athens from Persian hordes; courage, not just numbers, mattered. That Athenian hoplites had won without the crack troops of Sparta made the victory all the sweeter. Sixty years later the comic poet Aristophanes could still talk nostalgically of the old breed of *Marathonomachoi*, "the Marathon fighters," whose courage over the subsequent century was never later surpassed. In short, Marathon became a sort of shorthand for the triumph of traditional values, and was thought to have put an end to the Persian danger.[9]

Yet despite the immediate Athenian ebullience, Marathon proved not quite to be the final victory that it seemed at the time. A worried Themistocles, almost alone among Athenian leaders, drew quite different lessons from the victory—and all would prove vital for the survival of the Athenians in the years to come. While others celebrated the courage of the Marathon fighters, Themistocles felt the victory a fluke of sorts. He saw no grand strategy that had contributed to the infantry victory. There was no way that the hoplite victory at Marathon offered a blueprint for future military success against the huge maritime resources at the king's disposal.

Instead, to the mind of Themistocles, Marathon was merely a "beginning of far greater struggles"—in the way that the supposed war to end all wars, the "Great War" of 1914–18, was soon to be rebranded as a prequel First World War once an ascendant Germany invaded Poland in 1939 and started another global conflagration. Marathon was a probing attack, no more—given the greater resources of Persia that were still uncommitted to the war against the Greeks and were hardly diminished by the single, though humiliating, defeat. The loss of even 6,400 troops meant little in an empire of several millions. Themistocles immediately tried to warn his Athenians that unfortunately there might be no future Marathon victories in the face of "events still to come." Yet few Athenians wished to hear that ominous message at this time—the equivalent of someone warning the Americans in January 1991 that their brilliant four-day victory over Saddam Hussein was the beginning, not the end, of a far larger rivalry with a determined foe who would remain in power for twelve years into the future, until yet another American expeditionary force was sent into the Persian Gulf.[10]

In retrospect, Themistocles fathomed why the superior Persian forces had arrived in Attica in 490 after conquering both the islands of Naxos and Euboea without much Greek interference. Their choice and style of battle at Marathon proved perhaps unwise, but it nevertheless had been theirs alone. Had not Persian admirals under their general Datis—without worry about their Greek counterparts—determined when and where to fight? The Athenians and their few allies had been reactive, given their limited options. Yet with greater resources the Athenians might have fought at a time, place, and manner of their own choosing. Despite the Greek victory and the high enemy losses, perhaps more than two-thirds of the defeated Persian force had simply sailed away unscathed. They could easily come back. Sea power, Themistocles concluded, had enabled the Persians to arrive when and where they desired. In comparison, Athens by 490 still had only a small fleet and thus no comparable maritime lift capability. It took a keen contrarian mind, and a willingness to endure ridicule, to grasp that fundamental Athenian vulnerability at a time of infantry triumphalism.[11]

In the future, if an Athenian army had to march up and down the coast each time a Persian armada in the Aegean threatened the Attic coast, how could the city ever be truly safe without fortifications? Themistocles saw additional reasons why naval power made sense. The young democracy at Athens was only seventeen years old. It had hardly evolved beyond the culture of the traditional agrarian city-state whose backbone was a minority of landowning hoplite farmers. Most citizens, despite the radical notion of "power to the people," remained poor. Perhaps half did not own property. Aristocratic grandees like Aristides or Miltiades usually had managed to end up as the city's leaders, as the idea of political opportunity had not yet led to a notion of comprehensive equality.

To the mind of the radical Themistocles, the ideal of egalitarian politics would never come to fruition if the defense, and with it the prestige, of the city rested only with a minority of conservative property owners. Was there a way that Athens could still survive, even when its farmland was overrun, without need for countless Marathons? Why should security policy depend solely on those who could afford hoplite armor? How could the city remain safe against the Persian hordes when thousands of landless Athenians were not even mobilized for its defense?

In the ancient world, those who fought for the city-state usually ended up controlling it. Military strategy, in other words, simply reflected class realities. Wars, for radicals like Themistocles, were as much about internal politics as they were about national defense. Accordingly, using public money to pay thousands of poor to row in the fleet or build fortifications would strengthen the sinews of the new democracy. The poor would have their wages in silver coin and enjoy the prestige of protecting the city—while ensuring a permanent constituency for popular leaders like Themistocles.[12]

Themistocles had a final argument for sea power. Given the vast resources of the Persian Empire, the expeditionary force under Datis and Artaphernes in 490—while large in comparison to the Greek resistance—had actually been somewhat small. The Persian strike had intended to be merely punitive, concerned more with Euboea and Attica than the whole of the Greek mainland. But could the Athenians and their allies always count on such Persian half-measures in the future? Did not Darius' empire of some 20 million that stretched from the Aegean to India possess the means not merely to punish Athens, but to destroy it outright? If Athens were to be safe, Themistocles reasoned, it needed to reinvent itself, and almost immediately so, given the imminent threat. The Athenians required a large navy. A fleet in turn demanded a protected port and urban fortifications. Such investments likewise reflected an entirely new defense strategy more attuned to the nature of the enemy and in accordance with a growing democratic culture at home.

Yet the implementation of these radical ideas demanded rare political skills in order to warn his triumphant countrymen that the strategies that seemed unquestioned would prove suicidal. The career of Themistocles between Marathon and Thermopylae is similar to Winston Churchill's between the world wars—both were visionaries who were written off as alarmists and eccentrics by their contemporaries. Yet neither was fooled into thinking that prior victories had created permanent deterrence against a persistent enemy, temporarily down but by no means out. Instead, such mavericks knew that the once defeated already had far more assets than did their own victorious, but poorly prepared, democracies. In serial, unresolved conflicts, the initial victors can turn complacent in hoarding their advantages, the once defeated become audacious with more to gain than to lose—a logical enough fact that nevertheless few leaders appreciate.

After Marathon, each major traditional political figure who might have challenged Themistocles' new vision was either fined, ostracized, or came under public suspicion—Megacles, Miltiades, Xanthippus, Aristides. This growing infantry and naval divide between Themistocles and his more conservative rivals came to a head in 483, just three years before the arrival of the Persians at Salamis in a most unexpected way. A new, unusually rich vein of silver ore was discovered at the state-controlled mines at Laurium in southern Attica. That lucky find gave the Athenians an unexpected influx of sudden wealth. The resulting coined silver

The Olympias *is a modern replica of an ancient trireme. While contemporary ship designers have difficulty understanding just how the Greeks engineered their three-bank warships, the* Olympias *offers a good understanding of how Greek warships might have appeared as they sailed against the Persians at Salamis. Photo courtesy of the Hellenic Navy.*

would prove an opening for the impatient Themistocles to see his strategic thinking at last become state policy.[13]

Themistocles prevented the distribution of the windfall to the citizens on an equitable basis, as might have been expected in the egalitarian spirit of the young democracy (each citizen would have received an annual dole of about ten days' worth of wages). Instead, he somehow persuaded the assembly to build enough ships to ensure a fleet that would reach two hundred triremes. How a radically democratic politician could persuade his own constituents to pass up such easy money in the here and now in order to invest in an unproven naval program against a distant enemy, we are not told. But Themistocles' naval law proved a monumental turning point for Athens, not unlike, in the American experience, the passing of the Selective Training and Service Act of 1940 that squeaked by in the House of Representatives in August 1940 by just one vote—and just in time, on the eve of war.

Triremes were relatively novel warships that were becoming common in Aegean warfare. The radical design of three-tiered rowing benches resulted in unprecedented speed and power for ramming, but required careful training to ensure the fragile vessels were not swamped in rough seas and winds. Ostensibly the expressed threat to Athens was the nearby rival island power of Aegina, not the looming revenge of the Achaemenids. Why worry the assembly just yet with an apocalyptic vision of a huge Persian invasion?[14]

Themistocles no doubt always expected to use the new fleet and its conscripted crews against a second, massive Persian invasion that could arrive by sea at any time. But the war with Aegina, and the chance strike at Laurium, gave him the pretexts and the money to prepare for the looming existential Persian threat. By late summer 480, the Athenians may have built 170 triremes. Soon more than thirty thousand trained seamen protected the city from invasion.

William Tecumseh Sherman would later invent a new way of holistic warfare in attacking the civilian infrastructure of the slaveholding class. Matthew Ridgway would grasp that conventional warmaking might be more rather than less frequent in the age of nuclear deterrence. And David Petraeus was convinced that the conventional American military behemoth could nevertheless excel at counterinsurgency. In that same dissident vein, Themistocles had revolutionized the Athenian military and with it the entire Greek way of war.

History is replete with great generals who won unexpected victories. But rare are commanders who first built a military force ex nihilo, then crafted a national defense strategy, and finally drafted the tactical plan that achieved victory. Themistocles did all three and more. He was a veritable chairman of the House Armed Services Committee, secretary of defense, chairman of the Joint Chiefs, chief of naval operations, and four-star admiral all in one.[15]

The Persians Come Back (*Thermopylae and Artemisium, August 480 B.C.*)

The energetic and young king Xerxes (somewhere in his late thirties) assumed power on the death of his father, Darius, in 486 or 485. His mother, Atossa, was the daughter of the first Persian emperor, Cyrus the Great. And so Xerxes claimed royal preeminence through his maternal line in a way his upstart father never could, cementing his position among Persian elites as the rightful heir to the throne. He quickly determined to draw on the entire resources of the empire to avenge his father's failure. This time the Persian aim was to annex southern Europe across the Aegean as the westernmost province of Persia. Xerxes would crush the Hellenic resistance and end a bothersome Greece altogether.

By autumn 481 the Greeks got word that Persian mobilization was in full swing from Xerxes' western base at Sardis. The king might well cross the Hellespont into Europe within a year. Themistocles and his supporters immediately tried to prepare the Athenians for the danger. The endangered democracy finally passed various resolutions under Themistocles' leadership, recalling political exiles and preparing to mobilize the fleet for a combined Hellenic land and sea expeditionary defense.[16]

Once it was known to the city-states that Xerxes' forces were gathering in the western Persian provinces, the allied Greek leaders hastily agreed to meet at their own Panhellenic congress at the Isthmus of Corinth. Time had almost run out. There were still no forward Greek defenses to stop Xerxes before he built momentum and began to coerce into his alliance vulnerable city-states in the north. When the generals arrived, the usual bickering and delay characterized the Greek debate: Athens and Aegina needed to end their internecine war. Athens would be forced to grant supreme command of the allied resistance to the more esteemed Spartans, who nonetheless had far fewer ships. Spies were to be sent out to obtain more accurate intelligence. Invitations were extended to distant Greek states to contribute resources for a common defense.

Yet no concrete action followed. By early spring, the squabbling Greek states again met. This time they at last agreed to organize a combined land and sea force to fight as far to the north and as soon as possible to keep Xerxes away from the majority of the Greek population. But in April 480, Xerxes had already crossed into Europe with a combined force of hundreds of thousands of infantry and seamen. We do not know the exact numbers of the Persian muster; but to man a fleet of over twelve hundred triremes would require alone nearly a quarter million sailors. Most modern estimates put Persian land forces at somewhere between one hundred thousand and two hundred thousand combatants and support troops. In any case, Xerxes' grand expedition was the largest amphibious invasion of Europe until the 1944 Normandy landing more than 2,400 years later, and he claimed forty-one states had contributed to his muster. Scholars still do not quite understand how the Persian quartermasters solved the enormous logistical problems of feeding and caring for such a horde—one that dwarfed William the Conqueror's invasion of England in 1066.

The allied congress finally had sent a force of almost ten thousand

Greek hoplites and a large enough naval contingent to transport them up to Thessaly—an impressive number for the city-states, but one that could offer little real resistance to the huge forces of Xerxes. Nonetheless, the advance guard was supposed to keep the Persians from the heartland of Greece to the south. Themistocles was co-commander of this Panhellenic expeditionary force. Yet upon arrival, the position of the Greeks became untenable, even before they marshaled their forces for battle. At this early date, the alliance of mostly central and southern Greek states had embarrassingly little idea of either the geography of Macedon or the planned routes of the Persian invasion.

Themistocles and the Spartan Euainetos had even less inkling that the proposed line of defense up north in the Vale of Tempe between Mount Olympus and Ossa was topographically indefensible in the face of a large invasion. In one of the greatest blunders of the Persian War, the allies had come north unprepared, with too few troops, and too early—and co-led by Themistocles, known for his promotion of sea power rather than proven infantry generalship. The forces were certainly not equipped to camp, wait, and attempt to galvanize the anxious northerners for the expected Persian onslaught. They had no idea of the huge size of Xerxes' forces advancing toward them. In utter dejection, the humiliated Greek expeditionary force returned to the Isthmus well before the Persians even arrived, ostensibly to plot a second fallback strategy. But time was running out, and morale was almost shot. By late summer the Persians had swept through the north and were ready to enter central Greece through the narrow pass at Thermopylae. Panic set in. All eyes looked to the legendary Spartans to stop the enemy infantry onslaught.[17]

In response, somehow during their late summer religious festival of the Carneia, the usually blinkered Spartan leadership galvanized the Greek resistance and marshaled an ad hoc second Panhellenic land force of at least seven thousand infantrymen under the Spartan king Leonidas. He was to be accompanied and supplied by a combined fleet of nearly three hundred ships under the command of his fellow Spartan, Eurybiades. Themistocles enjoyed a quasiautonomous command in the fleet of almost two hundred Athenian triremes. He insisted that his Athenians would only serve at sea and not augment the hoplite defense at Thermopylae. The Greeks would have wished ten thousand Spartan hoplites at Thermopylae. But given that they had not shown up at Marathon during the Carneia, they were at least happy for a Spartan king, his royal bodyguard, and some Spartan ships under Eurybiades.

Hundreds of books and articles have been written about the Greek last stand at Thermopylae and the accompanying sea battle at nearby Artemisium. But for all the gripping drama of the heroism at Thermopylae, the gallant sacrifice of Leonidas, and the death of the Spartan three hundred (along with nearly eleven hundred Thespians and Thebans and several hundred other allied Greeks who earlier perished as well), Thermopylae—which, along with the simultaneous naval fighting at Artemisium, marked one of the largest combined engagements in military history—was nevertheless a terrible defeat. The loss of the pass allowed the victorious Persian army a wide-open route into the wealthiest of the Greek city-states. If a Spartan king could not stop Xerxes, who could?[18]

The successive naval collisions at Artemisium proved only a nominal Greek victory. Themistocles' aggressive tactics to draw the much larger but wary Persian fleet into the straits of Artemisium, his choice to engage in the unaccustomed late afternoon, and his reliance on speed, maneuver, and ramming, all continued to confound enemy triremes before they could deploy in proper order. By the naval battle's end, the allies had destroyed far more Persian ships than they lost. Sudden storms caught the retiring Persian fleet without adequate harborage and wrecked dozens more of the surviving triremes.

But despite the damage to the huge Persian armada, in both battle and in rough seas—perhaps six hundred triremes were lost altogether—it was the Greek fleet that retreated southward. Xerxes' wounded armada followed closely at their rear, supporting the land army that swept aside all opposition. For all Themistocles' own daring, he had overseen failed efforts in Thessaly and now at Euboia. How could the Greeks save Athens and the Peloponnese when even a naval victory and providential gale proved inadequate to stop the Persian juggernaut?[19]

A Spartan king was dead, his corpse decapitated and shamed. The holding forces at the pass were wiped out. Their bodies were desecrated and put on display by Xerxes. The survivors of the original seven thousand Greeks of the land defense had scattered in panic to their homes with the news the Persians were not far behind. The victorious, but crippled, allied fleet limped back to the bay at Salamis.

Perhaps half the Greek navy had been damaged or destroyed. Over a hundred triremes needed repair work. More ominously, most of the Greek city-states north of Athens had already joined the Persians or were making arrangements to do so. There would be no second Thermopylae. Xerxes' forces were growing again, the allies shrinking, and the king was supplying his forces from the "earth and water"—the symbolic manifestations of Greek surrender—of his Greek hosts. The Athenians' desperate appeal to field another Panhellenic army to stop the Persians on its northwestern borders with Boeotia was ignored by the Peloponnesian infantry. They preferred to stream home in defeat to the Isthmus.

Any Greek state that was not defended by the retreating alliance either was obliterated or joined the Persians. An overrun Thebes allied with Xerxes, a terrible loss for the remaining free Greeks given its excellent army. The polyglot forces of imperial Persia were more united than the Greeks who shared the same religion, language, and culture. The only debate for the dwindling resistance was over the location and nature of a glorious, but probably doomed, Greek last stand—even as Themistocles led the Athenian contingent home to rally what he almost alone hoped would be a Panhellenic naval response pledged to the salvation of his own city.[20]

Panic at Athens (*September 480 B.C.*)

The Athenians, during the Persian rush into Greece, had hastily consulted the oracle at Delphi. Their envoys received various responses from the always politically astute Pythia. The last and most famous reply from the wily priestess offered cryptic advice: First, retreat before the enemy; second, trust in a mysterious "wooden wall"; and third, put hope in a "Holy Salamis" and thereby the promise that the Greeks might at some date "destroy" the Persians.

Dispute broke out over the oracle's deliberately ambiguous meaning. For those Athenians who did not wish to fight at sea at Salamis—or were too poor or elderly to flee the city—the prophecy was either gibberish or perhaps recommended a defense on the Athenian Acropolis behind wooden walls of old doors, castoff furnishings, and rough logs. But Themistocles persuaded his fellow generals that Delphi's "wooden wall" could only refer to their own fleet of pine- and fir-planked triremes. Why, after all, would the oracle at Delphi call Athenian-held Salamis "holy," if she did not mean victory was assured there for the Greeks should they dare fight by sea? Whether Themistocles' agents had something to do with cooking up the prophecy, or twisting its interpretation, we do not know. But he certainly was not going to let the superstitious or pusillanimous thwart his plans to gamble all at Salamis, a strategy based on a decade of reasoning, not prophetic hocus-pocus.[21]

The real divide at Salamis arose over the proper way to defend the Athenians from hundreds of thousands of Persians. The enemy infantry and marine forces had not suffered a single defeat in the five months since their arrival in Europe. Two defensive strategies were hotly debated—the first among Athenians themselves, whether to protect the city proper or evacuate the population, and a second between the remaining city-states of the alliance over whether to fight at sea in the Bay of Salamis or to fall back southward even further.

Some of these deliberations were cut short when Xerxes arrived in Attica and quickly stormed Athens. The king's forces in short order had surrounded the Acropolis, where a diehard Athenian contingent proved that the oracle did not mean their futile barricade was any sort of literal "wooden wall." No prisoners were taken. Themistocles had previously introduced a decree to evacuate the city (a later version of the original proclamation on stone was first published in 1960) that directed the Athenians to the nearby islands and the northern Argolid. The city-state's defense was reduced to those who manned about 180 triremes in the Bay of Salamis, along with small contingents of hoplites.

The renegade Spartan ex-king Demaratus, now a Persian court adviser, had urged Xerxes to avoid Salamis. Instead, he argued, the Persians should sail around the Peloponnese to occupy the island of Cythera off Sparta. That way, Demaratus insisted, the Persians could avoid losses, tie down the Spartan army, and raise a revolt of the city-state's agricultural serfs, the helots—perhaps putting Demaratus himself back in power at Sparta as a puppet satrap king. With Athens in flames and the Greek fleet trapped in the straits of Salamis, however, such wise but cautious advice seemed timid to Xerxes. Instead, once the Greek armada was easily swamped here at Salamis, the Persians could simply land troops wherever they pleased in the Peloponnese. The plan was to pick off the few remaining city-states one by one.[22]

For their part, other Greek leaders had proposed several complicated alternative strategies before and after the retreat from Thermopylae. Many Athenians, for example, still wished to fight on the Attic plain, not at sea, in some sort of decisive infantry confrontation that might repeat the verdict of Marathon and save their city while restoring the prestige of the hoplite class. But that dream was quickly tabled after the disaster at Thermopylae. The rapidity of the Persian onslaught, the absence of willing allies, and the fact that King Xerxes this time had far more land forces than his father, Darius, had sent ten years earlier, for now all made another Marathon impossible. Those at Marathon had been outnumbered three to one. But the Persian land forces were at least ten times larger than the Athenian hoplite army. Only a few isolated pockets of Athenians remained holed up in the Attic countryside.[23]

The second option, of garrisoning the city proper, had already proved suicidal. The few who had remained at Athens to defend the wooden ramparts on the Acropolis were dead.

A third choice was simply for Athenians and the remaining allies to quit and join the Persians. Some Athenians were furious at the Peloponnesian city-states for abandoning them to the Persians without a fight. Many felt their cause was hopeless. Still, most at Salamis stayed firm. As long as the surviving Greek states had nearly four hundred ships, and the soil of the Megarid and the Peloponnese was still Greek, such surrender seemed premature, even if it meant tens of thousands of Athenians camping in the countryside without adequate shelter and food.

Most of the remaining allies, in fact, initially preferred a fourth and more defensible choice: to fight on land behind makeshift ramparts along the six-mile-wide isthmus. That strategy might save what was left of Greece to the south. The ships of Athens that way could retreat southward and engage the enemy somewhere off the coast of the Peloponnese. Who could object to that? The maritime Athenians, after all, earlier had not offered any of their ten thousand hoplites to fight at the shared land defense of Thermopylae. Now, in tit-for-tat fashion, the land powers of the Peloponnese preferred not to risk any of their own ships in the defense of an evacuated Athens.

Still, Themistocles wondered whether the Spartan proposals even served their own best interests. What then would prevent a Persian amphibious landing behind an isthmus wall (of the sort the turncoat Demaratus had in fact advised Xerxes to make)? Would not fighting in more open seas off the Peloponnese only give more advantages to a far larger enemy fleet? Why would the Athenians be willing to sacrifice any hope of recovering their city only to fight on behalf of Peloponnesians who clearly all along cared only for their own defense? More immediately, what would the assembled Greeks do about thousands of hungry refugees on Salamis, whose safety depended on the Greek ships in the harbors of the island? Who could restore morale after four successive withdrawals—from the Vale of Tempe in Thessaly, Thermopylae, Artemisium, and Salamis? An alliance that either loses battles or does not fight them finds it almost impossible to turn on its aggressor and cede no more ground.[24]

The squabbling Greeks before Salamis heard yet a fifth alternative—a most bizarre threat from Themistocles himself. He warned that the furious and betrayed Athenians would pull up stakes entirely. If the Athenians were to be sacrificed by their Peloponnesian and island allies, and a general retreat ordered to the south, then Themistocles would round up the city's refugees. He would sail them to distant Sicily and shuttle more than two hundred thousand Athenian residents near their colony at Siris—rebirthing Athenian culture in safety eight hundred miles to the west and ensuring that the Greeks' largest fleet would not fight for those still free in the Peloponnese.

"If you do not [fight at Salamis]," Themistocles warned his Peloponnesian allies, "then we quite directly shall take up our households and sail over to Siris in Italy, a place which has been ours from ancient times, and at which the oracles inform us that we should plant a colony. And the rest of you without allies such as ourselves, will have reason to remember my words."[25]

The final bad choice from among the far worse alternatives was for the remaining allies to fight a sea battle at Salamis. They would cede no more Greek territory. Instead, the admirals would preserve Greek unity and hope to cripple the Persian fleet—and with it any chance of escape of the massive army of Xerxes. Because there were finite supplies at Salamis, and thousands of refugees to feed, there was no time left for talk. The battle had to be joined almost immediately, even if most of the assembled admirals would have to give in to Themistocles' threats and override the original wishes of their own political authorities back home to retreat to a Panhellenic defense at the Isthmus.[26]

Holy Salamis (*September 480 B.C.*)

The historian Herodotus and the contemporary playwright Aeschylus, along with much later accounts in Plutarch, Diodorus, and Nepos, believed that the reconstituted Greek fleet was outnumbered by at least two or three to one. In fact, it may have been only one-fourth the size of the Persian fleet. There is no information how many reinforcement ships joined the respective naval forces after the mutual losses from Artemisium, or how many trireme hulls were repaired. But ancient accounts suggest that between Persian replacements and the growing number of "Medizing" Greeks, the enemy was still at least as large as when it had left Persia months earlier.

If some Greeks quietly slipped away from Salamis and headed southward, most stayed. Even after wear and tear on the fleet, and losses at Artemisium, if the Greek fleet did not number 366 triremes exactly, there still may have been well over three hundred Greek vessels at Salamis. They were waiting to take on a Persian armada of at least six hundred warships—although both Herodotus and Aeschylus record that the enemy fleet had been reinforced to more than twelve hundred ships. That huge figure cannot be entirely discounted, although it implies a quarter million Persian seamen to man such an armada. In any case, there may well have been well over two hundred thousand sailors assembled at Salamis, making it one of the largest sea battles in history.[27]

The Greek fleet, still under the nominal overall command of the Spartan Eurybiades, was less experienced than the imperial Persian flotilla. Greek triremes were heavier and less maneuverable, their crews greener. The king's armada was composed of various veteran contingents from Phoenicia, Egypt, Asia Minor, Cyprus, and Greece itself. Most of these navies had patrolled the Aegean and Mediterranean for years enforcing the edicts of the Persian Empire. Perhaps more Greek-speaking crews from Ionia and the Aegean would fight on the Persian than on the Hellenic side.

The alliance's best hope was to draw the Persians into the narrows between Salamis and the Attic mainland. Once there, the more numerous but lighter enemy triremes might prove vulnerable to the heavier, sturdier, and presumably slower Greek ships. Themistocles reasoned that the invaders also might not have enough room to maneuver and utilize all their triremes. Without more open seas, the Persians would lose the advantages of both their numbers and their superior nautical skill.

Surprise—and greater knowledge of currents and contrary winds inside the straits—would also aid the defenders. The unity of the Greeks versus the motley nature of the subject Persian armada, the psychological advantages defenders enjoy over aggressors, the hope that free peoples fight for their own destiny more stoutly than subjects do amid their subservience—all these, at least in Themistocles' mind, could become force multipliers and so might still trump Persian numbers.[28]

Various sources also refer to an improbable ruse on the part of Themistocles on the eve of the battle. He secretly sent his own slave Sicinnus on a mission to Xerxes, with a purported warning of an unexpected Greek withdrawal. The Persians might well have swallowed that strange story of Themistocles' treachery, given the rumors of Greek infighting and the well-reported Peloponnesian desire to go home. Themistocles' intention with the trick was threefold: First, he wanted to incite the Persians hastily to deploy and prematurely man their ships in the dark. Second, he hoped to fool them into splitting their larger enemy fleet to cover unnecessarily all the exits from the straits of Salamis. Third, Persian preemption would force reluctant Greek allies to commit to the sea battle and mobilize immediately in the face of the advancing Persian enemy. A fourth result, or so it was also alleged in antiquity, was that Themistocles could later claim that he had tried to do the Persians a favor, if they won, or if in the future he needed exile in a safe place. Apparently, the agreement to stay at Salamis had strengthened the position of Themistocles. In the few hours before battle, he began to exercise tactical authority despite the nominal overall command of Eurybiades.

In response, the Persians, without careful planning, rowed out into the straits of Salamis, just as Themistocles anticipated—but not before dispatching parts of their Egyptian squadrons to block the southern and western entrances to the strait. In short, Xerxes had sent some of their best contingents on a wild-goose chase to ambush a Greek retreat that never came. The result was the Persians could not make full use of their numerical superiority inside the confining narrows of the Salamis strait itself, where the battle was to be fought.[29]

Xerxes probably attacked just before dawn. As the September morning breeze picked up, the Persian fleet rowed forward in three lines against the Greeks' two, its captains worried that they "would lose their heads" should the enemy fleet escape. Quickly the attackers became disorganized due to the Greek ramming and the confusion of having too many ships in too-confined waters—and the shocking sight that the Greeks—the Athenians on the left wing, the Spartans on the right—far from fleeing, were heading en masse right toward them. Themistocles himself was at the vanguard of the advancing Greek triremes. Xerxes, in contrast, watched his Persians from afar, purportedly perched on his throne atop nearby Mount Aigaleos on the Attic shore. In the words of the dramatist Aeschylus, "The mass of ships was crowded into the narrows, and none was able to offer help to another."[30]

The sea battle was fought all day—most likely sometime between September 20 and 30, 480 B.C., perhaps on the morning of September 25. By nightfall half the Persian fleet was sunk, due both to poor tactics and leadership and to the superior morale and seamanship of the crews of the Greek triremes, who knew far better the tides and currents of Salamis Bay—and that defeat meant the enslavement of their families watching from the beaches. The surviving Persian fleet headed back to port and made preparations to flee back to Asia Minor before the Greeks demolished their pontoon bridge over the Hellespont.

The morale of the surviving fleet was shattered, despite their collective fear of the outraged king watching from above. The Persians suffered "utter and complete ruin." Although in theory the surviving defeated enemy still outnumbered the Greek fleet, the Persian armada was neither battleworthy nor eager to reengage the victorious Greek triremes. Perhaps more than eighty thousand imperial sailors were killed, wounded, missing, or dispersed—which would make Salamis the most lethal one-day naval battle in history, more bloody than even an Ecnomus, Lepanto, Trafalgar, Jutland, or Midway.

Ancient accounts record the macabre scene of the human carnage where Persian corpses were "battered by the surf, lifeless, tossed here and there in their cloaks." And given that most of the Persians could not swim, we should assume the Greeks speared any survivors clinging to the flotsam and jetsam, knocking them beneath the waves—"hitting and hacking them with broken oars and the wreckage of the ships." Ancient sea battles were usually fought near land, and with triremes that became partially submerged rather than sank outright. Nevertheless, the inability of Persians to swim and the likelihood that many were fully clothed perhaps made their losses much higher than among the Greek allies.[31]

Within weeks of the defeat, Xerxes left a ruined Athens. He sailed for the Hellespont in panic with survivors of the imperial fleet. A rearguard of sixty thousand infantry accompanied him by land. The king left behind his surrogate commander Mardonius, with a still sizable landed and cavalry force to continue the struggle the next spring and summer. The remaining Persian army quickly retreated northward for the winter through the pastures of Boeotia into northern Greece. The Athenian refugees for a time got back their burned-out city.

Although the Greeks had immediately declared victory after Salamis, a few months later Mardonius returned over the pass from Boeotia to reoccupy Athens. The population again fled, the Persians torching the city a second time. The brilliant victory at Salamis nevertheless did not prevent this subsequent Persian reoccupation. After camping in a deserted and largely ruined Athens, Mardonius then sent the Persians back into

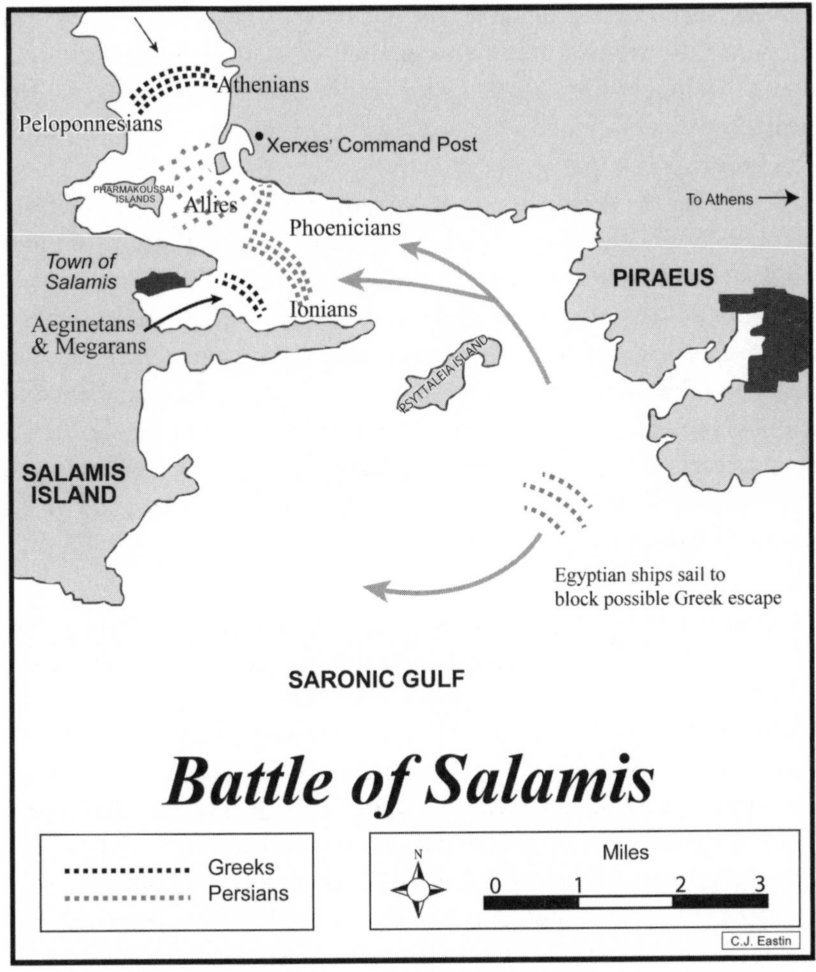

Boeotia yet a third time in late summer 479 to prepare for the expected Greek infantry counterattack. After the flight of Xerxes, some seventy thousand reenergized Greeks flocked to Plataea near the mountainous Attic border to finish off Mardonius. There, on a small plain near the Asopos River on the lower slopes of Mount Kithairon, the Greeks crushed the Persians, killed Mardonius, and watched the survivors scatter to the north.

With the storm and losses at Artemisium, and the subsequent naval defeat at Salamis, Xerxes may have lost cumulatively more than nine hundred triremes. Now with Mardonius' annihilation in Boeotia, perhaps as many as a quarter million Persian imperial infantry and sailors had perished in Greece. Rarely in the ancient world had so few killed so many. The cultural result was exultation in newfound Greek freedom: "No longer was there a bridle on the speech of mortals, for the people were set free to say what they wished, once the yoke of power was broken."[32]

Soon after the Persian defeat at Salamis, Themistocles vanished from accounts of the great campaign of 479 B.C. to mop up the tens of thousands of Persians who were on their own after the flight of Xerxes. Themistocles did not take part in the land battle, and he may well have fallen out of favor with his Athenian allies and his own countrymen, tired of his endless boasting of Salamis and his oversized ego. Instead, he stayed at sea pursuing enemy vessels along the coast of Asia Minor. He did not resurface prominently until the Persian Wars were over. Salamis was Themistocles' great moment, and when it passed, the war could go on largely without him.[33]

A Most Unheroic End (*Magnesia, Persian-held Asia Minor, 459 B.C.*)

About twenty years after Salamis, the legendary Themistocles, in his midsixties, was found dead—and in Persian-held Asia Minor, of all places. The rumors flew back across the Aegean that the old man had killed himself. The story went on that he was poisoned with some lethal concoction laced with the blood of a bull. Of course, the illustrious savior of Athens was not supposed to die like this, old, exiled, disgraced, as a would-be satrap no less, in pay to the very Persian Empire that had once sought to destroy his homeland.[34]

As an Athenian exile five years earlier, Themistocles had been ostracized, fled his native Athens, and earned a bounty on his head and a posse at his heels. The old man without a polis had serially worn out his welcome among a variety of suspicious Greek hosts—at Argos, Corcyra, Epirus, Pydna, Naxos, and Ephesus. Finally only his ex-enemies would welcome him in across the Aegean—the usual dénouement when a maverick had alienated both Athens and Sparta as places of refuge. Of course, many other Greeks of the age had turned traitor and joined the Persians, including the former Spartan kings Demaratus and Pausanias. Nearby Persian Asia Minor served as an ancient version of turn-of-the-century Mexico, the Aegean a sort of Rio Grande, across which prominent Greek outlaws often fled from various posses. Later the Athenian general Alcibiades served a Persian satrap Tissaphernes. But none of these infamous betrayers were as hallowed a figure in their time as was Themistocles. If nearly all great Greek generals—Miltiades, Pericles, Alcibiades, Epaminondas—given the jealousy inherent in the nature of ancient consensual societies, at one time in their careers were either tried, fined, or exiled, none had experienced quite such acclaim followed by such utter shame.[35]

While in Asia Minor for the last five years of his life (463–459), Themistocles had played on his former fame and knowledge of the Greeks to curry enough favor with the Persian king to win a well-paid imperial sinecure in Magnesia. King Artaxerxes, the despot who inherited the kingdom, supposedly shouted of the arrival of the self-made Athenian, "I have Themistocles the Athenian! I have Themistocles the Athenian! I have Themistocles the Athenian!" when he heard that the Greek hero had first entered Persian territory voluntarily rather than in chains. Apparently the famous traitor, even if past sixty, was proof to Artaxerxes that the Persians had at last evened the score at Salamis, well aside from the hope that the Persians were expecting to acquire dated Greek intelligence from the old captain.[36]

In the last year of Themistocles' exile in Magnesia, amid a new revolt of the Egyptian provinces, the Persians were once again at war with the Greeks—although fighting to hang on to their empire rather than to expand it in the west. In King Artaxerxes' mind it was probably past time for the refugee Themistocles to repay the king's five-year hospitality with active resistance against his own countrymen. Themistocles may have balked at that and thus finally killed himself in distress at the thought of joining the enemy. Or was he worn out by the ingratitude of the Athenians and simply could not stomach his rivals back home using the fleet that he created to win continuous glory as it once more carved away at the Persian Empire? It is impossible to know why he killed himself—if he in fact did commit suicide. (The story may have been a later Greek invention to explain Themistocles' despair over an unfair charge of treason.)

In any case, that Themistocles left Athens during its ascendance to enter Persian service at the start of the eastern empire's slow decline was only the culmination of his run of misfortune. Themistocles' father had once warned him about the fickleness of Athenian democratic politics—showing the young Themistocles the abandoned skeletons of ancient triremes on the shore, emblems of what happens to wartime heroes when their service to the state is no longer needed. Themistocles himself, always prone to a bit of self-pity and dramatics, often remembered that morality tale—and trumped it by comparing himself not to the keel of a rotting warship, but to the proverbial ubiquitous Greek plane tree, whose expansive shade is appreciated only when men seek refuge from the storm. In his defense, the litany of charges against Themistocles was probably personal in nature—part of an unfortunate aspect of an envy-prone Athenian democracy to bring down the preeminent and send its best military minds scurrying across the Aegean to find safety and lucre among the enemy Persians.[37]

The Road to Perdition (*Athens, 480–463 B.C.*)

The brilliant victory at Salamis (480) some twenty years earlier was not the capstone of Themistocles' career. Rather, it marked the catalyst for an even more radical subsequent agenda of transforming Athens itself—thereby offending most of the city's powerful landed families. It was almost as if Themistocles saw the victory over the Persians not as the end, but only the end of the beginning of an ambitious plan to reinvent Athens itself.

The postwar Spartan-Athenian alliance against Persia was over almost before the war ended. It certainly lasted no longer than did the equally unlikely Soviet-American pact following the common defeat of Nazi Germany. Themistocles' subsequent decadelong expansion of the fortifications of the city of Athens and enlargement of the fleet immediately provoked, by intent, the rival Spartans and their conservative sympathizers at Athens. Especially galling to Themistocles' rich and pro-Spartan countrymen was his ruse of going down to Sparta to agree to the utopian dream of an unwalled Greece. Ostensibly the Greeks agreed that that way, the returning Persians would never again have citadels to quarter in, while the city-states would not exhaust themselves in expensive sieges. Instead, without walls, all Greeks would remain in perpetual brotherhood, or at least fight it out through short, and less costly, decisive hoplite battles on the plains. But while the itinerant Themistocles was assuring the gullible Spartans of Athens's ecumenical pacifism in the new postwar era, his democratic supporters back home feverishly fortified their city and harbor in hopes of nullifying Spartan infantry supremacy.[38]

Themistocles also understood that walls in general weakened traditionalists. Fortifications meant less need for the city's own landowners to rally the Athenians to battle against any enemy that threatened their own farms. Instead, the city's new defenses divided the population more sharply into landed and landless classes. The new ramparts reduced political and economic clout for the traditionally powerful in Attica who held vulnerable farmland outside the walls, which could sometimes be sacrificed for the common good. Was not such realignment the demagogue Themistocles' real intent, after all—his agrarian critics charged—to reorder the class priorities of Athens, to favor the poor under the guise of new national defense strategies?

Fortifications were an even better way of meeting a formidable invasion than in panic evacuating and abandoning the city, as had happened before Salamis. Urban walls certainly required larger government expenditure; their construction tended to spread the wealth through the hiring of poorer workmen. These investments also transferred national defense to the fleet. That brought only further empowerment of the wage-earning poorer and more numerous rowing cohorts. Sea defense at Salamis had been the right choice at the time. But in the aftermath of the Persian retreat, Themistocles saw that his strategy could even be improved upon by evacuating in times of invasion only the countryside of its richer landowners—not, as in 480, sending the poor of the city into makeshift hovels on the surrounding islands.[39]

Most landowners understandably had long resented this decadelong divisive democratic agenda of Themistocles that soon after Salamis insidiously weakened the power of agrarian heavy infantrymen. In their eyes, the great divider had turned the city from one of "steadfast hoplites into sea-tossed mariners," as he used worries over national security for partisan domestic advantage.[40] Quite venomously, the conservative philosopher Plato, looking back over a century of radical Athenian history, much later wrote that the Athenians would have been better off to have lost sea fights like those at Salamis, even if they had saved Greece, rather than have such Themistoclean victories lead to the establishment of an extremist and unsustainable democracy severed from the land. It was Themistocles, Plato also complained, who had first "stripped the citizens of their spear and shield, and brought the Athenian people down to the rowing-pad and oar."[41]

Yet for a decade after the great Athenian victory, the upstart Themistocles lost no occasion to remind the Athenians that he alone had saved them. Only he had ensured them safety from future Persian attack. He continually sought to translate his own military prestige into remaking the very nature of Athens itself. His aim was to reject the old rural polis of the sixth-century Athenian lawgiver Solon and aspire to a cosmopolitan naval empire that would in time rule the Aegean under Pericles—more powerful and more majestic precisely because it would be more egalitarian. Themistocles had used guile to defeat the Persians at Salamis. But this time he was employing that same base cunning to marginalize Athenians at home.

As was the fate of many Greek visionaries, Themistocles' novel ideas instantly branded him a dangerous radical and earned him exile, yet within decades would be institutionalized by Pericles and others as official imperial policy. The fleet would only grow larger; even greater walls would connect the city to the port at Piraeus; and the poor would find even more avenues of state support. But that acceptance would come only after Themistocles' exile, and without full acknowledgment of his role as the creator of maritime empire. Themistocles, Plutarch concluded, "increased the power of the common people against the aristocracy, filling them with recklessness, once the control of the state came into the hands of the sailors, boatswains, and captains."[42]

It did not help the prophet of sea power that in a status-obsessed democracy, Themistocles was of mixed ancestry. While every freeborn Athenian male in theory aspired to an equality of result under Athenian democracy, good lineage, money, and family influence were, at least privately, still highly prized. Rumors claimed the mother of Themistocles could have been Carian or Thracian. Maybe she was even a prostitute or—who knows?—even a slave. His father was "not very well known at Athens." A Roman-era marble bust, now at the museum in Ostia, Italy, purports to be a copy of an original fifth-century-B.C. bronze sculpture of Themistocles: The face is unlike almost any other idealized portrait of Greek commanders, in showing a rather coarse figure with cropped hair and beard—more akin to a later Roman military emperor from the provinces of North Africa than a classical Greek hero.[43]

Apparently the family of Themistocles had little social clout, even if they did have some money. "Too obscure," Plutarch further sniffed of his father, "to advance his reputation." Later writers reveled in accounts of his earlier debaucheries and uncouth behavior to prove him an innate boor and profligate upstart. His appetites offered proof that Themistocles would, by virtue of his audacity, "be entirely great—whether for good or evil." At any rate, the name Themistocles in Greek meant "Famed for Right."[44]

In the traditional ancient Greek city-state, ideas and agendas were rarely judged entirely on their own merits, separate from the character, breeding, and background of the men who advanced them. Most ancient accounts of Themistocles' youth chronicle how he outsmarted the better-born. Both his intelligence and ruthless energy came naturally to Themistocles, what the historian Thucydides later acknowledged as his "native capacity." Thucydides, who likewise may have been of mixed Thracian ancestry, also claimed that Themistocles' talent lay in an inbred good judgment unrefined by experience or education. In truth, like most upstarts, he had to study and prepare far more diligently than did his more advantaged rivals to train his "infinitely mobile and serpentine mind." So, for example, Themistocles purportedly barked to detractors, "I may not know how to tune the lyre or play the harp, but I do know how to take a small and unknown city and make it famous and great." While Themistocles sought out the best tutors—such as Mnesiphilos, the material philosopher who became his lifelong confidant—he still consciously played on his lowly origins to cement his populist credentials among the Athenian *dêmos*.[45]

Usually Athenian democrats appear in the texts of Aristophanes, Plato, the Old Oligarch, Thucydides, Plutarch, and Xenophon as rabble-rousers. Their radically egalitarian ends were always used to justify their uncouth means. In that context, then, Themistocles frequents Athenian literature as the archetypical *polypragmôn*, the rascally busybody, who rose in Athenian society by his cleverness and limitless troublemaking. He was the antithesis to the more aristocratic and sober Miltiades, Aristides, and Cimon. Those were his chief rivals, and they were all bound by supposed landed reverence and privilege—and, in the case of Aristides, superior character and temperament. In any case, the biographer Plutarch records an entire corpus of popular abuse of Themistocles. In the Greek view, by the time Themistocles died, his deceptions and many ruses had ensured that Athens won the battle of Salamis, split the forces of the retreating Persians, and fortified the victorious city—and yet in retrospect were still seen as proof of his unsavory character.[46]

By the mid-470s, postwar Athens was mostly secure and on the rise. The city was well into an initial rebuilding of what had been lost in the burning of 480. Revisionism was the order of the day. The now distant victory at Salamis increasingly had become retroactively reinterpreted in the assembly as a logical manifestation of Athenian naval power, rather than, as was true a decade earlier, the most unlikely victory in the history of the Greek people. Some wealthier Athenians even claimed that Themistocles had really done little to ensure the Athenian victory at Salamis. They variously attributed the great victory to either the allies or the sudden arrival of Aristides and his hoplites. Odder still, the radical growth of Athenian influence in the Aegean between 480 and 471 in the public mind was beginning to become more associated with his conservative rivals Aristides and Cimon than with Themistocles.[47]

By 459, Themistocles was increasingly politically irrelevant. His reputation was fading among the people and being torn down by his aging rivals who still knew of it. It is indeed likely that Themistocles killed himself, a shameful thing to do in ancient Greek and Roman society—yet often favored by the most honorable figures in antiquity, from the mythical Ajax to the old Roman Cato. But as far as his problems with political rivals go, they were to be expected given Themistocles' achievements.

How Did Themistocles Do It?

Themistocles' multifaceted leadership entailed diplomacy, political partisanship, grand strategy, battle tactics, calm in combat, and unabashed cunning. Before the onset of Xerxes, he enacted measures that he believed might check Persian power, and events proved his belief correct. To the historian Thucydides, such "foresight" separated Themistocles from most successful Greek military thinkers of his age, who either had no comprehensive view of strategy or claimed such foreordained knowledge in hindsight. In three precise areas the advice of Themistocles proved critical in saving what had seemed surely lost.

1. *The building of the armada.* Had Themistocles earlier (483) not urged the Athenians to build their fleet with the sudden revenues from the unexpected strike at the silver mines of Laurium, there would probably have been no chance for a Greek defense at Salamis. Themistocles plowed ahead against the advice of most Athenians, quite contrary to the received infantry wisdom from the recent victory at Marathon. That he claimed the ships were necessary to defeat a nearby widely hated and tangible enemy like Aegina—Pericles later called the nearby island the "eyesore" of the Piraeus—perhaps made the radical measure more palatable. In short, Themistocles alone appropriated the money, invested it in a navy, and so had a fleet on hand ready to save Athens.

2. *The abandonment of the city.* Had Themistocles not persuaded the Athenians in September 480 to evacuate Athens and the surrounding

Attic countryside, their hoplite land army would have been wiped out in a futile Thermopylae-like last stand. An orphaned fleet would have retreated southward or westward. Had the Athenians stayed inside the largely indefensible city to withstand a siege, they would have likewise perished in toto or been forced to join the Persians. Nor after Thermopylae did Themistocles try to persuade the Greek allies to march northward to stop the Persians in the plains of Boeotia or Attica. Of course, Themistocles had fought at Marathon and co-commanded the failed defense at Tempe in the summer of 480. Yet he knew by mid-September that the gallant veterans of Marathon could not overcome ten-to-one odds. Even the infantry fight the next year at Plataea was a close-run thing—and winnable only after tens of thousands of Persians had been killed at Salamis or retreated home. The victory was also predicated on a massive mobilization of tens of thousands of Panhellenic soldiers, most of whom mustered only after hearing that Xerxes had fled Greece in defeat.

There were no other Athenians in the historical record who had advocated so radical a measure as trying to save the city by allowing it to be burned—twice. Later Athenians, most notably the general Nicias on Sicily, would rally their troops with reminders that "Men make a city, not walls," calling on the miraculous tradition of Athenian victory. Themistocles' postwar efforts to fortify Athens were followed by the efforts of Pericles after his death to build two extensive Long Walls connecting the city to the Piraeus. Both projects emphasized how determined subsequent generations were never to repeat the horror of 480 in abandoning the city along with its surrounding countryside.

The leader Pericles was a Themistoclean at heart. He argued that the best way to defeat Sparta in the Peloponnesian War (431–404) was to fight at sea after abandoning the defense of Athenian farmland against Spartan ravagers. But unlike Themistocles, Pericles advocated such a strategy only with the reassurance that the city and its port at Piraeus were safe behind stout walls, inside which the entire Attic population could find safety from enemy invasion.

3. *Drawing the line at Salamis.* Although most southern Greeks came to understand at the eleventh hour that Themistocles' logic was in their own interests in providing a forward defense for the Peloponnese and in keeping the Athenian fleet engaged in the Greek defense, there was still no guarantee that the Peloponnesians would fight at Salamis—given their near completion of a massive wall at the Isthmus. To read Plutarch's

Life of Themistocles is to review a list of ancient attacks on both the character and wisdom of Themistocles on the eve of battle. So two further actions of Themistocles were required to guarantee a fight at Salamis and then to achieve victory there.[48]

The ruse of Sicinnus persuaded the Persians immediately to rush into battle and thereby to force the wavering non-Athenian Greeks to stay and fight. Scholars are divided over the authenticity of the tale. But there is reason to accept the general truth of the ancient account: At the point when the alliance was about to break up, the news was announced to the Greek admirals that the Persians were already launching their triremes and thus all approaches in and out of the Salamis channel were to be blocked. Only then did the galvanized Greeks discover that they could no longer retreat to the Isthmus. The sole choice was either to fight immediately or surrender.[49]

Because Themistocles had persuaded the Persians into committing their ships into the narrow channels, it is probable that the actual plan of the Greek deployment was also his as well. The secret to the Greek success was to draw the cumbersome enemy fleet further into the narrows and thus ensure that it could not utilize its overwhelming numerical advantage. Themistocles had the Greek ships initially row backward. That induced the Persians to row further into the channel, on the assumption that the Greeks were in fact trying to flee as their fifth-column "intelligence" had indicated. When the two fleets collided, the Persians—again, as Themistocles had planned—were dispersed and not in good order, and unable to bring their full strength against the ordered Greek armada.

Controversy surrounds yet another supposed Themistoclean stratagem—the purported postwar second secret message to the defeated Xerxes urging him to sail home while Themistocles prevented the Greeks from reaching his bridges at the Hellespont first and destroying easy entry back into Asia. If this second effort at deception was also true, then it had the added effect of encouraging another split in Persian forces after the battle and drew off further Persian manpower. That meant at the subsequent battle of Plataea the following August, the enemy forces under Mardonius were not all that much more numerous than the assembled Panhellenic Greek army.[50]

Themistoclean Counterfactuals

The ancient verdict on the genius of Themistocles was unanimous. If his later career was checkered, his character dubious, and his end shameful, he remained the most gifted strategist that classical antiquity ever produced. Proof of that ancient assessment is found in imagining what might have happened had Themistocles failed to galvanize the Greeks at Salamis.[51]

There are no large islands immediately off the Hellenic coast to the south off the Isthmus of Corinth. Nor are there many bays or inlets on the northeastern shore of the Argolid peninsula to offer shelter for a retreating Greek fleet, in which to nullify the numerical advantages of the Persian armada. Even if the Athenians could have been convinced to leave Salamis and fight far to the south—perhaps transporting their refugees on Aegina and Salamis southward to join those already on Troizen—they were still down to only two poor alternatives of defense: a sea battle in the more open waters off the Isthmus, or a last-ditch land defense behind the fortifications of the Isthmus itself. Neither offered hope of victory. The former strategy would have probably meant being swarmed by a superior fleet in open waters; the latter option ensured being surrounded and outflanked by numerous enemy amphibious landings.

Herodotus reports a speech of Themistocles in which he rejected just this sort of a naval engagement off Corinth. Instead, he tried to convince the Spartan admiral Eurybiades of the merits of his strategy "to save Hellas":

> If you fight the enemy at the Isthmus, you will battle in open waters—just where it is to our worst advantage, since our ships are heavier and less in number. In addition, you will give up Salamis, Megara, and Aigina—even if we should win a victory there. And their infantry force will follow their fleet. And so you will lead them to the Peloponnese, and endanger all of Greece.[52]

In contrast, Themistocles added that a fight at Salamis would ensure that the Peloponnesians might delay their enemies from approaching the Isthmus and keep them far distant from their own territory. Only a victory at Salamis might save both Athens and the Peloponnese. Even a success at the Isthmus was too late for the salvation of Attica. The key for the Greek defense, then, was to keep its two greatest powers, Athens and Sparta, both committed to the spirit of Panhellenic defense after the catastrophic defeats and withdrawal from Thermopylae. Themistocles knew that tens of thousands of Athenians, both sailors and civilians, had not made it to Troizen and Aegina. Most were still stuck on Salamis. There they faced immediate enslavement or death if the Greek fleet abandoned them to the Persians, and they were largely without supplies or shelter if the Greeks delayed much longer.

Mnesiphilos, an Athenian elder, had also warned Themistocles earlier that should the Greeks not fight at Salamis, there was little chance that the Panhellenic armada would ever again assemble as one fleet, even at the Isthmus. "Everyone," Mnesiphilos predicted, "will withdraw to their own city-states. Neither Eurybiades nor any other man will be able to hold them together. Rather, the armada will break apart." For that very reason, Herodotus relates that the Carian queen Artemesia advised the Persians to avoid Salamis. She cautioned the king to wait and then gradually head south by land to the Isthmus. She further argued that a sea battle at Salamis would give the beleaguered Greeks one last, and unnecessary, chance to unite to stop the Persian onslaught.[53]

Nevertheless, the Peloponnesians in Herodotus' account clung stubbornly to the idea of a land defense. They were fortifying the isthmus even as their admirals debated for time at Salamis. At one point, Herodotus says that Themistocles (until he sent Sicinnus to dupe the Persians into starting the fight) had "lost the argument" with the Peloponnesian admirals. There is also good reason to believe, as Herodotus foresaw, that such an infantry defense would have failed.

Again, an intact Persian fleet could easily have landed troops to the rear all along the coast of the Peloponnese. A half century later, even with a fleet only a third the size of the Persians', the Athenians employed with success that strategy of seaborne raiding on the Peloponnese throughout the Archidamian War (431–421 B.C.). The meandering stone wall at the Isthmus, connecting the Corinthian and Saronic Gulfs, would probably have extended nearly six miles. In later Greek history, no defending force was able to keep out invaders from the north by walling the Isthmus. The Theban general Epaminondas between 370 and 362 B.C. on four occasions easily brushed aside resistance there, both on his southward and northward passages between Boeotia and the Peloponnese. Herodotus, then, seems correct in asserting that defense behind a wall at the Isthmus was no real alternative to a naval engagement off Salamis.

* * *

The Greek success at Salamis did not destroy the Persian fleet outright. Nor did the naval victory entirely rid Attica of the Persians. Rather, Salamis was the critical point in the war that turned a certain lost cause into a possible victory. Themistocles' triumph ensured that the Persians—absent their king, the imperial fleet sunk or in retreat, and their infantry demoralized—could not win the war outright under any conditions. The victorious Greeks had the advantages of logistics, knowledge of local terrain, and morale—and for the first time in the war, the "land itself became their ally."[54]

The Character of Themistocles

When Themistocles surveyed the dead Persians that littered the shores after the battle of Salamis, he told an acquaintance to feel free to strip them of their gold jewelry: "Help yourself—you are not Themistocles." A number of similar anecdotes about Themistocles attest to his sense of moral superiority, and his need to be appreciated by the Athenians whom he had saved. Ancient historians agree on some general themes in their discussion of the character of Themistocles—arrogance toward others, and absolute confidence in his own wisdom and leadership. Themistocles was not averse to scheming to ostracize his rivals. He freely faked omens to frighten the more pious into his fold. He sent duplicitous messages to the enemy. And he certainly tricked the gullible Spartans into allowing the Athenians to fortify their city.[55]

As a scrapper, he had learned that such unprincipled behavior was necessary in his unlikely rise to the leadership of the Athenians. As a new man, he was not invested in protection of the landed estates of the aristocracy and their mannered behavior. He had no allegiance to the Marathon men. He may not have had much compunction in abandoning the prominent tombs and shrines of the Athenian aristocracy in order to save the city proper. Both Herodotus and Plutarch associate bribery and deceit with almost every great end that Themistocles achieved (including, and especially, his year of generalship before and after Salamis). His dearth of ancient virtue explains why, after the incredible victory at Salamis, the principal Greek commanders there chose not to vote him the prize of excellence for his inspired leadership.

Sea power, fortification, and evacuation were originally unpalatable for aristocratic grandees. But these concepts for a pragmatic general like Themistocles were seen simply as useful or not. He was determined only to lead Athens and transform it into a radically democratic society that would naturally inherit the Aegean. The ancients were ambivalent about Themistocles: Unconventional strategies alone had saved Athens and augmented her collective power, but only a rogue like Themistocles could dream up and implement them. Salamis was a great victory, but it empowered Themistocles to change the nature of Athens for the worse.

Tactical insight on the battlefield, and even grand strategy, are not in themselves enough to restore the sagging wartime fortunes of a democracy. Themistocles' legacy was not merely enticing Xerxes to fight where he should not at Salamis and then drawing up a battle plan that would offer a good chance for his defeat. Rather, Salamis was the logical dividend of a far more complex Themistoclean vision. Under his leadership, the city would learn to privilege its majority population without land. Athenians would come to appreciate that ships were not merely superior assets to infantry and essential to maritime empire and defense, but they empowered the poor with wages and prestige. Under Themistocles' leadership, the Athenians would agree that Persia could be not only defeated, but utterly defeated, and in such a fashion that the resulting void in the Aegean would naturally favor the emergence of a new Athenian empire in its place.

Themistocles' vision would not only later provide the foundation for Pericles' maritime empire, but also, a half century later, for the forced evacuation during the Peloponnesian War that resulted in the destruction of a quarter of the population due to a plague that broke out in such close quarters. The great divider Themistocles also bequeathed an intensification of class strife between hoplite landowners and landless sailors. The near-centurylong animosity toward Sparta ultimately led to the defeat of Athens. Later conservative thinkers cited Salamis as the beginning of the end of the old polis of virtue, as the state began to redistribute money and create dependency. But that was all in the future. It was the responsibility of successors to embrace, expand, modify, or reject Themistoclean strategy that was aimed in his generation at thwarting the existential threat of Persia—and succeeded brilliantly at just that task.

Ancient observers also remarked on the superior morale of the Greeks at Salamis. The Greeks saw themselves as "slaves of no one." In the romantic tradition, rowers purportedly chanted out "Free your native land, free your children, free your wives, and free the seats of your fathers' gods and the tombs of your ancestors" as they sought to ram the king's ships. If the Greeks believed in their own innate superiority over the Persians,

Themistocles himself was convinced of the singularity of his own Athens. He was proud of his Hellenism, but at Salamis, Themistocles sought to save his own city and further the aims of what it was to be an Athenian—namely, to invent the Western notion of a state in arms that drew on the participation of all its citizens across class lines.[56]

What made Themistocles a great captain was his ability to craft strategy to reflect national character: Sea power not only embodied the city's real strengths, but would alone make Athens preeminent among the Greek poleis. It was, after all, about the only serious means by which to bring nearly half the population of Athens to the fore, given long-held Greek prejudices about status, land, infantry participation and equipment, and state defense. To further that aim of changing Athens into a naval power, Themistocles was better informed and more experienced than both his enemies and his associate commanders. No general in either fleet had such varied strategic and tactical experience in warfare of the ancient Mediterranean.

Xerxes was perched on a throne; Themistocles, in the fashion of Greek battle leaders, was in a lead trireme. Most Greek generals did not confide in slaves; Sicinnus was intimate with Themistocles, whose natural affinities were with the rank and file. Persian generals bowed to Xerxes; Greek commanders threatened to hit Themistocles. Themistocles was not just more of a soldiers' general than Xerxes, but also more than all his fellow Greek generals.

It was a habit of ancient historians to compare great captains of Greece and Rome to assess the most gifted. By the standards of ancient reckoning, Themistocles was considered preeminent, not merely because he was successful, but because his success seemed the dividend of a systematic military and military mind. Diodorus, following the fourth-century Greek historian Ephoros, lists a number of reasons why Themistocles was the greatest man Greece produced (*megistos Hellênôn*). With the fewest resources, Themistocles achieved the greatest results, not just in ridding the Aegean of the Persians, but also in dethroning the Spartans from their historic preeminent position in Greece and establishing the subsequent course of Athenian imperialism. His brilliance won the battle of Salamis, but also in peacetime led to Athenian naval hegemony.[57]

The historian Thucydides, not necessarily a fan of Athenian democracy himself, saw even more clearly how Themistocles had alone saved

Athens and "surpassed all others." In a long encomium, he claims Themistocles defeated Xerxes by his innate intelligence and the rare trait of foresight—the singular ability to see how things that should never happen might well indeed occur at least one time in the future. Had Themistocles lost, mainland Greece would have gone the way of conquered Ionia, where its sixth-century-B.C. Greek renaissance by the fifth had clearly stagnated under Persian rule. One need not be a cultural chauvinist to appreciate that Persian culture had very different ideas about personal freedom, democracy, the rights of the individual, and rationalism. Quite simply, without the savior general Themistocles, the world as we know it today might have been a very different place indeed.

Victory at Marathon in 490 had alarmed Themistocles while most others rejoiced. Defeat at Thermopylae had encouraged him when most Greeks fell into abject despair. Before salvation at Salamis there was no free Greece. After Themistocles' victory, there were soon to be few foreign enemies in the Aegean. His dream of an ascendant Athenian maritime empire was assured—and yet along with it a deadly rivalry with Sparta on the horizon.[58]

CHAPTER TWO

Byzantium at the Brink

The Fireman Flavius Belisarius—A.D. 527–59

An Obol for Belisarius? (*A.D.* 565)

Date obolum Belisaurio!

"Give an obol to Belisarius!" So a medieval fable spread about the poor beggar who had once almost alone saved the Byzantine Empire and helped ensure that it would endure for another nine hundred years.

More than a millennium after the exile, disgrace, and death of Themistocles, the legendary general Flavius Belisarius in his old age was supposed to have been reduced to a blind tramp, crying for coins in his wretched state to common passersby along the streets of Constantinople. This mythical end of the first man of Constantinople remained a popular morality tale well into the nineteenth century. Romantic painters, poets, and novelists all invoked the sad demise of Belisarius to remind us of the wages of ingratitude and radical changes in fortune, which we are all, without exception, prone to suffer. In Robert Graves's novel *Count Belisarius*, the old general is made to cry, "Alms, alms! Spare a copper for Belisarius! Spare a copper for Belisarius who once scattered gold in these streets. Spare a copper for Belisarius, good people of Constantinople! Alms, alms!"[1]

But even if a blind and mendicant aged Belisarius is a mythical tradition, the general's last years were tragic enough.[2] After stopping the Persian encroachment in the east (530–31), he saved his emperor from riot, revolution, and a coup d'état at home (532). Next he recovered most of North Africa from the Vandals (533–34). Then he directed, off and on, the invasion and recovery of southern and central Italy from the Goths (534–48)—only to be summarily recalled to Constantinople by his emperor Justinian. In all these victories, either defeat or stalemate had seemed the most likely outcome. Instead, the old Roman Empire of the Caesars was for a time nearly restored.

Then for the next decade (548–58), while war raged on all the borders of Byzantium, the empire's greatest general sat mostly idle. Belisarius, for all his laurels, nearly disappears from the historical record, as he was kept close at home by a suspicious and jealous emperor—worried that the popularity of his victories might lead to a rival emperor rising in the newly reconquered west.

As some sort of nominal senior counselor to the court of the increasingly paranoid Justinian, Belisarius was to be kept distant from any chance for more of the sort of conquest that had so enhanced his own reputation—even if that exile might mean an end to the ongoing military recovery of the Western Roman Empire abroad. But then suddenly, the general was brought back out of retirement a final time to save the nearly defenseless capital from a lightning strike of Bulgars under Zabergan in 559. His final mission accomplished, Belisarius was dismissed from imperial service for good. Stripped of honors, the old captain increasingly fell under court suspicion, given his great wealth, his Mediterranean-wide fame, and his appeal among the commoners of Constantinople.

By November 562, even his spouse, the aged court intriguer Antonia—her legendary beauty long since dissipated—could not save her general's military career. He was in his late fifties. The general had not held a major command abroad in twelve years since being replaced by the eunuch general Narses in Italy. Justinian put the retired and worn-out Belisarius on trial for his life on trumped-up charges of corruption and conspiracy to murder the emperor, whom he had served so faithfully for most of his life. He was imprisoned until found innocent in July 563. Thirty years of military service that had saved both the emperor and his empire counted for almost nothing. His once loyal former secretary and now hostile rival, Procopius, whose histories are our best source of Belisarius at war in the east, North Africa, and in Italy, may have been the court magistrate who oversaw his indictment and trial. In any case, much of the later work of Procopius is hostile to the general whom he once idolized.[3]

While we need not believe ancient accounts that Belisarius had been blinded and sat on display as a beggar, his last acquittal brought little relief. The would-be restorer of Rome's ancient glory died just two years later, about sixty years old in 565—a few months before the end of his octogenarian emperor, Justinian, who had done so much both to promote and to ruin his career. For nearly the next fifteen hundred years, the strange odyssey of Belisarius would serve as the theme of plays, novels, romances, poems, and paintings. The renown was due in part to his central and exalted place in the early chapters of the historian Procopius, an unbelievable career confirmed elsewhere in other sources. The general's victories, his serial arrests, and his court ostracisms all made him a larger-than-life character.[4]

At his death, Flavius Belisarius' imperial Constantinople—nearly wiped out by successive epidemics of bubonic plague, with Bulgars once again nearing the gates of the city, its Christianity torn apart by schisms and heresies, the great dome of the magnificent church of Hagia Sophia just recently restored from sudden collapse due to design flaws, the forty-year reign of its greatest emperor nearing a close—would nonetheless endure another 888 years. Its resilience had been in no small part due to the thirty-year nonstop warring of Belisarius—the last Roman general and the greatest military commander that a millenniumlong Byzantium would produce—who in a brief three decades had expanded the size of the eastern empire by 45 percent. Belisarius did not save a theater, or even a war, but rather an entire empire through unending conflict his entire life.[5]

A Civilization in Crisis (*A.D. 530*)

When the inexperienced, twenty-five-year-old Flavius Belisarius was first ordered eastward to Mesopotamia to preserve Byzantium's eastern borders from the Persian inroads, there was no assurance that an undermanned and insolvent Constantinople would even survive in the east. Salvation was not to be found in one or two battle victories against a host of enemies, but rather in long, costly wars in which Byzantium slowly reestablished its borders, assured potential aggressors that they would pay dearly for any future invasions, and sought to reclaim rich western provinces long lost to various barbarian tribes but critical to the original concept of Roman imperial defense in the Mediterranean.

Far to the west, "Rome" by the early sixth century had become no more than a myth. The Eternal City had been long before sacked by the

Visigoths (410), again by Vandals (455), and, two decades later, was occupied (476) for a half century by the Gothic tribes. Almost all of Italy was reduced to a Gothic kingdom, a thousand miles away from Constantinople in the east, with tribal leaders squabbling over what wealth was left from a millennium of civilization.

Visigoths had long reached and settled in the Iberian Peninsula (475). Vandals—barbarians originally from the area of eastern Germany and modern Poland—were recognized as the unassailable rulers of the former Roman territory of North Africa (474). The Germanic Franks increasingly consolidated their power in and around Gaul (509). For millions from northern Britain to Libya, life was not as it had been just a century before. The Roman army, Roman law, and Roman material culture west of Greece were all vanishing—or at least changing in ways that would be unrecognizable to prior generations. Newcomers from across the Rhine increasingly drew upon the intellectual and material capital of centuries without commensurately replenishing what was consumed.[6]

The emperor Diocletian had for administrative purposes divided the empire in the late third century A.D. In the early fourth century, Constantine the Great had founded the eastern capital of Constantinople on the Bosporus. Since then, Rome in the east had gradually developed a distinct culture of its own. Latin gave way to Greek as the eastern empire's official language. The future Byzantium relied not so much on the fabled legions for its salvation, but on its superb navy, and later on heavy mounted archers. Constantinople looked more often eastward and southward to Asia and Africa for its commerce and wealth. Unlike the west, the east had somehow survived the fifth-century Germanic barbarian invasions from the north—perhaps given the sparser enemy populations of the northern Balkans and the greater natural obstacles offered by the Black Sea, Hellespont, and Danube.[7]

Just as dangerous as foreign invasions were the multifarious religious schisms and infighting among Christian sects. Heresies and orthodox persecutions weakened resistance in the east to an insurgent Persia—and soon enough Islam. Constantinople would grow to over half a million citizens. Yet the empire's enormous and costly civil service, and legions of Christian clerics, often came at the expense of an eroding military. The administration of God, the vast public bureaucracy, and the welfare state translated into ever fewer Byzantines engaged in private enterprise, wealth creation, and the defense of the realm—at precisely the time its enemies were growing in power and audacity.[8]

By the time of Belisarius, no more than 150,000 front-line and reserve infantry and cavalry protected a six-hundred-year-old empire in the east that, even shorn of its western provinces, still stretched from Mesopotamia to the Adriatic in the west. If Italian yeomen had created the idea of Rome that had spread to the Tigris and Nile, Greek speakers who never set foot west of Greece kept it alive long after Latin speakers in Italy were overrun by Goths. Byzantine power, shorn of much of its Roman origins, still reached the banks of the Danube and the northern shore of the Black Sea and extended to Egypt in the south. By strategic necessity, some seventy thousand non-Greek-speaking "barbarians" were incorporated into the shrinking military. The empire relied as much on bribes and marriage alliances as on its army to keep the vast borders secure. Rarely has such a large domain been defended by so few against so many enemies.

What ultimately kept the capital, Constantinople, safe were its unmatched fortifications—the greatest investment in labor and capital of the ancient world. And the legendary walls would prove unassailable to besiegers until the sacking of the city by Western Europeans in the Fourth Crusade (1204). Nearly as important was the Hellespont, the long, narrow strait that allowed access from the Black Sea to the Aegean and Mediterranean and yet proved a veritable moat across the invasion path of northern European tribes. The well-fortified capital was surrounded by seas on three sides, and its navy was usually able to keep most enemy invaders well clear of the city itself.

For all the problems of the Byzantines, the eastern empire's shrinking citizen body was still known as "Roman." To moderns, Justinian's sixth-century Constantinople may seem corrupt and inefficient, set among a sea of enemies with a declining population, and itself beset by faction and often plague that would come to kill more than a million imperial subjects. But to ancients, life within its borders by any benchmark of security and prosperity of the times was far preferable to the alternatives outside.[9]

The Visions of Justinian

Consequently, even without the reintegration of western Europe and North Africa, Byzantium still controlled sizable territory consisting of much of modern-day Greece, the major islands of the Aegean and southeastern Mediterranean, the southern Balkans, Turkey, Syria, Lebanon,

Israel, Egypt, and Iraq. Within these borders, classical learning and traditions of Roman law still ensured citizens ample supplies of pottery, glass, building materials, food, and metals. Literacy remained widespread. Thousands of imperial clerks and scholars continued to publish scientific and philosophical treatises that both expanded classical scholarship and gave rise to continually improving agriculture, military science, and construction.[10]

Scholars have sometimes questioned whether Christianity—not just porous borders, Germanic tribes, punitive taxation, endemic corruption, inflation and debt, and constant civil strife—led to the fall of the Roman Empire in the west. Had Christian ideas of magnanimity and pacifism replaced classical civic militarism, while hundreds of thousands of otherwise productive soldiers and business people flocked to religious orders? The theory of Christian-caused decline, however, would fail to account for a near-millennium of continued rule in the Christian east well after the fifth century A.D. loss of the Roman west. Instead, in the eyes of Romans at Constantinople, belief in the Christian God had at last given their existence meaning and renewed determination to preserve their culture amid the collapse of Mediterranean Rome. The more the Eastern church was both beleaguered and persisted, the more its unassailable orthodoxy was considered critical to Byzantium's survival.

For a few visionaries like the future emperor Justinian and his lieutenant the young Belisarius, a tottering Byzantium should be not only saved but at all costs expanded. We do not know the degree to which Justinian from the beginning had systematic plans of restoring the lost western empire, or whether his successes in North Africa and Sicily led opportunistically to more ambitions in Italy in ad hoc fashion. Eastern Romans, in spite of their schisms and heresies, still believed that they had avoided much of the civil strife so destructive in the west. Byzantines had the more defensible borders, and a far more secure capital protected by massive walls and water on three sides, and so they, in time, could reconstitute much of the original domain of Augustus—or so at some point the young emperor Justinian may have begun to dream. That most residents of sixth-century North Africa and Italy might well have preferred to have been ruled by Vandals and Gothic tribes rather than see their lands devastated and depopulated for years in a war brought on by long-forgotten Greek-speaking foreigners was largely irrelevant to Justinian.[11]

Belisarius was to become rich from the spoils of his western conquests. He no doubt enjoyed the laurels of victory and the fame his military prowess ensured. But ultimately what drove him and thousands in the high echelons of Byzantine government and the military for more than thirty years against near impossible odds were both his faith in Christianity and his allegiance to the idea of Roman civilization and the gifts it had bestowed on millions. In other words, the generation of Belisarius fought relentlessly to reclaim the old empire because it believed in the idea of Rome—because it felt the restoration of the old way to be far better for their would-be subjects than the present alternative.

Flavius Belisarius the Thracian (505–27)

Little is known of Belisarius' early life before his entry onto the pages of Procopius' history. He first appears already a young officer in the imperial guard of the future emperor Justinian headed into Armenia with an army—"young and with first beard." In a striking mosaic panel in the sixth-century church of San Vitale in Ravenna, Italy (built not long after Belisarius captured the city), Belisarius, in simple civilian dress, appears to the right of his emperor Justinian. He stares out as a thin, dark-bearded young man of about forty, with thick, carefully combed black hair. The mosaic suggests more a scholar than a warrior.

In any case, Belisarius was born in ancient Thrace in what is now western Bulgaria, sometime between A.D. 500 and 505. He was in his early to midtwenties when Justinian became emperor and had previously served the future ruler in his personal guard.[12] Although the two would soon be at odds, there was some personal affinity between them that might explain why the young twentysomething officer, with little frontier experience, was sent out with an army to the eastern border to quell a Persian attack on the far reaches of the empire. Given his age, the relatively small size of his forces, and his lack of any experience fighting seasoned Persian troops, it is a wonder that the young Belisarius survived the frontier at all.

Both Justinian and Belisarius married powerful women—Theodora and Antonia respectively. Both wives' pasts were of supposed ill repute. That fact is often cited as explaining the inordinate influence that the two women held over their husbands, in a fashion atypical even of the lively early Byzantine court. Justinian and Belisarius were also both

Thracians by birth. Unlike most Byzantine elites, they were native Latin, rather than Greek, speakers. These affinities also may explain why both would share the notion that the lost distant western provinces and the old capital at Rome were key to Byzantium and could still be brought back inside the empire. But for such a grand notion to become reality, a shaky and nearly insolvent Constantinople would first have to ensure security on its perpetually contested eastern borders with Persia.[13]

Belisarius Goes East: The First War Against the Persians (527–31)

On the eastern borderlands—roughly in parts of modern-day western Iraq, Israel, Lebanon, Jordan, Syria, and eastern Turkey—the horsemen of the rival Sassanid Empire of Persia continually pressed the empire. Even in classical times, Caesar's Rome had been unable to pacify the Arab and Persian east in any permanent manner. Some of Rome's greatest losses—the deaths or capture of nearly thirty thousand legionaries at Carrhae (53 B.C.) and Mark Antony's serial defeats in the east (40–33 B.C.)—were at the hands of Parthian and later Persian armies. In general, due to the problems of land transport, scarce water, and great distances from the Mediterranean and Aegean, Romans preferred to work out general agreements with the Persians. These accords left much of the eastern frontier with only vaguely demarcated borders, along a line descending from the southeastern shores of the Black Sea nearly down to the Red Sea.[14]

Court accountants at Constantinople carefully calibrated the relative expenses of appeasement versus military action. They usually concluded that it was cheaper to pay an Iranian monarch to stay eastward than to march out eight hundred miles from Constantinople to stop him with an army. In any case, both Iranians and Byzantines had plenty of other enemies, and so in time they grudgingly acknowledged each other's civilizations; and they found their arrangements mutually acceptable for decades. But in 527 the Persian monarch Kavadh and the dying Roman emperor Justin dropped the old protocols of understanding. Kavadh claimed Justin had reneged on ceremonially adopting his son Chosroes (Khosrau) to cement a closer alliance. Justin, in turn, had tired of paying the bribe money and thought resistance to Persian demands could for once prove cheaper than the serial gold payouts.[15]

In reaction to the increasing tension, the Persians attacked the pro-Byzantine region of Lazica on the Black Sea. That aggression prompted a

The only known contemporary image of Belisarius is found on a surviving mosaic in the Byzantine basilica of San Vitale in Ravenna, Italy. This enlargement of the portrait of the bearded Belisarius depicts him apparently in civilian dress and perhaps about forty. Photo courtesy of Wikimedia.

In the mosaic of the basilica of San Vitale at Ravenna, the emperor Justinian (at the center and identified by a halo surrounding his crowned head) is portrayed with his imperial retinue. Belisarius stands on Justinian's own right with other military officers. To the emperor's left are church officials (the bishop Maximianus is next to the emperor) and members of the Byzantine court. Photo courtesy of Wikimedia.

retaliatory strike against Persia—if a slow-moving expedition could be so called—by the emperor. War was on. A series of expeditions went eastward, among them a northern corps led by the young, untried Belisarius and his co-commander, Sittas. The historian Procopius at the time explained the unusual promotion of someone so young to high military office by the fact that the hitherto obscure Belisarius was attached to the imperial guard of the general Justinian, nephew to the emperor Justin (518–27) and probable heir to the throne. He had surely not earned command by any prior feat of arms. The young Belisarius found himself in a near-hopeless war, far from home against far more experienced and numerically superior enemies.

At first Belisarius and Sittas, under the general command of Justinian, had mixed success along the frontier in Persarmenia, ravaging enemy territory before losing a pitched battle to the Persians. In just this first year of operations, the inexperienced Belisarius had done well enough to be in position as a commander to take advantage of two unexpected events. First, the other Byzantine generals, Belisarius' rivals, had fared even more poorly—or perished. Libelairus (the *magister utriusque militum*, or overall theater commander of infantry and cavalry) lost his nerve on hearing of the Byzantine setback in Persarmenia. He then retreated from an attack in the south at Nisbis, and thereby gave up his command. Then the regional commander in eastern Turkey and Iraq (*dux Mesopotamiae*), Timostratus, died. For unknown reasons, Sittas, not Belisarius, was probably blamed for the initial failure in Persarmenia. The result was that Belisarius replaced Timostratus and took over overall command of efforts at expanding operations to the south in Mesopotamia.[16]

Second, in August 527, the emperor Justin died. Belisarius' patron, Justinian, at last assumed power. The Byzantines committed far more resources to the Persian war, including a plan to build an extensive system of border forts and defenses to keep the Persians out of Roman territory. Again, Constantinople had neither the resources nor the desire to invade Persia, much less to topple the Sassanids. Instead, its limited aims were occasional hot pursuit across a new fortified line that might achieve some sort of deterrence and so bring an uneasy peace in the east without the costly bribes. The resulting savings would supposedly allow the funding of more important impending operations in the west, where most of the old Roman Empire had been lost.

Yet neither Justin nor his successor, Justinian, had yet quite conceded that the protection of the old eastern border with Persia—given the loss of resources from the Roman west—was beyond the power of their meager forces. The fact was that the grand strategy of the new young emperor Justinian—the notion of waging an eastern war to allow a subsequent, far more ambitious conflict to begin against the Vandals in the west—was courting disaster. The burden of two-front operations, from Gibraltar to the Euphrates, would plague all subsequent operations over the next twenty years. As Napoleon learned in 1812, and the Germans discovered in 1944, distant dormant fronts to the rear have a habit of awakening at inopportune moments to plague a bogged-down invader with multifarious battles.

Still, young Belisarius almost immediately proved worthy of his selection through two characteristics that would elevate his leadership above his contemporaries. First, he was calm in battle, and he knew instinctively the relationship between tactics and strategy and thus avoided wasting the limited resources of the empire in needless head-on confrontations that would lead to no long-term advantage. Second, Belisarius was skilled in counterinsurgency, in winning the hearts and minds of local populations by not plundering or destroying villages and infrastructure—an advantage in the dirty wars fought in the vast no-man's-land between Persia and Byzantium. Such restraint was rare among gold-hungry Byzantine commanders in the east. The result was that, even after initial defeats, Belisarius never lost an army or had hostile populations turn on his rear.

At Mindouos, the Byzantines under a joint command were repulsed when they rashly advanced and got entangled in concealed Persian trenches. The other commanders, Bouzes and Coutzes especially, were faulted for the defeat, while Belisarius managed to retreat with most of the cavalry intact. In subsequent efforts to fortify Mindouos, Belisarius was again defeated. He was forced to withdraw to the fort at Dara. Yet he was rewarded with promotion and immediately began retraining an army in expectation of a renewed Persian offensive. The Byzantines had lost a series of battles, but their forces had forfeited little territory and were still largely intact. Progress continued on their fortifying lines. And now a battle-tested Belisarius enjoyed authority over rival commanders.

Then at Dara in 530, along with his co-commander Hermogenes, Belisarius marshaled some twenty-five thousand troops against Persian forces at least twice that size. He was determined to decide matters through pitched battle. He had learned much from his previous defeats; this time, the commanders ordered their troops to construct elaborate trenches in front of their formations. They positioned infantry provocatively to the front and center, ahead of the cavalry on the wings—but reinforced at its rear with additional concealed horsemen. Belisarius figured that the enemy would be impeded by the trenches and confused by foot soldiers deployed so brazenly at his front. Perhaps the Persians would then slough off from his strong center to attack the wings instead. That way, as the enemy advanced and began to spread out, Byzantine cavalry, and hidden reinforcements behind the infantry, could swarm the enemy on its flanks.[17]

After an initial two days of skirmishing and futile negotiations, the battle began in earnest on the third day. The Persians added another ten thousand reinforcements. Belisarius had removed a cavalry contingent from his left wing and positioned it farther to the rear, hidden behind a small hill. When the Persians attacked on the right, they were surprised on both sides by the secondary mounted forces of the Byzantines. Over on the opposite side, the backpedaling infantry and cavalry on the Byzantine left held long enough for their mounted reserves to similarly hit the Persians on the flank.

Some five thousand elite mounted Persians were killed in just a few hours. In response, the less reliable Persian infantry in the center threw down their arms and retreated. Altogether, more than eight thousand Persian horse and foot soldiers were lost. A Byzantine expeditionary force—for the first time in memory—had defeated a massive Persian army in the east, and one nearly double its own size. The dramatic win at Dara gave the Byzantines a respite until the next spring, 531, when on Easter Day they met the Persians again to the south on the northern bank of the Euphrates River. Unfortunately, the lessons from Dara were not fully digested. Buoyed by the success at their prior victory, Belisarius' co-commanders believed that they no longer needed fixed positions, impediments and trenches, or the use of deception to defeat the Persians. Now, after Dara, they fooled themselves into thinking that the Byzantines were innately superior and could fight much more mobile Persian forces on almost any terrain and at any time they wished.

The result was disaster at the ensuing battle at Callinicum, fought on the banks of the Euphrates on April 19, 531, in what is now northern Iraq. With five thousand Ghassinid Arab cavalry and twenty thousand imperial troops, Belisarius recrossed the Euphrates and for once had a tempo-

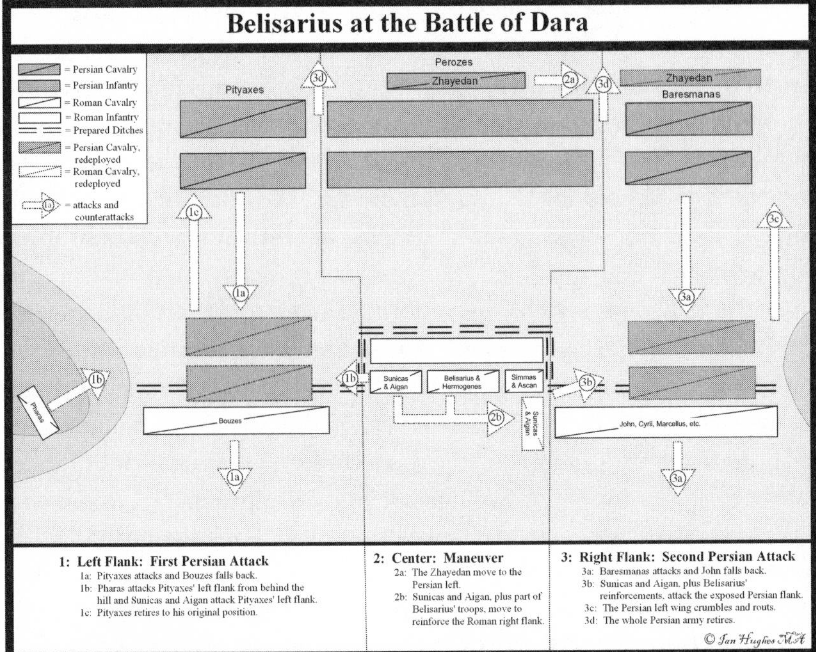

rary numerical advantage over a Persian army of about fifteen to twenty thousand. But the enemy was mostly mounted and mobile, and the Byzantines were recklessly intent on pursuing the enemy.[18]

Once across the Euphrates, the Byzantines oddly put their infantry on the left wing, protected by the river, and massed allied Arab cavalry on the right. Their own cataphracts (heavily armored cavalrymen) were in front of foot soldiers in the center. In the ensuing battle—our sources suggest that Belisarius tried to persuade his troops to hold off attacking—the Byzantines failed to detect a massing of Persian cavalry against their right wing, which soon crumbled, leaving the infantry facing the enemy with the Euphrates at their back. By the time the retreating Byzantines found safety across the river, they had probably suffered the greater casualties and lost any momentum won at Dara. Belisarius learned that in such border fighting, numbers per se did not always determine the outcome as much as tactics, morale, and generalship: Outnumbered Byzantines had won at Dara, and now similarly outnumbered Persians prevailed at Callinicum.[19]

At that point in the seesaw war, the fifty-year-old new emperor Justinian concluded that it was time for diplomacy (and payoffs). He negotiated an

"Eternal Peace" with the Persians (it was to last little more than seven years). He paid them eleven thousand pounds of gold, gave up some border territory, and recalled the thirty-year-old Belisarius to Constantinople to prepare for a new campaign far to the west against the Vandal kingdom of North Africa. Justinian was impatient for the calm in the east that was needed for him to turn toward the west. Chosroes himself wanted a truce to begin a radical shake-up in the organization of his Persian military.

Justinian had proved that his re-formed army could hold its own with the Persians even when manpower, geography, and logistics favored the enemy. The emperor had his peace, at the cost of a fixed annual tribute. In the near-constant fighting, Belisarius had learned how to deal with local populations and to use mixed contingents of allies—and to carefully deploy his limited forces against numerically superior opponents only when there was a good chance of success. Given the limited manpower of Byzantine frontier forces, losing an occasional battle was tolerable. Losing an army in the fashion of the old Roman campaigns in the east was not. Meanwhile, on the home front, the new emperor was still consolidating power, and yet finding it almost politically impossible to raise enough taxes for the planned new offensives in the west.

Belisarius Back Home: Riots and Rebellion at Constantinople (532–33)

Belisarius returned to civil unrest at Constantinople. He underwent an audit concerning the defeats in Persarmenia, and especially the losses at the battles of Mindouos and Callinicum. Yet Belisarius was absolved of any guilt—no doubt on the grounds that such setbacks were not fatal to the Byzantine cause on the border and he returned with peace at his rear. His critics were also wary of the young general's ties with the emperor and sensed that Belisarius was being prepped for future commands. The defeats could be ascribed to the laxity of his co-commanders, or perhaps the excessive zeal of his undisciplined troops, who had fervently urged their general to fight when Belisarius' instincts advised caution. Still, Belisarius had lost as many battles as he had won. And he had returned home through gold indemnities rather than victory.

His arrival at Constantinople was opportune. Justinian, in his fifth year of rule, had begun an ambitious reform of the civil service and tax system. The naïve emperor had hopes of firing bureaucrats, trimming expenses, and earning more revenue—again with an eye of readying capital for the reclamation of the western provinces. But in reaction, both civil servants and the wealthy, whose bribes traditionally ensured favorable court decisions, began to fight back. It was one thing to lose jobs and pay to ward off imperial bankruptcy, quite another to fund a huge optional war rumored to be planned in the west.

Throughout the summer and fall of 531, dissent most often surfaced through two factions that often acted as little more than armed gangs. The so-called Greens were identified with civil servants, tradesmen, and the commercial interests of the eastern provinces. The establishment party of the nobles and wealthy, with all the pretensions of the Graeco-Roman aristocracy, made up the more influential core of the rival Blues. These two opposing umbrella groups, often known as *demes*, were odd conglomerations of horse racing fans, political pressure groups, mafia-like patronage organizations, and Christian zealots all in one. They drew on popular support for racing in the Hippodrome to find captive audiences for their various political agendas and money-making enterprises.

Now furious about the prospective loss of patronage and increased taxes, the rival Greens and Blues joined in their anger toward Tribunianus, the court lawyer in charge of judicial reform, and John the Cappadocian, the praetorian prefect who oversaw the new taxation. The ultimate target, however, was the emperor Justinian himself, who was seen as blatantly cutting corners in order to prepare for a needless war in the west.[20]

In reaction, Justinian was forced to take action against the increasing violence of both factions. That further angered the more affluent Blues, whose social network he had often relied on for political support, while alienating for good the Greens, who sorely felt the cutback of state jobs. In a naïve show of bipartisan justice, Justinian had arrested and condemned to death seven ringleaders of both groups. At this point, after the inexperienced emperor had united rival gangs against himself, almost everything he would do proved counterproductive, and soon catastrophic.

By the new year, 532, two of the seven gang leaders had somehow survived the gallows—unfortunately, both a Blue and a Green—and sought sanctuary in a nearby church. Then the two factions joined in their demands that both be spared. Justinian could back down and appear weak; or he could take on the unified mob in the streets and risk outright civil war. When there instead followed only tepid imperial response, Blues and Greens became more emboldened, issuing a series of demands to suspend tax reform and arrest imperial grandees like John the Cappadocian, Tribunianus, and the city prefect Eudaimon. The mob was calling the shots and looking for some puppet to provide legitimacy for their ad hoc takeover.[21]

The more Justinian wavered, the worse the situation got. When the two factions next met for scheduled races in the Hippodrome in January 532, their common slogan was *"Nika!"* ("Conquer!"). Now in concert, the Greens and Blues began killing government officials, freeing prisoners, burning down churches (including the original Hagia Sophia), and surrounding the imperial residences. Soon the rioters proclaimed the reluctant Hypatius, the elderly nephew of the former emperor Anastatius, the new emperor, with the expectation that the weak figure would front for both parties.[22]

Justinian, besieged in his palace, still attempted to appease the rioters. He tried offering various amnesties, while promising investigations of imperial corruption. For five days, the emperor remained virtually surrounded. In some sort of depression, Justinian contemplated abdication—perhaps in the dazed fashion of a reclusive Josef Stalin after the Nazi invasion of the Soviet Union in June 1941, or the Shah of Iran's bewilderment in his final days of January 1979 as he lost his kingdom. According to ancient sources, Justinian's spirits were finally revived by his feisty wife, Theodora. She knew something of the low-life violence of the street and the fickle nature of crowds that respected strength but were emboldened by hesitancy. Theodora declared that she would rather die than cease being empress. Such braggadocio needed not be literally true, only to appear to be so to restore the mettle of her terrified husband. At last Justinian determined to fight back and restore order and obedience. The key was to separate the two factions in the Hippodrome, play one against the other, and make a violent demonstration to the mob of the power and anger of the emperor.

In a last effort to arrest the pretender Hypatius and quell the crowd, Belisarius with a few loyal bodyguards made a fateful decision to stake his emperor's survival on charging the mass of rioters in the Hippodrome. Fortunately for Justinian, even the outnumbered forces under Belisarius caused immediate panic among the motley insurrectionists. In turn, loyalist forces were encouraged at this belated sign of imperial defiance to join the fray—especially the general Mundus, who commanded some foreign mercenaries.

The court loyalist Narses had earlier begun buying off most of the leaders of the favored Blues, who suddenly began drifting away in small groups and returning home. Soon, when most of the grandees of the Blues were gone, Narses blocked the exits of the huge Hippodrome, leaving mostly Greens trapped inside. The heavily armed forces under Belisarius, Mundus, and Narses advanced. They met little resistance from the unarmed and panicked rebels. The emperor's troops were free to butcher the remaining rioters and unfortunate bystanders—and butcher them all they did. Thirty thousand were said to have perished in the Hippodrome—perhaps as many as the entire number of enemy Persians killed in the recent war by the imperial army in the east. It would be a trademark of Justinian's rule that more of his subjects died through plague and riot at home than abroad at the hand of his innumerable enemies.[23]

Soon the bumbling and reluctant interloper Hypatius was arrested and executed. Prominent treasonous senators and nobles were exiled. John the Cappadocian and Tribunianus were reinstated. The immediate result was that Justinian emerged stronger, wiser—and more ruthless. From now on he would listen far more frequently to his wife, Theodora, whose defiance had saved the emperor from his own loss of nerve. With the newfound cost-cutting financial reforms, a relatively quiet eastern border, and growing respect and confidence, Justinian could at last turn to North Africa.

Belisarius initially had been sent only to arrest Hypatius, but on his own initiative he had become the first of the three loyal generals to attack the rioters. That unexpected act in itself probably broke the rebellion. The soldiers' daring had saved Justinian and guaranteed Belisarius preeminence among Justinian's generals. Now a master of court politics, the newfound hero married Antonia, a lowborn libertine twenty years his elder with a number of children. She was not only a court insider, but also an intimate of the empress Theodora.

Which of the two women in the lurid history of Procopius appears the more cruel and depraved? It did not matter—Antonia's savvy and her intimacy with the empress cemented the previous natural affinity of the general and his emperor. In the end, Antonia proved a lifelong political partner with her far younger husband in what the historian Edward Gibbon famously called "a manly friendship."[24] The young Belisarius may have lost three of four battles on the eastern border. He may have failed to achieve a clear strategic victory over the Persians. But after the Nika riots he had proved absolutely loyal to his emperor—and shrewd about the relationship of military power to popular support. Moreover, as a Latin speaker and native of a more western province, Belisarius was an ideal commander to recapture the old Latin northern coast of Africa, and anything beyond that his emperor might envision.

Thus in June 533 the young Belisarius was entrusted by Justinian with his third great mission and set sail for Tunisia, with his new wife, Antonia, and his personal secretary, the court insider and soon-to-be historian Procopius. He was probably no more than thirty, but he already had earned a reputation as Constantinople's fireman, the first military responder to the empire's inevitable next conflagration.

Belisarius Goes South: The War in Africa Against the Vandals (533–34)

Throughout the fifth century, a succession of Germanic Huns, Visigoths, and Ostrogoths had overrun much of Roman western Europe as they picked off the western and northern provinces of the empire. Yet none of these northern barbarian invasions had proven as terrifying to the residents of an eroding Roman Empire as the onset of the Vandals. With not much more than a hundred thousand tribesmen, swift-moving Vandal forces had savagely swept southward and westward from their homes in modern-day eastern Germany and Poland. After migration west along the Danube in the early fifth century, the Vandals crossed the Rhine, ravaged Gaul, and settled in the Iberian Peninsula before, under their leader Genseric, swarming southward across the Mediterranean into the old Roman provinces of North Africa. If the warm southern Mediterranean was an odd place for such northern European tribes to settle, nonetheless by 439 they had taken Carthage and de facto ended Roman government in much of the old domains of Mauretania, Africa, Numidia, and Cyrenaica—parts of modern-day Morocco, Algeria, Tunisia, and Libya that for much of the fourth and the early fifth centuries had been considered immune from the more distant Germanic invasions.[25]

The Vandals—their purported propensity for wanton destruction gave us the later noun "vandalism"—were most infamous for their sack of Rome in 455, and for the failure of any subsequent Roman or indigenous Moorish force for a century to root them out of Africa. Unlike other Germanic and Slavic tribes, the Vandals exiled or murdered most elite Roman landowning citizens. They focused on piracy and raiding rather than expanding agriculture and commerce, and either forcibly converted most Catholics in North Africa to their own heretical Christian sect of Arianism—or killed them. Whether it was true or not, in the Roman mind, the Vandals were far more destructive than the Goths and had shown little inclination to resurrect the veneer of Roman culture under their domain.

In 468 the Vandals had destroyed a large eastern Roman fleet that had attempted to reclaim North Africa. From that time on, they were given their due from Byzantium, which had no desire to lose thousands in another hopeless war against such a murderous tribe. However, by the time of Justinian, after a century of pillage, Vandal kings recognized that their numbers were too small to guarantee their own security in the face of hostile Moorish tribes to the south and the establishment of Gothic kingdoms across the Mediterranean. They had done well enough pillaging and ending centuries of Roman rule, evading both Roman and then Gothic punitive pursuit. But as the booty ran out, the parasitic Vandals had not been able to create anything in its place comparable to the system of Roman wealth creation and governance in Africa that they had drawn upon for a century.

As a result, the Vandal kings began to seek an uneasy peace with Constantinople—on the general promise of a newfound tolerance for Catholics in Africa and agreements to respect Roman order in the eastern Mediterranean. But when the pro-Byzantine Vandal king Hilderic (523–30) was dethroned in a coup, his cousin, the usurper Gelimer, renewed the persecutions. Soon the supporters of the deposed king appealed to Constantinople—at precisely the time Justinian was planning to reclaim at least some of the western provinces, if not in pursuit of his grandiose idea of a restored Roman Empire in the west. The emperor had a good casus belli, relative peace at his rear, a growing treasury, a silenced opposition, and a young, energetic general to conduct an invasion.[26]

Yet the odds of success were still not encouraging. Once the armada entered the Mediterranean from the Aegean, the winds were largely unfavorable for westward sailing. The Byzantine fleet of some five hundred ships would have to land and supply an army among hostile populations more than a thousand miles from Constantinople. Even should Belisarius take back the Vandal capital at Carthage in modern-day Tunisia, he might still have to hold the province against numerically superior indigenous Moorish tribesmen. The Visigoths in Spain and the Ostrogoth kingdom in Italy were at best neutral; yet more often both wished to see Byzantium weakened.

Nevertheless the general set sail in June 533, along with Antonia, Procopius, and a large force of seamen, infantry, and cavalry. The armada numbered perhaps forty-five to fifty thousand, although only twenty thousand were front-line combatants. Belisarius had learned much on the Persian border and during the riots at Constantinople—to show both force and mercy among civilian populations, and not rashly to commit his usually outnumbered and sometimes poorly disciplined multicultural forces to battle in unfavorable circumstances.[27]

Despite a difficult three-month voyage to Africa—contaminated bread and bad water sickened or killed hundreds on the voyage, and a diversion of part of the fleet to Sicily was necessary to restore supplies—Belisarius landed in early September 533 with his forces intact, about fifty or sixty miles east of the Vandal capital at Carthage. His plan was simple: Belisarius would march his forces methodically westward—no more than about ten miles per day—keeping the fleet in sight to protect his right flank and sending out his feared Hunnish cavalry on his left as he rallied the countryside against the Vandal king.[28]

As Belisarius began to march westward through the coastal towns, he ordered his men to spare the native African villages. Byzantines enlisted both the Moors and what was left of the old Roman landowning classes, in a promised liberation from Vandal savagery and the visions of a more enlightened renewal of the former imperial rule. Belisarius envisioned an insurgent campaign of winning over the countryside, or, as he put it, "This is the moment when moderation brings salvation, while lawlessness leads to death." As a result he made a relatively uneventful march as "if in his own land." In some sense, it seemed an absurdity that a Greek-speaking Byzantine army, more than a thousand miles from home, less than a year after near civil insurrection, and with an enemy restless on its eastern borders, would even attempt to overthrow the heretofore dreaded Vandal kingdom—or that anyone in the west would wish to join such an empire in chaos. Yet Belisarius approached Carthage as if he were leading a consular army at the zenith of Roman provincial power.[29]

The shocked Vandals were scrambling under their chieftain Gelimer to put up some sort of resistance with a somewhat smaller force of ten to fifteen thousand, hoping to ambush Belisarius on the last leg of his march. They apparently anticipated that the Byzantine fleet would have to round Cape Bon out of sight of the army, where the coastal road crossed farther inland over hilly terrain to Carthage. Gelimer accordingly split his forces and assumed that once Belisarius descended into a low valley, he could be attacked front and rear from the mountains without hope of supplies or reinforcements from the fleet. Gelimer sent his nephew Gibamund with two thousand cavalry to hit the slow-moving Byzantines on the flank. Then his brother Ammatas would block the enemy advance. The main body under Gelimer would finally follow Ammatas to finish the pincer movement, surround Belisarius, and destroy his column in familiar territory.

Ten miles outside Carthage, on September 13, 533, at Ad Decimum ("at the tenth milepost"), Belisarius carefully established a secure camp. He then dealt piecemeal with each successive Vandal contingent, careful not to dilute the strength of his main forces. The historian Procopius saw Belisarius' genius in not deploying all his forces at the sight of each Vandal onslaught—together with the far too complex ambush of Gelimer—as largely responsible for the successive destruction of the various Vandal armies.

It was unwise for the Vandals, as a numerically inferior force, to trisect their strength in hopes of ambushing a larger column. Once the Vandal surprise attacks failed, there was nothing much left to block the steady advance of Belisarius on the capital. By day six of their march, the Byzantines were inside Carthage, repairing the ancient walls and preparing for a final battle against the reconstituted forces of Gelimer. In short, within a week of landing, Belisarius had accomplished what neither a Roman nor a Gothic force had been able to do in over a century—occupy the capital of the Vandal kingdom in North Africa. It was an example of blitzkrieg unmatched in the ancient world since the campaigns of Alexander the Great and Julius Caesar.[30]

Now in Carthage, over the next three months, Belisarius sent emissaries to win over the local Latin-speaking population, the Moorish tribes, and Vandals still loyal to the previous regime of Hilderic. Gelimer, in response, was reinforced by his other brother, Tzazon. The latter had just put down a rebellion in Sardinia and arrived to join the recuperating Vandals. The brothers hoped to retake Carthage from the west. On December 15 they confronted the Byzantines with a much larger force at Tricameron, seventeen miles outside Carthage. Belisarius had lost hundreds of his troops over the prior three months of firming up his occupation of the countryside. Now he was forced to station even more of his men to protect the captured towns from sporadic Vandal raids. So it is likely that some fifteen thousand Vandals under Gelimer at Tricameron may have initially outnumbered the Byzantine mounted force by perhaps five thousand or more.

Belisarius again deployed quickly and did not wait for the muster of his own infantry—cognizant of how the Vandals had fled at Ad Decimum when met with a sudden show of Byzantine nerve. The plan was for the heavy Byzantine cavalry on the wings to veer in and hit the Vandal center, after missile troops and horse archers had softened up the enemy, in hopes of breaking through before the Vandal flanks could surround Belisarius' smaller force. After at least two heavy Byzantine mounted assaults, Tzazon fell. The Vandal center weakened and once more Gelimer panicked and fled the field. By the time the Byzantine heavy infantry finally arrived, the Vandals were already in full flight.[31]

Over the next three months, Belisarius continued to root out the last vestiges of Vandal resistance in the west. He captured Gelimer and then finally was recalled to Constantinople—both to receive a triumph and to quash rumors that he wanted to set himself up as an independent strongman in a new African province. The emperor appreciated that Belisarius had established a clear pattern of winning generalship and seemed always to find a way to defeat Justinian's enemies, from the Persian frontier, to the streets of Constantinople, to distant North Africa.

In his new style of provincial warfare, Belisarius felt he could make up for the chronic shortage of troops through audacity and winning over the local population—anticipating modern notions of counterinsurgency warfare in which an outnumbered invader must enlist local adherents to a shared cause. So-called barbarian forces, as Belisarius knew, were led by magnetic tribal leaders. When these charismatic strongmen were targeted and fell in battle, their armies usually dissipated. The key was not to use his signature heavy cavalry in reckless fashion in unplanned pursuits, but to hit the enemy hard and quickly through focused and concentrated jabs, destroying its morale before it could use greater numbers to outflank and surround the smaller expeditionary Byzantine forces. In contrast, either alienating the locals or in static fashion preparing for a large set battle was a prescription for disaster.

The Mediterranean world was stunned at the fall of Carthage. Belisar-

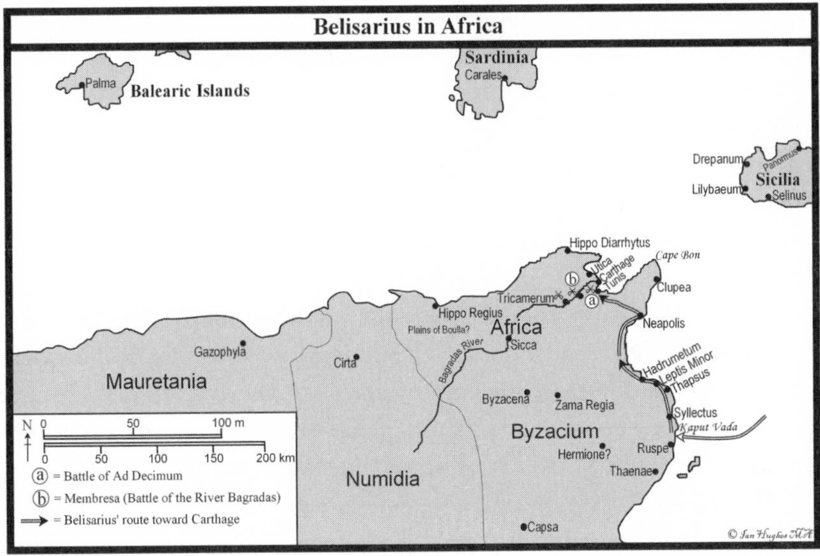

ius had landed in North Africa in June 533. Less than seven months later, his army had destroyed the century-old Vandal kingdom in Africa, captured the usurper king Gelimer, either killed, enslaved, or recruited into his army most of the Vandal population, established a new Byzantine province that might provide a base for future conquests in the west—and sent waves of terror through the Gothic hierarchy in Italy that it might be next in line in Justinian's apparent plan to pick off vulnerable provinces of the old Western Roman Empire. Byzantium was supposed to have followed the fate of Rome as a shrinking, corrupt populace gave way before hardier, growing, and more warlike tribes on its borders. Instead, Belisarius had somehow reversed the course of Mediterranean history and found a way for a small force of relatively affluent westerners to mold a successful expeditionary army of invasion against European tribesmen. As the general put it to his men before facing the Vandals, "Not by the number of men, and not by the measure of one's body, but by the valor of the soul, war is decided."[32]

Belisarius returned to Constantinople with the entire treasury of the Vandals—reputedly one of the largest hoards in the ancient world, the aggregate stash from some one hundred years of plunder in the western Mediterranean, much of it to be used to pay for the new church of Hagia Sophia. Those Vandals not scattered throughout North Africa were brought back with Belisarius to the capital and forcibly integrated into

Justinian's armies. The Vandal people quite literally had ceased to exist as an identifiable tribe and so disappeared from history.

The stunning achievement energized Justinian, at about the same time as the monumental church of Hagia Sophia was rising and as his historic reorganization and compilation of Roman law—the *Pandects* or *Digest*—was at last issued at Constantinople. Anything, it seemed—military, religious, legal—was possible for Justinian and his newly ascendant Rome.[33]

There would be occasional provincial uprisings and tribal revolts in Roman-reoccupied North Africa. The indigenous Moors, as well as what was left of the old Roman landowning elite, would grow to like their new Byzantine overseers no more than they had the Germanic invaders. Yet Byzantine power in North Africa would remain for more than a century—until the Islamic advances of the seventh and eight centuries swept westward from Egypt and incorporated the Maghreb into the growing Muslim caliphate.

Belisarius Goes North: The War in Italy Against the Goths (535–40)

After a year of adulation and a consulship in Constantinople, Belisarius headed again out west for the most important campaign of the emperor's intention to restore as much of the old Mediterranean empire as his resources would allow. His orders this time were to reclaim Italy and Sicily, and to ensure that the Moors did not overwhelm the newly reclaimed Roman provinces in North Africa.

Unfortunately, Belisarius would have less than half of the forces that had set out for Africa—in part because the emperor was deluded by the easy victory over the Vandals into believing Gothic Italy was equally vulnerable. In part, Justinian was also cautious because of the war closer to home against the Goths in Dalmatia. And in part, the emperor wished to guarantee that no one of his growing stable of generals was given too many resources that might at some future date threaten his power. He was still shaken, after all, from the Nika riots, when he had come within hours of losing both his throne and his life.

The so-called Gothic Wars in the Italian peninsula, in their various phases, were to last for nearly twenty years (534–54). The conflict would ultimately result in the near-complete annexation of Italy under Byzantine rule—and for a brief moment the near-recreation of the old Mediterranean Roman Empire. And yet the fighting would prove so exhausting to both invaded and invader that within little over a decade after the final peace (568), the Lombards would invade an impoverished Italy and undo most of the work of Justinian's generals there, just as Byzantine North Africa would later fall to the Islamic tribes.

The first phase of the war to restore Ostrogoth Italy to Roman rule would last five years (535–40). As in the Vandal war, the fighting began when Justinian intervened in a dynastic dispute—in this case, the murder of the friendly Gothic queen Amalasuntha—and sent Belisarius with 7,500 troops to remove the usurper Theodahad. Waged under the Byzantine propaganda of freeing long-lost kindred Italians from the "slavery" of the barbarian Goths, the war proved lengthy, complex, and costly.[34]

The campaign again underscored the genius of Belisarius in using extremely small forces to overwhelm the Goths and eventually take control of most of Italy and its seven million or so inhabitants. Until Belisarius' invasion, the Ostrogoths, like the Vandals, had terrorized Roman society for more than two hundred years since their initial incursions across the Rhine and Danube during the fourth century. The very distance that once had made Constantinople and the eastern empire more secure from the fifth-century barbarian invasions—originating from the northern side of the Rhine and western Danube—unfortunately ensured that it was increasingly difficult to resupply Byzantine troops fighting in far-off Italy.

Throughout the former western provinces there arose a certain mystique around the Goths—namely, that Germanic purity and hardiness had overwhelmed Roman decadence and frailty. Many Italians expected that subsequent Roman attempts to assert authority from distant Constantinople would surely prove no match against an innate Germanic ferocity. But whereas Italians may have been awed by the notion of Gothic invincibility, Belisarius was not. He saw instead traditional "barbarian" weakness of the sort his veterans had dealt with in the east and in Africa: an absence of unified command, reliance on mercurial tribal leaders, spotty logistics, lack of reliable sea power and naval support, and vulnerability to heavy armored Roman cavalry, especially the mounted archers that had proved so advantageous in the eastern wars against the Persians.[35]

Belisarius landed in Sicily late in 535 and quickly won over the island's population. By December, his paltry Byzantine forces had mopped up the remaining Gothic holdouts on the island without much of a struggle.

The terrified Goths at that point might have immediately ceded much of southern Italy to the popular invader. But another Byzantine army in Dalmatia across the Adriatic—under the commanders Mundus and his son Mauricius—was unexpectedly overwhelmed. Both generals perished. As a result, the Goths were given newfound optimism in resisting Belisarius, and were freed from worry of a relief invasion from the north by a second Roman army. Then, just as he prepared to invade Italy, Belisarius got wind of a revolt back in North Africa. He quickly returned to Carthage to put down a mutiny by a renegade Byzantine general, Stotzas. The latter had rallied garrison troops angry over the lack of promised pay, disputes over booty, and religious sympathies for Arianism.

Stotzas had a popular agenda of setting up a rogue Byzantine independent state in North Africa, and he somehow had managed to recruit some nine thousand Moors and Vandal holdouts to his cause. He was hoping to declare himself a king of Africa while Belisarius was bogged down in Italy. Yet with just two thousand loyal troops, Belisarius did not hesitate nor delegate, but on his own initiative landed at Carthage, galvanized friendly troops, saved the city, routed Stotzas, restored the province, and left the mop-up to the emperor's nephew Germanus. It was a little-remarked-on victory, but once again demonstrative of how the mere name of Belisarius was able to awe local populations and instill loyalty and morale in his own troops—and terror in his enemies. He quickly sailed back to Sicily to resume planning for the invasion of Italy, leaving Africa secure but in wretched shape after nonstop fighting between indigenous Moors, Vandals, and Byzantines.[36]

By late spring 536, Belisarius had landed on the Italian peninsula and taken the southern city of Rhegium. He went quickly northward to the stronghold at Naples and stormed the city after a costly siege, characterized by savagery on both sides. Now the road to Rome was open, and Belisarius lost no time in heading farther north. Meanwhile, a new Byzantine general in Dalmatia, Constantinianus, had retaken the offensive, routed the Goths, and threatened to enter Italy from the north or by sea from the east.

At this point, the usurper Theodahad was murdered. A new, more charismatic strongman, Vittigis, emerged to rally the Goths. Still, most of the native Italian population began to favor Belisarius and the Byzantine promise of a new united empire, perhaps in hopes that well over a half century of Gothic tribalism was coming to an end with a return of Roman rule under an enlightened western, Latin-speaking general, fueled by eastern money. On December 9, 536, Belisarius entered Rome. In just a year he had annexed much of North Africa and retaken Sicily and half of Italy. Byzantine power had advanced from its new bases in the Mediterranean, more than three hundred miles to the north, and caused widespread dissension among the Gothic ranks. All this Belisarius accomplished with an army not much larger than two traditional Roman legions, and largely within the strategic directives and limitations established by a distant and suspicious Justinian. With the Vandal fortune, Belisarius had probably paid for the cost of his operations through booty rather than imperial outlays. For a moment both Constantinople and Rome were again united under one emperor.

Rome may not have been the center of Gothic power. Yet the city was still relatively unchanged physically from its majestic days of Roman imperial power, and it remained home to some six hundred thousand inhabitants of various ethnicities and languages. Today the fifth-century "Fall of Rome" is a catchphrase for the end of days, but we rarely recall that after just sixty years of Gothic rule, the Roman general Belisarius in fact recaptured it from the proverbial barbarians, on the promise of an end to the Arian heresy and a return to a Roman grandeur of the old emperors.[37]

Belisarius quickly moved to secure the surrounding countryside outside Rome and ready the city's defenses for the expected counterattacks. He was responsible for defending the ancient capital with a minuscule command more akin to the urban police than a national army. Vittigis arrived to besiege the city four months later. From March 537 to March 538, the Byzantines were surrounded by various Gothic armies. The vastly outnumbered Belisarius was in nonstop action. He enrolled the citizenry into his defense forces and restored the old Aurelian ramparts. The Byzantines sent out constant sallies, and on occasion won and lost pitched battles before the city walls. Belisarius—in what would be a recurring scenario—desperately entreated Constantinople to send reinforcements, given that the enemy outside the walls may have numbered at various times over a hundred thousand besiegers. Yet he got no reply. Justinian did not regularly communicate with his generals, much less did he articulate to them any grand strategy of reclaiming the Roman west—either out of distrust or his own confusion over what his ultimate strategic aims actually were.[38]

Finally, as spring 538 approached, the Goth besiegers began to tire, especially as additional Byzantine forces appeared by sea. The result was that the enemy finally gave up and retired in March. After his brilliant defense of Rome, Belisarius then prepared to move farther northward with the new Byzantine reinforcements to complete the conquest of the northern Italian peninsula. But while Justinian had sent troops and more supplies, the emperor had established no clear central command authority in Italy—perhaps by intent rather than laxity.

As soon as Belisarius and rival generals focused on capturing Ravenna to end Gothic rule south of the Po River, disputes broke out as to how best to use limited resources to complete the conquest. Belisarius, the newly arrived eunuch general Narses, and John, the nephew of the general Vitalianus, bickered endlessly. They could not agree to unify Byzantine strength and storm the remaining northern Italian cities, most of which were far better fortified than the southern towns. And the farther northward the Byzantines went, the longer their supply lines grew from the Mediterranean—and the closer they came to the traditional centers of Germanic power and influence. Unity among the various small armies of the Byzantines was needed more than ever—at a time when many commanders wished to hunker down and loot their newfound provinces rather than risk stretching northward in an effort to reestablish a western province for Constantinople. Again, the problem lay back home with an emperor who had never quite decided whether he had the resources to restore in systematic fashion the old Roman Empire or merely would take what territories he could when a favorable occasion arose. Was the west to be part of a New Rome—or merely fragmented buffer states to offer security and loot for Constantinople? The answer seemed to depend on whether Justinian's armies were stalemated or on the move defeating their enemies.

The result of a distracted and divided command was that Milan was retaken by the Goths, mostly razed, and its Roman citizenry massacred, while the Byzantine relief forces were left squabbling. Finally, Narses, the Armenian eunuch general, was recalled. That move at last left Belisarius with overall nominal command. The final subjugation of northern Italy went ahead with the capture of the Gothic strongholds at Auximum (modern Osimo) and Faesulae (Fiesole).[39]

By May 540, Belisarius—now with loyal subordinate commanders, reinforcements, and control of the Adriatic—at last stormed Ravenna, the Gothic capital, and captured Vittigis. All of Italy south of the Po River was in Roman hands. Then Belisarius himself was recalled to Constantinople, ordered to bring back the captured Gothic king and his Italian treasury—and, most important, to address rumors that he had considered setting himself up as a conquering strongman independent of Constantinople.

Nonetheless, in a mere seven years, Belisarius had conquered western North Africa, Sicily, and most of Italy, almost doubling the geographical extent of the Byzantine Empire—and creating as many new problems as old ones solved. In the endeavor, the treasury at Constantinople was close to being depleted. The conquered lands were largely devastated and hardly able to become immediate productive sources of new taxation. Scarce imperial garrison troops were scattered from Carthage to Ravenna, more than a thousand miles from the capital. The old Vandal treasury waned as Justinian continued with his vast building projects. Indeed, to run this new expanded empire from the Atlantic to the Euphrates, Rome, not a distant Constantinople, as in the past would seem to be the more ideally situated capital. Belisarius himself had incurred jealousy and hatred from his rival generals, many of them increasingly well connected at Constantinople and eager to feed rumors to a paranoid Justinian.[40]

The conquered Goths had predicated much of their surrender on the assurance that the godlike Belisarius, as a sort of sympathetic proconsul, would stay on and guarantee Gothic interests. Yet he apparently either was disingenuous in his negotiations or realized only afterward that he could never honor such a promise. If such a proconsulship under Belisarius might have brought a chance of lasting peace to Italy, it also would have ensured the general's own demise at the court of Justinian. Meanwhile, Constantinople's opportunistic eastern enemies had broken the peace to strike on the frontier while Justinian was distracted in the west.[41]

As Belisarius was recalled home in 540, what, in fact, had the Byzantines accomplished in the west? Clearly, Africa and Italy had cost more than these new acquisitions might in the near future earn. To the north of Italy, Franks and Lombards were eager to capitalize on the demonstrable weakness of their traditional rival Goths, who, as they had acculturated to life in Italy, sometimes had proven to be as much a bulwark against the other, fiercer northern Germanic tribes as they had been incorrigible enemies of Roman civilization. Most importantly, a destructive precedent had been ratified in which the more Belisarius won land

and power for the emperor, the more Justinian sent out rival generals to undercut his own general's success. The more he added to the empire, the more costs the strapped empire incurred. If it were to be a choice—and it often was unfortunately seen at Constantinople in just those Manichean terms—between Byzantine conquest and an exalted Belisarius, Justinian usually clipped the wings of his most successful general and accepted the resulting negative effects on his wars.

But all that said, for a brief moment, most of the old Roman Empire—with notable exceptions in Gaul, Britain, and most of Spain—was reunited under a central authority for a last moment in history. The chief remaining rival heresy to Catholicism—Arianism among the Vandals and Goths—was on the wane. A new religious and political unity looked as if it were on the horizon. Belisarius had proven himself able both to defeat and to appeal to Moors, Vandals, and Goths as a fair proconsul rather than a vengeful conqueror, while managing to hold territory with relatively small numbers of troops. Had Justinian in 540 continued to place his trust in the young Belisarius' abilities, the Byzantines might have institutionalized the lost provinces within their imperial administration and the new unified empire might have endured.

Unlike Belisarius' return home after the destruction of the Vandal kingdom in Africa, when he arrived at Constantinople with the defeated Vittigis in tow, Belisarius was given no more public triumphs, despite unmatched victories in Italy. Byzantium's greatest general was still only thirty-six. He had been at war nearly nonstop for Justinian for the last fourteen years. Belisarius was a popular icon and already achieving mythic status among the populace at Constantinople—as famous for his military exploits as he was for his legendary character and personal habits. In an age of gratuitous cruelty and barbarism, Belisarius was noted, by the standards of his times, for his clemency, honesty, and lenient treatment of the conquered. Such mythmaking spread in the streets of Constantinople attesting to Belisarius the saintly conqueror, who personally attended his wounded, replaced the lost equipment of his soldiers at his own expense, and treated as sacrosanct the property of the residents whose land he marched through and fought on. His martial excellence had ensured everything from the funding to finish off Hagia Sophia to the recapture of Rome.

Whether or not Belisarius' legendary avoidance of alcohol, womanizing, and bribery likewise was true, it mattered little. The people seemed to have accepted all his virtues as gospel. When their general came home from the furthest borders of the empire, he brought peace, greater power—and plenty of plunder. But by 540 Justinian had two problems: a new outbreak of war to the east with the Persians, and a mature general more beloved and powerful than the emperor himself. The solution to both was to send Belisarius to the east to save yet another seemingly lost war.

Belisarius Goes East Again: War Again Against the Persians (540–41)

The "Eternal Peace" between the Byzantines and Persia in fact lasted just seven years. The uneasy truce was broken when the Persian king Chosroes once more crossed the Euphrates and began storming Byzantine-held cities on his way to Antioch on the Mediterranean. He had rightly assumed that the past six-year-long drain on Constantinople from warring in the west was an opportunity for some easy plundering of Byzantine territory that might earn even more lucrative bribes from Justinian to keep his eastern frontier quiet. More important, the Persians, in general, considered that they had been fooled into signing an armistice that freed up the Byzantines to profit in Africa, Sicily, and Italy. Newly acquired western treasure and manpower, Chosroes feared, might be redirected by Justinian toward the old conflict in the east.[42]

The Persian invasion once more reminded Constantinople of the dilemma that Byzantium and its generals faced in their quest to restore much of the ancient Roman Empire. Surrounded on all sides by enemies, Byzantium usually had two strategic defense choices. One, it had only enough strength to muster in a single theater to conduct a truly decisive war. Thus the successive acquisitions in Africa and Italy only invited Persian opportunism on the eastern border once Byzantine resources were focused elsewhere. In contrast, the second alternative of defending all of Byzantium's borders at once, without offensive operations designed at destroying permanently any one threat, also meant that its growing number of belligerents was never really defeated. Therefore, enemies usually were manipulated into uneasy armistices through bribery, dynastic marriages, and occasional regional fighting—all biding their time until they sensed a general weakness at the core.

After storming or forcing the surrender of the Byzantine-controlled cities on both sides of the Euphrates—Apamea, Beroea, Chalcis, Edessa, Hieropolis, and Sura—Chosroes finally accepted Justinian's offers of money to return to Persia. But on his long way back home from the rich and historic city of Antioch, which he had stormed and pillaged, Chosroes decided to grab in addition the key Byzantine border citadel at Dara. Once there, he broke off his siege only after receiving another thousand pounds of silver. The more the Persians threatened Byzantine cities, the more money they received to desist—and the hungrier they were for the next easy payoff.[43]

Justinian saw that bribes, supplied both from his own treasury and new plunder from the west, were only stopgap solutions, and that he needed to send out Belisarius to restore the border—almost a decade and a half after he went east on his first command. Justinian this way might kill two birds with one stone: removing a popular rival to the emperor at home while ensuring inspired military leadership abroad. Arriving from Lebanon, Belisarius reached Dara in June 540. There he prepared to enter Persian territory to teach Chosroes a belated lesson. Unfortunately, Belisarius quickly learned that Byzantine commanders far to the north on the eastern shores of the Black Sea had so maltreated local populations that Chosroes, while in Greek-held Lazica, had presented himself as a Persian liberator of indigenous peoples from supposed Byzantine oppression. There was again a sense in the east that spiraling Byzantine taxation fueled operations far to the west rather than being invested in security closer to home.[44]

Yet whereas the Persians sensed Byzantine division and uncertainty, Belisarius saw an opportunity: While Chosroes was in the north picking off Byzantine border towns, the Persian southern flank was for a moment poorly guarded. After an inconsequential battle outside the stronghold of Nisibis and a failed siege, Belisarius pressed further onward, down the southern bank of the Tigris to Sauranon. The Persian garrison there surrendered. And Belisarius now sent a raiding party across the Tigris to plunder formerly untouched Persian territory. In just a few months, once beleaguered Byzantine forces had now, if only symbolically, entered the territory of the Persian aggressor. But as the year ended, Belisarius retreated back across the border before Chosroes returned from the north. Lurid rumors had also reached the general that Antonia, newly arrived at the front from Constantinople, had conducted an open affair with their adopted son, Theodosius, in Belisarius' absence.

To top it off, a new and deadly type of bubonic plague was sweeping through the empire's eastern provinces and fell especially hard upon the army. The malady, brought on by the bacillus-carrying rat flea, would do more than any enemy to weaken the power of Byzantium at just the time its wealth and power were taxed as never before by Justinian's apparent vision of a new united Rome. Indeed, perhaps a million Byzantine subjects would eventually fall to the disease, paralyzing military operations in the fashion that the great Athenian plague of 430–429 B.C. had essentially ended the Athenian dream of winning the Archidamian War against Sparta.

Justinian's reign was to be marked forever by a dividing line not of its own making: expansion before the outbreak of the plague, and then desperate consolidation and occasional retrenchment after hundreds of thousands had taken sick and died. In some sense, the efforts of Belisarius in realizing Justinian's plans simply ended when the plague struck. Disease succeeded in curbing Byzantine power where Persians, Vandals, and Goths had failed.[45]

Belisarius returned to Constantinople to criticism that his successful Persian invasion had been prematurely terminated due to his own personal crises, and that his absence would only encourage another enemy attack. Few acknowledged that the Persians, after two years of warring, were at least sometimes on the defensive, much less that the plague-stricken empire no longer had adequate resources simultaneously to restore the old western Roman provinces and keep Persia on its side of the eastern border.

In the spring of the third year of the war, 542, Chosroes once again crossed the Euphrates with his largest army yet, then headed to the northwest through modern Syria. A weary Belisarius again set out from Constantinople and occupied Europum to block his advance. He then entertained some Persian ambassadors, selected his largest and most fit soldiers to stage ostentatious marches, and in general convinced the visiting officials that they were in mortal danger of having their king cut off and surrounded deep in Byzantine territory by his own near-superhuman troops. After further negotiations and some hit-and-run fighting, Chosroes withdrew and the three-year renewed Persian war ended quietly without much loss of Byzantine territory.

Belisarius was widely praised in his third major eastern campaign for chasing the Persians out without committing to a major battle or incurring much loss—especially at a time when the plague was killing Byzantine men far more than were Persian soldiers. He finally departed for Constantinople at year's end, despite news that thousands were dying each week in the plague-infected capital.

In his two-year war, Belisarius had chased the Persians out of Byzantine lands. He had killed more of the enemy than he had lost, while conserving imperial resources for yet another flare-up in the west. Belisarius' trademark tactics had proven successful throughout the empire. He was the sole Byzantine general, who, by quick advances and deliberate fighting on favorable terrain, could defeat or outsmart all sorts of numerically superior enemies. His outreach to local populations ensured indigenous support anywhere he campaigned and meant that he could push back the enemy at little cost while neither exceeding nor failing to meet his emperor's goals.[46]

Belisarius Goes West: The War in Italy Again (544–48)

The historian Procopius felt that when bubonic plague struck the capital at Constantinople, "nearly the entire human race came close to being wiped out." Soon the emperor fell sick, just as his commanders were concluding the latest round of the ongoing Persian wars with Chosroes through a mixture of bribes and adroit leadership. The generals at the front naturally assumed that the sixty-year-old Justinian would die, like most of the elderly who caught the plague. Therefore they met to discuss a successor, perhaps most logically Belisarius himself, or at least to exercise veto power over any would-be emperor back at Constantinople.[47]

The immediate problem for Belisarius was multifold: Justinian was ill, but not yet fatally so. Although the plague was usually equivalent to a death sentence, it might not necessarily prove true in the case of Justinian, given the careful treatment accorded the emperor. To entertain the offer of a supreme political post—or even a prominent veto in the imperial succession—would raise the old issue of Belisarius' loyalty in the fashion of the former Gothic request for the general to take over as a new western emperor, or the even earlier rumors from Africa that Belisarius had wanted to set himself up as an independent proconsul at newly acquired Carthage. Too many stories kept circulating that Belisarius sought high political as well as military office.

This was a dangerous game—well aside from the fact that the life of

Justinian was still in doubt and the generals were still in the east far from the latest-breaking developments at Constantinople. Should Byzantium's greatest general support the ascension of the empress Theodora, or a nephew who was Justinian's closest blood relative, or at least the official "court" order of succession—or allow his fellow generals in the field to float his own name? If Belisarius declined a subsequent offer of the emperorship and stayed loyal, as was his inclination, he still might be in danger, whether from a surviving Justinian who had heard disturbing reports of a seditious general, or from a widowed Theodora, who would resent his lack of support for her wishes, or from any new emperor and his clique, regardless of whether friendly or hostile to Justinian's supporters.

In the end, Belisarius did not join with the would-be plotters. Yet he still was summoned to Constantinople under a cloud of distrust as the emperor rallied and recovered. A confident Theodora took over the inquisition, and most of the wavering generals suffered the consequences. Belisarius was relieved of command and had his wealth confiscated. He could neither finish the Persian war nor head back west to stabilize the renewed Gothic conflict in Italy. Instead, for more than two years he was persona non grata in Constantinople, ostracized, impoverished, and under constant suspicion. All Belisarius could do was to wait for the emperor to regain his full strength and, with a clearer head, intervene on his behalf—or hope that his wife, Antonia, might win over his apparent archenemy, Theodora.[48]

Meanwhile back in Italy, during the four years of Belisarius' absence, the Byzantine commanders had flagrantly violated two cardinal rules of the general's philosophy of command: fair treatment of the locals, and honesty in all matters financial—especially concerning the division of booty and prompt payment of imperial soldiers' salaries. The results of poor Byzantine leadership were new offensives by a fresh and far more capable Gothic king, Totila. The Goth wisely played on both native Italian dissatisfaction and dissension within Byzantine ranks, posing as a national liberator who would throw off the renewed chains of Roman oppression. At least five Byzantine generals of different factions and ethnicities—Bessas the Goth, Constantinus, John the so-called Glutton, John, the nephew of Vitalius, and Vitalius—in the absence of Belisarius had forfeited much of what Belisarius had won by 540. While the divided command squabbled, plundered the Italians, and stayed safely ensconced in the major cities, the gifted Goth Totila was busy reclaiming much of Byzantine-held Italian countryside from the Po River to Naples.

A sick emperor, court intrigue, a Persian war, the virtual ostracism of Belisarius, and perhaps more than three hundred thousand dead from the plague at Constantinople—all of that ensured neither oversight of nor material support for the incompetent generals in Italy. If Justinian had unwisely and prematurely recalled Belisarius from Italy in spring 540, now, four years later and recovering from the plague, the emperor understood that whatever his own suspicions of the general's popular magnetism, he badly needed Belisarius to restore Italy.

So in spring 544, Belisarius, now forty, was once again returned to favor with the imperial court and ordered to Italy. But this time he departed with even less financial backing than in the past. Indeed, the general left not as before with a supreme command, but with the title of *comes sacri stabuli* ("commander of the royal stable") and a tiny force. His former secretary, the future historian Procopius, also did not accompany him and perhaps began to change his opinion of his erstwhile hero, given the perennial suspicion that seemed to surround Belisarius. Nonetheless, Belisarius made his way to Italy by land. He was relying in large part on what was left of his own money to hire imperial soldiers on the way westward. The generals in Italy concluded that the newly arriving Belisarius had not regained the emperor's complete confidence. More likely, they assumed that each of their Byzantine armies was still on its own, and so looked to the other to take risks against the Goths without much hope of help from a plague-ridden Constantinople.[49]

Along with the general Vitalius, Belisarius passed through Thrace and arrived in Dalmatia by May 544. There he headquartered on the Adriatic coast at Salonia. The two generals together had mustered little more than four thousand troops, smaller than a single traditional Roman legion. Nonetheless, Belisarius marched northward up through Croatia to descend into Ravenna in an attempt to keep the Italian cities on the Adriatic from either defecting to, or being besieged by, Totila's growing Gothic forces. Given that Belisarius had few troops, little imperial money, and no apparent power to unite the disparate Byzantine armies, he could do little more in the ensuing year than to try to keep the local cities around Ravenna free from the Goths.

Then, as Totila prepared to retake Rome, Belisarius sailed eastward back to Dalmatia—hoping to raise more imperial troops and win a direct appeal to Justinian for money and supplies. Finally, he took his small fleet on a circuitous route to reach Rome by sea, in hopes of supplying the city's defenders from the nearby Roman harbor at Portus. Justinian had still sent no aid, rightly worried about a new war with Persia and the drastic loss of manpower after the recent plague.[50]

Rome fell to Totila in December 546. Byzantine commanders, stationed throughout the Italian peninsula, had squabbled over its defense and were not willing to join Belisarius to save the ancient capital. After destroying much of the municipal walls, Totila then threatened to level the entire imperial city for its past anti-Gothic sympathies. He was dissuaded in part by messages from Belisarius, who was still nearby at Portus and who warned Totila that such nihilism would ensure revenge from both Goths and Byzantines.

Eventually, when Totila headed northward to Ravenna, Belisarius retook Rome. It was lightly defended—indeed, nearly empty, its defenses once more in disrepair. Belisarius' paltry number of troops was hardly able to man an adequate defense of the wall. Nonetheless, by May 547, Belisarius was inside the ancient capital and repairing the fortifications. This was the third year of his second Italian command, and yet Belisarius was right back where he had started—in a war that had gone on for twelve years after the Byzantines' once dramatic landing in southern Italy, coming after the brilliant victory over the Vandals in Africa.

The Goths under Totila returned and attempted to retake the city a second time from the Byzantines. Most of the Gothic chieftains were angry that Totila earlier had neither destroyed the city nor made adequate preparations to defend it from Belisarius' meager forces. This second Gothic siege failed. Totila was forced to head south to confront John, the nephew of Vitalianus, who was liberating Italian cities in Campania. The Byzantine generals may have been infighting and working at cross purposes, and their ranks depleted by plague, but when one found success, another rival often took the initiative. The result was that the war was not quite lost. Instead, the fighting reached an impasse for most of the subsequent two years, 547–48, as neither Goth nor Byzantine could drive the other out of Italy.[51]

Sometime in 548 Belisarius was once more recalled to Constantinople and replaced by the emperor's nephew Germanus. He arrived home in early 549 after five years of mostly inconsequential fighting. The war would eventually be won by Narses, an imperial insider and gifted general—at least until the invasion of the Lombards of 568 that would in time end the Byzantines' efforts at reconstituting the old Roman empire in the west. For the next five hundred years, Byzantium would cling to a few coastal enclaves in the south, as Italy was plagued by near-constant war between independent fiefdoms. Why Belisarius was recalled yet a second time from Italy—other than the serial and long-standing suspicions of the emperor Justinian—is not quite known. Our ancient sources offer a variety of possible causes. His well-connected wife, Antonia, had left Italy in 548 to lobby the court for more resources for her husband to finish the Italian campaign. But on the death of her ally, the empress Theodora, and the ascension of the emperor's favorite nephew, Germanus, Antonia may have sensed a power shift, and so instead lobbied Justinian to bring back her husband. Clearly with the demise of Theodora there was at last some chance that the earlier friendship between the two Latin-speaking northerners, Justinian and Belisarius, might be renewed.

In addition, there was always the recurrent threat from the east. The court at Constantinople may in a crisis have contemplated sending an experienced general to protect the border with Persia. Or perhaps Justinian thought he either needed a senior adviser at home, given the loss of his confidante Theodora, or wanted Belisarius where he could keep a close eye on him. In any case, Belisarius returned to Constantinople in late spring 549 to rewards, acclaim—and no further imperial service abroad.

With few resources and constant internal dissension, Belisarius had not only managed to delay Totila's onslaught, but also somehow to recapture Rome. His presence alone had saved Italy for the Byzantines, who would have otherwise been thrown out by 544. But after his departure, the Byzantines' position again deteriorated, and the dream of a unified Italy under Byzantium's control was for all practical purposes lost. Gone were the days of his first Italian tenure, when both the Goths and Italians were awed by his well-trained forces, his own personal support from the emperor, and his unbroken record of military success. Neither had any desire to welcome back the Byzantines. It would require a new commitment in resources and manpower—and a new supreme commander—to retake the peninsula.[52]

Once the plague abated somewhat, a recovered Justinian in fact would send more troops under the capable Narses. An elderly eunuch from the court was considered a far safer conqueror of Italy than the most beloved general in the empire at the height of his powers.

"This, too, I can bear—I still am Belisarius" (548–59)[53]

The resilience of Belisarius was legendary, as Henry Wadsworth Longfellow wrote of his sufferings in his poem "Belisarius." Now in his mid-forties, the general was given various honorific titles such as supreme military commander and theater commander for the east. These were positions of neither political nor military power, but each was necessary to assuage public concern over the fate of the most popular and famous Byzantine general. While some have suggested that the emperor once again wanted a recalled Belisarius nearby for advice, it seems more likely that Justinian—enfeebled by age, widowerhood, and disease—wished no repeat of the general's successful tenure in either the east or west, especially in hopes that his charismatic nephew Germanus might perhaps unite Rome following his death. Wars were either imminent or ongoing in Italy, Spain, and Mesopotamia—logical after a series of imperial and religious controversies and foiled coups. In short, there were simply too many opportunities for a dynamic rival to use against the Byzantine court.[54]

As Narses fought successfully in the west, and other generals were deployed eastward, Belisarius vanished from the historical record for almost a decade—akin to the exile of Themistocles amid the triumphs of his Athenian rivals in the postwar ascendency of fifth-century Athens, or the retirement of General Matthew Ridgway and his subsequent three decades of relative quiet following his salvation of Korea. A widowered Justinian was childless, in his late sixties, and, with the untimely death of Germanus in 550, now without an heir.

Then suddenly in 559, the general, aging and rusty from inaction, reemerges in contemporary sources. Ten years after his recall from Italy, and in the most peculiar circumstances—but in accord with his lifelong military skill and the suspicion that his success always garnered at the Byzantine court—Belisarius took the field for the last time. The plague had passed, but for years after, it had severely reduced Byzantine military manpower and curtailed Constantinople's availability to field an adequate home guard. The Nika riots had long reminded the emperor of the dangers of cutting the vast Byzantine civil service to pay for defense. Two decades of war in Africa, Italy, Mesopotamia, and Spain had drained the treasury—almost as much as had Justinian's grand plan to remake Constantinople into the greatest architectural wonder of the ancient world.

The result was that the Byzantine military was a shadow of its former self, scattered throughout the Mediterranean world and spread woefully thin in the east. An aged, lonely emperor had allowed the military to fall below two hundred thousand troops at precisely the time it was asked to protect a vast increase in imperial territory and manpower reserves were at their lowest. The theory of Byzantine defense apparently had been complete reliance on the massive walls of Constantinople—as well as attacking enemies far from home. Few emperors worried about an enemy assault on the capital itself.[55]

But that was precisely what happened in 559, when a detachment of Huns under the chieftain Zabergan split off from its main forces and crossed the Danube. With only seven thousand plunderers, he attempted a lightning-quick strike at Constantinople, convinced that the vast empire, after the plague, was hollow at its core. When the Huns reached the outlying villages near the walls of the city itself, Justinian went into a panic. He belatedly realized that all of his generals and armies were far too distant to recall. In desperation, the emperor called on Belisarius. The white-haired general was well over fifty and had not been in battle for years. The historian Agathias reports that as Belisarius "was putting on his breastplate and helmet, and equipped himself with his entire uniform from his youthful days, the memory of his earlier exploits returned and filled him with zeal." Yet Belisarius retained only three hundred or so of his veteran guardsmen, mostly deployed in largely ceremonial service and for his own protection. Nonetheless, Belisarius quickly took up the call and made arrangements to save the city—ignoring the irony that the emperor's best general was at home only because Justinian had foolishly recalled him from the distant Italian front.

At the village of Chettus, he organized a citizen defense force, spearheaded by his own three hundred veterans, and rustics eager to save their farms. The motley home guard beat back with heavy losses Zabergan and two thousand of his raiders. Constantinople was spared. The Huns withdrew toward the Danube. Belisarius' vastly outnumbered forces had once more bailed out his aged emperor through the tactical brilliance and personal magnetism of their commander. But the contrast between Justinian's panic and Belisarius' fortitude only furthered their final estrangement.[56]

Following his repulse of Zabergan, Belisarius was given little credit for his eleventh-hour heroics, and he was not allowed to pursue and finish off the enemy for good. Again, the elderly Justinian feared that to do so would swell grassroots calls for Belisarius to succeed him. The historian Agathias once again cites "envy and jealousy." But it got even worse than that. In 562, members of Belisarius' circle were accused of formally plotting against Justinian. By the end of the year, their captain was himself charged with treason, put under house arrest, his office and finances taken away—the third time that the emperor's jealousy had brought Belisarius into mortal danger.

It took another six months to establish either that the general was innocent of conspiracy, or that it was too dangerous to convict such a popular hero. At last Justinian restored his general's rank and privileges, but Belisarius was snubbed by the royal court. He would die within two years, in 565. Stories that he was blinded by the emperor and shamed by being forced to beg outside the Lausus Palace near the Hippodrome in Constantinople were probably mythical embellishments of his real enough humiliation. The end of Belisarius came just eight months before the emperor Justinian himself would pass away. Belisarius' widow, Antonia, eventually retired to a convent in her eighties—without anyone left to intrigue against or for.[57]

What had the old savior general accomplished in his some three decades of incessant fighting on behalf of Justinian's vision of a new united Rome? And had it all been worth it?

"The Name of Belisarius Can Never Die" (530–65)

Most of Belisarius' victories were to be overturned within a century. The Lombards invaded Northern Italy in 568, and only small regions in the south were saved by Constantinople. The Visigoths in Spain—a theater that Belisarius never campaigned in—rebounded. By 631, they had expelled the Byzantine outposts from the Iberian Peninsula. Most of Egypt and much of North Africa fell to Islamic armies by 711—at least in part because of the general impoverishment brought on by the destruction of the Roman and subsequent Vandal empires. Almost immediately after their successes, the Muslims then moved into Visigothic Spain.

Yet Byzantium itself—eventually to be surrounded on nearly all sides by Muslim enemies, and in growing rivalry with western Roman Catholicism—was to survive until 1453, nine hundred years after the death of Belisarius. The extension of Byzantine power under Justinian and Belisarius in some sense provided a critical buffer: When Islam spread from the Middle East, at least initially, it pressed at the periphery of the Byzantine Empire rather than at its core in Constantinople and northern Asia Minor.

The outbreak of bubonic plague in the early 540s that may have caused the deaths of a quarter or more of the empire's urban populations rendered Byzantium too weak to consolidate the victories of Belisarius in the west. It is one of the great "what ifs" of history whether Constantinople might have re-created a sustainable Mediterranean-wide empire without the epidemic.[58]

Along with the conquered provinces in North Africa, Byzantine conquests in Spain, Italy, and Sicily could have restored Roman prosperity and revenue, reunited populations, and offered successful resistance to the Lombards. Never had such an opportunity been thrown away as when Justinian pulled his support from Belisarius in the early 540s. The sixth century was supposedly a time when charismatic autocratic tribal leaders like Gelimer, Vittigis, and Totila overshadowed faceless incompetent Byzantine court insiders. In contrast, Belisarius himself was a magnetic throwback to an earlier age of Roman republican saviors—but unlike his adversaries, loyal to his civilian superiors. One of the great wonders of Roman history in the east is the remarkable fealty of Belisarius to his emperor, for all the rumors to the contrary. The history of decline in the west was often attributable to renegade generals marching on Rome—a fact perhaps well appreciated by Belisarius, who came and left home only when ordered by his emperor.[59]

Any final assessment of Belisarius' military genius—aside from the Jekyll/Hyde portrait offered by the historian Procopius—rests on four key considerations. First, his forces were almost always outnumbered, often polygot and multicultural, and in many cases mercenary. He usually was sent out to conquer entire provinces with armies smaller than twenty thousand men—and after the plague with even fewer forces. The great distances at which he operated from Constantinople, and the frequency with which he was forced to transport his armies by sea, almost always ensured that his armies were outnumbered by the enemy and plagued by logistics. Only a diplomat could have united such disparate contingents and found strength rather than sedition within such diversity. Despite stereotypes of mercenary disorder, in almost all of Belisarius' campaigns his own troops proved the most disciplined among friend and foe alike.[60]

Second, Belisarius almost never fought with unquestioned political support. He served as either a rival to Justinian's other favorite generals or under direct suspicion of the emperor himself. Almost every campaign required two paradoxical considerations: defeat might mean death or political exile, but victory could bring even a worse fate, through trial and execution on suspicion of imperial ambition.

Third, nearly all his wars involved counterinsurgency. Success hinged on his own ability to convince native Arabs, Africans, Germanic peoples, and Italians that they had more to gain from Byzantine rule and prosperity than under the tribalism of their own ethnic leaders—not an easy task when so many of Justinian's lieutenants saw provincial assignments as a mechanism solely for personal enrichment. In general, the task before Belisarius was to persuade neutral populations at peace in the east, Italy, and North Africa to join his own Byzantine forces—on the basis of some vague ancient notion of Roman commonality. Nostalgia about Rome was one thing, but in reality, invading Byzantine generals often ensured nonstop ravaging, random killing, and depredation for locals caught between warring armies. Belisarius' insight was that by offering security and humane treatment to indigenous populations, they became force multipliers in the struggles of Byzantium.

Fourth, Belisarius operated in a vast landscape of diverse weather, topography, and culture in which what brought victory in one area would not necessarily do so in another. His success from Mesopotamia to Carthage, from the River Po to the edge of the Sahara, came from flexibility of strategy and tactics while keeping his core military assumptions unchanged. That meant winning over the hearts and minds of the populace, maintaining high army morale by keeping soldiers well paid and fed, and assuring the court at Constantinople that defeat was his own while victory was the emperor's alone.

As general, Belisarius stressed the importance of interaction between officers and the rank and file. The duty of the commanders of Byzantium was to find the proper strategy of attack that fit their own meager resources, the particular distant landscape, and the size of the mostly superior enemy forces. Foresight was the key; as he reminded his outnumbered and green troops at the beginning of his second campaign against the Persians, "War tends to go well through good planning more than anything else."[61]

How, then, did Belisarius establish a blueprint for Byzantine defensive strategy for nearly a millennium? His greatest achievement was establishing a strategy similar to what B. H. Liddell Hart once called "tactical defense," or the ability to conquer territory without confronting the enemy solely through serial Western-style head-to-head slugfests. Rather, in Persia, Africa, and Italy, whether in sieges, raids, or decisive battles, Belisarius so positioned his forces that the enemy was almost always more likely to lose men than was his own army, whether it won or lost the engagement at hand. In Belisarius' view, the survival of the army, not particular victories on any given day, would win a campaign and prove critical to the security of the empire.[62]

Not only did allied provincials—Arabs, Armenians, Goths, Herulians, Huns, Moors, Vandals—provide critical manpower, but they brought needed diverse weapons and tactics, especially mounted archers, to the Byzantine military's inventory of forces. When Belisarius came west, neither the Vandals nor the Goths were prepared to deal with his mobile archers, who became force multipliers of Byzantium's chronically small armies. While Belisarius was charged with making offensive war—in North Africa, Sicily, and Italy—he often fought conservatively. That is, after acquiring a city or a base of operations, he began to win over the population and invest it with responsibility for its own defense against the inevitable counterassault.[63]

In nearly all his greatest victories, Belisarius was able to craft some sort of stratagem that mitigated his enemies' numerical advantages. For example, in Sicily he took Palermo by putting archers high on the masts of his ships to shoot down and panic the Gothic garrison. His troops captured a nearly invincible Naples by burrowing along the course of a long-abandoned aqueduct and taking the city from the inside. His defense of Rome against the besieging army of the Goth Vittigis involved not just brilliant tactics, but became a veritable "catalog of sixth-century military machinery." Whether it was prepping the battlefield at Dara with trenches or increasing the percentages of heavily armored horse archers in his army, Belisarius constantly sought to adopt, improvise, and invent to make up for what he lacked in manpower.

In the end, what are we to make of these victories over a rogue's gallery of brilliant ruthless foes—Chosroes the Persian, the Vandal Gelimer, Vittigis and Totila the Goths, and Zabergan the Hun—from well beyond the corners of the Mediterranean world? Belisarius usually lost small and won big. The victories at Dara, Ad Decimum, and Tricameron proved decisive; his losses at Tanurin, Callinicum, and at Rome neither ruined his army nor lost his war.[64]

A thirty-year career (529–59) saw the Last of the Romans fighting to save the beleaguered eastern empire in Mesopotamia against the Persians, only to return home to rescue his emperor Justinian from the Nika riots in the Hippodrome. Then he left for North Africa and in months destroyed the centurylong Vandal Empire whose ravages had so dominated the last thoughts of Saint Augustine. After that he sailed for Sicily, and for a time reclaimed the idea of a Roman Italy from the Mediterranean to the Po—only to go eastward again to meet the Persians, and then back again to a collapsing Italy, and then back to Constantinople to internal exile, trials, and humiliation, only while in forced retirement to save the city from a raid of Huns—and earn a final rebuke.

Remember the backdrop of Belisarius' frenetic campaigning. Byzantine power was collapsing. Chaos spread throughout the moribund Western Empire. A raging bubonic plague killed three hundred thousand in Constantinople and perhaps a million in the empire at large. A terrible earthquake collapsed the dome of Hagia Sophia. The onetime court supporter of Belisarius, the historian Procopius, turned on the general and would go on to smear him in his *Secret History*, as the emperor Justinian and his often lethal wife, Theodora, alternately rewarded, recalled, punished, ruined, incarcerated, and reprieved the old general. And throughout, Belisarius' conniving older wife, Antonia, a court intimate of Theodora, both tried to protect her spouse and at other times seemed as much against him as for him.[65]

The historian Procopius best summed up Belisarius' qualities that had led to victory in Libya and Italy: "In the dangers of war, he was constant without taking undue risks, while daring with cool calculation—both ready to strike quickly his enemies and yet cautious as well, depending on the needs of each particular situation. In these desperate conditions, he revealed a spirit that was full of confidence and not susceptible to panic. While during more favorable circumstances, Belisarius proved neither vain nor prone to softness. Moreover, no man ever saw Belisarius drunk." In the ancient assessment, Belisarius won because, like a Pericles, he understood that he had to encourage his rank and file when depressed and calm down the army when it was frenzied and overconfident in victory.

It has long been a habit to deprecate the achievement of Byzantium. "Byzantine," after all, became an English adjective meaning "overly complex to the point of being unworkable." Yet the classical roots of Western civilization survived in the eastern empire, while they were almost lost in the western. By the time of Constantinople's collapse in the fifteenth century, the west was resurgent and had been enriched by a continuous rediscovery of its classical heritage, often only through the agency of the stewards of Byzantium.

Rome—as the legendary catastrophes of Crassus and Antony attest—rarely enjoyed success on its far eastern frontier, where by contrast an outnumbered Belisarius kept the empire's border safe. Of course, Alexander, Caesar, and Napoleon ranged as widely as did Belisarius over the Mediterranean world and the east, but all three did so as authoritarian heads of state—both as general and emperor. Belisarius trekked across the ancient world as a general in service to his emperor and the Byzantine state. Prior great captains of antiquity fought for power, riches, land, and glory; Belisarius fought to reclaim old land that had once been Roman. We can argue over the moral nature of Belisarius' Byzantium—as we can over the nineteenth-century British Empire for which captains like Wellington crisscrossed Europe and India—but the quest of Belisarius was not for new colonies or new conquered peoples, but for the return of what others had taken. Justinian's dream of reconstituting a Mediterranean empire, reuniting Rome and Byzantium, was finally in vain. But that effort yielded a military blueprint for preserving Roman rule in the east for another millennium—thanks largely to his savior general, Flavius Belisarius.

That Belisarius fell afoul of his superiors may be a testament to, not a contradiction of, his achievement. Edward Gibbon, no romantic and no admirer of Byzantium, perhaps best summed up the character of Belisarius that explains much of his military success and lasting legacy: "The spectator and historian of his exploits has observed that amidst the perils of war he was daring without rashness, that in the deepest distress he was animated by real or apparent hope, but that he was modest and humble in the most prosperous fortune."[66]

CHAPTER THREE

"Atlanta Is Ours and Fairly Won"

William Tecumseh Sherman's Gift to Abraham Lincoln—Summer 1864

Who Was William Tecumseh Sherman?

Sherman was forty-four when he captured Atlanta in September 1864, a veteran who already had commanded in many of the worst battles of the Civil War—Shiloh, Vicksburg, and Chattanooga. He would fight in the war's last major battle, at Bentonville, just as he had its first, at Bull Run. As he went into Georgia in May 1864, Sherman still remained an utter paradox—both an insider with valuable political connections and an outcast who had met only professional failure before the war. He was a scruffy, unkempt westerner who brought a wealth of book learning and innate genius to the art of war. Pictures taken during 1864 do not suggest a robust young man of forty-four, but instead a troubled, almost angry middle-aged warrior in his fifties—face creased, hair wild, and eyes fixed away from the camera.

Sherman graduated sixth in his class at West Point in 1840. He was then stationed in a variety of locales in Florida, Georgia, South Carolina, and California, with duties from engineering to logistics. He married his foster sister, Ellen Ewing, daughter of the powerful, rich, and well-connected Ohio lawyer Thomas Ewing, who had raised him following the death of his own father. Yet despite his family connections, after resigning his commission in 1853 to enter the highly speculative banking world of Gold Rush California, Sherman met nothing but failure—and

In this famous Mathew Brady photograph of May 1865, a triumphant forty-five-year-old General William Tecumseh Sherman appears characteristically unkempt, with furrowed brow and modest uniform. Note the black sash on Sherman's folded left arm, in homage to the recently assassinated Abraham Lincoln. Photo courtesy of the National Archives and Records Administration.

was finally near bankruptcy. Unable to support his family, he subsequently tried law. Various business schemes followed before he won an appointment in January 1860 as the first superintendent of the new Louisiana State Seminary of Learning and Military Academy—only to resign a year later after Louisiana seceded and joined the Confederacy. After his first and only successful employment, Sherman headed back home to the north. Five months later he enlisted in the Union Army at the rank of colonel.[1]

After gallant service at Bull Run, Colonel Sherman was promoted to brigadier general and deployed as a second in command for the military district of the entire state of Kentucky. There Sherman abruptly experienced some sort of mental breakdown—in part from constant sleeplessness, asthma aggravated by cigar smoking, separation from his family, and perhaps bipolar depression, of which there was a family history; in part from the prescient but bleak realization that the new war to defeat the Confederacy would take years to win and cost thousands of lives—and that few of his superiors recognized this awful truth.

Only the intervention of both his wife, Ellen Ewing, and an influential younger brother, Ohio senator John Sherman (now known mostly for authorship of the Sherman Antitrust Act), landed him a second chance out west as a military subordinate to the ascendant Brigadier General Ulysses S. Grant. The latter, whom Sherman technically outranked, gave him a division command following his own successes at Forts Henry and Donaldson. Although Sherman's Ohio division was surprised on the first day of Shiloh, he nevertheless held firm against the huge Confederate advance, was slightly wounded twice, and had three horses shot from under him—and emerged after the Northern victory a national hero.

Prior to Shiloh, Sherman had referred to himself as a Jonah and confessed to contemplating suicide. Afterward, he had the confidence to appreciate that his own unique ideas about conflict in the industrial age were far more sophisticated and apt than those of most of his fellow Union generals, who mostly failed throughout 1862–63 to defeat their Confederate counterparts. In short, the horrific battle of Shiloh saved the career of William Tecumseh Sherman.[2]

Sherman had left the army in 1853, after most of his own generation from West Point had seen service in the Mexican War—Robert E. Lee, Albert Sidney Johnston, James Longstreet, George McClellan—and would go on to win prominent positions on both sides on the eve of the Civil War. But had Sherman really failed at all? In terms of professional employment, financial success, and reputation, he most surely had. Indeed, he could not even support his growing family in a permanent residence, and he counted on family acquaintances for any job he could find. But in the larger scope of learning the diverse requisite skills necessary to lead a hundred thousand men into Georgia, a young Sherman had not stumbled at all.

Quite unknowingly, by taking on and losing job after job, he had been engaged in a three-decade-long course of practical and formal preparation for generalship in a new age of mobile and total warfare. At one time or another, Sherman had refined his formal education at West Point with jobs as diverse as college administrator, banker, businessman, farmer, lawyer, and trader. He had visited and been deployed throughout much of the United States even as he was written off as a hopeless failure. At one point, Sherman confessed, "I was afraid of my own shadow."[3]

Sherman knew what it was to be broke, disgraced, and ridiculed; the *Cincinnati Commercial* had declared him "insane" after he resigned his command in Kentucky. Yet in all of his setbacks and abbreviated careers, Sherman had conducted himself honorably and was often a victim of circumstance—a fiscal panic and his bank directors' graft caused his financial demise in California. Secession and the looming war unexpectedly ended his bright career as a college administrator in Louisiana. By summer 1864, as commander in the west, he held no fear that either the public or his peers might not like him, much less think his ideas unconventional. Even in triumph at the war's end, Sherman raised controversy. In the viewing stand of the victory parade in Washington, he refused to shake the hand of the secretary of war, in rebuke to Edwin Stanton, who had unfairly castigated him for supposedly tolerating racist conduct toward emancipated slaves. But what did Sherman—who long ago had felt that he had nothing to lose—care about court scandal?

Marching thousands of soldiers and their supply train through the woods of Georgia to Atlanta required formal training in artillery, engineering, and mathematics, as well as acquaintance with the nature and costs of transportation, both by wagon and rail. Sherman's formal education allowed him to write clear letters and communiqués and to organize supplies and capital for his vast army. Dozens of menial jobs had given him firsthand familiarity with the resentments and anger of the common classes. There could have been no better résumé for leading a huge army into the woods of Georgia than that of the checkered career of William Tecumseh Sherman, bitterly though such requisite experiences had been earned.[4]

The Butchery (*August 1864*)

What a difference just a year and a half made. By late summer 1864, Northern excitement over the Emancipation Proclamation of January 1, 1863, had long vanished. Instead, angry Northern abolitionists were at loggerheads with President Lincoln. Copperhead Confederate sympathizers in the North hated both their president and his radical abolitionist critics—and often each other.

Few in a divided North remembered why in spring 1864 the public had worshipped the brilliant newcomer Ulysses S. Grant—the superman Grant who on that wonderful July 4, 1863, more than a year earlier, had brought them the magnificent victory at Vicksburg that cut the Confederacy in half, after nonstop victories at Fort Henry, Fort Donelson, and Shiloh. News of the taking of the key stronghold on the Mississippi at Vicksburg, along with the surrender of thirty thousand Confederates, had capped the celebration of the bloody repulse of General Lee a day earlier at Gettysburg.

Indeed, Grant's appointment to come east to command the Army of the Potomac in March 1864 had at once enthralled the nation. The rough-looking westerner seemed invincible and would bring a new toughness to the defenders of Washington. He certainly would not back down from Robert E. Lee as had past Union generals, who sounded like lions before, but kittens after, battle. Given his reputation for victories in the west, in spring 1864 the quiet Grant enjoyed celebrity status anywhere he went in Washington. Yet all that Grant mania was months—and nearly a hundred thousand Union dead, wounded, and missing—in the past. Besides the daily attrition of the Army of the Potomac through skirmishing and illness, a series of catastrophic set battles and sieges had changed the reputation of Grant the savior into the butcher of the Wilderness, Spotsylvania, Cold Harbor, and Petersburg. By June, even First Lady Mary Todd Lincoln had lashed out to her husband, "Grant, I repeat, is an obstinate fool and a butcher."[5]

By August 1864, consensus spread that Grant's superior, Abraham Lincoln—who, after some initial doubt, had easily secured the Republican Party's renomination in June—in little over four months would lose to the likely Democratic nominee in the fall election. That rival winner was most likely to be General George McClellan. President Lincoln had unceremoniously put him on ice after McClellan squandered numerous opportunities to move on Richmond following the marginally successful battle of Antietam in 1862. But the wily McClellan—removed from command of the Army of the Potomac in 1862 and given no subsequent important responsibility—had not resigned his commission. Instead, he had done his best to offer military credibility to the notion growing in the northern Democratic Party that an absolute defeat of the secessionists was either impossible or not worth the ensuing costs. The prospect of McClellan, the military expert, running against Lincoln, the novice—during times of horrific Union casualties—was gaining public appeal, especially since McClellan's losses of 1862 were ancient history and Lincoln's mishaps current events. Former generals can usually give up on wars far more easily, and with far less criticism, than other politicians. More important in the new antiwar narrative, the relieved McClellan had once gotten far closer to Richmond in May 1862—within seven miles during the Peninsula Campaign—and at less cost than had Grant in 1864.

If McClellan were elected in November, the war might well end with a negotiated armistice. Ideally, the Confederacy would agree to stop fighting once it understood that it could rejoin the Union without further acrimony—and retain slavery. Issues such as the expansion of slavery into the new western states could be readjudicated at some future date. Americans could end their rancor and agree that whatever differences they had over slavery paled in comparison to the mass slaughter of the last three years. The entire bloody Civil War, in this growing Democratic view, could be written off as a horrific tragedy brought on by intransigent New England abolitionists and die-hard Southern plantationists. Both extremists had unnecessarily dragged the majority of Americans, North and South, into a pointless war over their own respective obsessions with slavery—an institution that no doubt in the century ahead would eventually have withered away and died. President McClellan would heal the wounds of his predecessor's unnecessary war. The nation would become reconciled to the idea that, although millions of African slaves would have to continue their servitude for a while, at least there would be no more mass internecine killing. McClellan was too wise, at least initially, to be an open Copperhead who favored an immediate cessation of arms and the de facto granting of Confederate independence. But he seemed unaware that by 1864, the war had evolved into something far more than the original Northern effort to reunite the Union, but had come to be aimed also at ending slavery on all American soil. His early September acceptance letter to the Democratic Party that nominated him in late August 1864 is a textbook illustration of naïveté. McClellan promised simultaneously to reunite America, to increase the chances of ending the war, and to accept any Southern state back into the Union that wished to rejoin—without mentioning abolition as requisite for readmittance—as if, after three years of brutal fighting, most Northern states would allow slavery or any Southern states would wish to reenter without it.[6]

Yet McClellan sounded hawkish in comparison with his new and often embarrassing allies, the Copperhead "Peace" Democrats whom he represented. They were championed, most notably, by the seditious former congressman and newspaper editor Clement Vallandigham of Ohio. The latter barnstormed the Midwest crying Lincolnism to be "defeat, debt, taxation and sepulchers." By early 1864 a minority in some Midwestern states was at times thwarting the Union effort, encouraging draft resistance, sending out private emissaries to the Confederacy, and turning a blind eye to budding conspiracies to free Confederate prisoners. The word "miscegenation" first widely appeared in an American campaign as the Copperheads screamed that Lincoln favored not merely abolition, but a new mixing of the white and black races and permanent disenfranchisement of Southern whites.[7]

Since the states mustered their own militias to be incorporated into the Union army, a Copperhead legislature or governor could, in theory, insidiously curtail funding and hold back on its required military contributions. And while the Copperheads themselves, or their quiet sympathizers, did not have the votes to win national office, their support for a McClellan ticket might put the Democratic anti-Lincoln forces in power. That was especially likely if the Republicans were to continue to remain deeply divided, as news from the front got worse. The pulse of the war in Virginia governed all the politics of spring and summer. In general, as mostly westerners, the Copperheads were as much in sympathy with the enemy rural South, as with the supposedly allied industrial North with its fervent abolitionists. At other times, the more extreme Copperheads dreamed of seceding to form their own new western republic.

Well aside from the November election to come, the House of Lincoln was collapsing in every direction. First Lady Mary Todd Lincoln had exceeded her White House decoration budget by several thousand dollars. Worse still, she had diverted public funds to her own use through fraudulent bookkeeping. For most of the year, Mary Lincoln was desperately and stealthily seeking wealthy supporters to cover her debts in exchange for her husband's political patronage—offenses that would have led to impeachment attempts against a contemporary president. Graft was not far from the president himself.[8]

Lincoln was not in a good state of mind. In February, he told his close friend, the dying Illinois congressman and staunch abolitionist Owen Lovejoy, "This war is eating my life out. I have a strong impression that I shall not live to see it through." Lincoln may have suffered a mild case of smallpox in 1863, and not have regained his full strength. Neither Lincoln nor his wife, Mary, had ever quite recovered from the deaths of two of the four Lincoln sons in childhood. Disaster at the front only added to the burdens of personal tragedy and ill health.

There certainly had been disturbing incidents all year long, like the mysterious arson attack on the White House stables in February. A few months later there was an apparent foiled assassination attempt, as well as constant rumors of Confederate-inspired kidnapping plots. Little wonder that Lincoln seemed to go into periods of deep depression—finally to the point of having his cabinet sign letters of resignation that he placed in a White House safe.

If in early 1864, Lincoln had feared that he would not be renominated by the Republicans, after his June nomination he was increasingly convinced that he would not be reelected. By July the president was out on the ramparts at Fort Stevens during Jubal Early's Washington raid, almost intentionally, it seemed, exposing himself to Confederate sniper fire.[9]

Then there was the press. By early 1864, the attacks transcended political opposition and centered on Lincoln himself, calling him a naïf, incompetent, tyrant, butcher, baboon, freak—and far worse. The New York newspapers, other than the Republican *Times*, were the most vicious. Horace Greeley's *New York Tribune* simply reflected the pulse of the battlefield: a rare Union victory in 1864 won from him a sudden endorsement of Lincoln, while the increasing bad news from Virginia earned hysterical condemnation of the administration—often within a few weeks of earlier praise. Greeley, in the manner of a modern electronic commentator, was notorious not just for his fickleness, but also for the vehemence with which his present judgments contradicted his past assertions. Any rumor of military setback seemed to prompt a call for Salmon Chase, John C. Frémont, or Ulysses S. Grant to save the Union from Lincoln's ineptness and to run for the presidency on a united Republican victory ticket. Greeley himself spent the summer intriguing with McClellanites. Finally he was meeting even with Confederate emissaries in Canada in hopes of ending the war immediately.

The *New York Herald* under James Gordon Bennett was the largest newspaper in the North and by 1862 not so unpredictable as the

Tribune—it blasted Lincoln without exception. Along with the less influential Manton Marble's pro-Democrat *New York World*, Bennett could influence critical public opinion in the banking capital of the North, whose financiers' support for Lincoln's war was critical. In an age without the cell phone, Internet, e-mail, radio, or television, the New York papers, along with the monthly and weekly magazines and perhaps the *Chicago Tribune*, enjoyed almost a monopoly on the news. The only reason why the press had not yet prevented Lincoln from being renominated was that Union politics were at an impasse: as yet, no Republican or independent candidate had offered any better plan to stop the killing without rendering meaningless the past sacrifice of tens of thousands of Union soldiers. Continue the war and there would be more Gettysburgs; quit it and the hallowed sacrifice of Gettysburg would be in vain. Defeating a Southern army was one thing; defeating and occupying a vast area the size of Western Europe was quite another.[10]

Lincoln's fractious cabinet was more bitterly divided than ever. His political wisdom of early 1861 of bringing in a "team of rivals" of presidential hopefuls to keep an eye on their ambitions had come to seem like folly as the cabinet fell into a sort of chaos. Secretaries such as Edward Bates (attorney general), Montgomery Blair (postmaster general), Salmon P. Chase (secretary of the treasury), William Seward (secretary of state), and Edwin Stanton (secretary of war) were either intriguing with Lincoln's opponents, plotting to take Lincoln's job, fighting with one another, or indiscreetly lamenting to the press that their rustic commander in chief simply was not up to the task of winning a war in the east. The cabinet secretaries also knew that no American president had managed to be reelected since Andrew Jackson in 1832. Conventional wisdom certainly suggested that the amateur Lincoln was not the sort to pull off what others far more competent and experienced had not for more than thirty years.[11]

Things got even worse. Treasury Secretary Salmon Chase, a longtime influential abolitionist and increasingly disloyal to his boss, for months had been politicking on the sly with Radical Republicans, the most extreme wing of the party. Chase dreamed of wresting the nomination from Lincoln and winning the November election against the Peace Democrats on a more fiery platform of immediate universal abolition and a harsh occupation to be imposed on the rebel Confederates. Some of Chase's radical supporters wanted even more—perhaps a sort of permanent military subjugation and occupation of the South, or even repopulating the defunct Confederacy by poor Northerners, freed Southern blacks, and new immigrants. If more conservative critics wished a scaling down of the war, abolitionists urged a renewed existential struggle, one in which the culture of the losers would be obliterated, that of the winners made all-powerful.

Draconian punishment for Southern secession was also a backdoor way for abolitionists to gain permanent control of the U.S. Congress: Ex-Confederates would be denied voting rights; freedmen, as the sole representatives from a reconstructed South, would vote their thanks for Northern abolitionists by joining a now entrenched and permanent radical Republican majority. Both Northern Democrats and Republicans agreed that Lincoln was without a constituency—unable to offer leadership necessary to win the war, bring the slaughter to a close, or create the political consensus to slog on.

Only the unseemliness of a cabinet minister openly scheming against his own president had derailed Salmon Chase's efforts to subvert Lincoln. By June, Lincoln finally had enough and accepted Chase's pro forma resignation. In a near state of shock at the acceptance of his latest offer to resign—his three previous ones had been refused—the treasury secretary at last left the administration. But the evolving threat from the Radical Republicans far transcended Chase's own presidential aspirations. The abolitionist cause had already been taken up by the frontier hero and "pathfinder" John C. Frémont. The erratic Frémont was nominated on May 31 by a breakaway group of radical Republicans and war Democrats under the banner of the Radical Democracy Party. The unstable and conniving Frémont was mostly a symbolic protest presidential candidate. Yet he, too, might do his part to so weaken Lincoln and divide the Republicans that McClellan could win by uniting the Democrats.

While Chase, Frémont, and McClellan schemed on, Lincoln was worried about other Union generals coming to the fore. At various times, he sent out feelers to Ulysses S. Grant's friends to ensure that the once wildly popular general had no presidential aspirations before he was given the reins of all Union armies in March. Lincoln even inquired whether the incompetent, but still influential, radical General Benjamin Butler might be interested in replacing Hannibal Hamlin as his vice president. Hamlin, in fact, by June would not be renominated—and perhaps felt relieved. He had little influence with Lincoln anyway. Now, just in time, he could exit what seemed to be a losing ticket in the autumn.

By February 1864, flyers began circulating—the most prominent were entitled "The Next Presidential Election" and "The Pomeroy Circular"—listing high-ranking Republicans who had gone on record opposing Lincoln's nomination. These clumsy broadsides would not win Salmon Chase the Republican nomination. But once more, they contributed to the insidious narrative of a beleaguered Lincoln, whose former friends and supporters were as hostile as his proven enemies. In July, Lincoln pocket-vetoed the notorious Wade-Davis bill. The measure was a clumsy attempt to ensure a Radical Republican blueprint for postwar reconstruction that sought to destroy the remnants of antebellum Southern culture. By August there was a massive pro-McClellan rally in New York City. Observers noted that the worse the news of the war became, the better "Little Mac" looked.[12]

Lincoln reasoned that, in lieu of a dramatic Union victory, he needed either a Radical Republican on the ticket to quiet the base, or, contrarily, a Southern Union loyalist who could facilitate reconstruction and win crossover Democratic voters. Barring that, perhaps a loyal, successful general would do—to weaken either his right or left flank and restore his sinking military credibility. After the firing of Chase, the selection of the nondescript Andrew Johnson as his new vice presidential candidate pleased very few.[13]

Despite the criticism from the radical abolitionists, Abraham Lincoln himself had not changed much. He had not altered fundamentally his recent intent of serially abolishing slavery everywhere in the Union after the war in the interest of reuniting the country. But he had also not won the war after more than three years, and he could not adequately explain, in military terms, how he hoped to achieve victory as 1864 wore on—or why, as the South grew weaker, Union casualties mounted in each new month of the year. The country was $2 billion in debt. It was spending over $2 million a day on the war. Lincoln had desperate plans to call up another half a million northerners, in part by providing enough cash bonuses and incentives to ensure that veterans reenlisted after their three-year commitments expired. He was gambling on one final big surge to win in 1864 before his own political support vanished for good. A dramatic, timely victory by Grant would prove Lincoln and his agenda inspired after all, even as one more bloody defeat like Cold Harbor would confirm his incompetence.

From the beginning of 1864, Northern fortunes had deteriorated on the battlefield. Since spring 1861, about a quarter million Union soldiers had died in combat or from disease; almost two million Northern men had been taken from their jobs and enrolled in the Union Army. By 1864, a disturbing number of Northern voters no longer had any strong ideological beliefs other than to ally themselves with the winning political side—and the suspicion grew that by August 1864, Lincoln could not afford the mounting costs to defeat the Confederacy. From that one fact of military deadlock grew all of the doubts that Lincoln would not be president after March 1865.[14]

Changing Strategies (*March–August 1864*)

In August, another frequent visitor to the White House, the Pennsylvanian Alexander McClure, remarked of his visit with the president, "His face, always sad in repose, was then saddened until it became a picture of despair." Still the war went on. Yet the public did not appreciate that the advantages were still with the Union. No foreign powers had recognized the Confederacy. The Southern economy was slowly being strangled. The Union was producing new armies and war matériel at an astonishing rate—even as the North still could not defeat Lee's army, and was still having little luck on the battlefield beyond Virginia.[15]

The South saw that the rising antiwar mood of 1864 up north was the key to victory. If large areas of Alabama, Arkansas, Louisiana, Mississippi, Tennessee, and Virginia were under Northern control, the majority of the Confederacy, especially its large cities, was still unoccupied. Paradoxically, while the Confederacy was robbed of agricultural land, manpower, and some industry in its lost territories, the South also had more men to defend less ground, while the Union was forced to occupy and hold vast swaths of territory—the age-old military paradox that so plagued invaders from Napoleon and Hitler in Russia to the Koreans and Chinese who sought to cross the 38th Parallel and reach Pusan. The emperor Justinian may have had grand visions of a new Mediterranean Rome. Yet the reality for him as well was that more occupied land had to be guarded by always fewer troops.

The Confederacy—even in its reduced size, still far larger than most Western European nations—grasped that its new hope was to make the struggle so costly to northerners that various peace parties would defeat Lincoln in 1864 and vote in reasonable compromisers who would sue for an armistice. Riots and social chaos followed from the voracious manpower needs of Union generals, while the South had somehow, with far less domestic violence, managed to call up seven hundred thousand despite its much smaller population base.

Robert E. Lee, with his crack Army of Northern Virginia behind near-impenetrable barricades, finally began to understand that he was waging a political war. He no longer had to go north, losing thousands of men in search of the elusive big victory. Instead, survival meant success: Each month that his army endured and inflicted casualties on Grant's Army of the Potomac, the North became a little more likely to reject Lincoln and to grant an armistice in hopes of national reunification with slavery intact. As Lee put it, "Should the belief that peace will bring back the Union become general, the war would no longer be supported, and that after all is what we are interested in bringing about."[16]

The Killing Fields (*Summer 1864*)

Lincoln's political problems by August 1864 arose not from bad news at a particular theater, but from terrible reports from all fronts. Grant and Meade were being bled white by Lee in Virginia. Benjamin Butler was humiliated by far smaller enemy forces near the James River. An incompetent Nathaniel P. Banks almost lost his army in Alabama. And a slow-moving Franz Sigel got nowhere in the Shenandoah Valley.

Ostensibly the aim of these diverse operations was simultaneously to apply such pressure to the shell that at some point it would shatter and suffer a general collapse. The problem, however, with such a strategy was that Union armies were scattered for thousands of miles around the Confederate periphery, whose ever shortening interior lines made transference of troops and supply from one army to another suddenly far easier. In addition, too many of the Northern generals in charge of these offensives—such as Butler, Banks, and Sigel—were either militarily inexperienced politicians or utterly incompetent, or both. Finally, Grant was allotting precious Union troops to distant theaters of questionable importance under the command of known mediocrities, when a concentration of force was needed to take either Richmond or Atlanta.[17]

Indeed, the critical struggle remained between Robert E. Lee's Army of Northern Virginia and the Army of the Potomac, as both fought between, and sometimes above and below, the respective capitals at Richmond and Washington. Yet Lincoln's desperate "On to Richmond" strategy—to pour men into Grant's army so that he might either defeat Lee before the November election, or at least take the Confederate capital—had instead led to a bloody quagmire. The Union suddenly needed to take risks to show progress before the November election, but not so many risks as to lose the Army of the Potomac altogether. Such a bleak scenario was not unlikely.

In little more than three days of the so-called Wilderness Campaign (May 4–7), Grant's army suffered nearly 18,000 dead, wounded, missing, or captured soldiers. But unlike McClellan after Antietam, he pressed on against Lee. That obstinacy would impress subsequent military historians, but at the time, it was considered near-suicidal bloodletting. Next, in fierce fighting around Spotsylvania between May 10 and 21, Grant lost nearly another eighteen thousand men. Yet to prove to Lincoln that he was no McClellan, Pope, Burnside, Hooker, or Meade, who had all eventually retreated in the face of mounting dead, Grant boasted, "I propose to fight on this line if it takes all Summer"—another often-praised quote, but one that if uttered today would ipso facto spark an entire antiwar movement. Lincoln's problem was that a growing majority in the North feared that in fact the butcher Grant might just keep his promise and so cost them another 36,000 casualties with little to show for it.[18]

And he did. Grant's obstinacy was grounded in a strategy: He had done the proverbial awful arithmetic of inflicting substantial casualties that Robert E. Lee's Army of Northern Virginia could, in the long term, not sustain. The idea was that Lee, while in these successive battles suffering a percentage of losses against his overall strength similar to Grant, had far fewer reserves than did Grant and would thus quit first. But such calculations were in some sense still academic by mid-1864. In the here and now, the unexpected bloodletting—after the good news of 1863—had created a far greater hysteria in the North than in the South. The Northern public no longer cared about Lee's army. It only wanted an end to Grant's terrible losses. Perhaps the early retreats after stalemates by former generals were preferable to Grant's continued bloody impasse.

No matter—Grant kept it up. At Cold Harbor, between June 1 and 3, he nearly rendered the Army of the Potomac combat ineffective, through futile head-on charges against Lee's defensive works. In the slaughter—it seemed more like murder to those involved—he suffered another twelve thousand casualties. Grant's army had lost more than forty thousand soldiers dead, wounded, and captured in just thirty days. He pressed on to Petersburg. There, incompetence by subordinate generals led to a failed assault on the city and another eleven thousand casualties without gaining any traction in taking Richmond. A nine-month siege followed that would eventually cost the Union another forty-two thousand casualties.

In theory, "casualties" meant dead, wounded, missing, and known captured. But unlike modern war, a high percentage of the wounded perished or were so maimed as to be rendered unable to return to the front. The captured died in droves in Southern prisoner-of-war camps. The missing, if deserters, rarely returned, but just as likely they numbered those who had been ground up by artillery and never identified. In short, forty-two thousand "casualties" were nearly equivalent to the number of soldiers who disappeared from Grant's ranks for good.

Worse still, while the Army of the Potomac was locked in a death grip with Lee around Richmond, there was, for the moment at least, no effective Union army blocking Confederate advances through the Shenandoah Valley to the north of Washington. As a result, a confident Robert E. Lee ordered General Jubal Early to move northward up the Shenandoah Valley and to descend on Washington from the unprotected northwest. Early did so, and by July 11–12 he was on the outskirts of the city with nearly twelve thousand Confederate troops. A hesitant Early lost his brief chance of raiding inside the city proper, and he began withdrawing on the thirteenth. But the proximity of Confederate troops to the White House, while Grant was stalled outside Richmond and with little news at all from the west, confirmed the public feeling that something had gone terribly wrong. It was now 1864 and a Confederate army had gotten closer to the capital than at almost any time during the entire war. The president himself had come under enemy fire; the mood of the North was almost back to Bull Run again.

Amid such news, by August 23, President Lincoln reportedly remarked to a Republican supporter, "You think I don't know I am going to be beaten, but I do, and unless some great change takes place, badly beaten." Yet out west there was at least hope of a breakthrough before the election. A final Union victory in November 1863 at the vital rail hub of Chattanooga had secured southern Tennessee and left northern Alabama and Georgia open to invasion. William Tecumseh Sherman, commanding the three armies of the Military Division of the Mississippi, saw an opening. Sherman thought he could march freely into Georgia, then cut off or even take Atlanta—a key transportation hub and symbol of the secure interior of the Confederacy. He would outmaneuver the Southern armies, and perhaps by autumn split the Confederacy asunder—and thereby improve Lincoln's election chances even if Grant did not take Richmond.

By late summer, it became clear that Grant had little chance of entering the Southern capital before November. The stage was set for a growing paradox: As the nation looked to Grant outside Richmond to save Lincoln, the president's only possible salvation was with Sherman, whose operations in Georgia were less well known to the Northern public. Yet Sherman was a different, more unpredictable sort than Grant—an unlikely savior, given Sherman's reclusive nature and hatred of both politics and the press.[19]

Sherman Moves South (*May 1864*)

Well before the terrible Union summer in Virginia, William Tecumseh Sherman had planned to avoid the set battles that he feared might nearly wreck General Grant and his Army of the Potomac. Sherman had taken command of the Military Division of the Mississippi on March 18, succeeding Grant with the understanding that the two generals would be working in tandem, east and west, to crush the rebellion before the war-weary Northern public called it quits. Sherman thought that he could direct his western armies to outmaneuver, rather than charge head on against, his adversary General Joe Johnston and the Army of Tennessee. Such a strategy was far better suited to the wide-open spaces of Georgia than the narrow corridor between Washington and Richmond.

Sherman's forces instead would seek to trap and perhaps get to the rear of Johnston's army as it retreated southward. Then at some opportune moment, with his back to Atlanta, Johnston would be forced to either abandon the city or fight a numerically superior force under unfavorable conditions. Sherman would humiliate the South by freely traversing its homeland on the assumption that in the election year of 1864, perceptions of winning were nearly as important as piling up enemy corpses.[20]

In some histories of the so-called Atlanta campaign of spring and summer 1864, Sherman is still criticized for not seeking, in Clausewitzian fashion, the destruction of the main enemy forces under General Johnston, or for not heading in a beeline for Atlanta from the outset. But again, like Belisarius, he wished to avoid the sort of set battles that could ruin his army deep in enemy territory. If Grant was waging war directly against Lee's army in the field, Sherman, in contrast, would fight the Southern infrastructure that sustained its armies—and in the next year he would adduce lengthy explanations why this was the more efficient and even more moral course. Even if the Union could endure more of the sort of losses that would soon nearly destroy the Army of the Potomac, Lincoln's reelection chances surely would not survive simultaneous carnage in Georgia like that in Virginia. Of course, Sherman had explicitly assured Grant that he would not let elements of Johnston's army go eastward to reinforce Lee's forces protecting Richmond. But such a vague directive gave him ample latitude to wage his own strategic campaign in Georgia.[21]

Well before he set out on his road to Atlanta, Sherman had discussed with Grant, who had just assumed supreme command of Union forces, the rough outlines of their new grand partnership. Sherman, in Grant's words, was "to move against Johnston's army, to break it up, and to get into the interior of the enemy's country as far as you can, inflicting all the damage you can against their war resources." Once Grant and Sherman took the offensive at about the same time, in theory neither Lee nor Johnston could reinforce each other. That had unfortunately happened at the Battle of Chickamauga in late September 1863, when General Longstreet had arrived with more than two divisions after a nearly eight-hundred-mile railroad trip from the east in time to help defeat Union forces there.

Grant did not order Sherman explicitly to go after either Joe Johnston's Confederate army or Atlanta itself. Apparently the aim in the spring planning of 1864 was mostly to keep all reinforcements and attention away from Lee by causing havoc elsewhere in the Confederacy—as well as being a sort of Gallipoli campaign on the periphery that could divert attention from the mayhem in the trenches and might in and of itself lead to some sort of ultimate strategic advantage. Sherman at any rate assumed that his task was to tie down forces, ruin infrastructure, and seek to avoid losses while inflicting psychosocial mayhem on the Southern populace. He knew, however, that Atlanta was much farther from his base of operations than Richmond was from Grant's, and that his incremental advance would not immediately reassure the public that dramatic victories were imminent.[22]

As Sherman set out from Tennessee on May 7—roughly in time with Grant's own offensive in the Wilderness against Lee—the odds seemed against him. True, Sherman had more than a hundred thousand troops in his combined forces, the largest number of men he had yet commanded. He could rely on gifted subordinate generals like George Thomas (Army of the Cumberland), James McPherson (Army of the Tennessee), and John Schofield (Army of the Ohio)—far better commanders than most of those who served under Grant. Many of their regiments were made up from crack troops from the Midwest, especially homesteaders from Illinois, Indiana, Michigan, Missouri, and Ohio. They saw themselves as a different sort from many of the replacements filling up the ranks of the reconstituted Army of the Potomac. Or, as Liddell Hart once characterized Sherman's force as it left Atlanta for the sea, "the finest army of military 'workmen' the modern world has seen."[23]

Sherman's army was more comfortable at camping out and living off the land than was the Army of the Potomac, which had fought mostly on the border, never quite in the heart of the Confederacy. One eastern veteran, Rice Bull, remarked of the casual swagger of Sherman's western troops, "They all wore large hats instead of caps; were carelessly dressed, both officers and men; and marched in a very irregular way . . . We found their boast was that they 'put on no style.' They were a fine type of westerners; it was easy to see that at any serious time they would close up and be there . . . They expressed their opinion that we were tin soldiers. 'Oh look at their caps. Where are your paper collars? Oh how clean you look, do you use soap?' "[24]

Sherman understood that his numerical superiority could easily be offset by a skilled Confederate defense, bad weather, and rough terrain: "I also reckoned that, in the natural strength of the country, in the abundance of mountains, streams, and forests, [the enemy] had a fair offset to our numerical superiority, and therefore endeavored to act with reasonable caution while moving on the vigorous 'offensive.' " For most of May and June, Sherman's army in fact entrenched in mud and slept among downpours, incurring losses to illness and exposure—yet in the soldiers' eyes, these were still preferable risks to head-on charges against fixed enemy positions and bulwarks.[25]

Surprise would not aid the Union cause. Whatever his general orders, there was little mystery about Sherman's ultimate pathway to Atlanta. Sherman was initially dependent on the railroads, and four of them in Georgia ran into the city of some twenty thousand—the young and growing transportation and industrial hub of what was left of the Confederacy in the west. As Sherman put it, "I've been fighting Atlanta all this time. It's done more to keep up the war than any—well, Richmond, perhaps. All the guns and wagons we've captured along the way—all marked Atlanta." Atlanta was the great rail center of the South, one of its few munitions manufacturing sites, and a gateway to the Atlantic and Gulf port Southern cities. Sherman himself had written Grant at the outset, "Should Johnston fall behind the Chattahoochee, I will feint to the right, but go to the left and act against Atlanta or its eastern communications, according to developed facts."[26]

In addition to the perils of bad weather, mud, rough terrain, and the advantages that usually accrue to defenders, Sherman had to contend with a seasoned army led by an array of highly competent Confederate officers under General Joe Johnston, who had more than sixty thousand troops at his disposal and was adept in Fabian tactics of defense, bleeding an invader without committing to decisive battle. Johnston's subordinate generals—Leonidas Polk, John Bell Hood, Benjamin F. Cheatam, William J. Hardee, and Patrick R. Cleburne (perhaps the best division commander of the entire war on either side)—were more experienced than even Sherman's solid high command.[27]

In theory, as Johnston backtracked, his supply lines would shorten and he could galvanize an alarmed population. A fortified Atlanta might withstand for a while a besieging Sherman's army, while Johnston's intact mobile forces could maneuver around the Union rear to relieve the pressure. In contrast, as Sherman advanced on and around Atlanta, his circular lines lengthened. The growing need to station troops as occupation forces would further erode his strength. Or, as Sherman put his need to garrison conquered territory, "I am fully aware that these detachments weaken me in the exact proportion our enemy has gained strength by picking up his detachments."[28]

Sherman ultimately had to obtain his food and forage from faraway federal supply depots at Nashville, Tennessee. These in turn were further distant from an advance base at Chattanooga across the border. To Sherman's way of thinking, he probably could not stop Confederates to his rear from attacking his rail lines of support. But he could at least have on hand so many engineers, and so much extra track and timber, that he could rebuild infrastructure as quickly as enemy raiders might destroy it. Of all commanders on both sides of the war, no one matched Sherman's attention to repair and logistical details, as he pored over maps of Georgia and calibrated his army's anticipated progress with the necessary supplies. It was no accident that he set out into Georgia with forty thousand mules and horses and nearly six thousand ambulances and wagons and was confident that he could operate away from rail lines for days—and later weeks—at a time.[29]

The Long Slog (*June 1864*)

On May 7, Sherman moved his large army toward Dalton, Georgia, Johnston's base of operations. From May 7 to September 2, he headed ever so slowly southward—often at a snail's pace that would on average result in only a mile's southward progress per day over some four months. Yet for all his maneuvering and flanking, Sherman still headed southward and never retreated or ceased movement once the campaign started. His idea of advance was that three Union armies would descend from diverse directions and from the outset threaten Johnston with encirclement. There had initially been some Union fear of a preemptive Confederate attack from Dalton into Tennessee. Indeed, by late spring, Johnston had reequipped and reorganized the Army of Tennessee into an effective force who believed they might fight outside Georgia. But the South lacked sustained logistical support for any extended march far from its supplies. As Johnston knew, he could not afford to be cut off and trapped to the north, leaving Atlanta exposed.

As Sherman's three-pronged advance neared Dalton, Johnston felt his base was increasingly untenable. Even though he had occupied and fortified it for six months, within a week, Johnston simply abandoned his headquarters without a fight and drew back to Resaca. This was a critical move. At the very beginning of their long duel, Johnston had established that he did not quite know how to handle the unpredictable and highly mobile Sherman. Huge armies, dependent on rail, plowing into enemy territory were not supposed to outflank and outmaneuver so easily home-state defenders.[30]

Next, on May 13, Sherman's forces scrambled in vain to cut off any remnants of Johnston's army as it streamed into Resaca, in what would be the first pitched fighting of some fifteen or so running engagements to come. Now the awkward tripartite nature of Sherman's command, the dense vegetation and landscape, and Confederate skill combined to allow Johnston's forces to marshal successful defenses outside Resaca. There the main fighting raged between May 13 and 15. If the incautious Northerners had bumbled into the Confederate entrenchments when they assumed Johnston was still in headlong retreat, they next overreacted, and finally proved too timid in failing to pursue and cut off the retreating Confederates.

Apparently the normally aggressive Sherman was convinced that the two huge armies were still locked in a stalemate. In fact the Southerners were evacuating Resaca and vulnerable to encircling pursuit. Sherman's generals knew that a Confederate ambush and pitched battle were planned in the near future. Yet the where and when of the assault spooked them, and so they allowed Johnston to escape once again. In any case, Sherman uncharacteristically blamed General McPherson for a tardy pursuit: "Such an opportunity does not occur twice in a single life, but at the critical moment McPherson seems to have been a little cautious." Sherman would sometimes fault both McPherson and Thomas for not turning their flanking movements into encirclements and destroying rather than forcing back Johnston, and later Hood. He whined not so much out of self-aggrandizement, but rather from frustration that it was nearly impossible for his generals to realize his constant rapid-fire ideas in the short time he seemed to demand.[31]

By the evening of May 15, the outnumbered and entrenched Confederates had inflicted more losses than they had suffered (about four thousand Union casualties to roughly three thousand Confederate). Yet Johnston could afford them far less. While the ratios were favorable to the South, Sherman's casualties were easily made up by reinforcements that steadily poured into his army.

If Sherman missed opportunities to trap the exposed right flank of Johnston's army, he soon skillfully crossed the Oostanaula River, a strategic victory in itself. That gambit ensured that the Confederates had either to retreat even farther southward, or to risk having a Union army between them and their supplies. It mattered little that Johnston might claim he was preventing reinforcements being sent to Grant while drawing Sherman further from his Tennessee supplies, given that a huge—and growing—Union army was heading toward Atlanta while the Confederates either could not or would not stop it. The immediate danger to the South was now not the loss of Richmond, but of Atlanta.[32]

After Resaca, Johnston still neither counterattacked nor headed west into Alabama to get to the rear of Sherman's army. Both Sherman and Johnston believed that the slow Union descent into Georgia would soon validate their own respective strategies. Johnston took comfort that just as Grant neared but did not take Richmond, so, too, Sherman's approach to Atlanta would end in a costly stalemate outside the city. But by late May, events would confirm the wisdom of Sherman's strategy of advance and make Johnston's explanations for withdrawal seem like special pleading—especially his claims that by merely slowing Sherman, he would tip the balance of the November election in favor of the pliable McClellan. In fact, the more Sherman was faulted for missing opportunities to destroy Johnston's army, the more his own forces neared Atlanta with few losses—and the more his own troops rallied to their Uncle Billy as an iconic figure. There was simply not enough land between Sherman and Atlanta to ensure, at the present rate of advance, that he would not get there before the critical November election. In sum, Sherman was avoiding the decisive battle he could probably win, while Johnston was being pushed to force an engagement that he would surely lose. Johnston's tragedy was that he knew how to stall a general like Grant, but not one like Sherman.[33]

Johnston chose next to delay Sherman at Adairsville on May 17. At least three Union divisions formed up to meet him in a set battle. But Johnston soon discovered the terrain too expansive to allow his outnumbered troops an adequate defensive line. So once again, he withdrew. Where and when, those in a now worried Atlanta wondered, would it all stop?

Johnston choose to make his next stand at Cassville, a few miles to the south, purportedly for the long-hoped-for big battle that would trap Sherman deep in hostile territory. Even after two weeks of fighting, Johnston had access to more than seventy thousand troops in his general vicinity. On May 19, in the initial stages of fighting, Confederate troops inflicted heavy casualties on Sherman's forces. But in fear of being outflanked once again, the gun-shy Johnston broke off the battle, retreated across the Etowah River, and headed for the next line of defense at the Chattahoochee River.

Each time Johnston felt that he had drawn in and trapped one of Sherman's three armies, he soon began to fear that at least two others were at his flank or rear. While his forces neared Atlanta, Sherman's field of maneuver was widening around his encircled enemy. The tripartite nature of Sherman's army, especially its wide flanks and improving communication between the wings, made it almost impossible for a numerically inferior Johnston to achieve some Cannae-like encirclement.[34]

At first, the Southern government and public had forgiven Johnston for the withdrawals from Dalton and Resaca. Georgians assumed such withdrawals were needed preliminaries for the long-promised decisive battle and victory to come. The army itself was at first not at all demoralized by such tactical retreats. Sherman, after all, was still closer to Tennessee than to Atlanta. But after Johnston had promised to hold the line at Adairsville, and after achieving some initial success at Cassville, Johnston still had allowed Sherman in less than a month to halve the distance to Atlanta. Sherman was a mere fifty miles away from the city, and he still had more than five months of the campaigning season before the November election. When would he be trapped and destroyed deep in Southern territory?

For the next month, there ensued a predictable pattern of constant skirmishing in a huge theater without a single pitched battle of the sort that might decide the campaign. Sherman kept seeking to encircle Johnston and force his withdrawal, without in turn being pressured to storm fixed positions. Johnston wanted to keep contact with the invaders and wear them out as their supply lines lengthened and he pushed them into the wilderness of Georgia, shielding Atlanta. The closer Johnston was pushed back to Atlanta, and the more Sherman had to quit the rail lines and live off the land, in theory the better Johnston's chances became. Yet in a long series of battles in late May and June, the hoped-for decisive victory never quite came. Comparisons with Grant and Lee to the east no longer quite held. Grant was already outside Richmond and finding it nearly impossible to take the city; Sherman was still distant from Atlanta but making steady progress in a fashion that did not suggest he, too, would soon stall.[35]

The next of these bloody encounters came at New Hope Church on May 25, when Joseph Hooker's 20th Corps was ordered by Sherman to charge Johnston's lines, apparently on the mistaken assumption they were retreating rather than fixed and entrenched. Hooker, who was renowned for his audacious thrusts, was beaten back with severe losses. In two days, the Northerners atypically suffered ten times as many casualties as had Johnston's men. Yet it was Johnston, not Sherman, who retreated from New Hope Church.

On May 27 the two armies met at Pickett's Mill. Once again the Union army was defeated with severe losses. Johnston inflicted 1,600 casualties to his own losses of 500. Yet once more he, not Sherman, was forced to backpedal. On May 28, in yet another set battle at Dallas, Georgia, the overconfident Confederates under General Hardee foolishly emulated what the Federals had done at New Hope Church—and lost between 1,000 and 1,500 men in unnecessary charges against dug-in Union positions. Neither tactical retreat nor brief head-on assaults seemed to deter Sherman. The pressure on Johnston to find a magical remedy only increased, especially as Lee seemed to have figured out how to protect Richmond and bleed Grant white.

If neither side had been able to break the other's army in the first month of fighting, the landscape of battle nevertheless had still inched southward. Meanwhile, to the east, Grant had lost forty thousand soldiers, stalling in the Wilderness and again at Spotsylvania. Now Grant was to nearly ruin his army at Cold Harbor. News of the carnage perhaps emboldened Johnston to lure Sherman into Grant-like head-on charges.

As Sherman far away plodded southward, far closer to Washington the North once again failed in the Shenandoah Valley and at the James River in Virginia. The spreading gloom at the end of May inspired John C. Frémont to run on an independent Radical Democracy Party ticket. He had hopes of forcing the Republicans to dump Lincoln and run a stronger abolitionist. The only chance of good news was the slog in the Georgia woods.[36]

Fabian Tactics (*July 1864*)

After weeks of retreats, finally the natural advantages of interior lines of supply, along with friendly populations and the traditional desperation of the invaded, began to help Johnston. As Grant stymied at Cold Harbor—sixty thousand casualties in the Army of the Potomac since Grant began on May 1—and Lincoln was renominated at the Republican convention, both armies in Georgia maneuvered for position during the first part of June. They met again on July 9, launching a near-monthlong series of running battles around Marietta. Sherman initially failed again to outflank Johnston's entrenched lines. The Confederates were bolstered by the good highland ground of Kennesaw Mountain that gave them ideal defensive terrain, perhaps enough at last to stop Sherman altogether. Although Sherman was unable to get around Johnston and cut him off from the railroad, on June 22, John Bell Hood made an attack on entrenched federal lines at Kolb's Farm. Hood's corps was stopped cold, suffering fifteen hundred casualties and forcing Johnston once again to readjust his lines southward.[37]

Now, in an unexpected development—for the first and only time of the war—Sherman deviated from his long-accustomed strategy of flanking movements and unwisely chose to attack the dug-in Confederate lines on Kennesaw Mountain. Sherman found himself in the sort of bloodletting that he had not seen since Shiloh. Later he would lamely claim that the charge was necessary to establish the fighting credentials of his mobile armies. But in fact Sherman's defeat cost the Union three thousand casualties and was as ill-conceived as it was unsuccessful. The battle was over in a mere four or five hours as the Union brigades were "mowed down like grass."

Johnston was elated after Kennesaw Mountain. This was just the sort of one-sided battle that he had hoped all along to lure the impetuous invaders into. But Johnston still faced a disturbing reality. Despite near-incessant rain, swollen rivers, impassable muddy roads, and growing sickness among his ranks, Sherman's army remained far larger than Johnston's and kept in higher spirits. A chastened Sherman himself, for the duration of the war, would never order such a frontal assault again. Kennesaw became his first and last mistake in Georgia. Understandably, Sherman was all the more ready to return to his successful encirclement tactics that heretofore had gotten him more than halfway to Atlanta without such major losses. Unlike a Grant or a Hood, Sherman would not boast that he would keep to his head-on tactics, as if repeating a futile maneuver might somehow yield a different outcome.[38]

The result was that by July 5—despite the bad weather and the loss at Kennesaw Mountain—Sherman was at the banks of the Chattahoochee River. He was only nine miles from Atlanta and was preparing to cross the Chattahoochee and resupply his army by rail. His plans were to encircle Atlanta first from both east and west, cut off its rail lines, and then force the city to surrender or face starvation. The problem, however, was that there were still at least sixty thousand Confederates between Sherman's armies and the city—and no Union general quite knew what to do with Atlanta when it was captured.

Nonetheless, up north the public was keen to hear of success from Georgia as the proper antidote for the bad news from Virginia. As the strategist Liddell Hart put it, "Johnston was being steadily forced back, with a depressing effect to the morale of the Southern people and a most valuable tonic effect on the Northern public—in view of the impending elections. Wars can be won and lost in the hustings as well as on the battlefield. And all the time, too, Sherman was drawing nearer to Atlanta, more than ever the predominant goal in his mind."[39]

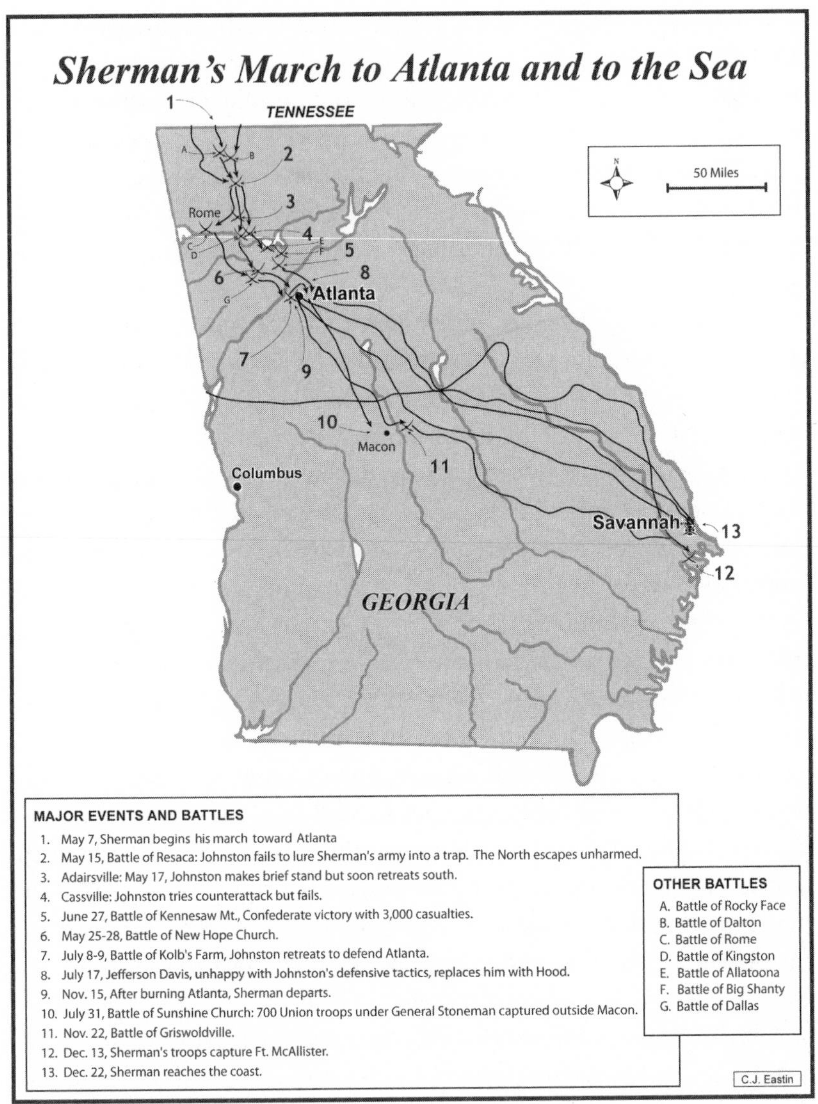

The Promotion of Hood (*July–August 1864*)

On July 17, 1864, in a move that would help to decide the Atlanta campaign, Confederate President Jefferson Davis finally had enough of retreating. He removed General Joe Johnston as commander of the Army of Tennessee, replacing him with fiery John Bell Hood. Davis rightly alleged that the tactics of Johnston had not stopped Sherman's advance to Atlanta, and both time and space were nearly exhausted.

Whatever one might think of his tactical sense, the Confederate John Bell Hood was a remarkable figure. Only thirty-three years old by spring 1864, Hood had already developed a prior formidable reputation for leading shock charges in the Peninsula campaign of 1862. Later, as a division commander, he lost the use of his left arm at Gettysburg. By September 1863, he was helping to break the Union line at Chickamauga, where he lost his right leg. In the aftermath, Hood was promoted to lieutenant general.[40]

Less than a year later, as one of Johnston's corps commanders and a favorite of Confederate president Jefferson Davis, Hood was once more clamoring for the elusive decisive winner-take-all battle against Sherman. Rumors circulated that Johnston had become gun-shy and hesitant, in part because of his slow recuperation during two years in Virginia from his own severe wounds. In contrast, Hood seemed all the more impatient for having lost a leg and the use of an arm. Age no doubt explained more: Hood was thirty-three, Johnston a tired but sober fifty-seven.

Even with Sherman less than ten miles from the city, Hood was still the wrong replacement for Johnston and exactly the wrong sort of Confederate army commander to stop Sherman's slow strangulation of Atlanta. For all his tenacity—at least three men were needed to strap the general to his horse—Hood had destroyed many of the divisions of which he had been given command. A third to a half of the men under his direct command were lost at each of the battles of Second Manassas, Antietam, Gettysburg, and Chickamauga. Sherman's subordinate commanders, especially those who knew Hood's character ("bold even to rashness") as fellow cadets at West Point, were eager to see Hood take over.[41]

Johnston let it be known that he surely had done better than Lee had against Grant. His relative numerical disadvantages were far worse than those of Lee, and yet he had lost proportionally far fewer troops. In his further defense, he had also forced Sherman to advance far more slowly to Atlanta than Grant had to the outskirts of Richmond in roughly the same time. Just as Lee had stiffened outside Richmond, so, too, would Johnston in front of Atlanta, where the advantages would increasingly accrue to the defense. Johnston's point was that, until his relief, he had been readying his army for a long war of attrition and fortified defense outside Atlanta that would stall and then wreck Sherman's army as Lee had nearly done to Grant. Why relieve him before his strategy had fully a chance to come to fruition?[42]

Hood later remarked of his appointment, "Was it General Johnston's policy to retreat till he had demoralized the army?" But Hood's immediate problem—other than the fact that the troops resented Johnston's abrupt removal—was not boosting morale, but finding a better strategy. Sherman was at the height of his powers, masterfully organizing and directing an enormous and constantly resupplied military machine of some hundred thousand veterans, who had grown in confidence with each mile they had advanced southward. Indeed, as Sherman neared Atlanta, he wrote as if he were a divine Nemesis, as if he were a tool to remind an entire people of the wages of their folly: "They dared us to war, and you remember how tauntingly they defied us to the contest. We have accepted the issue and it must be fought out. You might as well reason with a thunder-storm. War is the remedy our enemies have chosen." For the new commander Hood, it quickly became apparent that he was dealing not just with a good tactician and master strategist, but with a missionary as well, bent on teaching the entire South his version of a moral lesson. More mundanely, Hood would soon learn that the Confederate army outside Atlanta had only poor choices: either be outflanked and bypassed by Sherman, or be forced to fight head-on in unfavorable circumstances. Sherman's genius was that he usually controlled the conditions of battle, and somehow he had managed to supply his invading army far better than the defenders were provisioned on their home soil.[43]

Nonetheless, Hood was promoted to fight, and fight he would. He began the final round of the campaign in a series of three engagements within just ten days: at Peachtree Creek (July 20, nearly 5,000 Confederate casualties), Decatur/Atlanta (July 22, 8,500 casualties), and Ezra Church (July 28, 3,000 casualties). The battles were memorable—aside from the fact that Sherman's favorite army commander, General James McPherson, fell outside Atlanta—in that Sherman left the tactical details to his subordinates. Both sides suffered heavy casualties. But by the end of July, Sherman was ready to turn his full attention to the siege of Atlanta.

Most important, about eleven days after assuming supreme command, John Bell Hood's forces had suffered twice the casualties of Sherman's larger army, squandering sixteen thousand combatants without materially deterring the enemy. Now morale among the Confederates truly plummeted—with most soldiers nostalgic for the Fabian tactics of Johnston that were increasingly seen as about the only way to wear out the Sherman juggernaut. By the end of the battle of Ezra Church, decimated Southern troops—some three thousand were lost—sometimes would not follow the raised swords of their regimental officers into battle.[44]

Nor did Sherman rashly charge into Atlanta. Instead, in the final month, he systematically began cutting Atlanta off from all rail and wagon traffic, while bombarding the city. In theory, the Confederates at last were in the position that Johnston had once envisioned might turn the tide: a nucleus of thousands of troops, entrenched behind stout fortifications, housed among civilians in Atlanta, and guarded only by miles of thinning Union troops at the end of tenuous supply lines. Confederate mobile columns could leave the city and nearby camps to hit Sherman from the rear should he engage in a lengthy siege. Given that there was really no more army to outflank, Sherman finally had to choose between besieging and starving out the surrounded Hood in Atlanta or assaulting the city directly.

For most of August, Sherman sought pitched battle with Hood by daily shelling and sending cavalry out to cut the last rail link to Atlanta from Macon to the south. When his horsemen under Generals Stoneman and Kilpatrick proved unable to tear up the last rail line to Atlanta, Sherman sent his infantry out to destroy the tracks. As Sherman's troops seemed to leave his entrenchments around Atlanta, Hood and others in the city dreamed the Yankees were retreating back to Tennessee. Indeed, the Confederates and thousands in Atlanta began celebrating the defeat of Sherman's army on the assumption that the Yankees were dumbfounded as to how to stop the city's lifeline, out of supplies, and more worried about a counterattack from Hood.[45]

That fantasy dissipated almost immediately. Following the battle of Jonesboro on August 31, Sherman's forces finally severed the remaining rail artery from Macon. General Hardee's mounted forces were forced back into Atlanta, which lacked any source of fresh supplies. To prevent his troops from being trapped altogether, Hood pulled out the entire Confederate army on September 1, blowing up the city's munitions in a terrible conflagration even as Sherman's forces began entering the city the next day.

In less than fifteen weeks since leaving Tennessee, Sherman with relatively light casualties had taken the second most important city of the Confederacy. His army remained over eighty thousand soldiers strong—not that much smaller than when he had begun the Atlanta

In this colored lithograph by the Swedish-born illustrator Thure de Thulstrup, a mounted Sherman (on the right) gazes out from behind the breastworks at the Union shelling of a soon-to-be-captured Atlanta. Photo courtesy of the Library of Congress.

campaign. Of course, Sherman was not done; he was in position to cause far more havoc inside the heartland of the South. Indeed, Hood scattered from Atlanta with fewer than forty thousand troops—the Southerners in defense losing in the Atlanta campaign some thirty-four thousand casualties to the attacking Sherman's thirty-one thousand.

At the beginning of the struggle in spring 1864, Joe Johnston had originally been charged with ensuring that Sherman could not come east to aid Grant. But a somewhat different threat confronted the Confederates. There were very few forces between Sherman and the Atlantic coast—and so nothing to stop the victors from marching to the rear of Lee's army. As for Sherman, again historians would fault him for letting Hood escape Atlanta with the remnants of his army, when Union troops had virtually surrounded the city. But if he failed in one objective of destroying outright the Army of Tennessee, he succeeded in many others.

First, by taking Atlanta, Sherman provided an enormous emotional lift to a shaken Union as the November elections neared. In twenty-four hours, Sherman had essentially destroyed the candidacy of Democratic nominee George McClellan. Second, Sherman fought in a way that ensured his losses would be light at a time when Union casualties were unsustainable elsewhere. Third, Sherman had worn Hood's army down to less than half its original size. Fourth, he had prevented Hood from reinforcing Lee. Fifth, Sherman had positioned a large Northern army inside the South, where it could continue to raid and pillage the heartland as it headed eastward. And sixth, Sherman had saved Grant's sinking reputation. By taking Atlanta and giving deference to Grant, Sherman had enlightened the public about the Union's dual strategies of tying down one army in the east while encircling others in the west: Suddenly the bloodbath in Virginia could be reinterpreted as complementary to Sherman's quite different mobile warfare rather than antithetical and misguided.

In any case, after Kennesaw Mountain, Sherman was not about to risk another set battle against a desperate Confederate army. He would leave behind General George Thomas to deal with Hood if the latter went northward into Tennessee. Rather than being trapped in a destroyed city, Sherman was liberated—free to cut his supply lines, leave an Atlanta a wreck, ravage where he pleased, and live off the post-harvest Georgia landscape.[46]

"So Atlanta Is Ours and Fairly Won" (*September 1864*)

For a public sickened by the Richmond campaign, anything Sherman did that did not result in comparable carnage was welcome. But once Atlanta fell, everything changed. The reaction up north was electrifying. Sherman had taken a symbolic Southern city. His army was still intact. He was preparing even more campaigns. Who knew what the wily wild Sherman would do to the rebels next?

The once venomous press that had damned Lincoln, Grant, and at times Sherman was calling Sherman a national savior and a brilliant strategist who could not be stopped. All worries about the escape of Hood's army or uncertainties over Sherman's next move were drowned out by the public exultation. President Lincoln wrote Sherman the next day, "The marches, battles, sieges, and other military operations, that have signalized the campaign, must render it famous in the annals of war, and have entitled those who have participated therein to the applause and thanks of the nation."[47]

The papers, both pro- and anti-Lincoln, went wild. The pro-Lincoln *New York Times* blared, "The political skies begin to brighten." The *Chicago Tribune* boasted, "The dark days are over." The erstwhile Lincoln antagonist Horace Greeley in his *New York Tribune* announced, "Henceforth we fly the banner of Abraham Lincoln for our next president." A reporter for the *Cincinnati Commercial* wrote of the capture and destruction of Atlanta, "Grant walked *into* Vicksburg, McClellan walked *around* Richmond, but Sherman is walking *upon* Atlanta." In turn, the once cocky South that had been assured that Grant's terrible losses would usher in a Northern peace party was stunned. Most Confederates wailed that Lincoln would be reelected. The loss of Atlanta proved even more disheartening than that of Vicksburg or Gettysburg. The issue was not just the loss of Atlanta, but how and where Sherman could be stopped.[48]

The electoral effects were immediate. In an eerie happenstance, the antiwar Democrats had just met in Chicago on August 31 to nominate George McClellan. Abruptly "Little Mac" was put in the impossible position of either seeming churlish by downplaying Sherman's magnificent achievement, or praising it and thereby diminishing the reason for his own anti-Lincoln peace candidacy. The growing jubilation among the ranks of voting soldiers ensured that most would favor Lincoln—not an apparently has-been general, tainted by a Copperhead platform, who would throw away all the past sacrifice to make an unconditional peace with a spent South reeling and on the verge of collapse. The Union heretofore may have been sick of a losing war, but it was not sick enough to give up on what at last appeared to be a winning cause.[49]

Sherman himself was always acutely aware that the capture of Atlanta would be critical to Lincoln's success in defusing the recently nominated McClellan. In his memoirs, he recalled a conversation with Lincoln in which the president gave credit to Sherman for his reelection:

> The victory was most opportune; Mr. Lincoln himself told me afterward that even he had previously felt in doubt, for the summer was fast passing away; that General Grant seemed to be checkmated about Richmond and Petersburg, and my army seemed to have run up against an impassable barrier, when suddenly and unexpectedly, came the news that "Atlanta was ours, and fairly won."

In critiquing the importance of the McClellan candidacy, Sherman himself concluded of his capture of Atlanta:

> Success to our arms at that instant was therefore a political necessity; and it was all important that something startling in our interest should occur before the election in November. The brilliant success at Atlanta filled that requirement, and made the election of Mr. Lincoln certain.[50]

In a September 15 letter to his foster father, Thomas Ewing Sr., right after the capture of Atlanta, Sherman also pointed out that all the grand Union schemes hatched in March 1864 had until then come to naught—except his own: "The Grand Outlines contemplated these Grand Armies moving on Richmond, Atlanta & Montgomery Alabama, & Mine alone has reached its goal." Sherman was not much of a Lincoln partisan ("I suppose Lincoln is the best choice, but I am not a voter"), but he knew well enough that without Lincoln's reelection—the choice was either an unstable Frémont on the left or an appeasing McClellan to the right—his own efforts might come to naught.[51]

In a belated letter, nearly a month after the fall of Atlanta, the new Democratic candidate, General George McClellan, sent Sherman a word of congratulations: "Your campaign will go down in history as one of the most memorable of the world." His apologies for the tardy thanks reflected the embarrassment of his own position, given the sudden radical improvement in Lincoln's reelection chances.[52]

The Reelection of Lincoln (*November 1864*)

Despite the contemporary consensus, controversy still persists over whether the fall of Atlanta—coming more than two months before the election on November 8—by itself saved Lincoln's presidency. Skeptics point out that the tide had already turned somewhat by late summer. Admiral David Farragut, for example, had taken Mobile Bay on August 5, 1864. By the end of September, General Philip Sheridan had cornered Jubal Early in the Shenandoah Valley, and so devastated the rich Virginia landscape that it would never again serve as a Confederate conduit into Maryland and Pennsylvania.

Moreover, Lincoln would win the November election by over 400,000 votes, 55 percent of the votes cast, with a huge Electoral College win of 212 to 21. McClellan carried only New Jersey, Kentucky, and Delaware. Surely not all of Lincoln's success was predicated on the news of Atlanta's fall. While Lincoln won overwhelmingly among on-duty Union troops (especially in Sherman's army, where he won an 80 percent majority), the soldiers' vote probably did not provide the margin of victory. And even had Lincoln lost to McClellan, Little Mac might not have been able to quit the war without splitting the Northern citizenry in two.[53]

All that said, a shift of a mere 80,000 votes in certain key states would have won McClellan the Electoral College vote in an election that did not seem to break until September and October—and only on good news from the west. Moreover, it was not just Sherman's capture of Atlanta that restored Northern confidence, but the manner in which he took, occupied, and was planning to leave the city. By late August, most in the North, depressed over the near-destruction of Grant's army in Virginia, had forgotten the capture of Mobile. In addition, Sheridan's success followed Sherman's. While it enhanced the sense of momentum, Sheridan's devastation did not in itself foster a newfound Union confidence. Liddell Hart called all of these political considerations, both in the east and west, "the dark background to the final phase of Sherman's Atlanta campaign," adding, "Grant could do nothing, and any serious repulse to Sherman might have a fatal effect on public opinion. Caution was essential, yet success was equally so."[54]

As he occupied Atlanta, Sherman soon tired of being continually harassed by Southern cavalry and Hood's flying columns. He delegated the problem of Hood to the reliable George Thomas. Sherman was happy to see Hood go northward to meet the numerically superior and utterly reliable Army of the Cumberland under Thomas, thus enabling him to cut loose from Atlanta to head eastward. Yet he was wise enough to stay in Atlanta until after the election to avoid the implication to Northern voters that he had given up or been forced out of the key city—and to ensure that he did not begin a risky new campaign before the ballots were cast. After examining a number of possible marches to Southern ports, Sherman set out across Georgia soon after the election, on November 17, by cutting loose and living off the country. That gambit ("Let Hood go north, and I'll go south") made Hood's efforts at cutting Northern supply lines superfluous. Sherman believed that he could reach Savannah, after making Georgia "howl"; but he doubted that Hood could do the same in his northward march to Nashville.[55]

Sherman's Atlanta campaign and subsequent plans for further great marches helped to restore Grant's reputation among the Northern public. Whereas in spring 1864 the North expected that the hero of Vicksburg would shortly come east, take command of the Army of the Potomac, capture Richmond, defeat Lee, and end the war—perhaps within a hundred days—now, by the end of August, they had no such illusions. After the Wilderness, Spotsylvania, Cold Harbor, and Petersburg, Grant transmogrified into "the butcher" and lost the goodwill of the public.

But after Sherman took Atlanta and rumors spread that the city's capture was the beginning, not the end, of his extensive marching, Northerners gradually began to see Grant in a different, much more favorable light. As Sheridan, Sherman, and Thomas operated more freely and deeply in Southern territory (and without incurring great losses), Grant's campaign began to be seen as a necessary holding action—a gritty effort to tie Lee down, isolate the Confederate capital, and wear down the Army of Northern Virginia while other Confederate armies were routed and Southern soil violated by more mobile Northern forces.

The North would reelect Lincoln despite Grant's terrible losses—but only if the Union public could be convinced that such sacrifice would be capitalized on by generals like Sherman. As Sherman best put it to Grant in magnanimous fashion after taking Atlanta, "In the mean time, know that I admire your dogged perseverance and pluck more than ever. If you can whip Lee and I can march to the Atlantic, I think Uncle Abe will give us twenty days' leave of absence to see the young folks."[56]

Atlanta and Beyond (*November 1864–April 1865*)

History is replete with successful invaders—Xerxes at Athens, Napoleon in Moscow, the Germans inside the rubble of Stalingrad, the Chinese Communists at Seoul in 1951—who found their occupation of an enemy's defeated capital or key city of either little value or real peril, given that a large undefeated enemy force was still nearby and most of the occupied city lay in ruins or was without supply. In contrast, Sherman saw Atlanta as the beginning, not the end, of his Georgia campaign. Sherman was sometimes unsteady—especially between Bull Run and Shiloh, when he suffered severe depression. He often overstated his own case in his memoirs and unfairly deprecated the efforts of others. There were plenty of better battlefield tacticians on both sides of the Civil War—Lee, Longstreet, or Jackson, and Grant, Thomas, or Sheridan. He seemed surprised at Kennesaw Mountain—and both earlier at Shiloh and later at Bentonville. That said, no Civil War commander possessed a more astute appraisal of the nature of contemporary warfare, how to form and pursue grand strategy, and the critical nexus between war, civil society, popular support, and electoral politics. And few American generals have since.

After the capture of Atlanta, to the shock of its remaining residents and to the outrage of John Bell Hood, Sherman forced most to flee the city and set about garrisoning it as a depot for further operations. He neither apologized nor expressed one iota of regret for shelling the city on his approach. As he put it to John Bell Hood, in an exchange of letters after taking the city, "I was not bound by the laws of war to give notice of the shelling of Atlanta, a 'fortified town, with magazines, arsenals, foundries, and public stores'; you were bound to take notice. See the books. This is the conclusion of our correspondence, which I did not begin, and terminate with satisfaction."[57]

Sherman set out on November 17 from Atlanta on his famous five-week March to the Sea, reaching and capturing Savannah on December 21. From there, he undertook an even more arduous march through the Carolinas in an effort to enter Virginia at the rear of Robert E. Lee's Army of Northern Virginia. When the war ended in April 1865, Sherman had torn apart the South, humiliated the enemy, and caused massive defections from Lee's army as Confederate soldiers in Virginia heard constant bad news of a huge Union force running amok among their friends and family to the rear.[58]

Sherman, as an Ohioan with long residence in California, was at heart a westerner, familiar with navigation and supply over the new nation's great distances by wagon, train, and ship. He felt comfortable with like kind, especially marching, camping out, and meeting the challenges of wide-open spaces and rough terrain. After Bull Run, the first great battle of the war, Sherman never again fought in Virginia or Maryland—the meat grinders that would devour the Army of the Potomac.

Indeed, he would not return to the east until his final great march through the Carolinas. Pitched battles in the Richmond and Washington corridors were of an entirely different sort from the long marches through Georgia and the Carolinas, for which Sherman was far better suited. We do not know what Sherman might have done in Grant's place during the awful spring and summer of 1864, but he might well not have had the same avenues to enact his evolving ideas about modern total war as he did out west.

Misunderstanding Sherman

Sherman is often characterized as a heartless prophet of modern, total, and merciless war, with the burning of Atlanta or Columbia serving as a sort of precursor to Dresden or Hamburg. That characterization—fanned by Sherman's own vivid and occasionally hyperbolic use of nouns and verbs such as "cruelty," "hell," "ruin," "howl," "smashing," and "breaking"—is not accurate, if such a charge refers to the level of damage he inflicted on either the Confederate army or its population. In comparison to horrific battles elsewhere, few of the enemy—soldiers or civilians—died, either inside Atlanta or on his subsequent marches through Georgia and the Carolinas. Where Sherman, in the moral sense, proved a revolutionary figure was not in the killing of civilians or waging "total war," but through his radical notions of proper culpability in war.

It made no sense to him that the slave-owning plantation class of the Old South, which had plunged the nation into war, should be relatively free from the costs of combat while mostly non-slave-owning and poorer Southerners were dying in droves in northern Virginia. Sherman saw that the destruction of the Southern mystique of superior gallantry was essential to Lincoln's victory. Often in obnoxious fashion, he would instruct the South about the various dichotomies of the war. Industry and material advantage would nullify martial gallantry. The South's pride in Southern civic superiority would, so Sherman further assumed, be questioned by the fact of a hundred thousand Union soldiers tramping wherever they pleased.[59]

Sherman often tried to explain his evolving views in the context of the morality of the new age of warfare. In an August 14, 1864, letter to James Guthrie, a politician, railroad executive, and political ally, Sherman remarked as he neared Atlanta,

> We must, to live and prosper, be governed by law, and as near that which we inherited as possible. Our hitherto political and private differences were settled by debate, or vote, or decree of a court. We are still willing to return to that system, but our adversaries say no, and appeal to war . . . Other simple remedies were within their choice. You know it and they know it, but they

> wanted war, and I say let us give them all they want; not a word of argument, not a sign of let up, no cave in till we are whipped or they are . . . The only principle in this war is, which party can whip.[60]

More important still, for all the invective against Sherman, who was reviled as a terrorist in Southern papers, his ravaging was largely aimed at Confederate buildings, rails, telegraph systems, and the property of the slave-owning elite. For that he has never been forgiven, reminding us that Machiavelli warned in *The Prince* of the political repercussions of damaging property: "Men will sooner forget the death of their father than the loss of their patrimony." Yet Sherman's ultimate aims were to shorten the war and thereby save lives by marches that humiliated and demoralized the enemy population rather than butchering soldiers in head-to-head combat. He would be all the more hated the more he focused on property and the less he targeted Confederate soldiers. Or, as Noah Trudeau concluded:

> "Total war" implies a military operation meant to obliterate civilian infrastructure preparatory to imposing a new order on that society. Sherman had no such desires. His more limited goal was to make any continuance of rebellion so unpalatable to southern civilians that they would view a return to the Union as the lesser of two evils. The overwhelming force he applied made it clear to all that the so-called Confederacy lacked the wherewithal to guarantee personal security. Sherman's decision to add civilian property to the mix stemmed from his belief in collective responsibility and his determination to punish the Southern leaders who should have been looking out for the welfare of their people by finding an accommodation with him.[61]

For Sherman, like Clausewitz earlier, armies were political tools. He reminded the nation that an army and its civilian supporters were inseparable from each other. Yet unlike Clausewitz, Sherman did not see the need to find the enemy's main army and destroy it on the field of battle. The key was submission—whether materially or psychologically—of the entire civilian infrastructure that produced armies, a strategy not always predicated on set battle. Attack that civilian root, and its military fruit would die on the vine.

For Sherman, inconclusive wars often resulted even when armies simply gave up or in isolation were defeated—as if decisive battle was rarely decisive. In contrast, lasting peace was built through convincing an entire population that it had been both collectively defeated and humiliated, and that it bore the wages of its initial unwise aggression, and therefore that it should cease the production of war material and the contribution of men to the cause. Or, as Sherman put it once to General George Thomas, "I propose to demonstrate the vulnerability of the South, and make its inhabitants feel that war and individual ruin are synonymous terms." Much of later subsequent military history may well confirm Sherman's thinking that "hostile armies" were inseparable from "hostile people," especially when we reflect upon the ephemeral peace that followed the First World War, in comparison with the lasting peace after the Second.

Sherman was far more adept at ruining Southern morale without killing thousands of civilians than were his twentieth-century disciples. When Confederate armies did not meet him in huge pitched battles during the Atlanta campaign and the later March to the Sea, Sherman grasped how he had struck at the very nerve of the supposed military gallantry and dash of Confederate cavaliers. Or, as he once put it to a Southern acquaintance, "Your biggest armies in Virginia and Georgia lie behind forts, and dare not come out and fight us cowards of the North, who have come five hundred miles into their country to accept the challenge."[62]

Sherman is also known as a revolutionary in his uncanny appreciation of the material resources of the new industrial age. Even before the war began, Sherman saw that industrial production and material resources would be more a determinant than claims of superior bravery. In a prescient antebellum conversation with his friend and colleague David F. Boyd at the Louisiana Seminary of Learning and Military Academy (the precursor to Louisiana State University), Sherman—still residing in the South—let loose with a screed about the nature of war on the horizon:

> The North can make a steam-engine, locomotive or railway car; hardly a yard of cloth or shoes can you make. You are rushing into war with one of the most powerful, ingeniously mechanical and determined people on earth—right at your doors. You are bound to fail. Only in your spirit and determination are you

> prepared for war. In all else you are totally unprepared, with a bad cause to start with . . . If your people would but stop and think, they must see that in the end you will surely fail.[63]

Grant may have believed, though he never explicitly wrote, that the North's far greater population (22 million versus the South's 9 million, including slaves) meant that he could defeat the South even while losing three soldiers to Lee's two. But such arithmetic assumed that a more affluent Northern public would accept such losses until Lee quit. In contrast, Sherman looked to different statistics: the North possessed a 23–1 edge in manufacturing, a 10–1 superiority in arms production, well over twice the rail and telegraph infrastructure of the South—and a better informed and more fickle public. That meant that Sherman would have the resources to equip large armies to go into the South and waste the far more limited material resources of the Confederacy, while losing fewer soldiers in battle and thus maintaining public support.[64]

Grant, Hood, and Lee, like Sherman, finally grasped that rifled musketry, and soon the repeating cartridge rifle, along with far more lethal artillery, could destroy hundreds, even thousands of men in a few hours. But unlike Sherman, they were still not ready to abandon noble charges, head-on assaults—all the stuff of a once glorious Western way of war—that could prove suicidal. Since his horrific first day at Shiloh (April 6, 1862), Sherman had begun to craft a new manner of mobile warfare that could both bring victory and save his army from the oblivion of industrial warfare that would destroy tens of thousands of Americans at Antietam, Gettysburg, and Cold Harbor.

Later, in his formal analysis of the lessons of the Civil War, Sherman repeatedly stressed both the physical and psychological benefits of keeping soldiers moving. A sense of linear progress was critical, freed from the stifling strictures of a bureaucratic and noncombatant military to the rear. In other words, once in the field, "overwhelming necessity overrides all law." The more he could ensure that his men would have a good chance of surviving their victory, the more he could demand rigorous labor and physical sacrifice from them during his incessant marching. Only on the road, Sherman was the law, not his superiors Grant, Gen. Henry Halleck, or Lincoln.[65]

Sherman also appreciated the importance of new electronic communications. When the telegraph and mass-produced and circulated newspapers were wedded to a free society, suddenly news from the front could reach the public within days, if not hours—often raw and hysterically editorialized. That meant, in a consensual society, that casualties suffered at Shiloh, Antietam, or Gettysburg could incite panic and hysteria and overshadow the eventual story of tactical victory itself. A general in the new age of warfare could win a battle, but lose the public will to continue. All hard-won victories in their immediate aftermath could be seen as Pyrrhic. Sherman accepted that new fact of media influence—even as he railed against reporters as purveyors of doom who could destroy public support for any army by inexact and incomplete reporting.[66]

Lee and Grant may well have been better generals than Sherman, in the sense of deploying forces on the battlefield and keeping an iron nerve amid the bloodletting. But both nearly wrecked public support for their causes. It was Lee's misfortune that he had a disciple like the heedless John Bell Hood rather than like William Tecumseh Sherman, who might have caused havoc by slashing his way to the North, destroying the Union economy and morale—as Lee held down Grant and the Army of the Potomac in the east. Grant had a distant subordinate who made him look good; in contrast, Lee had one who made him look quite bad.

Yet in the end, as with most savior generals, the brilliance of Sherman's revolutionary strategic vision was overshadowed by the controversies over his supposed embrace of "total war." Military historians came to appreciate that Sherman had saved lives by bringing the war to a close; yet millions in the South, and nearly as many in the North, would forever deem him uncouth and barbarous. Sherman not only accepted that charge, but the additional one that his outspokenness had in some sense needlessly incurred it. In a letter to his wife, Ellen, he best summed up the paradox of wanting to explain to a nation what war was about while conceding the result would be unpalatable: "I know what I said will be gall and wormwood to some, but it will make others think." But then again, Sherman seemed almost to wish to shock the public, or at least be disliked by it; as he wrote his brother in the midst of the Atlanta campaign, "I was in hopes I could remain unpopular."[67]

The Sherman Way

What was the Sherman way? To lead troops from the front as unkempt-looking "Uncle Billy" or weather-beaten "Old Sherman," but only after the most careful planning and organization had ensured that the Army of the West would be both more numerous and better supplied than its enemy—and would suffer fewer losses. In the Atlanta campaign, Sherman was almost killed twice, at Adairsville and Cassville, where artillery and small arms fire shredded trees around his staff. Earlier at Shiloh, he was wounded in the hand and lost three of his mounts. In general, Sherman was impatient with stasis and understood that armies that do not move, erode. Those that do, gain confidence and are more likely to fight well and endure hardship.[68]

How did Sherman take Atlanta by September 2, without suffering costly casualties, and then prepare to march to Savannah—all deep in enemy territory with a variety of Confederate armies at his flanks and rear? Down to the mechanical level, Sherman was a master of practical details. Before Sherman set out, he calculated that 130 railcars were needed to travel southward from Tennessee each day he marched. To meet that need, Sherman commandeered railcars wherever he could find them, and finally shut down all civilian rail traffic. If his troops were well supplied with food and ammunition—and knew their general would ensure such supplies without interruption—they would march and fight well. More important still, Sherman could calculate how many railcars of stored matériel he might need when he left the logistical security of the tracks, and roughly how many supplies the local landscape might provide.

Soldiers fired rifles, but that was impossible without food, ammunition, and proper care. The historian John Marszalek best summed up Sherman's genius in planning the Atlanta campaign:

> He had come to see every Southerner, civilian and soldier, as the enemy; so too he considered every Unionist and every material good to be part of the war effort against the enemy. This ability to see war as total and to organize the vast resources to conduct that war made him the great military commander he showed himself to be that summer. Even before he began maneuvering his huge forces in battle, he had demonstrated military greatness.[69]

Unlike Johnston and Hood, who were not exactly clear about their ultimate aims other than stopping the enemy, Sherman not only planned to take Atlanta, but was already envisioning where and how his larger strategic ideas about industrial warfare would play out on marches to the sea and northward through the Carolinas. Sherman's famous exchanges with John Bell Hood right after taking Atlanta were soon quoted in newspapers and books as larger lessons about the nature of modern war itself. To Hood's objection that Sherman had first fired on Atlanta, where civilians were intermingled among his batteries, and then, upon its capture, ordered its population to be evacuated, Sherman in his reply described in brilliant fashion the new, expanded parameters of modern war and its rationale:

> In the name of common-sense, I ask you not to appeal to a just God in such a sacrilegious manner. You who, in the midst of peace and prosperity, have plunged a nation into war—dark and cruel war—who dared and badgered us to battle, insulted our flag, seized our arsenals and forts that were left in the honorable custody of peaceful ordnance-sergeants, seized and made "prisoners of war" the very garrisons sent to protect your people against negroes and Indians, long before any overt act was committed by the (to you) hated Lincoln government, tried to force Kentucky and Missouri into rebellion, spite of themselves; falsified the vote of Louisiana, turned loose your privateers to plunder unarmed ships; expelled Union families by the thousands, burned their houses, and declared, by an act of your Congress, the confiscation of all debts due Northern men for goods had and received? . . . If we must be enemies let us be men, and fight it out as we propose to do, and not deal in such hypocritical appeals to God and humanity.[70]

The stolid and straightforward George Thomas might have endlessly chased the retreating Johnston and Hood. Grant might have plowed straight for Atlanta, almost taken the city, and yet lost eighty thousand soldiers in the attempt. Each time a Southern general tried to go northward to threaten Union territory—Albert Sidney Johnston at Shiloh, Robert E. Lee at Gettysburg, John Bell Hood outside Nashville—he wrecked his army and ended up dead or retreating southward. Sherman knew how to keep his soldiers mobile, minimize losses, and take an all-important city like Atlanta, using it as a stepping-stone for greater things yet to come—and thereby winning Lincoln the election. More important, at his best he was able to translate his new philosophy of war into rhetoric that would soon galvanize the nation. Atlanta was not merely captured, but "ours and fairly won." Savannah did not merely fall, but was presented "to the country as a Christmas present." Georgia would not be dissected but made to "howl," in a "war so terrible" of "synonymous ruin" for civilians. His famous postbellum pronouncement that "war is hell" was simply a variation on what he had told the nation throughout most of the Civil War. As in the case of Themistocles, individual battles were not, for Sherman, ends in themselves, nor even theater operations that served strategic purposes, but elements of far larger sociological war.[71]

With Sherman stymied—or defeated—in Georgia rather than triumphant in Atlanta, Lincoln would not have been reelected. With President McClellan in the White House, there would have been enormous pressure to settle differences by permanent separation between North and South, or a return to a slave-owning Southern United States.

Quite simply, without Uncle Billy's men in Atlanta on September 2, 1864, the United States as we know it today might very well not exist.

CHAPTER FOUR
One Hundred Days in Korea

Matthew Ridgway Takes Over—Winter 1950–51

The Nightmare (*December 1950*)

Would all of Korea now be lost?

America's first major military defeat seemed inevitable. As Christmas 1950 neared, the shell-shocked United States was reduced to collective despair. Once ascendant American armies in Korea were on the brink of collapse. Certain destruction loomed from hordes of invading Communist Chinese troops. The hysteria almost paralyzed Washington. Left and right blamed each other for losing Korea or even going there in the first place. Rumor had it that Secretary of State Dean Acheson might offer to quit Korea entirely if the Chinese would likewise just leave the peninsula. Harry Truman had intervened to save South Korea in July 1950 on grounds that there would be no more appeasement to aggression, as there had been with Hitler at Munich. Now that resolution was beginning to seem hollow, if not embarrassing.

The senior ground commander of American forces in Korea was dead. The forces of the United Nations, foremost among them well over a hundred thousand American marines and Army infantrymen, were close to being annihilated by tens of thousands of fresh Chinese Communist infantry. Now, amid ice and snow, Americans were fleeing southward from North Korea as fast as possible. Gloom and panic buried even occasional good news. Few seemed to care that the U.S. Marine Corps on the east coast of Korea was in fact conducting a successful fighting retreat. Fewer still knew that the marines had killed more than fifteen thousand Chinese troops, along with another ten thousand through targeted air strikes. The entire attacking Chinese Ninth Army was rendered combat ineffective.[1]

Instead, disturbing details filtered back that shaky American troops of the Eighth Army on the western side of Korea had thrown away their equipment. Chinese intelligence reports stereotyped American infantrymen as "weak, afraid to die, and [lacking] the courage to attack or defend . . . They cringe when, if on the advance, they hear firing." Since the nineteenth century, Americans had chided the technologically backward Chinese and tried to persuade them to adopt Western religion, politics, and culture in order to evolve from poverty. Now the world seemed turned upside down: Sophisticated Chinese invaders were butchering American defenders—and with better weapons, training, and morale. General Peng Dehuai's Communist Chinese Army was not intent on merely pushing the Americans back into South Korea. He wanted to unify the entire peninsula under Russian and Chinese patronage.[2]

Throughout this bleak December, calls for the use of atomic bombs came from almost every quarter—as if the Korean conflict could be ended in the manner that Hiroshima and Nagasaki five years earlier had forced Japan to surrender. Talk spread of nationwide military mobilization and, at times, of an inevitable global nuclear war against what President Truman called "the inheritors of Genghis Khan and Tamerlane, the greatest murderers in the history of the world." Emergency legislation quadrupled defense spending. General Douglas MacArthur was silent about his failure to anticipate a massive autumn Chinese invasion. But he became loud about the need to bomb Chinese supply bases in Manchuria—including the demand to have a theater stockpile of at least twenty-six atomic bombs. Truman told the press that he would not rule out use of a nuclear weapon.[3]

In these first six months of Korean "police action," 14,650 Americans perished, most of them during the long retreat southward from the Chinese border during November and December 1950. In a matter of weeks, well over three thousand Americans had been killed or wounded. On a single day, November 30, 799 marines and Army personnel were lost—more than all the American combat fatalities in the Afghanistan war between 2001 and 2008. In panic the Americans were fleeing Chinese "hordes." As Matthew Ridgway later put it, "the blows fell and fell with such devastating suddenness that many units were overrun before they could quite grasp what had happened."[4]

This collapse was certainly not what the American people had bargained for, given their nation's uninterrupted record of overseas victories and the fresh memory of overwhelming triumph just five years earlier over the Axis powers. Nor was it what the public had been told would follow from the revered General MacArthur's recent brilliant landing at Inchon just a few weeks earlier in mid-September. Yet more than half of those Americans questioned in a November 1950 Gallup poll suddenly wanted the United States to use atomic weapons on enemy military targets to save American lives. By January 1951, about half the country would also conclude that going to war was a terrible decision.[5]

Somewhere between 200,000 and 340,000 Communist Chinese troops had unexpectedly crossed into Korea from Manchuria between mid-October and December 1950—their initial invasion for days largely undetected or even ignored by United Nations forces. By the end of the year, General Peng Dehuai had almost half a million North Korean and Chinese Communist forces under his theater command. A civil war among Koreans threatened to be the first front of a new World War III that in theory could quickly escalate to intercontinental nuclear exchanges, given that the Soviets had exploded a nuclear device a little over a year earlier and were seen as the absolute leaders of a vast monolithic Communist bloc. General MacArthur's intelligence officers had little idea that the Communist Chinese, in preparation, had transferred hundreds of thousands of their infantry forces from the coast opposite Taiwan to the Yalu River at the border with North Korea. The autumn 1950 Chinese invasion was probably the greatest intelligence lapse in postwar American military history, with far more immediately lethal consequences than either the surprise at Pearl Harbor or the flawed estimation of Saddam Hussein's chemical and biological weapons program.

Following the Chinese crossing of the Yalu, much of Asia suddenly seemed to be vulnerable to a Communist takeover. The spread from Eastern to Western Europe of the armies of the Soviet Union, in tandem with the aggression of Mao's China, loomed inevitable. If Korea could not be saved, how could a Japan, Taiwan, or even the Philippines hold out? If America, the world wondered, had freed Asia from the Japanese a mere five years earlier, how could it be that once ragtag Communists were liberating its nations from the liberators? And why were former allies now formidable enemies while former friends were lackluster allies?

For most of December, American newspapers and radio were aghast. Once nearly victorious armies in Korea were suddenly beginning to resemble the French disintegrating before the German blitzkrieg of May 1940. All the credibility and confidence gained from World War II dissipated. Fear and uncertainty replaced them.[6]

Amid this uproar back at home, Lieutenant General Matthew Ridgway, deputy chief of staff of the U.S. Army, got a late-night phone call on December 22, 1950, as he was enjoying a cocktail at the Washington home of a friend. Suddenly Ridgway was told that the ground commander of the Eighth Army, the distinguished World War II general Walton Walker, had hours earlier been crushed in a jeep accident. America's preeminent force in Korea suddenly had no commanding general on the ground. The theater commander and architect of the advance to the Yalu, the revered Douglas MacArthur, seemed stunned and unable to arrest the flight of American troops.

Hundreds of thousands of Chinese Communists had retaken the North Korean capital of Pyongyang on December 5—the allies had held it for only six weeks after taking the city on October 19, during the march to the Yalu. The Chinese had joined with re-formed and refitted units of North Koreans and together were nearing, or, for all Ridgway knew, perhaps already crossing, the 38th Parallel. That meant a threat to nearby Seoul, and indeed to all of South Korea. Ridgway was ordered to leave Washington immediately and to take command of what was left of collapsing American and United Nations forces as talk spread of another retreat to Pusan. Six years later, a reflective Ridgway recalled his apprehensions as he began a long multistop flight toward the battlefield: "The Army Commander was dead. The tactical situation was bad. I was in command, and on my answer to the question, 'What do you do?' depended something far more important than a grade in an instructor's book. On it hinged victory or defeat."[7]

Although he was a three-star general, and apparently near the pinnacle of the Army's Pentagon bureaucracy, Ridgway had received no official warning that he had been slated to be the next in line to assume command of the Eighth Army in Korea. His appointment was probably not initially supported by the then chief of staff of the Army, his boss, General J. Lawton (Joe) Collins. Ridgway certainly wanted out of the Washington bureaucracy. His loudly expressed views on the need to prepare for limited wars were antithetical to the cost-cutting Truman administration's naïve trust that America's new nuclear air power could deter all threats without the traditional expense of large conventional forces. Perhaps his appointment to save a limited war through conventional means was seen as a way of putting Ridgway's proverbial money where his mouth was.[8]

Ridgway was known as a strategic thinker, and as an experienced, if not a brilliant, World War II airborne corps commander in Europe. Few generals had seen as much combat. But Ridgway knew little about Asia in general or Korea in particular. And he had earned a growing reputation for being too outspoken for his own good. His immediate chief qualification, as deputy to General Collins, the Army chief of staff, was that from June to December 1950, Ridgway had tried, with some success, to restart the enormous Pentagon wartime machinery and get supplies and armament to a desperately outgunned and outmanned General MacArthur.

Ridgway was outranked and overshadowed at the highest levels by four-star heroes from the recent fighting in Europe such as Generals Omar Bradley, Mark Clark, Joe Collins, and Dwight Eisenhower. At his age, the odds were that Ridgway would not again obtain another senior command in the field. More likely, he assumed that he would end his career in a billet in Europe rather than stalking around in late middle age under bombardment on the front lines in wintry Korea. Nevertheless, Ridgway in a matter of hours was on his way to Tokyo.[9]

Anatomy of a Collapse (*September–December 1950*)

In autumn 1950, after six months of hard fighting, Americans had swept far north of the 38th Parallel in an all-out effort to rid Korea of Communists. They felt thereby that the West would send a message to both Soviet Russia and Red China not to subvert the postwar aspirations of emerging Asian states that were supposed to be free to determine their own futures through plebiscites. The unexpected turnabout at Inchon, where tens of thousands of North Korean troops were trapped and thousands destroyed, had restored the public's confidence in the previously unpopular and nearly disastrous "police action" of summer 1950. Americans had taken the wizard General MacArthur at his word that this new sort of limited war was both winnable and nearly over. Few remembered that the old general had long demonstrated a bad habit in the Pacific theater of prematurely declaring victory and scoffing at warnings of enemy offensives—often a prelude to disaster. They remembered only

MacArthur as a savior who had regained the Philippines and seemed to have done the same thing in Korea.

The Chinese People's Army all September and October had been brazenly ignoring the loud American triumphalism. Instead, Chinese generals had studied the always changing dynamics of the Korean battlefield that in just the latter six months of 1950 had seen the nearly seven-hundred-mile-long peninsula almost cleared of Americans—and in turn almost swept clean of their own allied Communist North Koreans and Chinese "advisers" and "volunteers." Yet the further northward United Nations forces had raced toward the Chinese border, the worse the weather and geography became. The north of Korea was more expansive, rugged, and mountainous than the south. Unfortunately, General MacArthur had not reconnoitered, and in fact knew far too little about, the environs of North Korea.

The nearer the Chinese forces waiting on the border found themselves to the encroaching front, the farther American-led infantry were from their own supply depots to the south. Like Xerxes on his way to his Salamis, the more exposed the advancing Americans became, the more overconfident they seemed—given the assurances of General MacArthur that many of his now victorious forces would be "home for Christmas." It was hard to know which was more ironic: MacArthur's uncanny ability to turn initial defeat into sure victory after the successful landing at Inchon, or to turn Inchon's subsequent victory into sure defeat at the Yalu. After the brilliant Inchon amphibious assault ("Operation Chromite") and simultaneous breakout from the endangered Pusan perimeter commencing on September 15, 1950, the American-led United Nations coalition had seemed certain to reunify Korea. On MacArthur's orders, the UN coalition crossed the 38th Parallel on October 7, eager to head northward to wipe out the fleeing North Korean aggressors. MacArthur felt that within another ninety days he could unite the entire Korean peninsula under a United Nations–sanctioned Syngman Rhee government in the south, allied closely to the United States.

Like General Custer at the Little Big Horn, the Americans after Inchon had eagerly sought to pursue the enemy. They had little clue that they were outnumbered and soon to be overrun and cut off by hundreds of thousands of skilled, fresh Chinese Communist troops, fighting near their own homeland and energized by revolutionary anti-Western zeal. Odder still, Americans should not have been surprised. "Red China," Matthew Ridgway later wrote, "had been threatening by radio almost daily—from the moment of the American surge after Inchon in September 1950—that it would come into the war if North Korea were invaded."[10]

If unification appeared a lunatic thought in late summer 1950, when American forces were a few miles from being pushed off the peninsula far to the south at Pusan, now, little more than four months after the start of the war, it seemed almost assured as they reached the Yalu River, well over six hundred miles to the north. General MacArthur had built up an army from a skeleton force of five hundred U.S. advisers and South Korean constabularies, had saved a beachhead at Pusan, and in a matter of weeks had gone on the offensive against veteran North Korean troops. There are few comparable turnabouts in modern military history in which a battered army in the space of weeks turns on, and then nearly ruins, its numerically superior aggressor.

Nevertheless, even with the Communists on the run in autumn 1950, reasons for disquiet were beginning to reach the White House and the Pentagon. If MacArthur persisted in his bellicose rhetoric and widely reported news conferences, the Chinese, if not the Russians as well, could intervene on news that Korea was to be united under an American-sponsored government right in their neighborhood, with American bombers based on their borders. The European allies—the British especially—feared that the humiliated Soviets might retaliate against an American crossing of the 38th Parallel by unleashing its divisions on a depleted Western Europe. Lord Salisbury in mid-November gave a sober speech warning that United Nations offensive forces so far north of the 38th Parallel violated a number of classical tactical and strategic principles, from insufficient manpower to tenuous supply lines.[11]

But MacArthur was still riding high both at home and abroad. Since the Communists had wished to destroy South Korea as an autonomous state, then why could not he in turn destroy the idea of an independent North Korea? What did weather, terrain, or empty Communist threats matter after Inchon? Indeed, once the Communists visibly got the war going, MacArthur may have welcomed the notion of sending Nationalist Chinese forces back into Communist China, or using atomic weapons to devastate Communist forces and industry in the region. Even a few civilians in the State Department, such as Dean Rusk and John Allison, had long called not just for "containment" but also for "rollback" and would support MacArthur as he headed northward as rapidly as possible.[12]

The Joint Chiefs of Staff were worried, but not enough to rein in

MacArthur's surge to the north. At the end of September, Defense Secretary George Marshall had cabled MacArthur that he had permission to go north as the situation dictated. "A more subtle result of the Inchon triumph," Ridgway later noted, "was the development of an almost superstitious regard for General MacArthur's infallibility. Even his superiors began to doubt if they should question *any* of MacArthur's decisions and as a result he was deprived of the advantage of forthright and informed criticism, such as every commander should have—particularly when he is trying to 'run a war' from 700 miles away."[13]

By mid-November, as the Chinese were crossing the Yalu in increasing force, MacArthur could still send out a communiqué boasting, "If successful, [the ongoing UN offensive] should for all practical purposes end the war, restore peace and unity to Korea, enable the prompt withdrawal of the United Nations military forces, and permit the complete assumption by the Korean people and nation of full sovereignty and international equality. It is that for which we fight." But even if MacArthur were right, it was hard to see how a poorly armed and trained South Korean military could defend the entire Korean peninsula against a million Communist troops on its borders without a near-permanent American presence in the tens of thousands.[14]

That the Chinese might mimic MacArthur's Inchon gambit in reverse—by widening the war with a bold move to likewise cut off an exposed enemy far from home—was lost on his generals. As Ridgway himself later wrote of MacArthur's inability to accept responsibility for putting his vastly outnumbered forces into a noose on the Yalu River, "It should have been clear to anyone that his own refusal to accept the mounting evidence of massive Chinese intervention was largely responsible for the reckless scattering of our forces all over the map of Korea." That was an apt description of the radical thinning of United Nations troops as they entered the ever widening geography of North Korea near the Yalu. And the de facto lack of communications between two Marine and Army forces as they marched northward up the two coasts made the American predicament even worse.[15]

Now in the bleak days of midwinter, with his forces reeling "all over the map of Korea," a shell-shocked General MacArthur warned that unless he was allowed to attack Chinese bases in Manchuria, the American cause in Korea was essentially hopeless. He went back and forth—sometimes promising complete victory, at others warning that a lack of resolve "would be the greatest defeat of the free world in recent times."

Meanwhile, the confused Joint Chiefs wondered, how might a lost war in Korea be saved by starting another war in China? They were further perplexed about whether MacArthur had been too wildly optimistic in declaring the war all but won in October, or too wildly pessimistic in all but declaring it lost in December—or both.

MacArthur did not mention to Washington, however, that he took for granted that neither the Soviets nor the Chinese would attack American air and supply bases in Japan or Taiwan. But that understanding assumed that the United States also had kept clear of Communist supply depots in Manchuria. The more an embarrassed MacArthur railed against a limited war, the more the cautious minds in Washington grasped that the Chinese and Russians were in fact also waging a limited war. And they, far more easily than America in the region, could escalate at will to other, far more vulnerable theaters.[16]

As the losses mounted, MacArthur began to lose his nerve. "The command," MacArthur warned, "should be withdrawn from Korea just as rapidly as it is tactically possible to do so." Finally, it was clear even to the blinkered Joint Chiefs that the mercurial general had gone full circle. By early January, MacArthur and others were reviewing wild contingency plans to evacuate all American forces to Okinawa, the Philippines, and Japan—a panic comparable to the Greek fright after Thermopylae, or Union hysteria after Cold Harbor.[17]

In fact, a self-serving narrative was developing out of MacArthur's isolated Tokyo headquarters: The problem had not been the general's reckless orders to his field commanders to race late in the year toward the frigid Chinese border. The disaster followed instead from the cowardly political decision in Washington restricting the scope of the war. MacArthur claimed that his problems were not that his land forces were vastly surprised and outnumbered in a neighborhood where the Communist Russians and Chinese could easily send hundreds of thousands of troops into the Korean theater. Instead, the disaster arose because he had not been allowed to widen the war into China, bomb Communist bases, and reserve the right to unleash America's nuclear arsenal if need be. When had the United States, the general wondered, not engaged in hot pursuit across borders to punish an aggressive enemy? And were not British spies in their Washington embassy passing on sensitive American strategic planning to the Communists?[18]

As things got worse, a once fawning press turned on MacArthur and trumpeted predictions of American doom. And by early January, the headlines of the *Chicago Tribune* blared, SMASH THRU THE 8TH ARMY LINE / Chinese Rout One Division and Advance Several Miles." The *Los Angeles Times* saw even less hope: REDS RACE SOUTH TO DESTROY U.S. FORCES.

Against this backdrop of the growing panic, Ridgway was taking over a seemingly hopeless command pawned off on him by his legendary superior, General MacArthur. The latter was ensconced hundreds of miles away in Tokyo fighting political battles with the Truman administration for his own legacy and reputation, hoping to preserve a possible future career in politics. If the Americans surrendered or were destroyed, Ridgway would be responsible for that defeat as supreme commander in the field—and MacArthur could use Ridgway's failure as proof that the war effort had been shorted by Washington. Yet if Ridgway were to be successful in restoring the front, the credit would likely go to the old strategist MacArthur, who still enjoyed nominal overall command. Faced with such a lose-lose situation, Ridgway flew to Japan to meet MacArthur himself.

Everything Gone Wrong (*August 1945–June 1950*)

The larger problem in Korea was not just the invasion of hundreds of thousands of Chinese Communist troops. Indeed, almost everything the United States military and State Department had done in Korea had gone wrong from the moment the Second World War ended. Adding to the general chaos of the postwar occupation—and in fear of Communist radicals—the Americans had initially retained hated Japanese colonial security forces to patrol the 21 million Koreans south of the 38th Parallel. Americans also clung to a naïve estimation of Communist postwar intentions in general, and still entertained an unwarranted deprecation of the quality of Chinese and Korean troops in particular. All that resulted in several contradictory and dangerous notions—that the Communist Chinese, for example, in the late 1940s were not bent on hegemony in Korea. And even if they were, they surely could not offer a serious military challenge to the United States.[19]

In the exuberance of the victories over Germany and Japan, American politicians also did not appreciate fully the sacrifices of both Soviet Russia and China in defeating the Axis powers. Much less did the Anglo-Americans grasp the ensuing sense of entitlement in their respective regions of influence that such massive Russian and Chinese human losses were felt to warrant. After all, the two former allies alone lost more of their population—nearly 40 million in the aggregate—than all other combatants on both sides of World War II combined, and they would fight tenaciously to carve out regional spheres of influence as the spoils of war and compensation for their dead.

As a result, the moment North Korea invaded the south on June 25, 1950, China had already repositioned some of its best units to be nearer the Korean border. More were to come from Manchuria—on the expectation of a wider conflagration. The Soviet Union seemed to have been in charge of much of the foreign policy decisions of its Communist clients—making the North Korean government a "Russian colony," as the June 5, 1950, issue of *Time* magazine had proclaimed shortly before the war. Meanwhile, Soviet and Chinese advisers and equipment poured into North Korea, confirming the American suspicion that no Communist satellite acted without Moscow's approval.[20]

American thinking about Korea was at first likewise unsophisticated. In the utopian theory of postwar reconstruction, Korea fell to the oversight of the newly created United Nations. But the UN had no real power to enforce its edicts without commitments of American military power—itself on the wane given the public's desire for a peace dividend after the sacrifices of World War II. With the end of the war, more in America had feared the return of another depression than worried about newly acquired overseas responsibilities. Under brokered postwar UN agreements, both Communist Russian and American occupying troops would depart the peninsula. The Koreans, north and south, would then be free to choose their leaders in supervised elections. Perhaps they would establish an independent—and unified—Korea for the first time since 1910.

In fact, neither Communist Russia nor China was going to allow another government allied with Americans near its borders. Russia felt that all of Korea belonged in its Communist orbit as its proper reward for entering the war against the Japanese, albeit late, on the side of the Allies. The power of the United States did not rest with fear of American boots on the ground—there were not many more than five hundred American troops when North Korea first invaded the south in June 1950. Instead, American deterrence rested solely on its already fading military reputation for helping to defeat Germany and Japan, along with its vast nuclear superiority over the Soviet Union, which had detonated its first nuclear bomb only the year before. Most observers in the Communist world, however, had studied rapid U.S. demobilization and thereby assumed that America's foreign policy would probably soon revert to its isolationism of the 1930s. With the European colonial powers of Western Europe bankrupt and exhausted by the war, opportunity was arising everywhere in the Pacific and Asia. Few cared that America had sponsored the new United Nations, or was helping to rebuild Europe, or even that its economy was booming in supplying a war-ravaged world.

In tactical terms, on the Korea peninsula in summer 1950, America was rightfully seen as a lightweight that had virtually disbanded its Second World War conventional arsenal in Asia. Scarcely 115,000 ground troops were spread over the Pacific and Japan as the public demanded defense reductions and a redirection in federal spending to new comprehensive social entitlements. At the very moment that global security demands mounted, with the rise of the Soviet Union and the demise of the British Empire, Secretary of Defense Louis Johnson slashed the Navy and tried to disband the Marines altogether. The latter scrambled to cobble together war surplus matériel, most of it obsolete, to maintain some sort of battle readiness.

The result by July 1950 in Korea was that the Eighth Army confronted a Soviet-supplied enemy with mostly outdated Sherman medium tanks and antitank weapons. Naval forces offshore were scant, especially amphibious craft. When the Communists assaulted the surrounded Americans at Pusan in July 1950, American artillery and recoilless rifle rounds bounced off their Russian-made T-34 tanks, of which the Communists had at least 150 supporting their forces. Somehow the military colossus of the Second World War in less than five years found its forces in Korea smaller, more poorly equipped, and far more demoralized than the army of an impoverished nine-million-person Communist North Korea. Unfortunately, this situation developed at precisely the time confident American diplomats were acting as if they enjoyed military parity, or even superiority, in the region.[21]

In this immediate postwar climate of unreality concerning America's military readiness, President Truman again considered conventional forces almost superfluous—given the existence of a nuclear arsenal that in one fell swoop had ended the war with Japan. "The concept of 'limited warfare,'" complained Matthew Ridgway later, "never entered our councils. We had faith in the United Nations. And the atomic bomb created for us a kind of psychological Maginot line that helped us rationalize our national urge to get the boys home, the armies demobilized, the swords sheathed, and the soldiers, sailors, and airmen out of uniform."[22]

For most American veterans, nothing could be worse than to be recalled to military service at a time of growing American postwar prosperity after years of combat in the wars against Germany and Japan. We now think of Harry Truman as a Cold Warrior who sought to save much of Asia and Europe from Communist domination with his advocacy of containment. But his undeniable Cold War zealotry was not always so evident in the immediate aftermath of the Second World War. Between 1946 and 1949, Truman was eager to demobilize U.S. conventional forces, divert the defense budget to social programs, and rely on America's nuclear arsenal to provide security. His secretary of defense, Louis Johnson, provoked a "Revolt of the Admirals" when senior naval leaders furiously objected to cuts in the carriers and naval aviation on the dubious proposition that strategic air forces alone, armed with nuclear weapons, could address far more cheaply almost any threat to American security.[23]

After losing nearly a half million Americans in the Second World War, the public also was naturally reluctant—a mere five years later—to go to war against former allies such as Russia and China to protect prior enemies such as Germany and Japan, which were to be covered under the new American nuclear umbrella and incorporated into regional military alliances. If the United States were to promote a new democratic postwar global order, then it fell to America to rehabilitate an unpopular Germany and Japan and restore both to the family of peaceful nations. Yet that would allow the Communist giants Russia and China the easier task of championing the victims, not the former perpetrators, of Axis aggression.

Given a weary public, some American diplomats were convinced that Japan was the only nation in the Far East that the United States could realistically protect through conventional military means. A few were even naïve enough to air that concession publicly. The usually careful secretary of state, Dean Acheson, in a speech on January 12, 1950, before the National Press Club in Washington, implied that South Korea did not reside within the American defensive sphere—perhaps an understandable caution given U.S. fear of an imminent Communist invasion of Taiwan. Not much later, the influential Senator Thomas Connally, a friend of Truman, asserted that the United States did not consider Korea vital to its strategy. Concerned parties in Asia made a note of all that. But even earlier, a 1947 Joint Chiefs of Staff study had likewise concluded that "From the standpoint of military security, the U.S. has little strategic interest in maintaining the present troops and bases in Korea." Senator

Connally in May 1950 had all but written Korea off as indefensible against the world Communist juggernaut: "Whenever she [Russia] takes a notion she can just overrun Korea like she will probably overrun Formosa when she gets ready to."

With senior U.S. officials airing such doubts, it was logically enough concluded abroad that the United States could probably not guarantee the survival of the nascent Syngman Rhee government in South Korea. U.S. equivocation may have in part persuaded Joseph Stalin, Mao Zedong, and Kim Il-sung that America might not even intervene against a Communist invasion from the north.[24]

The Joint Chiefs of Staff—none of whom had even visited Korea between 1946 and July 1950—were unanimous in agreeing that most of America's shrinking military capability should be directed at saving Western Europe. America's most influential postwar military planners—Omar Bradley, Dwight Eisenhower, and George Marshall—had far more war experience in European than Asian theaters. They all took seriously the warnings of their Western European counterparts not to deplete American strength in far-off tangential theaters. Soviet divisions vastly outnumbered their allied counterparts on the Asian continent—and could advance under a new Soviet nuclear umbrella. The power of the Red Army in the Second World War after 1944, and its destruction of the German Wehrmacht, were still on everyone's mind.[25]

In such a climate, strategic thinking in Asia had been largely left to the four-star general and hero of the Pacific theater, Douglas MacArthur—given the latter's long association with the Pacific and his preeminent record in the victory over the Japanese. Few questioned his proconsulship in Japan, assuming that the lack of postwar violence there was testament to MacArthur's diplomatic genius and military acumen. But the old general had not returned to the United States in over a decade. He had little insight into the thinking of either President Truman or his own Joint Chiefs—and none at all into the ramifications of the use of nuclear weapons. The mercurial MacArthur had five times turned down invitations to receive medals and honors in Washington. President Truman, who had never met the general, guessed that MacArthur was plotting to be drafted as the Republican presidential nominee in 1952. If that were true, then the general's accusations of Democratic appeasement of global Communism would be enhanced by his own quick victory over Asian Communists—reminding voters that he still alone preserved America's military prowess.

As a reclusive proconsul in Japan, MacArthur stayed ensconced in imperial headquarters in Tokyo. From there, he directed the postwar reconstruction of Japan, and nominally oversaw the less important Korean occupation by remote control. He had little notion that entering Korea with outnumbered, green American forces might invite an initial disaster. Yet, on the other hand, the equally naïve Communists had no idea that the Americans would ever intervene with forces large enough to stop their assault at Pusan.

MacArthur acted independently of both the Joint Chiefs and, increasingly, the Truman administration itself. Such autonomy was ill-advised, given that in 1950 he was seventy years old, and still defensive about a number of allegations of strategic ineptitude dating back to the surprise Japanese bombing of the Philippines, the later horrific costs in retaking the islands, and his earlier controversial flight from Corregidor. His intelligence sources were chronically defective. MacArthur was warned neither about the original June 25, 1950, North Korean invasion nor the subsequent massive Chinese attack of late November across the Yalu. Indeed, on October 15, 1950, in the midst of the American-led pursuit of defeated Communist North Korean forces, MacArthur had also assured President Truman at a much-heralded meeting on Wake Island that there was "very little" chance of Chinese intervention, since without Communist air support it would lead to the "greatest slaughter" of the enemy—at the moment that new Russian-supplied MiGs and pilots would soon challenge daylight American B-29 bombing missions.[26]

Even when the Chinese later crossed the Yalu, few in Washington were willing to question MacArthur. Ridgway related his own surreal conversation with General Hoyt Vandenberg, chief of staff of the Air Force. "'Why,' I asked him, 'don't the Joint Chiefs send orders to MacArthur and *tell* him what to do?' Van shook his head. 'What good would that do? He wouldn't obey the orders. What *can* we do?'"[27]

The politics and strategic landscape of Korea were also ostensibly hostile to the United States. Many liberated Koreans viewed America as increasingly pro-Japanese and unduly forgiving of past Japanese atrocities—which ranged from a brutal occupation of Korea to forced conscriptions of Korean youth and humiliating use of Korean women as prostitutes for Japanese soldiers. Postwar poverty was seen as better addressed by Communist largesse and a friendly—and nearby—China than a capitalist America that was on the side of the old colonialists. For many Koreans, there was not yet all that much difference between autocrats. The South Korean president, Syngman Rhee, was seen, not without reason, by many in the south as an antidemocratic, American-educated puppet, eased into power after the Japanese left. His far more brutal Communist rival Kim Il-sung was championed as an indigenous, revolutionary, and egalitarian figure who might spread a Chinese-style agrarian revolution.

While the south outnumbered the north in population, 21 million versus 9 million, and produced most of the peninsula's food on its more fertile and arable land, areas of the north for decades had been heavily industrialized, were more developed by Japanese colonialists, and were richer in strategic minerals. By 1950, North Korea was considered by Communists in both Russia and China as a valuable addition to the Communist bloc, and a necessary buffer state to the new Chinese government.

In logistical terms, Korea was over seven thousand miles distant from the continental United States, but conveniently right on the borders of both Communist China and the Soviet Union. Even if the United States were successful in preserving an independent South Korea, it would, as the Joint Chiefs feared, require a constant U.S. military deterrent presence for years. That might mean a permanent trip wire for a much wider Asian land war. While the Communist giants considered a compliant Korea necessary for border security, the largely unarmed Japanese feared that Communist reunification would turn the peninsula into a sword directed at their heart. Anti-Japanese sentiment sometimes trumped ideology on both sides of the 38th Parallel—to the detriment of the United States, which was an ally of Japan, and to the advantage of Russia and China, which were not.[28]

When Communist North Korean forces invaded the south with an initial wave of ninety thousand superbly trained troops, backed by Soviet-supplied tanks, and overwhelmed the ill-prepared forces of Syngman Rhee, it was unclear whether the United States would, could, or even should provide for an immediate defense. America was as unprepared to fight a land war in Asia in summer 1950 as it had been surprised by the Japanese navy at Pearl Harbor nine years earlier.[29]

On the Brink (*December 1950–January 1951*)

On Christmas Day 1950, six months after the North Korean invasion of the south, Matthew Ridgway landed in Japan. In just half a year, United

Nations forces had almost lost the war at Pusan, rallied to reclaim the South at Inchon, nearly finished the conflict by overrunning all of North Korea to the Yalu River—and were in danger of losing Seoul for a second time and with it all of South Korea. The next day, Ridgway met General MacArthur for a short briefing. Ridgway immediately found himself in an awkward position. MacArthur was his superior officer—whose own carelessness had contributed to the present fiasco on the Yalu and helped to bring Ridgway to Korea. The septuagenarian World War II hero was still wildly popular at home and had established a formidable public relations lobby both in Japan and the United States. He certainly had proven a superb proconsul in Japan. But as Ridgway knew from his recent tenure at the Pentagon, MacArthur was increasingly dismissed as a megalomaniac by many of the Joint Chiefs, who had long wanted to relieve him. How could a subordinate serve under such a figure at once responsible for both saving Korea at Inchon and nearly losing it at the Yalu?[30]

Yet even in the apparent collapse of the American cause, Ridgway grasped that once MacArthur had crossed the 38th Parallel, his two-pronged advance to the Yalu had not been entirely foolhardy. After all, he had sent United Nations troops to the northernmost tip of the Korean peninsula with astoundingly light losses—until the hammer of Chinese intervention fell. That fact told Ridgway that the Communists, at least the North Koreans, were not supermen. They could be pushed back again. MacArthur could sound unhinged in his rants about expanding the war, but, better than most, he understood the ultimate hegemonic intentions of both Communist China and the Soviet Union in Asia. The problem with the mercurial MacArthur was not his appreciation of the Communist threat and the misery it meant for millions under its sway, but finding the proper strategy to thwart it.[31]

In this meeting in Tokyo on December 26—later characterized as "detailed, specific, frank, and far-ranging"—the newly appointed Ridgway was ordered to withdraw to positions to ensure that Seoul not be lost for a second time. Yet he was still supposed to inflict enough damage on the Chinese to allow some measure of maneuvering for American diplomacy with the Communists. Although Ridgway had not yet landed in Korea and assessed the state of American forces, he wondered whether an immediate offensive might be allowable to MacArthur. "The Eighth Army is yours, Matt," MacArthur famously replied. In fact, MacArthur had no detailed plans for how to stop the Chinese advance. He seemed more interested in fighting a public relations battle with Washington.

On arriving in Korea, Ridgway quietly learned that his hopes of immediate offensive operations were in vain. Instead, he discovered that the catastrophe was even worse than reported. His Eighth Army was in shambles. Many of its officers wanted out of the theater altogether. Keeping the advancing Chinese out of South Korea was out of the question. That Seoul would fall a second time to Communists was simply a matter of when and how. The real worry was instead whether growing panic would stampede UN forces back to Japan, losing them even their refuge at Pusan in the south. Ridgway, the World War II veteran, had not experienced American confusion since the ill-fated Operation Market Garden or the German assault through the Ardennes during the Battle of the Bulge.

The initial Chinese assault (dubbed the Chinese First Phase Offensive) between October 25 and November 24, 1950, had already cost the Americans 27,827 casualties, including nearly ten thousand killed and missing in action—far more lost than in the infamous battle for Iwo Jima. For a brief period until late November, sophisticated Russian-made MiG-15s had given the Communists virtual air superiority along a corridor near the Chinese border. There may have been three hundred or so such aircraft stationed in neighboring Manchurian airfields. Slower, vulnerable propeller-driven B-29 heavy bombers—whose fire raids had struck terror in Japan five years earlier—were increasingly confined to night attacks against the north, given that American postwar jet fighters were not up to the MiG-15's standards and could not protect the B-29s. Once-shattered Communist North Korean divisions had been refitted and resupplied in China. Now they were again far more confident and battle-ready than were their South Korean counterparts, who had started the war six months earlier with scarcely enough equipment for 65,000 troops.[32]

Ridgway spent the frigid waning days of 1950 visiting his corps and division commanders in the Eighth Army. What he found appalled—but also informed—him. Morale was shot. Rumors circulated of traumatized American troops cheering as they had retreated once again south of the 38th Parallel. Republic of Korea allied troops almost ran over Ridgway himself as he got out in the road and vainly tried to stop their fleeing columns.[33] Vast supplies of weapons and materials had simply been abandoned in the north, robbing entire brigades of their firepower while augmenting the stocks of their Chinese pursuers. American GIs—accustomed to enjoying ample supplies of matériel in the latter years of

World War II—were often outgunned by Soviet-supplied superior tanks and airpower. Wrong-headed "scorched earth" orders had resulted in the destruction of roads, bridges, and railways in the north. Yet such a strategy was not very effective, given that the Chinese often advanced mostly on foot.

Such wanton destruction instead had demoralized once friendly Korean populations. Losses of infrastructure would also come back to haunt the mobile Americans if they were ever to go back on the offensive and return to the north. General MacArthur, distant from the battlefield, moreover had no real appreciation of Chinese tactics and organization. Instead, his commanders clung to the notion that enemy columns, like conventional European armies, could easily be targeted by American bombers and stopped through airpower alone. In reality, most Chinese advanced off the main routes in difficult terrain. They often attacked under cover of darkness, and they took masterful advantage of poor weather that hampered air sorties.

American troops, in a fashion also reminiscent of the frostbitten days of the Battle of the Bulge, were inadequately prepared for the brutal Korean winter. Many freezing soldiers had thrown away their helmets in preference for the rare, warmer woolen caps. Some units in their desperation had discarded virtually all their bayonets. Soldiers lit roaring campfires to ward off frostbite, identifying their presence to Chinese infiltrators during frequent after-dark engagements. American victories in World War II had relied heavily on massive American tactical support and strategic air superiority. But neither was assured. Targets were restricted by political considerations. And the Chinese brilliantly timed their advances to coincide with rough winter weather.

Americans were also confused by the unconventional tactics of Chinese invaders. They blew bugles, whistles—almost anything that made noise—when attacking. Some trained propagandists shouted taunts in English. All had been conditioned by months of intensive anti-American propaganda to despise their enemies and "the Wall Street house-dog General MacArthur." Most units preferred nocturnal attacks. And they almost always sought to infiltrate American lines well camouflaged, or, in a few cases, wearing American uniforms. The terror of the Chinese came not just from numeric superiority, but from the sense of the unknown and mysterious, embellished by Communist propaganda, in the way perhaps that Hernán Cortés's conquistadors were at first baffled by the tactics and appearance of their Aztec adversaries at Tenochtitlán, or many of the Greeks in the years before Marathon, according to the historian Herodotus, had feared even to look upon Persian troops. Thousands of Chinese marshaled behind the lines to stockpile supplies, safe from American artillery. Then during the night they frantically marched to predesignated attack points, fresh and undetected.

Americans often went to sleep thinking the Chinese were miles away from the front (and they often were), only to awaken and find that thousands of enemy soldiers had almost magically infiltrated their lines during the night. Moreover, Chinese usually aimed their thrusts at seams in the United Nations lines, either at suspect South Korean divisions or, more frequently, at the gray areas between South Korean and American forces where command responsibility was unsure and American firepower less likely to concentrate.

Fighting Communists was a new American experience. At first, officers concluded that a rabid ideology, when mixed with stereotypical Asian discipline, had created an almost mystical challenge unlike any other in American military history. Americans back home knew that just five years earlier, the Soviet Red Army had beaten the Wehrmacht on the Eastern Front, and that even more recently, Mao Zedong's Chinese Communists had defeated the better-supplied Nationalist forces of Chiang Kai-shek. These facts contributed to the public impression that Communist fanaticism was a force multiplier to which the Western democracies had so far found no answer. In short, the Chinese Communists enjoyed the same sort of inflated ideological and ethnic reputation that the Japanese had won after Pearl Harbor and Wake Island until Guadalcanal.[34]

Ridgway also found an absence of American command coordination. That was to be expected after the death of General Walker, and given that General MacArthur was far away in Tokyo. But worse still, Army General Walker as commander of the Eighth Army, and Marine General Almond as head of Tenth Corps, had sometimes worked at cross purposes. There was no real supreme ground commander in Korea, given that General MacArthur allowed his friend Almond to act independently of Eighth Army control. Both Walker and Almond had been headstrong leaders but were often prone to impetuousness. The physical barriers between east and west Korea, intraservice rivalry, and the vastly different rates of advance of the two American armies made it hard for either force to reinforce or cover the other once the Chinese came across the border. It was almost as if there were an Army war and a Marine war, the two quite independent of each other—not long after President Truman and Defense Secretary Johnson had wished to reduce or even disband the Marine Corps.

Serving alongside the Americans were some thirty thousand allied troops, mostly from Britain, Europe, Greece, and Turkey. They were disheartened and had lost confidence in American leadership. Most had been originally sent largely on the assumption that after Inchon, the war was about over and all but won. They expected peacekeeping roles in the trail of the successful American advance. Now, instead, many of the Canadian, Dutch, French, Greek, and Turkish detachments reached the front during the unexpected massive Chinese counterattack in late November and December—at the very moment when their American sponsors were in headlong retreat.

Indeed, despite a UN Security Resolution authorizing the use of force to repel Communist aggression, only sixteen nations would eventually send troops. Almost all of them were reluctantly persuaded to do so, perhaps on the implicit argument that otherwise both the Truman Doctrine and ongoing Marshall Plan aid programs were not quite assured. In total, only forty thousand non-American foreign troops would fight for South Korea—in comparison with 5,720,000 Americans who would over three years at some point be rotated through the Korean theater.[35]

British officers had no idea why MacArthur in October 1950 had pursued the Communists past the more defensible "waist" of Korea near the 39th Parallel in a wild-goose chase to the Chinese border. They were equally bewildered as to why the panicked Americans in December had simply fled southward toward the far less defensible 38th—once more neglecting the opportunities at the waist to establish formidable lines of defense while easily outrunning their pursuers, who were without motorized transport and still miles behind them. Too reckless an advance was trumped by an even more reckless retreat. Later Truman regretted that he had let MacArthur reject the sober British advice, pointing to the 39th Parallel on a map and supposedly lamenting that he had not stopped the American advance at the "neck of Korea."[36]

A depressed Syngman Rhee was sure that United Nations troops could not save Seoul. This time most likely they would abandon him and the Korean peninsula altogether. Rhee was prescient: Back in Washington a nasty political fight was brewing between left and right in Congress. There was no unified support for continuing the war, but clear indications that in the 1952 election to come, "Who lost Korea?" would be the central campaign issue. President Harry Truman, soon-to-be presidential candidate General Dwight D. Eisenhower, Senator Joseph McCarthy, Secretary of Defense George Marshall, and General MacArthur himself all had differing agendas, without agreement about what the United States' common aims were—or how much blood and treasure Americans were willing to pay for what most still saw as a far distant optional war. In fact, the war threatened to destroy the political careers of all five high-profile generals and politicians.

Ridgway wanted to know whether the Soviet Union would pile on and soon send in troops for the final kill, then turn on Japan and Formosa. If the forces of the United Nations stopped the Chinese offensive, should they resume the advance of autumn 1950 and try to unify the entire Korea peninsula under the control of a single democratically elected leader, or go back to the two-state status before the war? Were atomic weapons necessary, or were there even enough of them available to be effective against a vast country like China, and if so, had the newly nuclear Soviet Union reached strategic parity with the United States? Ridgway soon learned that almost no one in Washington had answers to any of those questions—even as he wished to raise far more like them. Just as Grant's disastrous 1864 offensives had wiped away the optimism of the prior summer and sent the Union into a defeatist mood, so, too, the Chinese invasion now rendered Inchon a distant memory and a real defeat an immediate possibility.

Salvation (*January–April 1951*)

What immediately followed in late December and January was predictable. In just two weeks the Eighth Army in the northwest had retreated back across the Imjin River and was once again south of the 38th Parallel. America's second army in Korea to the east, the Tenth Corps, had meanwhile fallen back southward to Hungnam. For some reason, before Ridgway took over, UN forces in the east were ordered to be evacuated hundreds of miles by sea, perhaps all the way back to Pusan, abandoning swaths of hard-won territory that were not yet even occupied by the Communists.

To Ridgway, the problem was not just that there were no longer many

United Nations troops in the north, but that those in the south were exhausted from a demoralizing extended retreat. A thin line of troops was guarding Seoul, outnumbered three to one by an oncoming Chinese-led army eager to clear the peninsula entirely of foreigners. Back in the United States, there was more loose talk—much of it inspired not just by MacArthur supporters, but also by leaders in Congress and President Truman himself—of using atomic bombs to stop the seemingly unstoppable Communist attack. Ridgway had informally asked MacArthur to authorize the possible use of poison gas once he arrived and fathomed the extent of the collapse of the American forces.[37]

Alarmed Europeans clamored for restraint. They feared a general nuclear conflagration, diminished U.S. resources for the defense of Western Europe—and the real possibility that the Americans might lose in such an unfavorable theater and thus encourage Communist expansionism elsewhere. The Labour Party–controlled British Parliament was furious that British soldiers might soon find themselves pawns on a nuclear battlefield. Elders in the British government hastily persuaded Prime Minister Clement Attlee to fly to Washington. There Attlee voiced heated objections to almost every element of American foreign policies toward both Koreas and Red China—in vain trying to cajole the Truman administration to make peace with the Chinese in hopes that they would soon prove independent from their Soviet sponsors and settle for some sort of prewar boundary at the 38th Parallel. In general, the Americans were still confident that they could weaken worldwide Communism in Korea, the British equally convinced that an American defeat would empower it.[38]

President Truman was furious. He felt betrayed, given MacArthur's rosy reports of an imminent and utter Communist defeat at their meeting on Wake Island in early October 1950. He was angrier still at the dissent coming from the front lines, where MacArthur and others were busy diverting blame away from themselves. Finally, on December 5, just weeks before Ridgway's appointment, in exasperation he had issued the following order: "No speech, press release, or other public statement concerning foreign policy should be released until it has received clearance from the Department of State." President Truman added that all commanders were "to refrain from direct communication on military or foreign policy with newspapers, magazines, or other publicity media in the United States."[39]

Yet was the situation really as bleak as MacArthur and the Joint Chiefs believed, or Truman feared? To Matthew Ridgway's mind—and nearly his mind alone—the answer was clearly no when he arrived on December 23, 1950, in Korea. Optimism, if grounded in logic rather than blind hope, was critical for restoration. And no one was more rational in those dark days than Matthew Ridgway. First, despite the fear of "Chinese hordes," there was not such a great numeric disparity, at least if one considered the entire Korean peninsula and its larger environs—and the vast superiority enjoyed by American-led United Nations forces both at sea and in the air. As the army reeled backward, it was often forgotten that MacArthur still had nearly 550,000 ground, air, and naval forces at his theater command. Included in the Eighth Army and Tenth Corps alone were over 178,000 American infantry and marine troops. The Communists did not seem to take into account that the United States had vast naval and air resources based nearby in Japan and in the Philippines. They could be easily supplied, and facilities there were nearly impregnable from attack, given the superiority of the American fleet and strategic air force. The problem for General Peng Dehuai's combined Korean and Chinese Communist forces was not that they did not outnumber the United Nations coalition, but that they did not outnumber it enough to counterbalance overwhelming American firepower and supplies.[40]

True, the enemy had reached the outskirts of Seoul by the New Year with total forces in the peninsula numbering nearly half a million North Korean and Chinese troops. But the Communists were for the most part becoming tired, sick, cold, and daily more distant from their thinning supply lines, which were under constant UN attack. They certainly did not have adequate artillery to support their huge forces. As they pressed their attacks, the Chinese bunched up—as if the disheartened Americans would not have adequate firepower to break up such formations. Never in modern military history had such a large army marched so far without guaranteed air superiority, or indeed much air or artillery cover at all. That lapse would soon be their undoing, as Ridgway realized. Were the Chinese really the Genghis Khan–like warriors of myth that frightened the Eighth Army into running back from the Yalu—or instead poorly clothed and fed Chinese conscripts who had lost the advantage of surprise and were colder and hungrier every mile they advanced southward from the Yalu?

Postwar analysis from the Communist side has emphasized the ongoing crisis in Chinese supply, which was pounded by U.S. air forces and artillery. By the new year, Peng Dehuai was already requesting a hiatus in offensive operations from his Chinese superiors. Few in the Chinese government appreciated the heavy toll on his forces from American air and artillery barrages; the Red Army's superiors back in Beijing were proving as out of touch with the battlefield as were their American counterparts in Washington—a problem familiar to weary frontline generals in many wars.

Most of the Americans' problems, Ridgway concluded, were caused not by mere numbers or enemy superiority. Instead, the United States army in Korea had been plagued by lack of good leadership. It also suffered from a divided command, murky objectives, poor public relations, public indifference at home, and a sudden and unwarranted panic at the appearance of the ideologically driven Chinese. Indeed, in recent years, historians have reexamined the precipitous withdrawal of the Eighth Army from the Yalu under General Walker and have argued that such a lengthy and rapid retreat was not necessarily foreordained, or perhaps completely necessary: "The rank-and-file might have responded had the leadership been up to it. But it was not. Eighth Army as a whole panicked and fled; it was a shameful performance." Much of the subsequent two years would be spent trying to regain areas so readily given up by Walker during his precipitous retreat.[41]

In some ways, the evacuation of the marines on the eastern side of the peninsula was even more shocking, given that the 1st Marine Division had fought a successful retreat to Hungnam and had established a defensible perimeter, inflicting twenty-five thousand Chinese casualties during its withdrawal. Ridgway saw that the marines, at least, had been as much ordered as forced to retreat. He also concluded that even if the Eighth Army had soon to abandon its thin line along the Imjin River, roughly along the 38th Parallel, and evacuate Seoul a second time (January 3–4, 1951), he would still not be overly concerned. The key was to trap and destroy large numbers of Communists, even if that meant fighting for a time south of the capital. Ridgway had confirmed there were already four fallback lines of trenches and barbed wire, all mined and guarded by artillery—in succession all the way back to the stronghold at Pusan if necessary. Yet he felt that such a long withdrawal would not be necessary, given that soon the enemy would overrun its base of supplies and begin thinning as it dispatched soldiers to occupy ground—just as the Americans themselves had experienced on the way up to the Yalu. Somewhere in the Chinese command, there was a counterpart to the reckless MacArthur, an overconfident zealot who was wildly demanding that his stretched Communist columns could nevertheless race all the way to Pusan.

Other considerations gave the calm Ridgway even more optimism amid the general gloom, despite his unfamiliarity with Korea. While General Walker had been a fine Second World War armored commander under General George S. Patton, and while his accidental death had been tragic, Ridgway carefully began to sense that Walker may well have been as impulsive in retreating past the 38th Parallel as he had been in advancing beyond it—far outracing the pursuing Communists, losing contact with the enemy altogether, creating the impression that defeated troops had no chance against throngs of Asian Communists, and needlessly destroying infrastructure in retreat.

Later historical assessments have agreed with Ridgway. "There is little doubt," one historian of the Korean War concluded, "that there was a 'bugout' mentality among many men in Eighth Army in December 1950. They wanted to be going south fast and keep going. The command echelon of Eighth Army also seems to have wanted to put a lot of distance between themselves and the Chinese in early December 1950—in order to save the army, they usually said."[42] Walker's tragic demise, in an ironic sense, relieved Ridgway of the worry that his own radical restructuring of the Eighth Army was a referendum on Walker's serious faults that had contributed further to MacArthur's flawed command. Ridgway was free to reinvent the Eighth Army, while Walker was canonized—perhaps in the tradition of General Simon Bolivar Buckner, whose untimely death on Okinawa in July 1945 aborted an uncomfortable but growing consensus that his unimaginative strategy had led to thousands of needless American casualties.

Moreover, by mid-December 1950, the growing replacement of slower F-80 Shooting Stars with late model American F-86 Sabres signaled the end of the enemy MiG-15's brief air superiority. If Ridgway could hold on, and Americans could recapture bases near the 38th Parallel, the B-29s and propeller-driven fighter bombers might resume, with jet fighter escort, the daylight bombing of the north—especially of vulnerable Chinese supply lines—without interdiction by enemy jet fighters.[43]

Ridgway also knew that despite superior morale, and some fine Soviet weaponry, Chinese Communist forces were ill-equipped. Some

Communist forces were without adequate food and medicines and armed with only grenades. Soon, massive American resupply would guarantee further advantages in artillery, tanks, machine guns, and supplies. Ridgway immediately saw the paradox of Korea in a way that MacArthur somehow did not. If in late November 1950 the well-supplied Americans could not get sufficient socks, shoes, caps, jackets, and rations to their troops far to the north on the Yalu, how could the less organized Chinese do any better for their own cold and hungry soldiers outside Seoul? While most in the West were terrified of the Chinese, Ridgway saw that the cold and geography affected both sides equally, and the enemy would probably suffer more than the better-clothed Americans. Later, Chinese internal assessments of poor supply, outbreaks of disease, the toll from air attacks, frostbite, and lack of supplies all supported Ridgway's hunch that the Communists were in dire straits and would not be able to go much farther south than Seoul.[44]

The genius of Ridgway would be found in restoring morale and allowing the Chinese to extend their lines as they rushed headlong to the south. The key, then, was to rebuild, gradually withdraw intact, stock up, and wait for the moment when exposed Chinese columns would be most vulnerable to counterattack—hopefully far north of Pusan, and before the American public gave up on the war. If the Chinese had crafted a new, terrifying way of fighting, so could the Americans—one tailored precisely to address Chinese weaknesses. By establishing fortified lines, ringed with minefields, supplied by air, replete with plentiful artillery, and under constant bomber cover, Americans would bide their time and soon obliterate oncoming Chinese light infantry.

Moreover, Ridgway, again perhaps alone, saw that in this sort of limited war, holding ground was not so important. America could find success without necessarily going all the way back to the Yalu River to reunite the peninsula. Instead, killing off Communist forces would teach the Chinese (and by extension the Russians) the lethality of American firepower and the strength of the country's will. Success in Korea might create a deterrent that would extend even to Western Europe. That would remind both Stalin and Mao of the wages of taking on American airpower and artillery.

Were South Korea to be restored with defense guarantees, were the Chinese and North Koreans to lose hundreds of thousands without achieving any of the objectives of the July 1950 invasion of the south, and were the Americans to establish a means of checking Communist

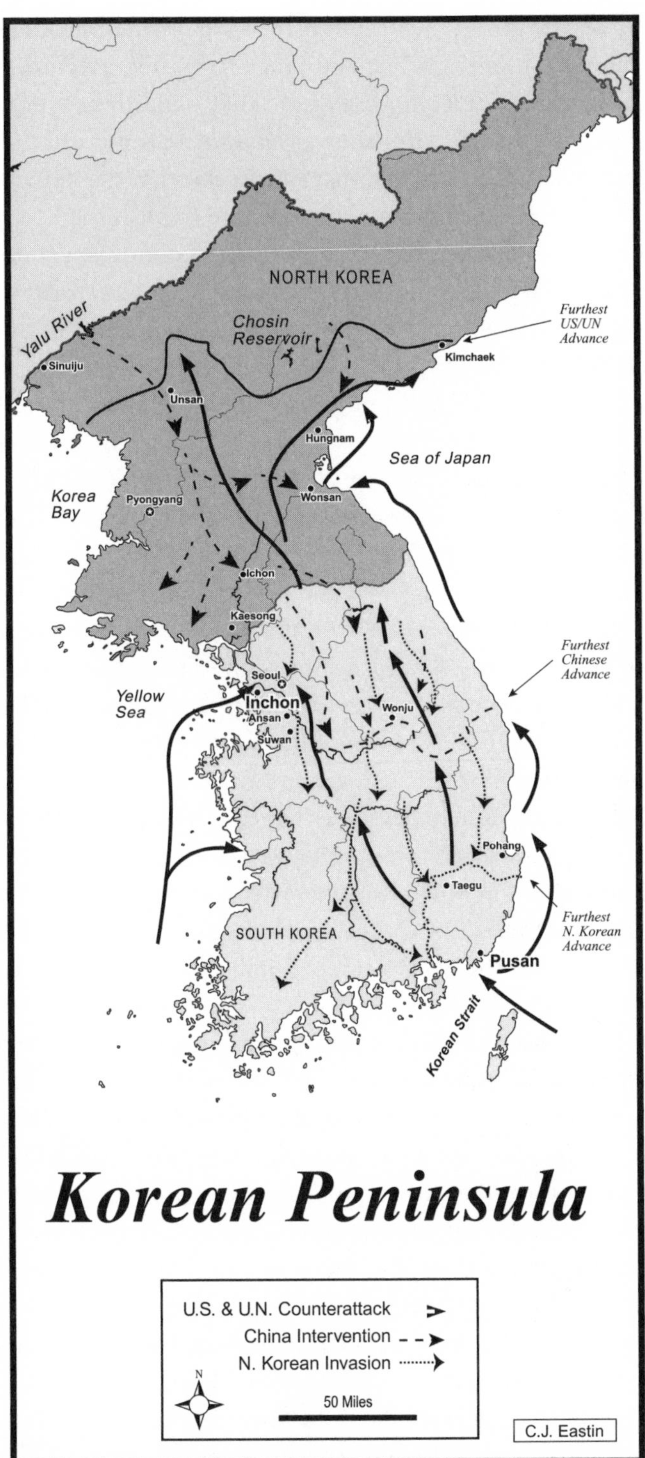

NORTH KOREA
Yalu River
Chosin Reservoir
Sinuiju
Unsan
Kimchaek
Furthest US/UN Advance
Hungnam
Sea of Japan
Korea Bay
Pyongyang
Wonsan
Ichon
Kaesong
Furthest Chinese Advance
Seoul
Yellow Sea
Inchon
Ansan
Suwan
Wonju
Pohang
Taegu
Furthest N. Korean Advance
SOUTH KOREA
Pusan
Korean Strait
Korean Peninsula
U.S. & U.N. Counterattack
China Intervention
N. Korean Invasion
N
50 Miles
C.J. Eastin

offensives on the ground—without provoking a wider nuclear war and while keeping Western Europe and Japan safe—then victory could be achieved after all. Ridgway would see to that—and thereby educate the public that a stalemate in a limited war far away in Korea was more a victory than a defeat. Ridgway, in other words, saw that the ultimate objectives of the North Koreans and Chinese were to push the United States out of Korea and reunite the peninsula under Communist control. And yet if he were to try the same in reverse, it might prove strategically untenable, given the geography of Korea and its distance from the United States. During the Battle of the Bulge, Ridgway had been one of the few American generals who had almost immediately grasped the folly of the German offensive—undertaken without proper supply, reserves, or air support—and in Korea he sensed the same opportunities for counterattack and American advantage against the present Chinese offensive, likewise when most others did not.

Ridgway also calmly reviewed the prior first six months of the war (June to December 1950). He realized that in just two weeks in June and July 1950 after the North's surprise invasion, the United States held the Pusan perimeter through a massive buildup of men and matériel. Then, less than a month after the Communist attack, the United States had, before the entrance of enemy jets, achieved air superiority over the entire peninsula. And just ninety days after North Korea crossed the 38th Parallel, the Communists were outnumbered and surrounded at Inchon. Four months after the North Koreans' attack, they were facing annihilation at the Yalu. Indeed, by October 1950, the North Koreans had ceased to exist as effective fighting forces. China had changed the equation, coupled with loss of morale on the part of Americans, who went from the promise of "home by Thanksgiving" or "by Christmas" to confronting hundreds of thousands of new enemies in the frigid north. The one constant in this strange seesaw war was American firepower: its lethal artillery and constant air strikes, coupled with Korea's relatively bleak open terrain, meant that the strung-out Chinese might pay the terrible price, whether on the offensive or in retreat.[45]

Finally, Ridgway sensed that the growing political animus between MacArthur and Truman had led to a directionless policy on the ground in Korea. To Ridgway, two considerations were thus paramount: First, keep out of the political fray, without either undercutting his superior, MacArthur, or spouting off about administration politics limiting his own options; second, utilize the preoccupations of his superiors to gain a free hand in restoring sound strategy and tactics to the front without intrusive oversight. So while MacArthur from Tokyo kept sending to his select Republican supporters back-channel doom-and-gloom appraisals of the front he rarely visited, Ridgway on the battlefield quietly remained upbeat. In direct communications, he assured the somewhat confused Joint Chiefs that far from the war being lost, his Eighth Army could soon restore South Korea entirely to the 38th Parallel.[46]

In about eleven weeks after Ridgway's arrival, Seoul was recaptured from the Chinese and North Koreans. In little more than three months, South Korea was in fact saved and its borders restored to or beyond the 38th Parallel. As Ridgway summed it up, "In less than *three months* . . . the Communist thrust into South Korea had been met and brought to a stop, and the invading forces all but destroyed. In less than *two weeks* the Communist offensive, begun on New Year's Day, was halted. And in exactly *three weeks* from the second evacuation of the South Korean capital on January 4, 1951, the United Nations Command passed over to the offensive."[47]

As Americans regained their confidence in early 1951, Ridgway found himself fighting on almost every diplomatic front. MacArthur did not always welcome Ridgway's good news from the battlefield that could contradict his own bleak narrative, that the politicians had wrecked his marvelous offensive to the Yalu. The mercurial and politically expedient Joint Chiefs at first expected all American forces to be evacuated from Korea, then in an about-face Seoul to be quickly retaken, then again the 38th Parallel to be restored, and then perhaps modest American advances beyond it—all these contortions predicated solely on Ridgway's own prior battlefield success. Truman backed Ridgway's efforts—but in part mostly for leverage against MacArthur and to ensure that in time the latter could be replaced by a successful, less controversial commander. Others like General Dwight Eisenhower and General James Van Fleet would come to praise Ridgway's "tremendous victory." But after Korea was saved, both began to fault him—as a ground commander in Korea and theater overseer in Tokyo, and for not repeating MacArthur's folly of heading up to Manchuria, or at least advancing to the 39th Parallel. As a general rule in the Korean War, when Americans faltered, critics immediately claimed they had been too foolhardy; and when they successfully advanced, the same opportunistic critics railed that they had not properly capitalized on their success.[48]

If Ridgway did not always receive ample credit from superior officers, the Pentagon quietly came to appreciate his amazing achievement. Before Ridgway's arrival, there was desperate talk of invading China, inviting Taiwanese troops into Korea, and using atomic weapons. Yet once the Americans retook Seoul, all such desperate planning quietly ceased. Secretary of the Army Frank Pace visited Korea and summed up Ridgway's brief four-month command of the Eighth Army before he assumed MacArthur's old role as supreme commander in Tokyo: "Matt, you have worked not only a military miracle, but a spiritual one with this army."[49]

Even more controversially, a confident and victorious Ridgway persuaded American leadership not to press for the entire reunification of Korea, one of the most fateful decisions in American military history. When North Korean strongman Kim Jong-il in the new millennium boasted about sending a nuclear rocket toward Hawaii and promising a Seoul "in flames"—nearly sixty years after the Korean War armistice—that determination to stop at the 38th Parallel was still rightly questioned. A present-day unified—and non-nuclear—Korea would have extended to millions more a quality life, enriched the world with even more goods, and vastly reduced the chance of nuclear war in the Pacific. Yet in fairness to Ridgway's decision to stop at the 38th Parallel in spring 1951, a few considerations need to be emphasized.

What made him a great savior general, in the manner of Belisarius or Sherman, was his recognition that the risks he ran—rushing to turn the American army from defense to offense in a matter of days—would not be fatal to his cause should the unforeseen occur. In contrast, going far into North Korea not only might end in failure, but in theory result in such a failure as to endanger the entire American effort to save a viable South Korea.

The Joint Chiefs instructed both Ridgway and Van Fleet in May 1951 to hold roughly at the 38th Parallel—in response to diplomatic decisions about the larger strategic picture in the Far East and in reaction to the loss of public support for another offensive stage of the war. Had they thought and ordered otherwise, Ridgway would have dutifully led the offensive northward. In other words, the decision was not Ridgway's alone—even though his personal view that it was unwise to reinvade the north had in turn influenced the Truman administration not to risk another race to the Yalu.

Ridgway was not in command in summer 1953, when the final armistice was signed. Critics of his decision two years earlier to stop at the 38th Parallel had plenty of opportunity to restart the war and drive the

Communists back beyond the Yalu—had they believed Ridgway was wrong that there were not sufficient American forces, United Nations support, approval of the American people, and surety that China and Russia would not send massive reinforcements to prevent the loss of the North. As Ridgway himself put it,

> At the end of the campaign, our battle line would have been stretched from 110 miles to 420 miles, and the major responsibility for holding it would have been ours, for it would have been beyond the capability of the ROK [the Republic of (South) Korea] army. The questions then would have been: Will the American people support an army of the size required to hold this line? Will they underwrite the bloody cost of a Manchurian campaign? Will they commit themselves to an endless war in the bottomless pit of the Asian mainland? I thought then and I think now that the answer to these questions was "No."[50]

The Ridgway Record (*April 1951*)

The enemy tested Ridgway immediately. The Chinese resumed attacking just as he arrived at the front. Between December 31 and January 5, the Communists began a third phase of their offensive, following both the October crossing of the Yalu (October 27–31, 1950) and the second-stage massive concentration against the Eighth Army (beginning on December 9, 1950). Seoul fell again on January 3–4, at the end of Ridgway's first week on the job. But unlike the retreat from the Yalu, Ridgway withdrew slowly under heavy air and artillery support, hoping the advancing Chinese would butt up against nearby prepared lines and be easily targeted by air strikes. They were. By January 15, their offensive sputtered and wore itself out—just ten days after the American loss of Seoul. More than eight thousand enemy troops were lost to American bombing alone.

As the Chinese and North Koreans tired, Ridgway's new army readied for his first counteroffensive. This time troops were assured that their officers were acquainted with Chinese tactics. They had firm supply lines, and, if successful, they would not rush pell-mell again across the 38th Parallel to ensure approving headlines back home. The subsequent American turnabout was nearly unbelievable. On December 26, 1950, Ridgway had officially taken command of the retreating Eighth Army. On January 15, during "Operation Wolfhound," United Nations forces had ceased their retreat and sent reconnaissance patrols to reestablish contact with the enemy. Ten days later the Eighth Army and Korean counterparts turned around and headed north back to the Han River. In three weeks, Korea was an entirely different war. Suddenly the cruel winter cold was not America's enemy, but its ally.

On February 5, 1951, "Operation Roundup" saw the Tenth Corps advancing on the eastern flank. The fourth Chinese offensive, far from pushing the United Nations contingents back to Pusan, stalled on February 17. In response, a counteradvance, dubbed by Ridgway "Operation Killer," helped to set the stage for the collapse of North Korean and Chinese forces south of the Han River. It was followed by yet a third American-led offensive, "Operation Ripper," in which the Eighth Army retook Seoul on March 14 for the second and final time, while the Ninth and Tenth Corps, under difficult conditions, crossed the Han to the east.

Ridgway had under his direct command some 150,000 American and South Korean front-line combat troops. His aggregate allied theater forces on the ground almost matched the combined Chinese and North Korean armies. As word got out of Ripper's success, Ridgway was deluged with congratulations from Generals Eisenhower and Bradley, Dean Rusk, and George Marshall—who all at various times had approved and disapproved of crossing the 38th Parallel, as the situation changed.

By April 5 there was yet another advance, "Operation Rugged," in which the American-led coalition recrossed parts of the 38th Parallel and occupied a new front dubbed "Line Kansas." A Chinese "Fifth Phase" offensive only temporarily pushed the Americans southward, who regrouped and fought their way back to their previous positions. In Ridgway's view, only such a steady series of offensives could get the Eighth Army back to, or slightly beyond, the 38th Parallel before the peacetime public back home revolted entirely at the staggering human and material cost of the war—and at some point would call an end to such a back-and-forth war of advance, retreat, and advance.

Truman finally relieved General MacArthur on April 11 and promoted Ridgway in his place—a move the president had long wished to make, but now found politically and militarily feasible given that the United Nations forces were once again at the 38th Parallel. General Ridgway had saved Korea. He had not criticized Truman's limitations on theater operations. And he had established a cadre of officers who were convinced that they could preserve the Rhee government without widening the war to China. MacArthur may have been an icon in America, but he was increasingly felt to be irrelevant on the ground in Korea—again, due to Ridgway's restoration of the American cause.

Truman also astutely wagered that after public anger over MacArthur's firing quieted down, an irate American people might soon come to the same conclusion. With the failure of the fifth Chinese offensive, and the appointment of General James Van Fleet to take over Ridgway's field command of the Eighth Army, Ridgway's promotion to theater commander ensured there would be no more public strategic arguments between military leaders and the Truman administration. In short, Ridgway's direct command of the battlefield ended after less than four months—with a stabilized front and United Nations forces in control of nearly all of South Korea. The war was back where it started six months earlier, something the Communists had never anticipated.

There would be off-and-on fighting around the 38th Parallel for the next two years, as both sides sought military advantage to influence the chronically stalled armistice talks that had begun in June 1951. In April 1952, after more than sixteen months in Korea and Japan, Matthew Ridgway was promoted to Supreme NATO Commander in Europe and left the Korean theater entirely, a year before the final armistice agreement. Eighth Army commander General Van Fleet would also be transferred before the armistice; he left Korea nine months after Ridgway, in February 1953. The Korean War for all practical purposes ended with the signing of the armistice treaty on July 27, 1953, with Generals Mark Clark and Maxwell Taylor in command of a mostly quiet front roughly along the 38th Parallel.

What had Matthew Ridgway actually done in roughly one hundred days on the ground, between late December and early April 1951, to ensure this remarkable turnaround that had saved South Korea?

Most important, he sparked a radical change in morale. Ridgway was at first appalled when he arrived at the front: "The men I met along the road, those I stopped to talk to and to solicit gripes from—they too all conveyed to me a conviction that this was a bewildered army, not sure of itself or its leaders, not sure what they were doing there, wondering when they would hear the whistle of that homebound transport."[51]

How did he turn the defeated in spirit to confident attackers? Ridgway immediately embarked on two sweeping changes. He insisted that soldiers be resupplied far more rapidly with warm clothing, hot food, regular mail service, and up-to-date weapons. One-third of the American troops, he discovered upon arrival in Korea, lacked proper winter protection. His concern with comfort was not intended to reward soldiers for retreating, but rather to demonstrate concern for their ordeal—and, more important, to ready them for the offensive challenge ahead. A restoration of fighting spirit, Ridgway argued, is something that "cannot be imposed from above, but that must be cultivated in every heart, from on up. It is rooted, I believe, in the individual's sense of security, of belonging to a unit that will stand by him, as units on both sides and in the rear stand by all other units."[52]

Ridgway forbade the use of the common slang term "bug out" to describe the collapse of the Eighth Army at the Yalu, even as he sought to ensure that it never happened again. Soldiers who met him on arrival found him "courteous." He publicly managed to praise MacArthur, even as he was determined never to repeat his superior's rash advance to the Chinese border—a decision made hundreds of miles away without knowledge of morale, terrain, or weather. Ridgway changed both strategy and attitudes without giving the impression that both General MacArthur and General Walker had committed grievous errors. Walker was dead and MacArthur in the midst of a political campaign of sorts; Ridgway felt that criticism of either would be a simple waste of time.[53]

Soon the defeated Eighth Army would be asked to fight in a more aggressive and more dangerous fashion, often in the hills away from supply depots below. "It was not their doing," Ridgway lamented, "that had brought them far under strength to this unfortunate country with major shortages in weaponry and insufficient clothing and food, and had spread them across an area far too wide for them to maintain an effective front." One of the hardest tasks for a general is to ask a defeated army to go back on the offensive when it is assured that it will suffer for the immediate future even more casualties before it eventually suffers less in victory. If the men could see that their commander was as cold as they were, walking among them, and dressed and eating like them, they would appreciate that their officers were one with them.

Ridgway was even more concerned about the defeatist mood among Walker's officer corps: "Every command post I visited gave me the same sense of lost confidence and lack of spirit. The leaders, from sergeant on up, seemed unresponsive, reluctant to answer my questions. Even their gripes had to be dragged out of them and information was provided glumly, without the alertness of men whose spirits are high."[54] He approached the problem in the same fashion that all successful generals have done. First, he would lead subordinate officers by example. The

Eighth Army main headquarters was 150 miles behind the lines; Ridgway moved it to the front. He immediately began driving to and flying over the advanced positions, meeting division commanders within his first few days of command—in much the same way that Major General George S. Patton had restored morale and confidence to shattered and retreating American forces under the command of a far distant and incompetent Major General Fredendall at the Kasserine Pass in February 1943.

Ridgway, just as Sherman had schooled himself about the topography of Georgia, memorized the battlefield and mastered the terrain: "Every road, every cart track, every hill, every stream, every ridge in that area where we were fighting or which we hope to control—they all became as familiar to me as the features of my own backyard."[55] Ridgway relieved several high officers—at one time or another the generals of at least five divisions—whom he deemed defeatist or "mediocre." The Pentagon was not pleased that Ridgway was promoting colonels and sending back sacked generals for whom there were no pre-retirement billets in Washington. But Ridgway pushed to reenergize the existing leadership with offensive zeal. "Don't want to see your defense plans," he told commanders in the field, "want to see your attack plans." He demanded that field officers, like his central command, get close to the fighting. Colonels and generals were to visit other battlefield posts to integrate tactics and support.[56]

He insisted that the Joint Chiefs and the political leadership back in Washington cease leaking to the press contingency plans for a retreat to Pusan or off the peninsula. Instead, he said, they should let it be known that the Americans would retake Seoul. Ridgway made his nonnegotiable objectives clear almost immediately to the shaky South Korean government.[57]

"Corrective measures," Ridgway argued, "could not be confined to Korea alone, however, for some of our major weaknesses had their roots in failures at home."[58] In response, by late January 1951, Ridgway had drafted a comprehensive manifesto, "Why Are We Here? What Are We Fighting For?" He had its talking points distributed to all the soldiers under his command. Because during the fiasco of December, soldiers loudly had complained that they had no business in a barren wasteland fighting Chinese while their South Korean allies often ran from the fight, Ridgway felt the entire American presence in Korea needed a uniform and easily referenced rationale. Why, after all, would a mechanic from New Jersey or an Iowa farmer risk dying in the bloom of youth in Korea to keep his far distant nuclear-armed homeland safe? Ridgway argued that what would win Korea was not just superior discipline and matériel, but confidence in American civilization and national purpose. If soldiers did not believe, they would not win.[59]

In his characteristically upbeat message to the troops, Ridgway systematically covered all the reasons for American intervention in his newly released manifesto: legal—the United Nations had authorized, and the U.S. Congress had funded, the defense of South Korea; moral—the Americans were fighting to preserve the freedom of the Korean people, to whom they had given their word and bond; political—his command was struggling to ensure Western freedoms to anyone who was willing to fight alongside for them, in what had become a global struggle to oppose a Communist creed that sought to end the freedom of the individual; and practical—the fight inside Korea was simply part of a larger war in which America was threatened by aggressive Communist totalitarianism. How well the United States fought abroad would determine to what degree it was safe at home. Or as Ridgway put it, "The real issues are whether the power of Western civilization, as God has permitted it to flower in our own beloved lands, shall defy and defeat Communism; whether the rule of men who shoot their prisoners, enslave their citizens, and deride the dignity of man, shall displace the rule of those to whom the individual and his individual rights are sacred."

Modern critics often caricature Ridgway's lofty rhetoric about Western civilization versus savagery—inasmuch as he tried to persuade his troops that the stakes were no less than the survival of Western culture, that Korea was the stage for a Manichean struggle between godless world Communism and liberal Christian democracy. Even his contemporary civilian superiors expressed unease with Ridgway's brutal labels for his offensives—names like Operation "Ripper" and "Killer"—that might unduly frighten the American public about the nature of a supposed "police action."

But Ridgway knew that this kind of war was new to American soldiers, not seen since the turn-of-the-century insurrection in the Philippines. It was simple to grasp the urgency of an existential global struggle like World War II. Asking soldiers to go into battle on behalf of "containment" was less easy to explain. Better, Ridgway felt, to emphasize how cruelly the Communists fought, and how such savagery was integral to their plans for global domination. That larger, more existential struggle might motivate an American soldier in a way that the doctrine of American geopolitical containment surely would not.

As part of this effort, early on Ridgway pushed to integrate the troops under his command—an issue that had been under consideration for nearly a decade and enjoyed the support of the Truman administration but had stalled through bureaucratic infighting, congressional opposition, and lethargy within the Army. Yet as Ridgway began to repel the Chinese assault, his moral authority grew, and by April 1951 he began integrating African Americans in the Korean theater into previously segregated units under his command. By July, most combat forces were integrated, and by the end of the war, all U.S. armed forces were for the most part desegregated.[60]

Ridgway's optimism soon proved infectious. Even by late January, Army Chief of Staff General J. Lawton Collins was reporting back from a visit to Korea that morale had almost immediately improved. Soon MacArthur himself was mixing in occasional upbeat appraisals in his otherwise gloomy reports. True, the improved American spirit in itself did not overnight stop the momentum of thousands of Chinese as they stormed into Seoul. But as stated, Ridgway noted that advantages were already accruing to the allies—increased troops, better equipment, new and superior weapons, more supplies, shorter lines of supply, more training for the South Koreans—that would soon tip the scales back in favor of the Americans.[61]

Ridgway changed tactics as well. He spread out his officers to hills and rough terrain. Advance would not be confined to roads. Soldiers would fight the Chinese at night. Unit commanders at the front would themselves have control over tactical air and artillery support. Control of terrain was to be considered fluid. Hurting the enemy rather than merely protecting a fixed line was the key. "There was nothing but our own love of comfort that bound us to the road. We too could get off into the hills, I reminded them, to find the enemy and fix him a position. I repeated to the commanders as forcefully as I could, the ancient Army slogan: Find them! Fix them! Fight Them! Finish Them!"[62]

Ridgway, as promised to his officers in December, now in the new year would dress like, live among, eat with, and become one with the nearly frozen troops on the ground. "Ridgway's concept of leadership," David Halberstam correctly concludes, "was better suited for a more egalitarian era. He intended not to impose his will on his men, but to allow the men under him to find something within themselves that would make them more confident, more purposeful fighting men. It was their confidence in themselves that would make them fight well, he believed, not so much their belief in him."[63]

Finally, Ridgway won over the press in a variety of ways, after his initial efforts to block real-time reporting. When the lines held, he gave credit to subordinates. When MacArthur flew in to take credit for much of what Ridgway had accomplished, the latter tactfully sent private memos back to MacArthur's headquarters in Tokyo suggesting that the general's boasts of quick restoration of the theater and impending offensives might violate confidentiality and tip off the enemy—sound military advice that the publicity-hungry but militarily astute MacArthur could accept without loss of face. Matthew Ridgway understood the power of imagery, especially the notion of confidence that an optimistic commander exudes. In the spirit of Patton's pearl-handled pistols, Ridgway charged about with a grenade on one shoulder strap, a medical kit on the other—a veritable "Prince Hal in suspenders and airborne jump trousers." When some press accounts described the medical kit as a second matching grenade, his men dubbed Ridgway "Old Iron Tits."

So be it, Ridgway thought, if it sent the public the message that they had a fighter on the ground to stop the Communists. Appearances mattered—if MacArthur looked like a stodgy, grandfatherly grandee poring over a map, a robust Ridgway would instead appear as if he was either off to or emerging from the front lines, in need of explosive power to stop the enemy and ready to treat his own wounds in the ordeal. He roamed the battlefield with his men in the manner of a scruffy Grant or Sherman, but chose also to demand the most minute details from his officers in the field, in emulation of George S. Patton or the Duke of Wellington, a man of order who might impose his mastery of order upon an amorphous and disorderly army. If he was heroic in his insistence of keeping at the front and risking his person, Ridgway was also "antiheroic" in his leadership style by trying to convey to his men that their general was dressed like them and would share the same dangers, one way or other.[64]

Ridgway's picture would appear on the covers of *Life* and *Newsweek* over the next two years, and he was plastered on the front page of all the major papers. The Ridgway square jaw, erect posture, and enigmatic expression—part grimace, part smile—conveyed exactly the right image to disheartened troops and a weary home front: a can-do American unworried about either the freezing cold or the hundreds of thousands of Chinese on the peninsula, neither depressed that the war was to be lost

General Matthew Ridgway arrived in Korea at age fifty-five in mid-winter. Here, in Grant-like fashion, the determined Ridgway appears with winter cap and in the dress of a common soldier, with his trademark grenade strapped to his right shoulder. Photo by Carl Mydans/Time & Life Pictures/ Getty Images.

nor falsely jubilant that it was already won. In contrast, MacArthur played constantly to the cameras, but he instead appeared aged, tired, and frail—and in fact was all three. Since no one seemed to accept responsibility for the orphaned war, Ridgway filled the void and often thereby earned the unfair charge of narcissism—in the fashion leveled at both "Uncle Billy" Sherman and "King" David Petraeus.[65]

Who Was Matthew Ridgway?

When he assumed command of the Eighth Army in December 1950, few American officers were better qualified for the multifaceted challenges in Korea than Matthew Ridgway. He was fifty-five years old and had been in the Army since 1917, almost thirty-three years—a graduate of

West Point, and son of a West Point graduate. At forty-nine, Ridgway had parachuted into Normandy on D-Day as commanding general of the 82nd Airborne Division after a distinguished record in Italy. Later he commanded a corps during the disastrous failed Allied attempt to vault over the Rhine (Operation Market Garden) in September 1944. Ridgway fought against the German Ardennes Offensive, known more popularly as the Battle of the Bulge, and he had helped restore American lines after a near collapse—a similar winter temporary disintegration analogous to the later Korean bug-out, and also followed by overreach and vulnerability to a counterattacking enemy. Ridgway finished the European theater as an airborne corps commander and was promoted to lieutenant general. In both Europe and Korea, Ridgway found himself on the front lines and on isolated occasions in actual combat. Based on his past performance, the trademark live grenade attached to his chest was not for mere show.[66]

His philosophy of war was Thucydidean: Because human nature remained constant and transcended changes in culture and technology, the principles of war remained eternal. They were unchanging—whether fighting against Germans or Communist Chinese, whether in the age of gunpowder or in the new nuclear age. Personal leadership, the closer to the front the better, was as important in Korea as in the past—both to anticipate crises and in demonstrable fashion to share hardships with the rank and file.[67]

Yet Matthew Ridgway could not have been an easy person to know. If he seemed a soldier right out of central casting—formal, ramrod-straight, and in excellent physical condition—he was also a stern, often self-righteous moralist, judgmental and outspoken in his tastes, a man respected and admired rather than liked or enjoyed. He found MacArthur a publicity-mad egotist. Yet in his own, more understated way, Ridgway successfully courted the press and framed the American recovery around his own indomitable will. Before Korea, Ridgway had argued successfully to defer a poorly thought-out and potentially suicidal airborne assault on Rome in September 1943 in the last hours before the planes were due to take off. He had landed on D-Day and helped to save the scattered and error-plagued airdrop. It was Ridgway who would later persuade President Eisenhower not to send ground troops to save the French at Dien Bien Phu.

At times, Ridgway's loud Puritanism seemed at odds with his own private life. He married three times. He idolized his young third wife, yet

General Douglas MacArthur is photographed here in Manila in 1945, five years before the outbreak of the Korean War. MacArthur was one of the most photographed figures of the postwar era and enjoyed sizable support for a 1948 presidential run—making Ridgway's task to save MacArthur's war a diplomatic and military minefield. Photo courtesy of the National Archives and Records Administration.

left for Korea without even telling her exactly when he had departed. While he confronted superiors with blunt talk, Ridgway had a sense of detachment about himself that ensured his principles would outweigh career considerations. That very self-control may have led, in the fall of 1945, while he was on postwar occupation duty, to a serious heart attack. After blacking out and waking up in a hospital, Ridgway rejected his doctor's advice that he be relieved of duty and return immediately to the United States for extensive tests. Instead, after a brief recuperation, he promptly went back to work—and went on to live for another forty-eight years.[68]

Despite the general consensus that Ridgway was the "perfect" soldier, at one point almost every senior officer who mattered in Korea was suspicious, jealous, or hostile to him. MacArthur claimed credit for his success and gave private interviews deprecating Ridgway's abilities while assuring Ridgway personally and publicly that he had MacArthur's full support—a duplicity Ridgway himself only years later came to fathom. Indeed, MacArthur freely lampooned Ridgway to the media. He called his strategy of incrementally regaining ground from the Communists as "an accordion war," implicitly to be contrasted with MacArthur's swashbuckling Inchon gamble and march to the Yalu to end the conflict for good.[69]

Dwight D. Eisenhower would later write a book wrongly claiming that General Van Fleet, not Ridgway himself, had retaken Seoul—a month before Van Fleet had even arrived in Korea. Van Fleet would suggest that he was later stopped by Ridgway from realizing MacArthur's dream of reuniting Korea. After Ridgway's later testimony before a Senate hearing that Eisenhower's planned defense cutbacks endangered national security, and because of near-constant fighting with the administration over its proposed massive budget cuts to the Army, Eisenhower did not reappoint Ridgway for a second term as Army chief of staff. Ridgway retired at sixty in 1955, in some bitterness at having been on the bad side of the most popular and influential American of the age. His friend and former subordinate General Maxwell Taylor would replace him and find success in implementing many of Ridgway's ideas about more flexible military responses in the nuclear age, given his superior political instincts and more engaging personality. We forget today that the subsequent half-century tradition of fighting "limited wars" in the nuclear age was first established by Matthew Ridgway, though it is rarely credited to him. At best, for decades Ridgway's achievement was largely forgotten. At worst, generals and politicians in hindsight blamed him for not reuniting all of Korea, although most at one time or another had early despaired of saving even the south.[70]

Ridgway and Eisenhower would subsequently clash again over possible intervention in Vietnam, and over a score of other issues: Ridgway's criticism of Eisenhower's neoimperialistic notions about Southeast Asia; Eisenhower's failure to defend military officers from the demagogic tactics of Senator Joe McCarthy; and Ridgway's adamant argument that nuclear weapons did not preclude the possibility of conventional war or the need for large conventional ground forces. Since Ridgway may not have been the first choice of Chairman of the Joint Chiefs Joe Collins to replace General Walker, it was not always clear whether Ridgway could rely on Collins's unwavering support. Even when he was promoted to theater commander to assume MacArthur's billet, Ridgway was not consulted about his own replacement to lead the Eighth Army, General Van Fleet. The latter, in fact, was neither Ridgway's favorite nor even considered particularly friendly, but he nonetheless was a talented commander who would work well with his superior.[71]

The blunt-talking Ridgway earned controversy for the rest of his long postwar career. As NATO commander he offended Europeans by surrounding himself almost exclusively with American officers, apparently in the belief that there was no advantage in disguising the reality that the United States contributed an inordinate amount of manpower and treasure to the alliance. Few subsequent supreme commanders have followed his chauvinistic example. Always the iconoclast, he would be pilloried by the right as too liberal in his reluctance to commit U.S. ground troops abroad, while the left saw him as hopelessly reactionary; he was caricatured both as an ossified defender of military tradition and as a rebel within the brotherhood of officers. Conservatives came to believe that he had stopped unnecessarily at the 38th Parallel; liberals felt he was too promiscuous in his use of lethal force, causing collateral damage among Korean civilians.

During the 1960s, Ridgway set out his past differences with military icons like Eisenhower, MacArthur, and Van Fleet, and his own contemporary unease with the Vietnam War, in two memoirs, in part drawn from a series of magazine articles such as *Soldier: The Memoirs of Matthew B. Ridgway* and *The Korean War: How We Met the Challenge; How All-Out Asian War Was Averted; Why MacArthur Was Dismissed; Why Today's War Objectives Must Be Limited*. In the latter, the lengthy subtitles announced Ridgway's didactic intentions to shed light on the complex character of Douglas MacArthur, who is sometimes savagely derided for theatrics and ego but nevertheless praised for his astute strategic and geopolitical sense. During the Vietnam War, Ridgway offended hawks by loudly explaining why an optional land war in Vietnam was unfeasible and unnecessary. He probably disturbed doves even more by insisting that we must win any war that we undertake, even if it was begun foolishly and was poorly conducted. The cultural upheaval of the 1960s and 1970s repelled him, especially the attacks on the United States government by antiwar protesters at a time of national conflict.

Without the support of Matthew Ridgway, it is doubtful that combat brigades in Korea would have been so successfully racially integrated. Yet the reformer who had pushed for racial integration within the ranks during the Korean War—calling segregation both "anti-American and un-Christian"—later loudly opposed the full integration of women into the armed services. Even more adamantly, he fought the volunteer army, insisting that military service was critical to inculcate democratic values among the nation's youth—and, more controversially, to prevent decadence among idle and comfortable teenagers.[72] Ridgway was not shy in promulgating traditional views on military service that were becoming largely repugnant to a modern audience—namely, that military preparedness and sacrifice were critical to a society not merely for its protection and survival, but also to ward off the dangers of affluence and leisure, which always tend to enervate a prosperous democratic people in times of peace.

Yet in the dark days of the early 1950s—when the Soviet Union had exploded nuclear bombs (an atomic bomb in 1949, a hydrogen bomb in 1953), when China and much of Korea, like Eastern Europe, had gone Communist, when there were both Communist witch hunts and plenty of Communist sympathizers inside the government—Matthew Ridgway provided a needed antidote to Douglas MacArthur's insubordination and attempted usurpation of civilian control over the military. One of Ridgway's first acts as MacArthur's replacement in April 1951 was to issue a directive to all senior American ground, naval, and air commanders in the theater to remember their commitment to civilian oversight—and not to exceed limitations placed on their commands by those in Washington worried about the outbreak of World War III.[73]

Later, Ridgway saw his reinforcing of respect for civilian oversight as one of his greatest achievements: "Once a policy is set, however, it is the military man, in keeping with the oath he takes and with the very phrasing of his commission, who should either execute that policy or resign from the service. General MacArthur would have introduced a wholly different doctrine from this." Without the genius of Matthew Ridgway and his restoration of Korea, it is hard to imagine that Truman either would have been confident enough to have relieved MacArthur, or, having once dismissed him, would have eventually won back some grudging public support for his controversial decision. In that sense, Ridgway saved the Truman presidency. That nuclear weapons were not used in Korea was largely due to the skill and sobriety of Matthew Ridgway.[74]

Ridgway's personal life after Korea was as checkered as his professional one. As a public defender of traditional American values, Ridgway was not merely married three times and divorced twice, but was wedded finally to a spouse twenty-three years his junior. He and his wife, Penny, lost their only son, Matthew, to a freak accident in Canada. After that tragedy, Ridgway never quite recovered his optimism. By the late 1960s he usually waded into popular controversy only to offer blunt, often insightful, but in the end polarizing, if not cranky, assessments. His two daughters from a second marriage remained mostly estranged from him until his death.

Matthew Ridgway finally received the Presidential Medal of Freedom in 1986, at the age of ninety-one—thirty-five years after his remarkable tenure as commander of the Eighth Army in Korea. In his citation, President Ronald Reagan remarked of Ridgway, "Heroes come when they're needed; great men step forward when courage seems in short supply." Ridgway's contemporaries George Marshall and Omar Bradley earlier had praised him as one of the finest American soldiers America produced.

Yet even then controversy followed the old iconoclast. The year before, Ridgway had been invited by then president Ronald Reagan to accompany him on a controversial visit to the German military cemetery at Bitburg, where, it was belatedly discovered, some Waffen SS troops were buried. Rather than cancel the goodwill ceremony between the American and German governments, the Reagan administration—amid growing popular anger in the United States—had desperately searched for a senior American officer who might go to Bitburg and salvage the ill-advised visit. Ridgway, as one of the highest-ranking surviving American Second World War generals, met former adversary Luftwaffe General Johannes Steinhoff. Both placed wreaths on the graves of the dead in a public ceremony of reconciliation, a token that seemed to have offered moral cover for the embarrassment of the Reagan administration's poorly researched choice of cemeteries. In turn, Ridgway's gesture was seen by a cynical press that had forgotten Korea as justification for the long-overdue award from a grateful Reagan.[75]

Five years later, after the awarding of the Medal of Freedom in 1986, Ridgway received the Congressional Gold Medal, just two years before his death. But four decades after Korea, most Americans had forgotten the details of the horrific winter of 1950–51, Ridgway's tenure in Tokyo, and his long battles to avoid both a strategy of a monolithic nuclear response and a large ground war in Asia. They did not remember the Korea of 1951, whose salvation had long been overshadowed by the tragedy of Vietnam.

Dwight Eisenhower and Omar Bradley are often considered America's preeminent twentieth-century American military heroes, George S. Patton as the embodiment of American audacity. Douglas MacArthur is enshrined for his return to the Philippines. Matthew Ridgway might have outshone them all—had Korea not been a "police action" more comfortably forgotten, and had he not, in his subsequent long life, been so blunt and unpredictable in his assessments.

At a time of increasing wealth and leisure at home, when in the early 1950s Americans were already beginning to express doubts about both the morality and competency of their culture, Matthew Ridgway was a throwback to an earlier age of little self-doubt. To Ridgway, the American system was superior to all others, its Constitution was near perfect; and its people were freer and more prosperous precisely because of an exceptional national character that encouraged and rewarded rugged individualism. True, he fought furiously in Korea to save the geopolitical stature of the United States. But in both his speeches and his communiqués, Ridgway made clear that the war was a larger referendum on his own civilization—one that he was not about to lose, either for himself or for the people who had sent him so far from home.[76]

A Korea Still Divided

More than a million Korean civilians perished in the horrific three-year-long war. Some estimates double that number. Over two million Communist Chinese and North Korean troops were killed or wounded, though the full extent of their losses has never been published. South Korean and United Nations forces suffered a million and a half casualties. The United States suffered 157,530 killed, wounded, or missing, among them 36,516 combat fatalities—and spent more than $500 billion in today's dollars—to save only South Korea, and not, as once envisioned in autumn 1950, to reunite the entire peninsula. Altogether, more than 4 million Korean, Chinese, American, and allied troops and civilians perished in the war, at a minimum. Carpet bombing and massive shelling had decimated Chinese ranks but also resulted in frequent collateral damage to friendly populations. Sometimes American animosity toward North Korean and Chinese Communists became racial and made subsequent relations with South Korean allies problematic.

This war—unnecessary to some—ended three years later right where it had begun, at the 38th Parallel. Why did so many hundreds of thousands have to die only to return to the status quo ante bellum—a Communist-backed dictatorship in the north, and an American-supported authoritarian government in the south? General Matthew Ridgway's answer was that the costly effort had stopped Communist aggression. Americans had given the South Koreans a chance to find their own destiny. And for the first time in the nascent Cold War, a stand in Korea had reminded the Communist bloc that the United States could and would protect its allies.[77]

Matthew Ridgway saved Korea from an unmitigated military disaster not of his own making. In the process, he realized his earlier ideas of how to contain Asian Communism without resorting to either nuclear weapons or a wider land war. Before Korea, Ridgway had made the argument for a strong conventional army in an age when too many dreamers and cost cutters alike wished to retreat to a fortress America protected by a nuclear Strategic Air Command. Very rarely has any American general (other than William Tecumseh Sherman and David Petraeus), in so short a time, radically changed tactics at the front while integrating such operational doctrine in a wider strategic framework of fighting.

The truth was that just as Ridgway had been a rare operational optimist during his one hundred days as the head of the Eighth Army, as theater commander, he became pessimistic concerning the American ability to unify all of North Korea against overwhelming Chinese numerical superiority while maintaining public support for a major drawn-out Asian war that risked becoming nuclear. Ridgway the tactician felt that the reformed American army could go back to the Yalu, but as a strategist he feared that its success would mean a never-ending and ultimately unsustainable commitment.[78]

Ridgway and the Verdict of History

There are few parallels in modern American military history to Ridgway's radical restoration of a lost war in so short a time. Even if one argues that the conditions of Ridgway's appointment were, in hindsight, somewhat favorable—an arrival when Chinese forces were nearing exhaustion at their furthest point away from their supplies, followed by subsequent rapid promotion to theater command in Tokyo before the acrimony arose over whether to press far beyond the 38th Parallel—someone had to take shattered forces and use them to quell ascendant ones.

The winter and spring 1951 American offensives are analogous to the Battle of Midway and Guadalcanal that were turning points in the Pacific war, coming less than a year after disaster at Pearl Harbor. In similar fashion, Ulysses S. Grant, at his victories at Fort Henry, Fort Donelson, Shiloh, and Vicksburg, restored the western front, and indeed the Northern cause itself, during the Civil War. General Creighton Abrams had stabilized Vietnam by 1973 and allowed the Paris peace talks to proceed on the basis of a two-state solution. Yet Ridgway's victory in Korea was different from other restorations, in that he rescued an entire war with geopolitical significance—not just a campaign or theater.

Should the Chinese-led offensive have continued unimpeded southward past Seoul, the United States, as planned, would have withdrawn from Pusan to either Japan or Taiwan. Such a defeat would have ensured thousands more American casualties, the loss of more equipment, and the extinction of the South Korean government. The Soviet Union would have had to become even more bellicose to match the rising stature of its client Mao Zedong's victorious Red Chinese army and to maintain its mantle of exporting global Communism.

There would have been no South Korean miracle—no Hyundai, Kia, or Samsung global brands, no evolution to democracy. Millions more Koreans would have had their lives reduced to the wretched misery that is the norm of contemporary North Korea—a country that, had it the combined population and resources of the entire Korean peninsula, would have posed a far greater threat than does the nuclear North today. An emboldened China would have turned its attention to Taiwan—convinced that a defeated America could not, or would not, send troops to protect its friends. A Chinese invasion of Taiwan could either have led to the annexation of Taiwan outright, or probably served as the catalyst for a nuclear response from the United States.

Instead, the enormous losses China suffered in Korea between January and April 1950 from American artillery and air strikes left an indelible impression on its leadership about confronting U.S. forces—and might explain its later reluctance to intervene overtly in Vietnam in the fashion it had in Korea. According to historian Bin Yu, himself a veteran of the People's Liberation Army, "The most important lesson that China learned from its engagement in the Korean War is to avoid or prevent such a war in the future, or both. Although it fought the war into a stalemate with the most powerful military in the world, Beijing paid a tremendous price economically, diplomatically, and strategically."

In retrospect, at least a few of Ridgway's peers acknowledged, if belatedly, his stunning achievement. General of the Army Omar Bradley much later remarked, "His brilliant, driving, uncompromising leadership would turn the tide of battle like no other general's in our military history." After witnessing Ridgway in the field, one colonel summed up the opinion of more junior officers in Korea by remarking of his turnaround that it was "one of the marvels of military history." Forty years later, at Ridgway's May 1993 funeral, Chairman of the Joint Chiefs General Colin Powell could still declare, "Every American soldier owes a debt to this man."[79]

That both South Korea and Taiwan are today successful democracies, that MacArthur's vision of an all-out war to roll back Asian Communism through the use of nuclear arms did not come to pass, and that the United States military still fought successful conventional wars abroad at the height of the Cold War nuclear standoff are largely due to the still underappreciated miracle brought about by General Matthew Ridgway—all in just those hundred days in Korea.

CHAPTER FIVE

Iraq Is "Lost"

David Petraeus and the Surge in Iraq—
January 2007–May 2008

"The Willing Suspension of Disbelief" (*September 10–11, 2007*)

The questioning grew sharper and the speechmaking windier. September 11, 2007, was turning into a long day on Capitol Hill for the bemedaled, rather diminutive general back from Baghdad to report to a skeptical Congress for a few hours.

General David Petraeus, Commander of Multi-National Forces–Iraq, nevertheless thought that he had good news about the months-long surge of about thirty thousand additional American forces into Iraq to quell rising violence. The four-year-long effort in Iraq, deemed lost to internecine mayhem and foreign-inspired terrorism, had gradually since February begun to stabilize. Or at least that is what Petraeus and his staff believed. In his first year of supreme command in Iraq, David Petraeus already thought he could explain to his civilian overseers why and how the controversial surge had brought about this encouraging change of events—and why they should not give up on the strategy when it was showing concrete results.

The additional troops—initially dispatched early in 2007 following President Bush's January promise to send more help to the theater—were in place by June. Petraeus was prepared with charts and statistics to reassure doubting congressional leaders that the beefed-up American presence—along with his command's changes in tactics—had at last hit on the right formula to turn around the violent country.

The surge was working, if ever so slowly. His combat teams had swept out of their compounds. They had decentralized their operations and concentrated on protecting Iraqis from sectarian violence and ensuring the delivery of basic services. Petraeus sought to explain to his overseers why his change in tactics and greater manpower would lead to fewer American deaths, fewer Iraqi deaths, and fewer terrorist incidents. Such progress would only accelerate, if the surge was still funded and supported at home, or so Petraeus argued to Congress. The unpopular Iraq War, in other words, was not yet lost.

Along with the American ambassador to Iraq, Ryan Crocker, Petraeus reviewed the metrics of the first eight months of the surge. The good news ranged from increased electrical production to fewer U.S. losses in the last two months. They were summarized by Petraeus's confident assurance that "The military objectives of the surge are, in large measure, being met." The general went on to explain how radical Islamic terrorists of all stripes were suffering grievous losses in Iraq. "Coalition and Iraqi forces," Petraeus emphasized, "have dealt significant blows to Al Qaeda–Iraq." At the same time, Petraeus added, "We have also disrupted Shia militia extremists." American casualty figures, at least, were starting to bear out the general's confidence. September 2007 would end in less than three weeks with 68 American deaths that month in Iraq. That was down from the war's highest toll of 126 fatalities in May, and soon to drop to 23 in December.[1]

One reason for the good news, according to Petraeus's testimony, was that the Iraqis themselves were also fighting better than ever: "Iraqi Security Forces have also continued to grow and to shoulder more of the load." But his optimism went beyond just the battlefield. Petraeus's counterinsurgency strategy was improving the lives of everyday Iraqis who might see Americans at last as partners rather than occupiers. Because of additional positive signs of growing Iraqi political stability, good figures on economic improvement, and reduced civil violence, Petraeus finished his testimony with a glowing summation: "Our country's men and women in uniform have done a magnificent job in the most complex and challenging environment imaginable. All Americans should be very proud of their sons and daughters serving in Iraq today."

Ambassador Crocker shared the cautiously optimistic appraisal of the surge's effects, albeit with a disturbing warning to the wavering Congress: "I cannot guarantee success in Iraq. I do believe, as I have described, that it is attainable. I am certain that abandoning or drastically curtailing our efforts will bring failure, and the consequences of such a failure must be clearly understood."[2]

Had the general and the ambassador convinced skeptical senators and representatives that widely unpopular President George W. Bush's January 2007 desperate gamble to send more troops into the Iraqi inferno had begun to pay off? Given the political dimensions to the issue, it was more complicated than a simple yes or no answer. Many Democratic would-be presidential luminaries on the other side of the Senate hearing table—Senators Joe Biden (D-DE), Hillary Clinton (D-NY), Chris Dodd (D-CT)—had not only voted for the war in October 2002, but subsequently chastised the Bush administration for not sending enough troops to secure the peace.

In October 2002, pro-war speeches by Senators Joe Biden, John Kerry (D-MA), and Harry Reid (D-NV) were among the most passionate in calling for Saddam Hussein's removal for violating past accords and seeking weapons of mass destruction. In fact, these former supporters of the war had once couched their support for his removal as a continuation of the Clinton administration's official call for regime change. For them, a public grilling was to be a marquee occasion to prove to a country, turned off by the unexpectedly violent and costly Iraq War, that they were as antiwar as they had been pro-war just four years earlier.

Iraq in the public mind had descended from a brilliantly conceived three-week victory by April 2003, to a terrible mishap plagued by too few troops in early 2004—to what, exactly, now in September 2007? Few were certain. Whereas there once had been millions of parents of the war, it was now a veritable orphan.[3]

In the questioning to follow—perhaps the most acrimonious congressional hearings about an ongoing war since deposed General Douglas MacArthur's appearance to review the Korean War nearly sixty years earlier in May and June 1951—Petraeus's testimony was met by near-universal skepticism. Although the military in Iraq did not calibrate the success or failure of the surge by the number of U.S. casualties, nonetheless, 2007 was on track to record the most U.S. fatalities in the entire history of the war—despite a clear tapering off of American losses in August and September 2007. Nevertheless, 904 Americans would die by year's end. Even more might perish in 2008, as thousands of Petraeus's troops left fortified compounds and began to intermingle far more with the civilian population. Was not the previous strategy of General Casey and General Abizaid—one that emphasized a lower military profile—the right one in a politicized climate that worried more about American battle casualties than about quelling ethnic and sectarian violence?

At times, some senators displayed open scorn for Petraeus and his surge—perhaps because the September 2007 hearings had roughly coincided with the kickoff of the 2008 presidential campaign. Moreover, Petraeus was not just supreme commander in Iraq, but had become a symbol of a wider strategic and political effort to justify the Iraq War. Lame-duck president George W. Bush was at his most unpopular since assuming office, with the Republicans in disarray after their shattering losses in the 2006 congressional midterm elections that had proven a referendum on an unpopular war. A sharp antiwar stance seemed a requisite for any serious Democratic presidential contender. Most senators at the hearings intended to make the most of their free televised time in showing the nation how Petraeus—and indeed the Bush administration—was wasting more blood and treasure in the hopeless quagmire in Iraq.

Petraeus's televised inquisitors knew well enough that the most recent polls showed that 64 percent of the American people did not approve of the Iraq War. Few interrogators were about to buy any of Petraeus's rosy scenarios when most Americans did not. Almost immediately upon the conclusion of the testimonies, senators would do ad hoc interviews outside the hearing room that began with flamboyant dismissals of Petraeus's optimism.[4]

In late 2007, Senator Hillary Clinton in most polls led all her Democratic rivals for the 2008 party nomination. After Petraeus finished his testimony, she grilled the general and essentially called him untrustworthy: "I think that the reports that you provide to us really require the willing suspension of disbelief. Any of the metrics that have been referenced in your many hours of testimony, any fair reading of the advantages and disadvantages accruing post-surge, in my view, end up on the down side."

It was hard to tell whether Clinton was accusing Petraeus of deliberately distorting data, or simply offering a disingenuous and false analysis of the otherwise reliable information that he had supplied to Congress. She seemed to be worried that her chief Democratic rival, Barack Obama—who was not a senator in October 2002 when Congress (including Senator Clinton) had authorized the use of force to remove Saddam Hussein—had emphasized his far earlier antiwar pedigree. In any case, she had been on record by early 2007 as wanting a unilateral American withdrawal from Iraq: "You've got to know when to hold 'em, and know when to fold 'em. It is my judgment that it is time for us to disengage from Iraq."[5]

Most presidential hopefuls did not bother much with questioning Petraeus or Crocker at all. Senator Obama, for example, lectured both witnesses for seven minutes without pausing for a reaction from either—or posing a question. He concluded, "We have now set the bar so low that modest improvement in what was a completely chaotic situation, to the point where now we just have the levels of intolerable violence that existed in June of 2006 is considered success, and it's not. This continues to be a disastrous foreign policy mistake."

In fact, candidate Obama's present assessment was rather mild compared to his earlier negative assertions. But it fairly represented a growing American weariness with the five-year-old war. He had greeted the announcement of the Petraeus surge in January 2007 with an especially pessimistic forecast: "I am not persuaded that 20,000 additional troops in Iraq is going to solve the sectarian violence there. In fact, I think it will do the reverse." If there was any doubt of Senator Obama's contention that the surge was not only not working, but making things worse, he had made his views even clearer four days later following the hearings: "I don't know any expert on the region or any military officer that I've spoken to privately that believes that that is going to make a substantial difference on the situation on the ground." In January 2007 he had already called for all American combat forces to be completely withdrawn from Iraq by March 31, 2008—with the departure of troops to start before the surge had even begun. Even as the surge had proceeded, Obama persisted in declaring the troop increase a failure—to the approbation of both a growing antiwar base and a majority of Americans. While campaigning in New Hampshire on July 20, 2007, for example, Obama had stated as fact the surge's failure: "Here's what we know. The surge has not worked."[6]

By the time of the hearings it was clearly advantageous for candidate Obama's budding foreign policy reputation to remind the country that he had long predicted the present failure. Now on national television, he, like other senators, was not prepared to let General Petraeus get away with what he felt was a false impression that the surge was working or that his own earlier prognostications were flawed.

A more seasoned presidential contender, the Democratic chairman of the Senate Foreign Relations Committee, Senator Joe Biden—who had visited Iraq frequently—on the day before the hearings had preempted Senator Clinton's dismissal of Petraeus's testimony by assuring the country that Petraeus was "dead flat wrong." The next day, during the actual proceedings, Senator Biden questioned the general's statistics, provided his own anecdotes about the impossibility of traveling in Iraq, and tutored Petraeus on the senator's own partition plan to set up contiguous independent Kurdish, Shiite, and Sunni enclaves—a trisection proposal that he would soon push through the Senate on a nonbinding resolution that was to be largely forgotten as the violence subsided.[7]

The influential Senate majority leader, Harry Reid, while not a member of the Senate Foreign Relations Committee, had already gone further than any congressional critic of the war. In April 2007—five months before the hearings—Reid had proclaimed that "this war is lost and the surge is not accomplishing anything." Not much later, Reid, like others, once again questioned Petraeus's optimism on the surge: "He's made a number of statements over the years that have not proven to be factual." Meanwhile, outside the hearing, committee member and presidential candidate Senator Dodd scoffed that Petraeus was engaging in "happy talk."[8]

The senatorial consensus was that General Petraeus was not telling the truth, even under oath—an appraisal shared by many liberal House members as well. The chairman of the House Foreign Affairs Committee, Tom Lantos of California, blasted Petraeus and Crocker with more euphemisms for dishonesty: "We can no longer take their assertions on Iraq at face value." Petraeus and the surge were a political hot potato as public opinion continued to swing sharply against the war. The general was in danger of being reduced to a partisan defender of an unpopular administration rather than a military officer trying to win a lost war for his country.

Some of the popular reaction was just as harsh about Petraeus himself. Perhaps the nadir came on the very first day of his testimony. On September 10, 2007, the *New York Times* ran a MoveOn.org ad—at a generous discount of less than half the normal advertising rate and contrary to its own policies of not accepting ad hominem ads—with the provocative headline GENERAL PETRAEUS OR GENERAL BETRAY US? The ad went on to suggest that the general was a liar and perhaps even traitorous: Petraeus was supposedly a commander "constantly at war with the facts," in "an unwinnable religious civil war." The ad further predicted that "Today, before Congress and before the American people, General Petraeus is likely to become General Betray Us."

Few senators, and fewer even in the media, could appreciate that in fact the surge was already starting to bring some calm to Iraq, despite the increase in violence for the twelve-month period following mid-2006. Indeed, though 2007 would prove to be the costliest year since the start of the war in terms of lost American lives, combat fatalities nonetheless would be more than halved in 2008—and then halved again in 2009. Even more telling, by the time of the September congressional hearings, Iraq civilian deaths had, as Petraeus pointed out, already dramatically plummeted in just a year, from 3,389 in September 2006 to 752 in September 2007. These figures did not necessarily suggest that the insurgents were losing the struggle—only that the American military had a chance to gain more time to stabilize the country.

There was still no indication in September that in just a few weeks' time, American casualties would abruptly drop to twenty-three dead in the month of December 2007. That would be the lowest monthly figure since early 2004, when the violence had erupted into open warfare. The more Petraeus attempted to convince Congress by his own preliminary data that the incipient surge was beginning to work in calming Iraq, the more his inquisitors ignored his testimony and played to the general public anger.[9]

The entire mood of the country—and well beyond America's shores as well—had been polarized since before the war began, in a fashion not seen since the Vietnam War years or perhaps the pre–Civil War era. Michael Moore, the controversial documentary filmmaker, had seemingly wished for an insurgent victory—comparing the insurgents in Iraq to Americans' revolutionary forefathers. Apparently, Moore envisioned American casualties as a sort of penance for our unwise and immoral involvement: "The Iraqis who have risen up against the occupation are not 'insurgents or 'terrorists' or 'The Enemy.' They are the REVOLUTION, the Minutemen, and their numbers will grow—and they will win. Get it, Mr. Bush? . . . I'm sorry, but the majority of Americans supported this war once it began and, sadly, that majority must sacrifice their children until enough blood has been let that maybe—just maybe—God and the Iraqi people will forgive us in the end."

Even greater anger against the war had emerged in a variety of venues. A 2004 novel by Nicholson Baker, *Checkpoint*, contemplated the assassination of the wartime commander in chief George W. Bush—a topic again taken up in a later film shown at the 2006 Toronto Film Festival, the International Critics Prize–winning "mockumentary," Gabriel Range's *Death of a President*. In a 2004 op-ed in the British *Guardian*, one Charles Brooker had wished out loud for a return of John Wilkes Booth and Lee Harvey Oswald ("Where are you when we need you?"). This global animus toward George W. Bush seemed to rub off on any civilian or military official who agreed that the controversial decision to go into Iraq did not necessarily need to end in the loss of the country to insurgency and an abject American withdrawal. Many officers privately no doubt objected to the strategic rationale of going into Iraq in the first place, but still felt that the only thing worse than fighting a poorly conceived war was losing it.[10]

But how exactly had a previously little-known and apolitical General David Petraeus ended up in this maelstrom of trying to save an orphaned war—one authorized by both houses of Congress, once supported by 70 percent of the American people, and just a few years earlier seen as the centerpiece of the Bush administration's successful efforts to destroy the nexus between Middle East authoritarians and international terrorism?

From "Mission Accomplished" to Abject Nightmare (*March 2003–December 2006*)

There was a variety of reasons, some understandable and others less so, why the public welcomed this second, and clearly more controversial, post-9/11 war. As a practical matter, the prior Afghanistan intervention—begun eighteen months earlier, on October 7, 2001—had seemingly gone brilliantly, with 88 percent of the public voicing support even as experts warned that the country was "the graveyard of empires" and could never be kept free of the Taliban. Yet the last cadres of the ruling Taliban were expelled from most of the cities of Afghanistan by December 17, 2001, just nine weeks after the invasion—at a cost of only twelve American dead. By January, Afghan tribal elders were meeting in Europe to form a quasi-constitutional state. In 2001, the notion that Taliban diehards would still be killing Americans a decade later seemed remote.

The United Nations had sanctioned the occupation of Afghanistan. European members of NATO, as they had in the Korean War, pledged to send peacekeeping troops to oversee what appeared to be an amazingly abrupt transition from theocracy to some sort of democracy. If Afghanistan had been liberated in less than nine weeks, with a consensual government in place in four months, then Saddam's Iraq—which the U.S. military had already defeated easily in 1991—in such a comparative calculus might be overrun in a three-or-four-week "cakewalk," followed by an interim government within a year. At least that was the thinking among some of the more optimistic proponents of the war and perhaps the public at large.[11]

On October 11, 2002, the U.S. Congress approved, by wide margins in both houses, a joint resolution authorizing the use of force to remove Saddam Hussein. In some sense, this act was merely a restatement of a prior 1998 congressional authorization for "regime change" in Iraq, supported and signed by Bill Clinton. Apparently a majority in Congress felt that after twelve years of a cold war with Saddam Hussein, characterized by constant patrolling of Iraqi airspace, it was time to confront the regime—especially given Saddam's occasional support for terrorists of various sorts in a post–September 11 climate. At the time, many of America's traditional allies—the United Kingdom, Italy, Spain, Poland, Australia, and others—accepted that the American decision to force Saddam Hussein to comply with UN resolutions was the right one, even if the UN Security Council finally balked at authorizing a war to remove the Iraqi regime, and there were loud NATO dissenters such as France and Russia.[12]

The U.S. Congress accordingly cited twenty-three causes for war. Almost every writ imaginable was included in the resolution for the use of armed force. The congressional checklist ranged from Saddam's genocidal practices ("by continuing to engage in brutal repression of its civilian population thereby threatening international peace and security in the region") and his subsidies to terrorists of all stripes ("to aid and harbor other international terrorist organizations") to his trying to kill former president Bush and opposing the enforcement of UN resolutions ("attempting in 1993 to assassinate former president Bush and by firing on many thousands of occasions on United States and Coalition Armed Forces engaged in enforcing the resolutions of the United Nations Security Council").[13]

Most of these congressional authorizations were strangely ignored by the Bush administration over the next five months, at least in a general debate over the wisdom of removing Saddam Hussein. Instead, the administration would commit what turned out to be the most grievous error of its eight-year tenure, by focusing on only one theme of the wide-ranging twenty-three congressional proclamations: the danger of Saddam Hussein's weapons of mass destruction. Apparently administration planners thought that an existential danger might rally the public to war in a way that Saddam's prior acts of genocide, attempts to kill a U.S. president, cash subsidies to Palestinian suicide bombers, or sanctuaries for wanted international terrorists would not. The result was that in the short term, most Americans believed that their government was moving to obliterate supposedly vast WMD stockpiles in Iraq.

The WMD argument was compelling, but the administration had in effect put all their eggs in one basket. The war was sold on an effort to strip Saddam of his WMD arsenal—a dubious proposition given the inadequate intelligence surrounding the closed Baathist police state. Despite a growing antiwar movement, and the failure to prove a connection between Saddam and the 9/11 terrorists, the public was convinced by the Bush administration's insistence on the dangers of WMDs that the war was necessary. It also trusted that it would be no more difficult than had been the removal of the Taliban, with a consensual government rapidly installed in Saddam Hussein's place. Worse still, when WMDs were not found as anticipated, the administration did not rely on the other writs of the congressional decrees, but instead post facto changed the reason for the war to a new emphasis not approved by Congress—namely, spreading freedom and liberty in the Middle East.

Nonetheless, the first few days of the Iraq War confirmed prewar confidence. Donald Rumsfeld's successful strategy in Afghanistan of a "light footprint" was repeated once more against Saddam Hussein. Fewer than two hundred thousand American and coalition troops quickly marched into a country of 26 million from Kuwait, brushing aside most organized resistance. Saddam's Baathist government was removed in less than three weeks (March 20–April 9) in an effective campaign that cost just 139 U.S. military personnel. "Shock and awe" pyrotechnics were supposed to have sent both the Iraqi military and civilian population into panic without causing substantial material damage that might impair postwar nation building.

Critics who had either predicted another Vietnam quagmire or argued for a half-million-man force comparable to that of Gulf War I at that initial point seemed to have been proven wrong. Numerous Iraqis appeared jubilant as they toppled Saddam Hussein's Baghdad statue. Kurdistan was liberated amid a sea of pro-American euphoria. There were no mass disruptions on the Arab street. Nor did global Islamic terrorism

Three soldiers from the 1st Battalion, 7th Marines (1/7), armed with M16A2 assault rifles, enter one of Saddam Hussein's Baghdad palaces during the first weeks of Operation Iraqi Freedom. Photo by Lance Corporal Kevin C. Quihuis Jr., courtesy of the Department of Defense.

spike. Iraq seemed relatively calm. Oil prices soon returned to normal levels. On May 1, 2003, George Bush gave a formal victory speech on the aircraft carrier *Abraham Lincoln*, declaring major combat operations over in Iraq—beneath an enormous banner triumphantly proclaiming MISSION ACCOMPLISHED. The commander in chief had just won two wars in the Middle East, against the region's most violent regimes, at the cost of only 151 American fatalities.[14]

Almost immediately the initial rapture faded. The idea of "mission accomplished" proved premature and soon embarrassing. The expected large stockpiles of weapons of mass destruction failed to materialize. That fact was especially awkward to the Bush administration because the rationale for war had not emphasized the majority of quite different congressional authorizations. Instead, enormous depots of conventional artillery shells and bombs were uncovered—and left unguarded—providing the enemy with the ingredients for thousands of future improvised explosive devices.

Saddam Hussein and his sons were nowhere to be found. Compounding the confusion, General Tommy Franks, the CENTCOM (United States

Central Command) commander in charge of the U.S. presence in the Middle East, who had overseen the invasion, abruptly announced his intention to retire on May 22, 2003. He gave the impression that he wished to leave Iraq before the unexpectedly escalating violence marred his swift victory over Saddam—and tarnished his postmilitary prospects in the private sector. By 2004, Franks had already published his memoirs. As the violence was heating up, he had written a wish list of regrets—a host of "I wish that's"—followed by laments over the inability of the State Department and Pentagon to work together. The former general Franks in print regretted the lack of an international conference on rebuilding Iraq, the "melting away of the Iraqi army," and so on—all without apparent recognition that his own retirement had added to the confusion amid an ongoing insurgency. More regrettably, General Franks, at a key moment when proven U.S. leadership was needed in Baghdad, had ordered the withdrawal of the Coalition Forces Land Component Commander (Lt. Gen. John Abizaid) and his headquarters from Iraq, and then compounded the error by ordering its replacement with the understaffed and poorly led Coalition Joint Task Force 7 (under the newly promoted Lt. Gen. Ricardo Sanchez).

Meanwhile, the first American regent of Iraq, Lieutenant General (Ret.) Jay Garner, lasted in his position only a few weeks, after terrorism increased, lawlessness prevailed, and his calls for prompt Iraqi elections were determined to be unrealistic. Few later knew what to make of Garner's brief tenure—whether he had been inept or carefully crafting plans that might have worked had he been given a fair opportunity and not undercut by infighting in the administration. What was increasingly apparent, however, was that a growing fight between Secretary of State Colin Powell's State Department and Secretary of Defense Donald Rumsfeld's Pentagon over how postwar Iraq should be run would only escalate—and be played out quite publicly in the press.

By May 11, 2003, Paul Bremer was appointed the new proconsul, with vastly expanded powers. Bremer was a former managing director of Kissinger and Associates. His own background did not include Mideast expertise. His appointment and residence in the heavily guarded Green Zone enclave did little to dispel rumors of American neocolonial ambitions in the oil-rich Gulf. It was also unclear at first to whom, exactly, he reported, whether President Bush, the State Department, or Secretary of Defense Rumsfeld. Soon, however, it became clear that Bremer answered more or less directly to the president, and that meant that he usually bypassed the Pentagon in his initial decisions—even though the military, rather than their civilian overseers, were still far more engaged in organizing resistance to the insurgency. That ensured a dangerous bifurcation between civilian and military efforts in Iraq. Secretary of State Colin Powell was purportedly voicing concerns about his administration's messy war off the record, both at home and abroad. In just a few weeks the so-called reconstruction seemed as disorganized as the military campaign had been nearly flawless. As the violence increased, those in Congress and the Pentagon with prior, but largely private, doubts about the war sought more explicit redemption from the press, as if they were not responsible for the ramifications of a war that they had opposed.[15]

In addition to problems of a unified military and civilian command, the Turkish Parliament at the final buildup to the Iraq War had unexpectedly denied the American 4th Infantry Division transit into Iraq from the north. That rejection in hindsight did not seem to be too harmful in the first weeks after the victory over Saddam Hussein. Yet soon the initial absence of Americans in the Sunni-controlled provinces would have lasting consequences for the course of the occupation. The eventual result was that thousands of crack American troops never entered northern Iraq as part of an expected pincer movement, leaving many of the recalcitrant Sunni provinces of Iraq simply untouched when the formal shooting stopped. NATO ally Turkey soon proved at best a neutral, and at worst tried to exercise veto power over Kurdish regional autonomy—in ominous signs of an increasing estrangement from its traditionally close relationship with Washington.

Millions of Sunni Iraqis had no reason either to fear or respect relatively small numbers of postwar American occupation troops who were careful not to ignite another war. Some began to act on that increasingly obvious fact of American caution. The notion of an American military "light footprint" had seemed to be working well in "postwar" Afghanistan and again during the initial three-week Iraqi war. Yet with the official fall of the Baathist government, thousands of humiliated Iraqis began to fathom that they had given up without much of a fight. The majority still had never seen any U.S. troops—either during the three-week war or now during the occupation.

As the postwar chaos spread, Bremer increasingly distrusted the frail Iraqi Interim Authority and the provincial Iraqi Leadership Council. By the time the more permanent Iraqi Governing Council was established in July 2003, Bremer's Coalition Provincial Authority had managed to dissipate most notions of the Americans as liberators rather than foreign colonial occupiers. Iranian and Gulf oil money, respectively, fueled warring Shiite and Sunni insurgents, sometimes in league with former Baathist officers, sometimes under the guidance of transnational terrorists—and sometimes simply fighting each other as much as the Americans. Chaos of any kind weakened the impression of U.S. resolve and undercut America's evolving mission not just to remove Saddam Hussein, but also to leave a constitutional government in his place as a model for broader Middle East reform.

At home, American analysts were divided over the proper responses to escalating violence. Some argued for an influx of additional troops to restore order; others were convinced that the problem was instead too much of an already high American profile that had needlessly provoked Iraqi sensibilities. If many liberals had never wanted to go into Iraq, many conservatives had wished to bomb it and leave. Most felt that the Bush administration had underestimated tribal factionalism and had been more interested in moving on to remove other terrorist-sponsoring regimes than in staying on to nation-build in Iraq—a Wilsonianism once rejected by mainstream conservatives and Bush himself during the 2000 presidential campaign.[16]

Conditions on the ground were getting worse. Already by summer 2003, the American occupiers, even as they increased the number of their patrols, were beginning to play defense in a psychological sense, careful not to restart a full-scale war by sending in more troops and thereby jeopardize their brilliant original three-week victory. While it was understandable that American commanders would move their headquarters into Saddam's easily defended and empty palaces, the compounds soon proved to be easily caricatured by critics—especially the most ostentatious, the Al Faw resort in the suburbs of Baghdad. The impression grew that the Americans had removed one authoritarian only to install themselves as replacements in his monstrous residences. The initial American reputation of overwhelming power insidiously eroded. Looting of Iraq's infrastructure went on unchecked until June 2003, when rules of engagement were finally altered to allow for the use of deadly force in guarding critical facilities. Improvised explosive devices began shredding thin-skinned American Humvees—a vehicle designed for behind-the-lines transport, not for frontline battlefield patrolling. On May 23, Paul Bremer had ordered the disbanding of the Iraq army and the expulsion of prominent former Baathists from the Civil Service.

Ideological cleansing might have seemed a wise move to ensure the long-term loyalty of a new army and bureaucracy. Yet the expulsions were proving disastrous in the short term. Unemployed, poor, and armed young Iraqis wandered the streets, fueling new rifts between Sunni supporters of Saddam Hussein and now ascendant Shiite nationalists. Indeed, some 385,000 Iraqi troops, and another 335,000 members of various Iraqi police and security forces, were cashiered without chance of quick reenlistment—despite a belated American attempt to issue back pay in July 2003.[17]

Tens of thousands of these unemployed former Baathists with military skills found work as insurgents and terrorists. Soon Iraq's 26 million citizens were no longer sure whether the outnumbered Americans and their allies could stabilize the country, and many began to offer concessions to the apparently ascendant terrorists. The American authorities also did not appreciate that just because hundreds of newly hired Iraqi bureaucrats and officers had no prior ties with Saddam Hussein, that did not necessarily ensure that they were competent, or that they had been driven out of government service only on ideological grounds rather than malfeasance and incompetence. Was it worse to reemploy experienced Baathist bureaucrats or to hire thousands of inexperienced opponents of the Hussein regime? No one seemed to know.

Soon al-Qaeda sensed an opening and pronounced Iraq the central theater in the jihadists' war against the West. Osama bin Laden and Ayman al-Zawahiri both urged terrorists throughout the Middle East to flock to Anbar and Ninewa Provinces to drive out the infidel occupiers. As violence increased in Iraq, once-silenced antiwar critics at home rebounded to argue that the war—supposedly sold fraudulently at its inception—was clearly lost. The occupation and reconstruction were proving as ineptly planned—and thirty times more costly—as the initial three-week war was inspired. Yet there was good news among the chaos: In July, the two murderous sons of Saddam Hussein, Uday and Qusay, were hunted down and killed in Mosul, and the Iraqi Governing Council began functioning as a precursor of the upcoming democratically elected government.

No matter—even former loud supporters of the war argued that the failing postwar occupation justified their reversal of position into even more prominent antiwar critics. The Iraq War was becoming almost as divisive as Vietnam had been. In response, on July 3, 2003, a defiant President Bush said of the insurgents, "bring 'em on." They did. By August, terrorists had bombed the Jordanian embassy, and soon the United Nations headquarters, killing the popular UN envoy Sergio Vieira de Mello.[18]

Far worse was still to come in spring 2004, when the good news of the capture of Saddam Hussein (December 2003) had worn off and the Jaish al-Mahdi rebellion, inspired by the Shiite radical cleric Muqtada al-Sadr, began to spread across south central Iraq. Now the Americans were dealing with both Sunni—Saddam Hussein loyalists as well as al-Qaeda supporters—and Shiite insurgencies. Mass bombings struck the Italian barracks as the terrorists began targeting particular foreign contingents in hopes of shattering the coalition's unity and sending these smaller deployments in disgrace back to Europe. American helicopters were occasionally shot down, and insurgent missiles were fired at incoming transport jets, imperiling resupply efforts. The impending American presidential elections of 2004 ensured that the increasingly violent war in Iraq became a polarizing wedge issue.

Widespread revelations of undeniable prisoner abuse at the coalition-controlled Abu Ghraib prison in Baghdad in late April 2004 tainted American professions of idealism and dovetailed with ongoing criticisms of the detention facility at Guantánamo Bay, Cuba. Yet if Abu Ghraib enraged many Americans, the seemingly directionless course of the war infuriated even more. Impotence seemed the order of the day: Iranian sailors with impunity captured a small British contingent; suicide bombers struck at foreign contract workers; and terrorists began to capture and execute foreigners in macabre video beheadings. There was a growing consensus across ideological lines that the war was waged halfheartedly and yet immorally all at once.[19]

Just prior to the first Abu Ghraib disclosures, al-Qaeda-affiliated Sunni terrorists murdered four U.S. security contractors in Fallujah. Soon videos of their burned and strung-up corpses were flashed across the world. That atrocity prompted a Bush administration vow to retake the troublesome city. The formal siege of Fallujah began on April 4. The assault quickly made good progress, until Paul Bremer, under pressure from the Iraqi interim government, recommended a series of pauses and ceasefires before calling off the engagement altogether on May 1—with terrorists still in de facto control of the city. The Americans had, it seemed, ceded Fallujah to insurgents and killers as a safe haven—and would very soon have to spend more blood and treasure in retaking it after the November election.[20]

In fact, Americans did just that, reentering the city on November 9, 2004, in Operation Phantom Fury. They recaptured Fallujah by the fifteenth, in the bloodiest single U.S. military urban battle (106 coalition forces killed, over 600 wounded) since the siege of Hue City during the Tet offensive of winter 1968 in Vietnam. The second battle for Fallujah was a decisive American victory and wrought havoc on ex-Baathists and al-Qaeda, but it brought no reassurance to the public—given that the city should have been pacified in April. Like the battles of the Tet offensive, Fallujah was an American victory that somehow led to enemy propaganda advantage. Lives on all sides had been needlessly spent in taking a city that had subsequently been given up—with the foreknowledge that it would have to be retaken when the political climate made such a vital operation more feasible.[21]

At the heart of public discontent and political opposition to the conflict—as in every war—was always rising U.S. casualties. The so-called peace had seen a steady increase in U.S. losses following the conclusion of the "war"—from 486 dead in 2003 to well over eight hundred fatalities in each subsequent year (2004: 849; 2005: 846; 2006: 822). While the number of Americans killed monthly in action had in fact spiked in 2005 (it would rise only on one occasion again, during the first year of the surge), the rising toll steadily eroded public support. By the midterm elections of 2006, nearly three thousand Americans had been lost—a figure small in comparison to the killed and missing even in some single battles in history such as Belleau Wood, Iwo Jima, and Chosun, but felt now to be enormous in times of a supposed postbellum reconstruction.[22]

From late 2003 through 2006, the U.S. effort found itself in a race against time at home and abroad. Could the heralded Iraqi nationwide elections in January 2005, a growing non-Baathist and reformed Iraqi army, and a rapidly adapting American military quell the insurgencies and foster a new democratic Iraq—before Baathist renegades, al-Qaeda terrorists, Iranian-sponsored Shiite militias, and Kurdish nationalists tore apart the country, or American public support for the war collapsed altogether at the news of rising casualties? What exactly, critics asked, was the United States trying to do in Iraq?

The administration waited until November 2005 to publish, in Matthew Ridgway fashion, a formal declaration of its strategic aims ("The National Strategy for Victory in Iraq"). The manifesto was mostly a plan of "clear, hold, and build," but one designed to turn over the country as fast as possible to the Iraqis without resulting in chaos.[23]

Yet the fourth year of the occupation, 2006, seemed even bleaker as U.S. casualties climbed to their highest levels yet. President Bush later called the summer of 2006 "the worst period of my presidency." More than a thousand roadside bombs were being detonated per week. Counteracting the nightmarish IED became an understandable American obsession. New Shiite and Sunni death squads terrorized civilians, when they were not busy blowing up Americans, and carved out entire urban centers that became no-go zones for Americans.[24]

Finally, back in Washington there was a Revolt of the Generals. Prominent critics—retired Major General Paul Eaton, retired Lieutenant General Gregory Newbold, Major General John Riggs, Major General Charles Swannack, retired General Anthony Zinni, and retired Major General John Batiste, among several others with long experience and distinguished service in the Middle East—derided not just operations in Iraq but the entire idea of going to war there in the first place. All gave military credence, whether by intent or not, to the antiwar movement's contention that an ill-conceived war was unwinnable and should be ended.

The generals had gone public—in the *New York Times*, in *Time* magazine, and on television—with scathing denunciations of the situation in Iraq, and they were largely canonized by the media. While their critiques were diverse, all seemed to focus upon a shortage of troops, an atmosphere of denial of reality in Washington, and the micromanaging of the war by Secretary Rumsfeld, whom they blamed for the rising violence and called upon to resign. Yet their critique was not uniform or always consistent: Were these high-ranking officers and retired generals calling for new tactics and greater commitment to save Iraq, or simply concluding that the American experience in Iraq was a mistake from the beginning, with ill effects on the military, and that Iraq was no longer worth saving?[25]

In the second national referendum on the conflict after the presidential election of 2004, Republicans paid the political price for their adherence to the war, losing both houses of Congress in the November 2006 midterm elections. Secretary of Defense Donald Rumsfeld, who had planned to leave if Republicans lost the midterm elections, resigned, seemingly under pressure, even as a radical shake-up of the military leadership in Iraq went ahead. That Rumsfeld left after the elections rather than before seemed to characterize the Bush administration chaos. Republicans in Congress lamented that they had received no pre-election boost from his departure—a commentary on how dismal their confidence in a political comeback had become.

CENTCOM commander General John Abizaid and the theater forces commander in Iraq, General George Casey, either retired or were kicked upstairs. Abizaid was replaced by Admiral William J. Fallon in March 2007. Casey was followed by General David Petraeus in February 2007. It was the consensus that almost all high American civilian and military officials in Iraq from 2003 to 2006—Generals Abizaid, Casey, Franks, and Sanchez, as well as Paul Bremer and Jay Garner—had failed to grasp the nature and dimensions of the Iraq resistance movements.

In February 2006, Sunni terrorists had blown up the golden-tiled dome of the thousand-year-old Shiite al-Askari mosque in Samarra. That spectacular operation set off even more sectarian violence between Sunni and Shiite factions—and drew in more money and support from their respective foreign patrons. The bombing also had disrupted the Casey-Abizaid plans to continue troop withdrawals, and it seemed to call into question the entire strategy of American scheduled departures. True, Saddam Hussein had been finally captured (December 13, 2003), tried and convicted (November 5, 2006), and executed (December 30, 2006), but in such a grotesque and humiliating manner that his demise only seemed to polarize Iraqi factions and discredit the idea of democratic justice.[26]

The more a beleaguered President Bush talked of freedom as a universal value that would resonate in the Middle East, the more Americans and Iraqis alike saw the result only as chaos and mayhem. By late 2006 George Bush's calls for "freedom" and "democracy" in Iraq were seen as naïve and wishful at home, and yet as colonialist, Machiavellian, and conspiratorial in the Arab world. Liberals saw no political advantage in supporting a conservative's idealistic calls for supporting democracy in the Middle East; conservatives felt that one of their own was sounding too much like a naïve Wilsonian internationalist rather than a realistic statesman.

The president had once emphasized the positive ripples of Iraq in the surrender of weapons of mass destruction by a worried Muammar Gaddafi regime in Libya, the house arrest of Dr. A. Q. Khan in Pakistan and the dismantling of his nuclear export franchise, the Syrian withdrawal from Lebanon, and protests for human rights in many Middle East countries, but by the end of 2006 his critics bitterly countered with the

Hamas election in Gaza, the rise of Hezbollah in Lebanon, and the Israeli-Lebanese war of July 2006 as negative fallout from the war. Neither proponents of democratization nor antiwar pessimists seemed to grasp that American policy, whatever its general contours, was more likely to be effective when the United States won wars and seemed preeminent, and more likely to falter when it appeared to be losing conflicts and rendered militarily impotent.

In December 2006, the bipartisan, presidentially appointed Iraq Study Group released its ambivalent findings. The group urged the United States to secure the country, and yet argued for a plan for a foreseeable end to American occupation that was not predicated on calming the country—reflecting the reality that no one really agreed how many U.S. troops were needed in Iraq and for how long. Each side of the war debate championed those elements of the commission's deliberately ambiguous conclusions that confirmed their own views. The antiwar movement was no longer confined to just the hard left, but encompassed mainstream Democrats—and a growing number of Republicans angry that the war had already lost them both the Senate and the House in the 2006 midterm elections and would soon perhaps lose them the presidency as well in 2008.

Most books and articles on Iraq that appeared between 2005 and 2006 forecast an American defeat characterized by an unending civil war, a wider regional conflict, Somalia-like chaos, or the emergence of an anti-American Iraqi autocrat. By fall 2006, classified intelligence estimates had concluded that al-Qaeda controlled virtually all of Anbar Province.[27]

The Origins and Implementation of the Surge (*2006*)

From the moment of Saddam's fall, a wide divide had grown over how best to reconstruct Iraq.[28] The most influential strategy eventually came to be identified with General John Abizaid, the chief of Central Command, and General George Casey, the senior ground commander in Iraq. The latter, in the wake of the Abu Ghraib prison scandal of April 2004, had replaced Lieutenant General Ricardo S. Sanchez in June. Sanchez had seemed unable to prevent such lapses and was often unaware of the public relations disaster that Abu Ghraib had become. Despite being the most junior three-star general in the entire U.S. Army, Sanchez had been appointed to command all ground forces since mid-2003—apparently on the theory that such an untried officer could easily conduct mop-up operations in a calm postwar environment. Yet, in less than a year, it was clear that Sanchez had been overwhelmed by the task.

Casey and Abizaid had concluded that a continued large U.S. presence provoked insurgencies and ensured Iraqi dependency. Instead, the better way to achieve peace in Iraq and foster U.S. interests would be to begin steadily withdrawing American troops. At each scheduled reduction in American forces, the Iraqis would be required to step up to replace them. The pace of transformation would not always be contingent on actual events on the ground, but rather become a catalyst for them. After all, violence was always endemic to Iraq, and American soldiers would be seen as the problem rather than the solution. If the American training wheels did not come off the Iraqi experiment, they argued, the new democracy would never learn to ride on its own. But by late 2005 one U.S. military consultant in Iraq summed up the situation about as bleakly as imaginable: "Those who remain behind to fight over the rotting carcass of the Iraqi state will be the survivors of a process of political Darwinism: ruthless, merciless, and not averse to engaging in ethnic cleansing of the Other."[29]

Ostensibly, both top generals had reflected the views of their bosses, Secretary of Defense Donald Rumsfeld and the collective opinion of the Joint Chiefs of Staff. All the top brass worried about U.S. commitments elsewhere and about overstretched assets. More important, the theory of a light footprint had seemed to work well in Afghanistan and during the first few weeks after the Iraq War. Perhaps, then, emphasis on nation building was a cause of, not the solution to, the violence? Such a "get in and get out" strategy was also better in accordance with Rumsfeld's larger views of a light, fast, and more mobile armed forces and reflected his own skepticism about the practicality of democratization and nation building in the Middle East—doubts that had always put him at odds with grand neoconservative strategists and others in the Bush administration.[30]

Indeed, at first the Casey-Abizaid build-and-hold strategy had seemed to improve the situation, as American casualties declined somewhat. But in February 2006, after the attack on the iconic al-Askari Shiite mosque in Samarra, sectarian violence escalated. Shiites and Sunnis began to battle each other daily and at times combined against Americans and their allies, who were appearing impotent in efforts to reestablish security. Nonetheless, until the end of 2006, the prevailing American strategy remained a preplanned steady drawdown from 140,000 troops to an envisioned 60,000. The killing of the terrorist Abu-Musab al-Zarqawi in June 2006 and the appointment of a new effective American ambassador, Zalmay Khalilzad, and new Iraqi cabinet officials all seemed to give the Casey-Abizaid strategy a second wind.

Perhaps the two most prominent proponents, within the active military, of the Casey-Abizaid approach were Generals Shoemaker (chief of staff of the Army) and Lute (chief of operations on the Joint Chiefs). The former Special Forces officer and influential consultant Michael Vickers pointed out that the Casey-Abizaid small imprint strategy was actually the key to counterinsurgency: a "less is often more" profile would curb anti-Americanism and force greater responsibility on the part of the Iraqis. In contrast, the idea of sending a few thousand more troops into the Iraq quagmire was not one shared by many top-ranking generals other than the maverick David Petraeus and his own small circle of advisers.[31]

If the first choice was politically untenable, the second would be strategically disastrous. Yet the status quo was clearly not working. That again left this fourth and final option of surging between twenty thousand and thirty thousand troops. At the same time, a group of dissident officers also advocated an accompanying change in tactics from the current counterterrorism (going after known terrorist insurgents) to one of counterinsurgency (protecting the civilians to deny insurgents necessary support and sanctuary). The surge was not to be considered a Vietnam-like escalation (that tarnished word was deliberately avoided), since it would be small and declared temporary, but would still be just enough of a push to allow a window of calm to reenergize the Iraqis to craft their own defense while American tactics and strategy radically shifted. The metaphor was often one of a small push to send the Iraq reconstruction to the summit, after which it could coast downhill on its own.

Who, then, thought up the strategy, planned its details, and won over President Bush in the latter months of 2006—contrary to public opinion and without necessarily the early support of the secretary of defense, the senior American ground commander in Iraq, the supreme commander in the Middle East, and most of the Joint Chiefs of Staff? The advocacy group was informal and ad hoc. It was composed of civilians, a few sympathetic administration officials, and some active officers and retired military officials. The common tie was shared support for David Petraeus's insistence on more American boots on the ground in Iraq, and more emphasis on undermining the appeal of insurgents than on protecting

U.S. forces or simply hunting down and killing terrorists. Petraeus became a symbol of doubt both about the pessimistic conclusions of the Iraq Study Group and about the incremental changes in the current status quo offered by other critics such as General Pete Chiarelli.[32]

Petraeus had earlier enjoyed some success in quieting violence as a two-star general in charge of the 101st Airborne Division's occupation of the Mosul region of Iraq between 2003 and 2004. In fact, he had developed a sort of cult status—both among local Iraqis and the Western media—in distributing vast amounts of reconstruction money to bypass the fossilized occupation bureaucracy. In the process, Petraeus earned from Iraqi beneficiaries the nickname "King David" for his singular discretionary authority in the region. That epithet, however, was also cited by American critics as proof of his unchecked ego and ambition—and of his near constant need for media attention. It did not help matters when Petraeus later told reporters for the *Washington Post* that his role in Mosul had been "a combination of being the president and pope."

In April 2004, General Petraeus returned to Washington, where he gave a largely upbeat review ("Iraq appears much more manageable on the ground than it does from afar") to the Washington Institute about his success in Iraq, highlighting his earlier efforts at reconstruction, counterinsurgency, and training the new Iraqi army. But whether he knew it or not, such high-profile positive assessments back in Washington were not widely believed by the media. To the degree that Petraeus sounded credible, his emphases on adaptation and constantly changing strategies seemed to confirm that American postwar plans had been from the start innately flawed and in need of constant reassessment.[33]

After being promoted to lieutenant general in charge of the Multi-National Security Transition Command and given chief responsibility by Secretary Rumsfeld for training a new Iraqi army, Petraeus had almost immediately discovered that the Coalition Provisional Authority under Paul Bremer had made little progress in creating an effective new Iraqi military. Petraeus would have to begin from scratch by finding scores of new Iraqi officers whose loyalty transcended their tribal affiliations. He was not shy about describing these challenges in a series of essays and interviews detailing how his own successful efforts in Mosul at nation building and counterinsurgency might serve as an exemplar for all of Iraq.

The high profile of Petraeus as a freelance thinker had won over several correspondents in Iraq and even some media critics of the war back home. After all, support for the reformer Petraeus seemed to square the circle of being against the war and the administration that waged it without being against the troops or the idea that Iraq could still be calmed. In July 2004, *Newsweek* ran a cover story on Petraeus entitled "Can This Man Save Iraq?" written with almost gushing praise: "His fans believe he's a new-style officer for a new type of warfare, where battles can be won with superior technology and firepower, but true victories can be secured only by good peacemaking and politics." At the same time, the attention raised eyebrows among Petraeus's military superiors that he was stealthily feeding journalists criticisms of the status quo at their own expense, if not angling for supreme command itself. General Sanchez, the supreme commander at the time of Petraeus's selection to oversee the training of the Iraqi army, later expressed resentment of the latter's supposed political grandstanding: "The administration was spinning the event to make it look like Petraeus was coming to Iraq to salvage a failed military effort. It was all political maneuvering ahead of the upcoming presidential election." It apparently never occurred to General Sanchez that his cynical appraisal of Petraeus's politicking in 2004 could be both true and yet irrelevant, given the latter's far greater appreciation of what had gone wrong in Iraq.[34]

By 2006, supporters of General Petraeus were determined to save Iraq by going around the Joint Chiefs and top administration officials. In their favor, they were largely exempt from the normal media disdain accorded supporters of the war. While surging was unpopular to most critics, the change in strategy was also clearly a rebuke to George Bush and the status quo. Whether Petraeus knew it or not, his own advocacy had found a media seam. Journalists hostile to the Bush administration could focus on Petraeus's critique of the war, even if their eventual antiwar aims were quite different from his.

Most prominent among the advocates of the surge strategy were Dr. Fred Kagan, a historian and resident scholar at the American Enterprise Institute, military analyst Dr. Kimberly Kagan, retired General Jack Keane, National Security Advisor Steven Hadley and many of his staff subordinates, and the so-called COINdinistas—military officers and Pentagon consultants who had long argued for the need for organizing civilians to oppose insurgents rather than merely going after them without due regard to the consequences on the larger civilian environment. These were highly educated and battle-tested colonels and lieutenant colonels associated with Petraeus such as Sean MacFarland, H. R. McMaster, Michael Meese, Peter Mansoor, Bill Rapp, and other officers including Derek Harvey and Mark Martins. Whether formally part of the official Joint Strategic Assessment Team or not, many of these Petraeus protégés had Ph.D.s and had taught at West Point—and informally as early as September 2006 had originated the idea of surging and changing completely U.S. strategy. They enlisted other outside advisers and consultants such as John Nagl and David Kilcullen, who had long written about quelling insurgencies. And while they all could be credited with helping Petraeus to craft the details of the new strategy, their advice would have remained largely academic without a charismatic supreme leader like Petraeus to ensure theories became fact.

Vice President Dick Cheney and his staff became prominent inside advocates of Fred Kagan's and Jack Keane's initial AEI surge lobby, and the vice president's staff all along did much to help win the president over during December 2006. Bush himself soon became a vocal supporter of a change in strategy—in direct opposition to most in his own State Department and Department of Defense and many of the Joint Chiefs, with the exception of the chairman, Marine General Peter Pace. The former secretary of state, retired General Colin Powell, was an outspoken opponent of the surge. Well before the Bush formal announcement of the reinforcements, in a wide-ranging December 2006 interview with *Face the Nation*, Powell flatly declared that America was "losing in Iraq" and a "surge cannot be sustained." He went on to declare, "It's very difficult to see how the American Army can impose its will in this sort of conflict."[35]

Even before the surge was fully implemented, many of Bush's staunchest supporters and former hawks publicly voiced consternation over the escalating violence and saw no hope that a surge or anything else would save Iraq. In November 2006, on the eve of the surge, some of the most prominent supporters of the war—Kenneth Adelman, David Frum, and Richard Perle—voiced pessimism and blamed the incompetence of George Bush (a "failure at the center"). A little over a month after the announcement of the surge, the former ambassador and consultant to the Kurdish government, Peter Galbraith, flatly announced, "President Bush's plan has no chance of actually working. At this late stage, 21,500 additional troops cannot make a difference. U.S. troops are ill prepared to do the policing that is needed to secure Baghdad . . . At best, Bush's new strategy will be a costly postponement of the day of reckoning with failure." While Secretary of State Condoleeza Rice and Secretary of Defense Donald Rumsfeld were not initially vocal opponents of the surge, they evidently believed, albeit for different reasons, that the Casey-Abizaid strategy of a light footprint might still be the least risky proposition.[36]

The three elements of the surge advocacy group in redirecting U.S. strategy—to be summarized in an American Enterprise Institute formal report on Iraq—were, first, to deploy twenty to thirty thousand troops as reinforcements. The second was to secure supreme command of the Iraqi coalition for General Petraeus. And third, the reformers wanted to supplant many of the existing methods of fighting the war—as well as the military and, if need be, civilian overseers of the current Iraq policy of reconstruction. Retired General Keane served as an informal three-way liaison between those outside government, the active military, and the Bush administration. The catalyst that suddenly had empowered the unlikely group of outsiders was the election rebuke of November 2006 that pushed a desperate President Bush to reexamine the current strategy. While the advocates of the surge conceded that the public was weary of the war, they nevertheless believed that most Americans would come to support an escalation if it offered any hope of victory.[37]

Years after both the invasion of Iraq and the decision in late 2006 to send a small reinforcement of twenty to thirty thousand, it is almost impossible now to reconstruct precisely the support for, and opposition to, such a radical decision. In the culture of Washington, those who were for the war often claimed they were against it when casualties mounted, and those who were not early advocates of the surge later claimed its patrimony after it worked. Finally, positions were often changed a third time as Iraq was either considered won or still not worth the price—an argument that continues to this day. Nonetheless, all factions agreed on one fact. By early 2007, General David Petraeus had assumed responsibility for either saving or abandoning the lost war in Iraq. He was not merely the highest-ranking military officer on the ground in Iraq, but was now looked to by both the administration and the nation at large as the last hope for avoiding a catastrophic American defeat.

"The New Way Forward" (*January 2007–November 2009*)

On January 10, 2007—nearly four years after the invasion of Iraq—President George Bush formally decided to back the Petraeus group. He outlined a new strategy known as "The New Way Forward," the official title of the program. In a nationally broadcast television address, Bush promised that at least five additional army brigades and two marine battalions (that is, about twenty thousand troops, with additional personnel such as military police, engineers, and aviation units that would bring the total closer to thirty thousand) would be sent right away to Iraq, to be stationed mostly in and around Bagdad and Anbar Province. "So America will change our strategy to help the Iraqis carry out their campaign to put down sectarian violence and bring security to the people of Baghdad. This will require increasing American force levels. So I have committed more than twenty thousand additional American troops to Iraq." At that moment in the polls, the president enjoyed an average 28 percent approval rating. Only Harry Truman and Richard Nixon at their lowest points had been more unpopular sitting presidents. Over 66 percent of Americans opposed sending any more troops to Iraq.[38]

That additional manpower was to facilitate a new effort at securing neighborhoods, protecting the population, and expanding basic services. Bush promised security for Iraqis to participate in their new democracy and to revive the economy—in contrast to the prior strategy of stationing American troops in fortified compounds from which they ventured forth to patrol neighborhoods and attack terrorist suspects. Up to now the mission had been mostly "force protection" (not losing American soldiers in battle) and "counterterrorism" (killing anyone who was trying to kill our own). But now, in Ridgway fashion, there were six new talking points that summed up the Petraeus strategy: "Let the Iraqis lead. Help Iraqis protect the population. Isolate extremists. Create space for political progress. Diversify political and economic efforts. Situate the strategy in a regional approach."[39]

The protocols sounded almost more sociological than military, the product of a university rather than of a battlefield. They ranged from entering previous no-go zones to more widely dispersing troops in Iraqi neighborhoods. In addition, the president formally announced that General Petraeus would succeed General George Casey as commanding general of multinational forces in Iraq. In general, Bush's announcement was greeted by disdain. Senator Joe Biden a week later introduced a Senate resolution opposing the surge. Senator Obama added another, calling for a mandatory phased troop withdrawal. Yet among a small number of analysts and officers, and the shrinking number of war supporters, the news of a surge at last brought relief—and even greater hope that the taciturn Petraeus would be at last given a chance to win the peace.[40]

By June 2007, all five new brigades were in Iraq. With some 150,000 aggregate ground troops at his disposal, Petraeus was at last fully implementing the long-promised strategy. He tasked them with securing Baghdad, the surrounding Sunni areas in Anbar Province, and the mixed Sunni-Shiite Diyala Province. Quite abruptly, counterinsurgency strategy became the new American gospel throughout Iraq. Past tribal violence and anti-American terrorism were no longer to be consistently considered proof of lasting enmity. Instead, once-hostile civilians were invited back into the government. Insurgents were coaxed to either lay down their arms or, better yet, switch sides, through a variety of financial inducements and political strategies. The message went out that Americans were not going to leave according to predetermined and political timetables, but only when the new Iraq democratic state was secure and free of its enemies.

In these first few months of the surge, both American and Iraqi casualties skyrocketed. That was not surprising as high-profile patrols increased and coalition forces went into previously no-go insurgent strongholds. Back in Washington, even though the surge was just weeks old, nervous members of the administration began worrying about the political fallout over possible failure. Republican senators and congressional representatives, still smarting from the 2006 midterm rebuke, pressured for some sort of political settlement—even without progress on the battlefield. The new CENTCOM commander in the Middle East, Admiral William J. Fallon—before his removal a year later—did little to facilitate the strategy or the sending of more troops into Iraq, perhaps reflecting the resentment of the Joint Chiefs, who, after all, had suffered an end run by surge proponents.

Yet for all the politicking, by midyear 2007 there was some sense that the surge was gaining momentum in securing the country. The additional numbers of American troops had helped, but the change of tactics was even more important as Lieutenant General Raymond Odierno, commander of Multi-National Force–Iraq, began reassigning even pre-surge troops out of their forward operating bases and into smaller outposts inside Baghdad's neighborhoods. In the past such a conspicuous presence was seen as needlessly provoking Iraqi sensitivities; now ubiquitous Americans (with their Iraqi counterparts alongside) on the streets and sidewalks were intended to reassure civilians that they would be safe when they either joined Americans or fed them intelligence about insurgents and terrorists in their midst.[41]

Baghdad was not only Iraq's largest city and capital, but symbolic of the entire country. With new surge troops, General Odierno soon began to ring the city. Five brigades through much of 2007 were monitoring entry and exit, hunting down bomb factories and weapons caches, and organizing small urban renewal projects. But these preventive measures did not mean that the Americans did not seek to kill the enemy. In fact, while the media focused on stepped-up efforts at providing security and nation building, Odierno and Petraeus ordered a new all-out assault on terrorist enclaves. The names of the operations—Phantom Thunder, Phantom Strike, Lightning Hammer, Arrowhead Ripper—were reminiscent of General Matthew Ridgway's own similarly branded offensives in 1951 to counterattack the Chinese and regain respect for American lethality. At the end of 2007, in Anbar Province, at the center of the violence, nearly seven thousand weapons caches were confiscated and thousands of terrorists killed. The Sons of Iraq, a popular Sunni movement to expel al-Qaeda, had helped to enlist over a hundred thousand militiamen—including thousands of Shiites—to join in operations with Americans against the terrorists. These new allies were an unexpected boon for Petraeus, even if their support was sometimes fraught with controversy, given that many of the Sons of Iraq had American blood on their hands as former insurgent terrorists—and were now receiving up to $300 a month as paid constabularies.

As a result of their movement into Iraqi communities, for the first time in the war, the number of American dead exceeded one hundred over three consecutive months, from April through June, 2007. Iraqi civilian losses stabilized and then fell to levels not seen since the insurgency and Shiite-Sunni strife had begun in earnest in 2006. To uninformed observers, getting out of the safe compounds seemed to translate into getting more Americans killed. Pressure mounted back home. In June, Senate Majority leader Harry Reid and Speaker of the House Nancy Pelosi (D-CA) warned President Bush that the Petraeus half-year-old surge had already failed: "As many had foreseen, the escalation has failed to produce the intended results . . . The increase in US forces has had little impact in curbing the violence or fostering political reconciliation." Almost immediately, the Democratically controlled House of Representatives went on record opposing the surge in a February 16, 2007, House Concurrent Resolution. Only a filibuster by a minority of senators prevented passage of the nonbinding resolution. Senator Barack Obama had a few days earlier called the surge a "reckless escalation" and had gone further still by introducing legislation to remove all U.S. combat troops by March 2008.[42]

Then quite abruptly the violence began to taper off. American fatalities in July fell below a hundred. They would never exceed that monthly number again for the duration of the war. By fall 2007, Iraqi losses tapered off as well. Insurgents were increasingly hunted down and killed or captured, thanks to new cooperation from war-weary civilian informants. Although few prominent leaders in Congress had believed Petraeus's September 2007 assurances that promised benchmarks—reduced levels of violence, more government services, and fewer American losses—were being met, it was clear by year's end that almost all were exceeded in fact. In late December 2007, the well-regarded Brookings Institution scholars Michael O'Hanlon, a foreign policy senior fellow, and Jason H. Campbell, a senior research assistant, returned from Iraq to report to often stunned audiences that violence had dropped to 2004 levels and that the Petraeus pacification policy was in many areas already working.[43]

Iraqi government officials cited their own reduced casualties and the extension of government control over formerly insurgent territory. It was difficult to tell whether the so-called Anbar Awakening that had begun in spring 2006—in which Sunni tribal leaders turned against both al-Qaeda terrorists and ex-Baathists in their midst—was independent from, or fueled by, the subsequent American change in tactics and determination to stay and pacify Iraq. In June 2006, Army Colonel Sean MacFarland, along with Marine officers, had first met with Sunni tribal leaders in Ramadi and promised them aid. The subsequent surge incorporated the Awakening under Sheik Sattar, as well as the so-called Sons of Iraq—most prominently both by supplying them with money, and through biometric data distinguishing them from current terrorists and killers in their neighborhoods.

Tribal leaders had also by mid-2006 developed a healthy—and cumulative—respect for U.S. military lethality. Most were sick and tired of gratuitous al-Qaeda cruelty and extortion. Some were even eager for the American military to advocate their own seemingly neglected interests with the new Shiite-dominated Maliki government in Baghdad. Petraeus's subordinates, laden with cash and reinforcements, tried to exploit all those fissures in isolating the terrorists—well before the president authorized greater troop levels. The emergence of Iraqi counterinsurgent forces would soon coincide with the arrival of more Americans.[44]

The second year of the surge, 2008, proved even more successful. In

July 2008, only thirteen American soldiers were lost. Baghdad turned mostly quiet—just thirteen months after the deployment of more American troops. Media accounts conceded that most political and economic benchmarks promised by Petraeus—under dispute throughout 2007—were being met and passed by late 2008. Oil production exceeded 2 million barrels per day. Rates of increases in Iraq's GDP reached 7 percent per annum. Sunnis returned to parliament; former Baathists vowed to reenter politics. Almost all public criticism of Petraeus vanished. Indeed, the anti–Iraq War protests themselves dried up, which might have suggested to the enemy that there was no longer any chance that domestic opposition would result in a sudden withdrawal of U.S. troops.

Suddenly, by midsummer 2008, Iraq was no longer a key issue in the presidential race. It disappeared from the front pages of most newspapers and was no longer the lead story on the evening network news channels. Calls on the Democratic side for an immediate withdrawal were quietly dropped; campaign websites were scrubbed of their antiwar platforms. Even the acrimonious charges of the September 2007 hearings were forgotten. A new fallback antiwar position spread that Iraq was no longer "lost," but that the current quiet had come too late and cost far too much—and could not be sustained. The evaluation of the surge quickly found itself embedded in election-year partisan politics. War critics insisted that it had not worked soon enough; supporters argued that Bush's gamble redeemed the entire occupation. Such squabbling would go on until mid-2008, when the radical downturn in violence was then beyond dispute.[45]

Political bickering remained not over whether Iraq had drastically improved—it most unmistakably had—but whether such unforeseen success could really be attributed to General Petraeus and/or his surge. All sorts of alternate exegeses were advanced—some in part quite true, some transparently partisan revisionism: The U.S. announcement of not giving up had ipso facto convinced allied Iraqis to regain their confidence and the insurgents to lose their own. The early 2006 "Arab Awakening," which saw thousands of former terrorists join the Americans in Anbar Province, almost alone had tipped the scales in reducing violence before the arrival of American reinforcements. The Iraqi hatred of al-Qaeda was such that by 2007 open civil war had erupted throughout Iraq, and the Americans simply piggybacked onto antiterrorist sentiment.

Still other critics of the surge argued that by 2007 the Americans had cumulatively killed so many insurgents and terrorists that there was bound to be a turn of the tide, one that only happened to dovetail with the appointment of General Petraeus. Just as importantly, the Iraqi Security Forces, years in the making, finally reached critical mass in 2007 and were able to shoulder far more of the war effort. The world spike in oil prices sent extra billions into the Iraq economy that improved daily life. Diplomatic outreach and tough negotiations convinced Iran, Syria, and the Gulf monarchies to stop funding their respective terrorist appendages at previous levels of support. In short, reasons to account for the turnaround without necessarily directly crediting Petraeus or the strategy that sent him there seemed endless.[46]

Although traditional military analysts sometimes claimed that Petraeus had not taken the war to the enemy, in truth he and General Odierno killed and captured more enemy insurgents than at any other period of the conflict. It was largely seen as politically suicidal to boast of enemy losses—due to the memory of inflated body counts in Vietnam and sensitivity to newly allied and formerly hostile Iraqis. But one unemphasized feature of Petraeus's public focus on nonkinetic operations and civilian outreach was a new latitude given to hunting down and killing al-Qaeda–related terrorists. By the end of 2008, American forces had killed or captured tens of thousands of them—there were soon twenty-four thousand prisoners in Camp Bucca alone—in addition to inflicting well over a hundred thousand casualties since the beginning of the war. Or, as one counterinsurgency officer later reminded Petraeus, "There was a lot of killing for the first six months of the surge in Iraq—you could call it compellence theory." Was it incidental or integral to COIN strategy that public attention on social and economic reconstruction deflected focus away from more controversial increased killing of the "irreconcilable" enemy troops who had no intention of quitting—which in turn was essential in reassuring civilians to step up and participate in the new democracy? The question of what tactic actually brought the peace was never really answered; but it remained undeniable that the U.S. military had killed more insurgents than ever before—at a time when public attention was focused on the arguably less important aspects of nation building and winning hearts and minds.[47]

King David

David Petraeus was an unlikely American warrior, and an even more improbable partisan lightning rod. He was at once bookish, academic, and athletic, but of unassuming size and sometimes appearing tired and stooped. Petraeus had graduated forty-third in his class—in the top fifth percentile—at West Point in 1974, and then somewhat controversially two months later married his girlfriend, Holly Knowlton, the daughter of the superintendent, General William A. Knowlton, herself equally intellectual and a gifted graduate of Dickinson College. General Knowlton was a highly decorated combat veteran and polymath. He spoke several languages and was widely read among the officer corps—a role model who stressed to his new son-in-law the importance of combining academic training with military service. Whether or not Petraeus knew it at the time, he was already being pushed into an untraditional military that emphasized academic training rather than just armor, artillery, and traditional infantry combat experience while gaining a reputation for careerist savvy that would grow more controversial in later years.[48]

In this regard, three traits—or rather paradoxes—characterized the next twenty-five years of Petraeus's meteoric ascendency to the very elite of the American Army's officer corps: (a) excellence in every imaginable assignment, but none of them as yet in actual wars; (b) unmatched intellectual preparation and academic training that tended to complement Petraeus's superb physical condition; and (c) ambition to acquire the most challenging, prestigious, and diverse appointments possible, a drive that occasionally grated on rival officers of similar rank and earned suspicion from his superiors. Young David Petraeus was usually the smartest guy—and the most fit—in the room. Often he acted as if he knew it. And almost always both those realities annoyed peers more even than they impressed superiors.[49]

Just nine years after leaving West Point, Captain Petraeus graduated in 1983 as the top student at the U.S. Army Command and General Staff College at Fort Leavenworth, Kansas. His academic work suggested that Petraeus would prove to be among his generation's most gifted army tacticians. Four years later, in 1987, he earned a Ph.D. in international relations from Princeton University's Woodrow Wilson School of Public and International Affairs, writing a dissertation on the deleterious effects of Vietnam on subsequent military operations—especially the American military's incurring a troublesome, but understandable, lack of self-confidence. While still in his early thirties, between 1985 and 1987, Petraeus was proving an ascendant officer, scholar, and teacher at West Point. His subsequent multifaceted assignments shared a common theme of developing strong personal friendships with high-ranking officers, all

At the height of the surge in July 2007, General David Petraeus tours the streets of Baghdad, in camouflage and body armor—his four-star rank distinguishable only by the stars on his cap and chin flap. Photo ©Thomas Dworzak/Magnum Photos.

the while showcasing his organizational and intellectual skills at the company, battalion, and brigade level.

After finishing Ranger School with honors, Petraeus had served in a light infantry brigade and as an assistant operations officer in a mechanized unit at Fort Stewart, Georgia. In 1988–89, Major and Dr. Petraeus was posted in Germany, under the stewardship of an old mentor, General John R. Galvin, in another combat billet as an operations officer to the 3rd Infantry Division and its 1st Brigade. Petraeus had been attached to some of the most powerful generals in the United States, and so logically next took on a post as assistant executive officer to the U.S. Army Chief of Staff, General Carl Vuono, in Washington, D.C. Superiors were impressed with his energy and academic excellence; rivals again saw a fast track based on developing friendships with four-star generals, Ivy League academics, and politically well-connected assignments.[50]

When Lieutenant Colonel Petraeus at last became a battalion commander, he was almost killed in 1991. A soldier under his command accidentally let off an M-16 round into his chest. The gaping bullet hole required emergency chest surgery—performed by future Tennessee senator Dr. William Frist—to repair a leaking pulmonary artery and vein and to resection a portion of the lung. Once recovered, Petraeus spent the latter 1990s as a colonel in various posts in both the 101st and 82nd Air Assault Divisions. He might have died again in 2000 in yet another noncombat accident, when his parachute incompletely opened and he fractured his pelvis in a rough landing. When Petraeus was promoted to brigadier general, he had almost been killed twice in the field—and yet had not seen battle.

Whether consciously or not, David Petraeus for two decades had been preparing himself neither for conventional warfare nor for counterterrorist special operations—nor even for classic jungle or rural insurgency. Instead, he had prepped for large-scale postbellum occupation and reconstruction in highly urbanized, extremely hostile populations—exactly what Iraq would be like in 2003.

As a two-star general, Petraeus had served in the Balkan peacekeeping operations during 2001–2002 and there sharpened his ideas about counterterrorism before leading the initial assault on Baghdad as commander of the 101st Air Assault Division. His first formal combat assignment almost immediately became widely publicized, thanks to Pulitzer Prize–winning journalist and embedded reporter Rick Atkinson's account, *In the Company of Soldiers.* In the postwar occupation, Petraeus drew more admiring reporters to Mosul who were happy to contrast his approaches with those of supposedly less imaginative, more traditional commanders. He gladly informed reporters that his brigades, in a manner consistent with his own peacekeeping experience in Haiti and in the Balkans, were employing counterinsurgency techniques rather than solely hunting down terrorists. Few others were as successful in the dark days of the early violence between 2003 and 2005 that followed the removal of Saddam Hussein.[51]

An increasing number of reporters conceded that while the military bureaucracy was clueless about the budding insurgency, Major General Petraeus had set himself up in Mosul like a successful Roman proconsul. He was overseeing the reestablishment of everything from the urban university to the city council. Petraeus disbursed millions of dollars to more than four thousand projects ("money is ammunition")—often without the oversight of Paul Bremer, the head of the Coalition Provisional Authority, who had been monitoring civil affairs for the year after May 2003.[52]

Petraeus saw Iraq as a challenge to his own thirty years of experience and training; others saw his proclamations of success as implicit endorsement of the unpopular Iraq policies of the Bush administration. That was never more true than on September 26, 2004, when Petraeus wrote a progress report in the *Washington Post* reviewing his own performance ("Now, however, 18 months after entering Iraq, I see tangible progress. Iraqi security elements are being rebuilt from the ground up.")—just six weeks before the November U.S. presidential election. Many Democrats felt that officers like Petraeus were losing the election for John Kerry, who was blasting Bush's conduct of the war. Nonetheless, few could argue that Petraeus's efforts at training and equipping more than 160,000 Iraqi military and police recruits in counterinsurgency were a formidable feat—despite the spike in violence to come in 2006.[53]

Then Petraeus was inexplicably withdrawn from Iraq back to the United States, to be given a controversial assignment from the latter part of 2005 until February 2007 as commanding general of the U.S. Army Combined Arms Center at Fort Leavenworth, Kansas. Some suspected that rivals within the military had managed to send Petraeus to Leavenworth to sideline his probable rise to a four-star rank. Yet even thousands of miles away from the Iraq theater, the Petraeus mystique still grew. Reporters, for example, saw the appointment as somehow symptomatic of the inept Bush administration occupation: The only "thinking man" who had any success was purportedly crudely shuffled out to the backwaters of the American Midwest. When mavericks objected to Bush's losing strategy, the critique went, they were apparently sent home. But Petraeus's assignment may not, in fact, have been politically driven, given the importance of the Leavenworth appointment. In any case, the assignment provided him a rare chance to reflect on his past experience in formulating future ideas on how to defeat the Iraqi insurgents.

At Leavenworth, Petraeus more or less oversaw strategic and tactical thinking and training for the army's entire officer corps—especially incorporating lessons learned in Iraq in terms of official military counterinsurgency thinking that could be uniformly applied throughout the Middle East and South Asia. Along with Marine Lieutenant General James N. Mattis—whom Petraeus would subsequently serve both over and under in Afghanistan—Petraeus shepherded the military's publication of Field Manual 3-24, *Counterinsurgency*, the new bible of dealing with insurrections such as those ongoing in Afghanistan and Iraq. Mattis himself had commanded the 1st Marine Division during the assault on Baghdad and had seen that ad hoc counterinsurgency strategies were critical in winning over the population. In part, his early advocacy reflected why the Marine Corps for most of the reconstruction had proven effective in stabilizing their assigned areas of the occupation.[54]

Petraeus disseminated those lessons in the context of securing Iraq in two widely read articles that would be later published in the winter 2006 and fall 2008 issues of *Military Review*: "Learning Counterinsurgency: Observations from Soldiering in Iraq" and "Commander's Counterinsurgency Guidance." Twenty-six highlighted talking points in the latter essay were clearly intended to be a practical guide to securing Iraq. Sympathetic observers figured that it was only a matter of when, not if, Petraeus returned from his Kansas sabbatical to Iraq.[55]

The Twenty Months

How had David Petraeus—from his February 2007 return to a violent Iraq as supreme commander of the multinational forces to his mid-September 2008 departure from a more or less quiet country—pulled off such a stunning reversal?

The first challenge was political, both at home and in Iraq: to ensure that the new Democrat-controlled Congress did not cut off funds for his last-ditch efforts to save Iraq. But that high-wire act simultaneously also required that he not show ingratitude for the president's vote of confidence in him—and, indeed, for his own meteoric rise. As the noted military correspondent John Burns put it at the time, "For General Petraeus, being cast as the president's white knight has been a mixed blessing." Burns emphasized that Petraeus was careful to cast himself as the servant of both Congress and the president, hoping to invest both in his own success and thereby preclude any demands on his own particular loyalty.[56]

Wisely, Petraeus avoided domestic politics and ensured that his subordinates did not directly engage congressional critics or bask in administration praise. The result was an end to talk of cutoffs; congressional funding continued. Bush was delighted in the salvation of his war; meanwhile, many in the Democratic Congress felt that their past harsh criticism had led to necessary changes. Most strikingly, public attitudes about Iraq slowly began to change. In February 2007, 67 percent of the public felt that the war was going badly. But just a year after the arrival of Petraeus, Americans were split 48 percent to 48 percent over whether Iraq was faring well or poorly, an unexpected turnabout that might provide political cover for wavering supporters.[57]

In Iraq, the politics were trickier. A Shiite majority long oppressed by Saddam Hussein had come to power through American-sponsored elections—to the dismay of a once privileged Sunni and Baathist-tainted minority with strong ties to the rich nearby Sunni-dominated Gulf sheikdoms. The challenge was not just persuading the government of Shiite Nouri al-Maliki, who had become prime minister of Iraq in May 2006, to move beyond retribution for Baathists and to treat his Sunni countrymen equitably. It was unfortunately far more complicated than that. Petraeus also had to ensure that the wily Maliki would also act against his own supporters, specifically thousands of Iranian-supplied Shiite terrorists organized by the fiery demagogue Muqtada al-Sadr, who wished to turn Iraq into a Shiite theocratic client state of Iran. Thanks to Maliki's acquiescence, for much of Petraeus's tenure, Sadr was either quiet or in exile, especially after he had provoked a fight with the far more revered Shiite cleric Ayatollah Ali al-Sistani—and lost the confrontation. And, in fear of government crackdowns—and convinced the U.S. military might well kill him—Sadr finally at last ordered a stand-down of his militias by August 2007. Looming behind these religious fault lines inside Iraq were even greater regional challenges: It would do no good to remove Saddam Hussein's threat to the oil-exporting Sunni Gulf sheikdoms only to replace his Baathist dictatorship with a Shiite-dominated elected government, in name a democracy, in reality a client state of theocratic Iran.

Petraeus also had to turn the Sunnis of Anbar Province against the Sunni fundamentalists of al-Qaeda and various former Saddam supporters. Those gymnastics meant a de facto Sunni alliance with the Shiite-dominated government that was often shunning Sunni parliamentarians. For the most part, Petraeus was able to induce each faction to suppress

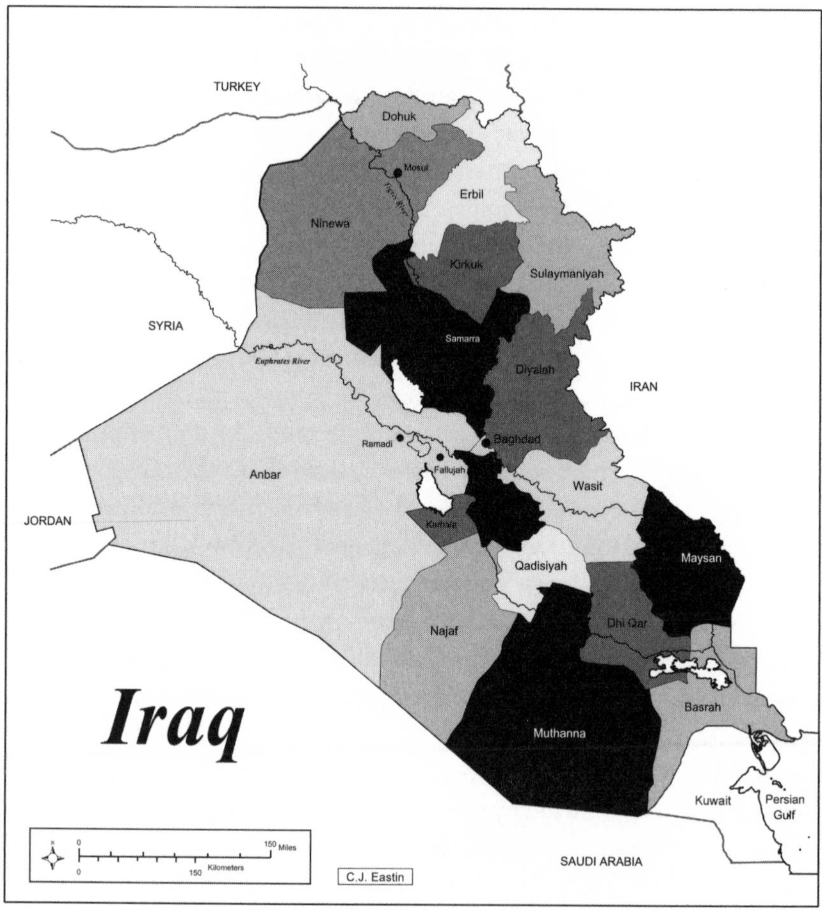

its own extremists while transitioning to a Shiite-dominated government in a Sunni-dominated neighborhood—with a new, more deadly U.S. military eager to enforce these new protocols of understanding.

That violence from both Shiite and Sunni militias waned was testament to Petraeus's political skills, which were enhanced by the inspired diplomacy of the American ambassador, Ryan Crocker. Early on, Crocker had grasped that security rested on assuring the more influential but less numerous Sunnis that they would not be oppressed by the new Shiite-led government; on convincing the Shiites that democracy gave them predominant power but not the right to do to the Sunnis what Saddam had done to themselves; and on convincing the Kurds that semiautonomy would be as prosperous for them as independence would be suicidal. Crocker and Petraeus developed a good partnership, and the former soon earned the reputation as the premier U.S. ambassador and diplomat at large in the State Department. Under the Petraeus-Crocker team, gone were the baleful days of the infighting between Paul Bremer and his military counterparts. The importance of Crocker was highlighted by the lack of any comparable diplomatic figure in Afghanistan, where for the next few years, from 2009 to 2011, American diplomacy would be at odds with its own military, estranged from the Karzai government, and unable to enlist the full support of neighboring Pakistan.[58]

Petraeus surrounded himself with gifted subordinates and colleagues who invested in his success. General Raymond Odierno had been unfairly tarred early in the war by the press as an unimaginative bullet-headed hard charger of the old school as commander of 4th Infantry Division. Petraeus thought otherwise, realizing that the caricature was not only unfair, but perhaps even valuable in bringing Odierno's military bona fides on board to present counterinsurgency as a no-nonsense way of defeating the enemy. Odierno stayed on as Petraeus's senior ground commander in Baghdad. He proved a master of counterinsurgency and provided continuity as Petraeus's eventual successor. To some observers, Odierno was one of the key reasons for the success of the surge. In any case, he took the fight to the terrorists as never before and let others label his ferocity as part of counterinsurgency.[59]

One key to regaining public support was curbing American casualties, especially losses to improvised explosive devices. Such mayhem was especially demoralizing given its random nature, and the fact that Iraqi insurgents otherwise were usually beaten badly in any firefight they engaged in with the U.S. military. Despite spending $10 billion to stop the roadside bombs, the Pentagon's technological experts could scarcely keep up with the insurgents' ability to fabricate ever larger and more sophisticated explosives. Petraeus saw that the solution ultimately lay with the Iraqis. He had to get his men outside the compounds, embed them within Iraqi communities, and develop human intelligence to break up the bombing teams and develop communities to the point where the explosions were seen by Iraqis as counterproductive. Stop the IEDs, and for the most part the war was sustainable, as the insurgents increasingly avoided firefights with U.S. troops. As a stopgap measure, Petraeus insisted on receiving thousands of MRAP heavy vehicles, designed especially to curb the effects of IEDs. While such trucks were clumsy and hard to maneuver, in the short term their greater armor and superior design certainly saved lives.

Important to this teamwork was the image of David Petraeus as everyman. He gave credit to others. To the media he insisted that he was neither a Bush advocate nor a reformer sent to undo the mistakes of the past—"I am not an optimist or a pessimist," he would declare, "I am a realist." His uniform was almost indistinguishable from his enlisted men's; his habit was to visit almost every outpost of the sprawling American occupation. Within a matter of months, in early 2007, the character of Petraeus became as important as his tactical insight. Petraeus had accrued moral capital, in the way that the name of Themistocles or Belisarius was synonymous with competence, Sherman's honor was unquestioned, and Ridgway's integrity was legendary.[60]

Down from Olympus

David Petraeus turned over his by then relatively quiet command on September 16, 2008, to the gifted General Raymond Odierno, and then returned from Iraq to widespread adulation. Just two weeks later, on October 31, 2008, Petraeus assumed command of CENTCOM in Tampa, Florida, the most prestigious and important regional theater of operations in the post-9/11 military—directing counterterrorism operations in some twenty countries as well as overseeing the combat theaters in Afghanistan and Iraq.

There had been no major terrorist attack since September 11, 2001. Iraq was relatively quiet. The fighting in Afghanistan still remained off the front page. In theory, Petraeus could enjoy a well-earned, relatively quiet administrative post as he oversaw operations from Florida that were largely successful—at least in part because of doctrines he had promoted and used with demonstrable results in Iraq. Given that he was the most popular American general in a generation, Petraeus could no doubt expect to be offered either the chairmanship of the Joint Chiefs of Staff or the supreme command of NATO, the usual capstones for such a singular career.

The public certainly felt an enormous sense of gratitude to Petraeus for turning Iraq around. He immediately became almost as respected as Dwight Eisenhower following World War II, or perhaps more than Colin Powell during the early 1990s. *Time* magazine had judged Petraeus one of the one hundred most influential people of 2007. Several newspapers and magazines followed suit throughout 2007 and 2008, along with various awards and honors. As Petraeus left Bagdad in late summer 2008,

Secretary of Defense Robert Gates praised him by asserting that "history would regard Petraeus as one of the nation's great battle captains." By January 2010, David Petraeus was consistently cited in polls as one of the most widely revered men of his generation in the United States. In early 2011, a guest *Wall Street Journal* opinion editorial advised that Petraeus should be promoted to five-star general, an honor not bestowed since Omar Bradley had been made General of the Army in 1950. Senator Lindsey Graham likewise raised the issue of a Petraeus fifth star and thought there might be bipartisan congressional support for it.

An April 2011 poll ranked Petraeus as the most popular of all potential Republican presidential candidates for the upcoming 2012 election—even though he had emphatically earlier denied, in Shermanesque fashion, to Washington reporter David Gregory any intention of running for president: "No way, no how." His Gallup poll favorable-to-unfavorable ratings were an unheard-of 61 percent to 7 percent. By the end of Barack Obama's first two years in office, Republicans yearned to see Petraeus join the presidential race—if somewhat unsure exactly what Petraeus's politics were. In any case, in comparison with all the great twentieth-century American generals, perhaps only Dwight Eisenhower matched Petraeus's political savvy and understanding of the press and uncanny ability to seem liberal to Democrats and conservative to Republicans.[61]

Yet within months, the mass adulation of Petraeus began to fade—in a way reminiscent of William Tecumseh Sherman's retreat into the shadows following the end of the Civil War and his adamant disavowal of any political aspirations. The Republican primary fight returned to normalcy as political veterans vied for the nomination and Petraeus reiterated his uninterest in running for political office—and made it known for most of 2012 that he was also not interested in the Republican vice presidential nomination. Petraeus himself sometimes stepped into political controversy as the new CENTCOM commander. For example, in March 2010, he told the Senate Armed Services Committee that "a perception of U.S. favoritism for Israel" was hampering U.S. efforts throughout the region—a common sentiment often voiced by former U.S. generals who usually dealt far more frequently with Arab militaries and heard their constant criticisms of pro-Israel U.S. Middle East policy.

As CENTCOM commander, Petraeus was directly in charge of turning around Afghanistan as well—a theater that seemed to have suddenly gotten worse in 2009 even as Iraq had continued to quiet. If America had supposedly "taken its eye off the ball" by launching a war in Iraq, would the quiet in Baghdad not mean that the U.S. military could have its eye on the ball on a single front in Afghanistan, and thus a similar quiet should likewise follow there? Petraeus was in some sense already in the awkward position of not fully basking in the calm he had produced in Iraq, while inheriting the chaos of a war he heretofore had had nothing to do with. No matter—the public expected another successful surge. Petraeus no doubt would again become the savior general of Afghanistan who did what others could not.

Originally President Barack Obama had campaigned on the quieter Afghanistan as the "good" war that was a logical and direct retaliation for 9/11—and one that had far more United Nations and NATO support. But now it was becoming far more unsettled than George Bush's "bad" theater in Iraq that Petraeus had once saved and that Vice President Joe Biden was proudly proclaiming might "be one of the great achievements of [the Obama] administration." Indeed, in the Obama administration's first eighteen months, more Americans died in the upsurge in violence in Afghanistan than had been lost during the entire first eight years of the war. It was almost as if Petraeus's old work in Iraq was claimed by others, while the old mess of others was now his own new responsibility. In addition, promising as a candidate to fix Afghanistan did not necessarily mean that as president Barack Obama wished to risk recommitting to Afghanistan in the manner in which the surge had once salvaged Iraq—given that it was unclear whether the two theaters were all that similar.[62]

In June 2010, senior Afghanistan ground commander General Stanley A. McChrystal was abruptly relieved of command by President Obama for indiscreet remarks to a *Rolling Stone* magazine journalist about the Obama administration's allegedly inept conduct of the war. With two supreme commanders gone in just a year and a half from Afghanistan—General McKiernan had been relieved just months earlier—President Obama needed continuity and stability. So he asked the national hero Petraeus to step down from his CENTCOM post and take over active command of the ground war in Afghanistan. Quite unexpectedly, Petraeus was appointed commander of U.S. and NATO forces in Afghanistan on June 23, 2010, and was directing operations by July 4. Petraeus, in characteristic confidence, reflected on the appointment by comparing himself to the savior generals Grant, Ridgway, and Slim, who in World War II had saved the allied effort in Burma: "I've had a certain affinity for leaders who have been given seemingly lost or at least very difficult causes."[63]

Yet new command soon proved a thankless job. For all the challenges posed by Iraq, it was Afghanistan that had always posed much more challenging problems for long-term stability and the creation of constitutional government. The terrain was far more difficult, with towering peaks and snow. The country was landlocked, without ports of access. Neighboring Pakistan, a volatile nuclear power, was at best an unreliable ally that was nonetheless essential to American resupply. The country's borders with Iran, Pakistan, and the former Soviet republics likewise afforded sanctuary and free passage to insurgents of various sorts. Afghanistan was impoverished, without the oil that boosted Iraq's economy. Illiteracy and tribalism, as well as a thriving drug trade, made counterinsurgency a far different proposition than in more literate Iraq. There were more NATO allies in Afghanistan than in Iraq, but they operated under far more restrictions, nation by nation, on the rules of engagement. As a rough index of their comparative levels of security, during the first full month that Petraeus took over in Afghanistan (July 2010), there were eighty-eight coalition deaths, compared to only four fatalities in Iraq.

At first, Petraeus sought to apply the same sort of "inputs" that had saved Iraq, requesting a surge of forces, replicating his counterinsurgency and civilian reconstruction teams, and urging that his old counterinsurgency partner, General Mattis, replace him as CENTCOM commander. But again, it soon became clear that a popular President Obama, who inherited a deteriorating situation in Afghanistan from the Bush administration, did not quite feel the same urgency to take enormous risks to save the ten-year-long war effort in Afghanistan as had a desperate and unpopular George Bush in the case of Iraq in 2006. If most of the old Bush conservative base had supported escalation in Iraq, the new Obama liberal core did not especially favor a similar effort in Afghanistan. Nonetheless, a surge was ordered; but quite unlike the escalation in Iraq, its psychological effects were somewhat nullified by Obama's announcement of firm dates for unilateral withdrawals of U.S. troops.

The lack of clear success of the Afghan surge between 2010 and 2012 now began to raise questions about the circumstances of its model, the 2007 Iraqi surge: If more troops and a change in tactics in Afghanistan were not turning the war around, had such developments really ever worked in Iraq? In other words, when the surge did not immediately save Afghanistan—despite undeniable successes in Helmand and Kandahar

Provinces—it strengthened revisionist arguments that the Anbar Awakening and general disgust with al-Qaeda, not the surge, had secured Iraq. And thus without a commensurate "Afghan Awakening," sending more troops and protecting the population would have little effect.

In any case, by 2011, the American public, after a decade of support, had lost most of its zeal for war, and the public concern over a surge in Afghanistan was not what it had been earlier in Iraq. President Obama had not met with his commanders in Afghanistan until months after taking office, and the administration seemed more concerned with leaving the country than with defeating the Taliban and leaving behind a stable government.

The Taliban had also learned a great deal over the decade, especially about American tactics in Iraq. It was proving a canny enemy who saw that IEDs were the best way to maim Americans and demoralize the public in the sparsely settled terrain of Afghanistan. U.S. helicopter and fighter sorties were employed far more frequently than in mostly urban Iraq—and far more often hit civilian targets, forcing Petraeus to apologize for collateral damage. Targeted drone assassinations of suspected terrorists in Pakistan were a favored tactic of the new administration, and their sometimes wayward strikes made counterinsurgency efforts in Afghanistan all the more difficult—especially against a wily enemy that knew the propaganda value of collateral damage. Pakistan proved a far more effective sanctuary for terrorists than had Iran or Syria in the case of Iraq; Pashtun tribesmen considered both sides of the border their ancestral home. In Iraq, the United States had removed a mostly secular dictatorship without religious support; but in Afghanistan, U.S. forces had toppled an Islamic theocracy. The latter fact made it more difficult to isolate Islamic fundamentalists from the general population.

After only a year, without the envisioned calm in Afghanistan, Petraeus gave up his command on July 18, 2011, to assume a new civilian post as director of the Central Intelligence Agency. Rumors had spread that Petraeus was growing dissatisfied with the Obama administration's policies over troop levels in Afghanistan, but had, after some discussion, decided neither to resign nor to go public with his unhappiness. At one point, Petraeus was supposedly said to have warned of the Obama administration's efforts to muzzle his military assessments of Afghanistan and relations with Pakistan, "They're fucking with the wrong guy." Yet, in some sense, the political handlers in the administration may have surmised that the reputation of General David Petraeus by mid-2011 was not what it had been at the end of 2008. The CIA appointment was often interpreted by the media as a way to ease the popular but frustrated Petraeus into a position of power and reputation befitting his status—but without providing him the means to embarrass the president over the deteriorating situation in Afghanistan or to launch a political career, given that he was working inside rather than parallel to the Obama administration.[64]

The penultimate years of the brilliant career of David Petraeus bore an uncanny resemblance to Belisarius' final ceremonial offices—close to but without ultimate power. In vain he had privately opposed the withdrawal of all U.S. troops from a quiet Iraq in December 2011 and the continual announcements of a planned complete drawdown from Afghanistan. Petraeus was no doubt still largely seen by some in the Obama administration as a "Bush general," even while conservatives saw him as a newly reformulated Obama appointee. Bob Woodward, the widely read Washington insider journalist, echoed the old charge of Petraeus's supposedly "endless campaign of self-promotion" that led to ever more appointments and press coverage.[65]

Although in theory he could have served as CIA chief while in uniform, Petraeus instead either was advised to leave the military, or chose to retire from the Army on August 31, 2011. He was only fifty-eight years old. It was rumored that Petraeus, after leaving Iraq, had preferred a post on the Joint Chiefs—in the fashion of laurels given to earlier generals of similar stature such as General Colin Powell. With the appointment of General Martin Dempsey as chairman of the Joint Chiefs, Petraeus was passed over—again, amid rumors that the CIA post was considered the proper cul-de-sac for generals with possible political ambitions. In any case, the Obama administration had given Petraeus a key post on its own team and simultaneously denied him more prestigious military assignments. Of his desire to serve as chairman of the Joint Chiefs, retiring Secretary of Defense Robert Gates had warned Petraeus, "Forget about it." The public was never apprised why its most successful living general should not warrant the military's highest post.[66]

The frantic twenty months to save Iraq had taken a toll not just on the country, but perhaps on the person of David Petraeus as well. In February 2009, just four months after returning from Iraq, CENTCOM commander Petraeus was diagnosed with prostate cancer and underwent a two-month regimen of radiation treatments. Questions arose again about his health the following June when he momentarily collapsed during a hearing of the Senate Armed Services Committee—a fainting spell he attributed to dehydration. Petraeus now appeared in photos without his customary camouflage of a soldier in the ranks; in formal military dress, the general seemed almost encumbered by his vast array of medals. That effect of seeming out of place and uncomfortable was only magnified when he was photographed in a civilian suit and tie. Many remarked of his wearied appearance.[67]

Within a brief three-year period, a relatively young David Petraeus had ended his illustrious military career in a stalemated Afghanistan and switched jobs without leaving an impression of singular success at either. He was assuming control of a CIA infamous for tarnishing the reputations of many who had tried to harness it—an agency whose failures surface in the media, but whose successes usually remain classified, and whose director during scandal and catastrophe is usually first to be blamed and last to be exonerated. In that regard, the stunning and unexpected resignation of David Petraeus from his CIA post on November 9, 2012, after an admission of an extramarital affair, and right after the U.S. presidential election, shocked the nation—and at the time when this manuscript went to press remained a mystery that may involve far more than issues of adultery. Ostensibly he had helped save Iraq under the auspices of an unpopular Bush administration, and then was put into nearly the same situation in Afghanistan as the war worsened and President Obama's poll numbers dipped. The mess of Afghanistan had overwhelmed every American general sent to quiet the country since the upsurge in violence in 2008. In truth, the wars abroad, and the so-called war on terror at home, were no longer daily issues of national concern. Success earned generals neglect in the media, failure only occasional accusations.

If the fates of other controversial savior generals—and in particular, the scandals that forced David Petraeus from the CIA—are any indication, it is likely that our modern Ridgway's fortunes peaked in the darkest hours of 2007–2008, when one rare American—along with his brilliant cadre of civilian and military advisers—was able to save a war deemed lost by almost everyone around him. Or, to paraphrase the Roman poet Ennius of Quintus Fabius Maximus, "The Delayer" (Cunctator)—another savior general who in the late third century B.C. kept the Roman Republic alive after its four losses to Hannibal at the disastrous battles at Tricinius, the River Trebia, Lake Trasimene, and Cannae and who was equally criticized for not waging war in terms of just trying to kill enemy soldiers—*unus homo nobis cunctando restituit rem*: "one man by delaying restored the state to us."

We shall see whether Iraq shall stay won, as the United States, in a somewhat surprising decision, could not agree with the Iraqi government on establishing a small permanent American presence and so abruptly pulled out all its remaining troops from the country at the end of 2011. Nonetheless, in the final month of the American occupation—December 2011—not a single American soldier died, and the nascent Iraqi democracy was relatively free of violence as its oil production and revenues soared. Iraq's relative stability was David Petraeus's legacy and remained in sharp contrast to the Arab dictatorships throughout the Middle East that tottered and fell during the so-called Arab Spring of 2011, followed by general chaos and violence—all against a backdrop of hopes that some sort of constitutional government would survive in Iraq.

For now, we know only that without David Petraeus, the American effort in Iraq—along with the reputation of the U.S. military in the Middle East—would have been lost long ago.

Epilogue: A Rare Breed

Mavericks and Loners

What common traits helped these diverse generals to save lost wars? Were their profiles any different from the generally agreed-upon criteria of command excellence that are so often attributed to brilliant generals like Alexander the Great, Julius Caesar, Hannibal, Napoleon, Wellington, or Grant?

There is certainly no typical profile of shared age, class, or political view of a savior general. Ridgway came to Korea at fifty-five, an age at which Alexander the Great was long dead. Sherman cut no figure like the Duke of Wellington on a horse. David Petraeus first saw combat in Iraq in his early fifties, at an age when a declining Napoleon was in exile and dying. Themistocles was of birth as low as Caesar's was aristocratic.

By definition, a savior general like a Themistocles, Ridgway, and Petraeus started on the defensive. If they were to take the initiative to the enemy, it was often in a wider landscape of pessimism and near hopelessness, as Belisarius learned when he went both east and west, and Sherman did when he kept heading south amid the gloomy spring and summer of 1864. The ability to envision a great new offensive campaign or to plan a dramatic opening invasion to a war may well require different talent from salvaging an entire conflict.

The best-known Great Captains are like grand medieval architects and master builders who out of nothing raise majestic spires. Yet the savior generals resemble more closely the unsung engineers who were called in to fix a poorly built and now cracked dome, or an ill-designed buttress before the resplendent but unsound edifice crashed down in ruin.

The savior generals display commonalities of character and disposition that encouraged contrarianism of all sorts—professional, political, and social. When Ridgway arrived in Korea, he quickly discovered—against the consensus that an invincible Chinese enemy had crushed outnumbered and outgunned Americans led by the brilliant Douglas MacArthur—that the American army was not so much beaten militarily by Chinese and Korean forces as it was poorly equipped for winter weather, panicked, terribly led in the field, and without confidence in the nature of its mission. Uncertain American strategy, tactics, and operations, not Chinese supermen, had led to the horrific losses. In less than one hundred days, Ridgway rectified those lapses. He soon ended up back across the 38th Parallel, with the Chinese invaders even more exhausted and overextended than the Americans had been in the north during November 1950. Where the Joint Chiefs and soon even General MacArthur saw hopelessness, Ridgway instinctively sensed opportunity, but worried that he alone embraced such optimism.

Less than a third of the American public by late 2006 thought a surge of troops could salvage the Iraq War when David Petraeus was being considered for promotion to command of all ground forces in Iraq. Petraeus, and his small circle, understood that after four years of warring, Islamic terrorists and ex-Baathists were vulnerable to the strategies of counterinsurgency. They had suffered far more casualties than had the Americans. Even as the media suggested Americans had lost the support of the Iraqi people, Petraeus sensed that the insurgents, not the U.S. military, had alienated their base Sunni population and so were now vulnerable to new counterinsurgency tactics. To obtain for Petraeus supreme command in Iraq, his supporters had to outflank the bureaucracy and chain of command on the premise that Petraeus was right and most others wrong.

This natural independence of mind and need to reject past conventional thinking were critical, and were probably innate rather than merely acquired characteristics. There had to be unusual self-regard in the wily half-Athenian scrapper Themistocles or the once unstable Sherman to assume that most others were unable to save a nearly stalemated or lost war. Belisarius apparently thought that his name alone might make up for chronic shortages in manpower and matériel. "King David" Petraeus and Matthew Ridgway arrived in theater as if their entire prior lives had been requisites for their few months of salvation. Neither shied away from publicity.

Hollywood created the genre of the Western on the premise of the tragic hero, the loner or misfit in times of peace whose singular fighting qualities alone can save the town when called upon by its beleaguered community. The foundation of great American Western films—*The Searchers, Shane, High Noon, The Man Who Shot Liberty Valance, The Magnificent Seven*—is the willingness of bothersome outsiders to save frontier civilization, fully cognizant that their efforts will be less than fully appreciated, and that their controversial presence will no longer be appreciated, or perhaps even useful, in the calmer times that they had delivered. Riding off into the sunset does not only express the consensus of the saved town that such outsiders are no longer needed. It is an acknowledgment, too, on the part of the saviors of a sort of detached superiority that they can do in war's darkest hours what most others either could not or would not—or a tacit admission that they have less to offer in times of accustomed peace. Note here that I do not suggest nihilism is in the DNA of savior generals; by all accounts, they functioned within their respective military systems and were contrarian rather than renegades and bomb throwers.

Assuming responsibility for a lost rather than uncertain war requires a different magnitude of physical stamina, and one that usually cannot be sustained for more than a year or two under such grueling pressures. Sherman may have eschewed postwar political life because his great marches had left him numb and wearied after 1865. He certainly sounded far more skeptical and tired than did Grant, who had ended the war's final months with far less success.

Perhaps Themistocles could never quite recapture the singular mental concentration and effort that were needed to rally the Greeks to win at Salamis. He played no part in the subsequent great Hellenic victory at Plataea a year later and probably enjoyed a reduced role in naval operations after Salamis. At some point, David Petraeus realized that his tenure of endless nights without sleep in a collapsing Iraq was not sustainable in the long term. That Belisarius did not foment unrest against Justinian between his frequent recalls might suggest that all those breakneck marches and endless voyages to collapsing fronts had left him exhausted.

He certainly disappeared from the historical record for a decade after his last recall from Italy.

Preparation

Savior generals are not mere cowboys. Most were keen students, even scholars, of war. If while in the shadows they garnered little notice, they nevertheless used their time in obscurity to systematically review contemporary tactics and strategy of an ongoing losing war. In their prior tenures, they were open to innovation and experimentation without the burdens of supreme military command. As outsiders in their ideas about sea power, logistics, total war, or counterinsurgency, they were largely left alone when the war went well—only to receive a sudden call to arms at a time of near defeat, when more conventional choices were long exhausted.

Long before Themistocles took control of the Athenian fleet in 480, he had been the architect of Athenian naval supremacy—a strategist before he was a heralded admiral. David Petraeus literally helped to write the book on counterinsurgency before applying those principles as supreme ground commander in Iraq. Most of what Sherman accomplished in Georgia and the Carolinas had its roots in earlier, smaller raids during his successful advance to Meridian, Mississippi, in 1863. He had learned a far different lesson from his ordeal at Shiloh in 1862 than had his superior Ulysses S. Grant. If Sherman's peculiar views about total war in the modern era were rarely known or irrelevant during the ascendancy of Grant in 1863, then they were deemed vital to the Union by late 1864, when Grant's alternate preference for shock battles had almost destroyed the Army of the Potomac. The emperor Justinian called forth Belisarius to end the Vandal Empire in North Africa only because of the general's prior success in restoring the eastern Byzantine front and crushing insurrectionists during the Nika riots at Constantinople. Belisarius had proven to his emperor that he knew how to do much with little. When most strategists were deprecating conventional forces in the new age of nuclear superiority, Ridgway not only saw that new limited ground wars would be more, not less, frequent, but also thought deeply about how to win them without resort to the bomb. If he once wrote mostly ignored memos about conducting conventional wars at the Pentagon, he suddenly was asked to put theory to practice in December 1950.

Given their preparation out of the limelight, savior generals were not easily caught up in the hysteria of apparent easy victory. In the general public euphoria over other generals' successful conventional strategies—hoplite triumph at Marathon, the Union victories at Gettysburg and Vicksburg, MacArthur's stunning victory at Inchon and race to the Yalu, and the brilliant three-week removal of Saddam Hussein—the soon-to-be savior generals resisted conventional wisdom. Instead, they waited their turn, and when it came, they were determined to get to the front, reconnoiter firsthand, and dispel group consensus that did not accord with what they saw and heard from men on the ground.

Most generals assume that every great victory is naturally to be followed by an even greater one; but savior generals are philosophers of sorts who worry about the idea of ying and yang, nemesis and karma—and so do not think that a Marathon, Dara, Gettsyburg, Inchon, or crushing of Saddam Hussein is necessarily the final chapter. They instead realized that previous and accustomed victory often leads to arrogance and, in turn, complacency or even a sort of paralysis, ending in catastrophe. Nothing in war is static—yet few leaders in the moment of triumph remember that fundamental truth about conflict. Overconfidence blinds the winning side to the need for constant reassessment and readjustment to meet the ever-changing conditions on the battlefield.

The Enemy with a Thousand Faces

Some enemies are not just formidable but abjectly terrifying. Before the victory at Marathon, the Greeks, or so the historian Herodotus remarked, feared even to look upon the Persians. Rumors of the decapitation of the Spartan king Leonidas at Thermopylae perhaps only added to the sense of dread that hung over the defeated Greeks who retreated to Salamis. The chronically outnumbered Byzantines likewise felt such apprehension about their myriad fierce tribal enemies such as the Goths, Vandals, and Huns, and an array of Persian and Arab enemies to the east, whom bribes, not force, usually alone had warded off. By 1864, a growing number in the demoralized North were beginning to believe the myth that the South simply had bred a better warrior class, one so adept at arms that it still might nullify the vast advantages in technology, numbers, and supply enjoyed by the North. Many feared that no Northern generals could match Confederate luminaries like Robert E. Lee. In Korea, the sudden influx of hundreds of thousands of Communist Chinese created sheer panic among retreating American troops. Sudden tales of "hordes" of fanatical supermen who in eerie fashion blew trumpets and baited their enemies on loudspeakers quickly spread among demoralized United Nations troops. After hundreds of Americans were blown up by Shiite and Sunni Muslim extremists in Iraq, many in America felt there were simply few antidotes either to suicide bombers or to improvised explosive devices—the trademarks of a premodern enemy that bragged it loved life far less than the more comfortable postmodern Americans.

What is remarkable in all these cases was how little such dread affected generals like Themistocles, Belisarius, Sherman, Ridgway, and Petraeus. They did not belittle their enemies' fighting prowess, but simply saw that their own side's prior problems were not due to larger-than-life foes, but to deficiencies in their own forces. In other words, a Sherman or Ridgway did not really worry about the martial reputations of their enemies, only about ensuring that their own forces were so well trained, motivated, and organized that they could defeat any conceivable adversary. Themistocles' sailors who rowed in the Bay of Salamis that day believed they could beat back any armada—whether the Great King's or not. What did it count whether Ionians, Egyptians, or Phoenicians served in the king's fleet? For Belisarius, once he had created a successful Byzantine way of war, it did not matter whether he employed it against Persians, Arabs, Vandals, Goths, or Huns.

A great general peels the veneer of invulnerability from a winning enemy, and he does so by convincing his own men that victory is entirely within their own purview. In short, the problem is never seen as a particular adversary, only an army's sense that enemies are abstractions, given that victory or defeat is always fluid, never fated. By the time Uncle Billy's army took Atlanta, it no longer resembled the tentative force that had left Tennessee five months earlier, but felt that it could march through the South with impunity and itself win the war outright. The Chinese of spring 1951 were as terrified of the Americans as the American forces that Ridgway inherited in December 1950 had been of the Chinese as they crossed the Yalu.

Grand Strategy

Superior generalship can save an army. But to infuse it with a sense of victory, generals convince their armies that they will not just defeat the enemy, but do so in a fashion that will ripple far beyond the theater. The sailors at Salamis were not just fighting Xerxes, but were themselves emissaries of a new sea power that would help decide the entire Persian War. Belisarius' men were not just defending the borders of Byzantium, but at some point sensed that they were the instruments of a larger vision of their general and emperor in restoring a lost Roman Empire in the west. Sherman's men did not just take Atlanta before the election, but in attacking the infrastructure of the Confederacy were determined to "make war so terrible" that the Southern population would prefer peace, and to make the supplier of arms as legitimate a target at the rear as was the user at the front. Ridgway pushed the Communists out of South Korea. In the process, he taught the West that it could fight and win a distant limited conventional war in the age of nuclear annihilation. Before Petraeus quieted Iraq, "counterinsurgency" was an abstraction to most of the American people; afterward, the public believed their sons and daughters could defeat far-off insurgents on American terms.

These generals saw their tasks as transcending the immediate war. They were not just to beat the enemy on a particular day, or even during a given campaign, but also to craft a means that would defeat the enemy to the point of winning the war, and thereby to provide a blueprint for others to do so as well. After Petraeus left Iraq, counterinsurgency was accepted as the means for the remaining Americans to keep Iraq quiet. Sherman introduced to the American way of war the idea that targeting the enemy's morale and material reserves should not be confined to the front—with devastating consequences in the century to follow. Themistocles created the Athenian fleet and the way to use it successfully; even those who despised him saw that his vision might found an Athenian empire.

Savior generals were fine writers and skilled communicators, advocates of causes much larger than merely defeating an enemy on the field of battle. Petraeus is an accomplished author. So was Ridgway, who drew on history to inform his key decisions in Korea. Sherman's memoirs, letters, and communiqués show a level of insight superior even to Grant's. Themistocles seems to have mastered the Athenian Assembly well before he did the navy.

War on All Fronts

The savior generals saw civilians as key to their victories. For David Petraeus, the aim was not just to kill the enemy, but rather to persuade (or hire) both Sunni and Shiite tribesmen to turn on the insurgents and terrorists in their midst. That also meant persuading everyday Iraqis that neither foreigners like the Americans and their allies nor rival religious groups posed as much of a threat to their own safety as did radical Islamists in their own environs. His predecessors either did not fully grasp that fact or were so overwhelmed by the endemic violence that they had neither the time nor the resources to win over the population.

Matthew Ridgway found himself in a civil war, in which he had to fight alongside South Koreans against North Koreans and their Communist Chinese allies—at a time when all Koreans were puzzled that the United States was an apparent ally of the hated Japanese, and almost all Americans back home were tired of Asia in general. Rebuilding Korea went on even as Ridgway was often destroying it.

William Tecumseh Sherman operated mostly in hostile territory after May 1864. For all the contemporary disparagement of him as a "terrorist," Sherman was savvy enough to target mostly the houses of the wealthy and the infrastructure of the Confederacy while sparing the lives of Southern noncombatants. Yet there was an important qualifier: he would make war so terrible to the architects of the Confederacy that the deleterious effects would trickle down to even average Southerners who were often exempt from Sherman's direct ire.

Belisarius and his small army could not have overthrown the Vandal kingdom without convincing North Africans that his invaders were restorers rather than conquerors. At any given time in the east, in Africa, or in Sicily and Italy, Belisarius would have lost the war had the indigenous population turned against him.

Themistocles took an entire people to war by evacuating Athens, not just seamen in the fleet. Sherman insidiously targeted the manifest symbols of Southern wealth and authority—plantations and Confederate buildings—as he sought to remind the mostly poor and non-slave-owning local populations that he was not their real enemy. Ridgway was careful to remind Koreans that their common enemy was Communism, not other Koreans per se in the north. Petraeus knew of these lessons, and so he assumed that Iraq would not be quiet until those he protected from insurgents joined in to protect his forces as well—despite vast differences in nationality, religion, and language.

Two common themes emerge. As far as the civilian populations are concerned, generals won their hearts and minds not by rhetoric or reprisals, but by convincing locals that they had much to lose by further opposition—and far more to gain through cooperation. As for the military, it was always to be seen as a fish that had to swim and breathe in a civilian sea.

Saved—but Not Won?

The title of this book is not *The Victorious Generals*, although all five profiles most surely deal with victories. Nonetheless, Salamis was the beginning of the end for the Persians, not *the* end—a final Greek victory to be won only at Plataea a year later where Themistocles played no part. Persia was quieted, never conquered, by the fifth-century Greeks. An exiled Belisarius was not in Italy when Narses finally pacified the peninsula. It was Grant, not Sherman, who accepted Lee's surrender in Virginia. Ridgway never fulfilled MacArthur's vaunted aim of reuniting Korea—and was in Europe when the war finally ended. David Petraeus was gone from Iraq when the last American troops left the country, and he remained almost mute about the prospects of the country's uncertain future as violence returned.

In all these cases, the aims of the savior commanders were limited. Their role was to restore a theater, to give other generals and politicians the opportunity to recover victory or at least avoid defeat. Because Themistocles was not an Alexander, Belisarius not a Caesar, and Sherman not a Napoleon, taking over an entire war and ensure that it stayed won, both militarily and politically, was beyond their responsibilities. Matthew Ridgway resurrected a nearly lost South Korea; whether UN forces could or should have moved across the 38th Parallel in a second invasion was ultimately left to President Dwight Eisenhower and the Joint Chiefs. David Petraeus saved Iraq; but after December 2011, when the last American troops left, it was up to Iraqis themselves and the Obama administration to protect a nascent constitutional government. At the death of Belisarius, Byzantium controlled most of the Mediterranean—to be preserved or forfeited by subsequent generations.

Magnanimity

Savior generals did not fault the prior generals who had nearly lost the war. Instead, a Themistocles or a Ridgway praised predecessors whose ideas were ensuring defeat, even as they quietly proceeded to reject their methods of war making. Sherman gave much credit to predecessors even as he adopted policies antithetical to theirs. David Petraeus said nothing much that was critical of his predecessors General Ricardo Sanchez or General George Casey. It was the genius of Matthew Ridgway that he found a way to reject the tactics and strategy of Douglas MacArthur even as the latter took credit for what to the outside observer should have been seen as rebuke.

Such magnanimity in turn allowed even greater leeway for needed radical innovation. Colleagues became invested in the success of the maverick, whose failures were his alone and whose successes were to be shared by others. In 2004, burly General Ray Odierno was unfairly caricatured by the media as "Old Army" and a practitioner of unimaginative shoot-'em-up tactics that had helped lead to open insurgency in Baghdad. By 2007, during his second deployment, he was reinvented as the newly appointed General Petraeus's right-hand man and considered an adept practitioner of the sophisticated arts of counterinsurgency. "Modest and humble" were the adjectives the historian Edward Gibbon saw as key to Belisarius' success. The same adjectives apply to the thinking of all the savior generals, who, despite their undeniable egos, were careful to share the laurels that they had largely won on their own. To read Sherman's letters is to appreciate his serial disavowals of envy of Grant. In the moments when he was deified, he credited Grant; when Grant was unfairly criticized, he took the blame himself. The famous quote by Sherman about Grant reflected Sherman's magnanimity: "He stood by me when I was crazy, and I stood by him when he was drunk; and now, sir, we stand by each other always."

Soldiers' Generals

The savior generals were amateur sociologists of a sort, too. They understood concepts such as national character and what their own forces were best—and worst—at. As leaders of constitutional societies, they knew especially the constraints of public patience. The people were for or against the war not solely on ideological or political grounds, but more often as a result of *perceptions* of losing or winning—given that an unsuccessful war was inevitably to be costly to the people themselves, whether in higher taxes, lost loved ones, fewer entitlements—or moral outrage. Unpopular wars turned popular with quick victories—but devolved into sure defeat with continued stalemate. In democracies, then, time in war was of the essence; in consensual societies, the desire to bring the troops home begins the moment they leave for the front.

That incessant demand for rapid success in turn required aggressive tactics—Themistocles challenging the Persian fleet, Sherman methodically driving into Georgia to capture Atlanta before the election of 1864, Ridgway upon arrival in Korea demanding that his division commanders offer plans for offensives, and Petraeus surging in Iraq. Many mediocre generals ultimately come to distrust, if not despise, the politicking of their civilian superiors; savior generals usually understood and dealt with the public constraints that limited their overseers' options. They are, after all, creatures of politics, sent in to win back public approval.

Note here the key role of spouses—sources of support that were often underappreciated—Antonia probably kept Belisarius from Justinian's executioners on more than one occasion. Sherman would never have received a second chance at Shiloh had his influential, rich, and savvy wife, Ellen Ewing, not politicked on his behalf and restored her husband's sinking spirits—going so far as to meet with Lincoln himself. By all accounts, Ridgway at last found happiness with his young, beautiful wife, Penny. And Holly Knowlton Petraeus was not just a general's wife, but also an informed and trusted confidante, a daughter of a general who probably knew as much about the politics of the U.S. army as her husband—a role that the media did not fully appreciate when Petraeus was engulfed in postbellum extramarital scandal. If it is critical for a savior general to be a contrarian, such independence is made far easier when he has a loyal—and connected—spouse.

Regardless of their class upbringing or the exalted status of their rank, savior generals adopted the profile of an egalitarian on the battlefield to lead by example. No Persian could distinguish Themistocles from any other trireme commander at Salamis. Sherman was scruffier than most of his subordinate officers. Ridgway, with live grenade and medical kit hung on his chest, was indistinguishable from a sergeant. Petraeus out of camouflage appeared aberrant. None had the look of a plumed Alexander or Napoleon.

All this was contrived—but not wholly contrived. A savior general really was a man of action. He looked restless, appeared to relish combat, and was as vigorous and often as warlike as his men. Petraeus often challenged officers and enlisted men half his age to outrun or outexercise him. Sherman's mess was as crude as his soldiers'. If such generals were to ask their men to take new risks to salvage victories, then they must be willing to share the ensuing dangers, and, like a Sherman or Ridgway, appear almost indistinguishable from the men they led. It was no accident that Themistocles, Belisarius, Sherman, Ridgway, and Petraeus on almost any day of their commands could easily have been killed, so close were they to the front and so unconcerned were they for their personal safety.

Retreat into the Shadows

Unexpected successes won these visionaries public acclaim. But they also raised their stature from minor theater commanders almost overnight into national political figures—often with unfortunate personal results. Such radical change in fortunes often clouded perceptions of why these contrarians had been suspect in the first place for most of their careers, and thus perhaps explains why in the calm of peace their reexamined lives would so often end in controversy and sometimes in unhappiness. Many, after all, were reckless and had difficult personalities, large egos, and eccentric habits that became once again apparent in peace after having gone largely unremarked in the context of war. One can be as uncomfortable in public life as he is adroit on the battlefield. David Petraeus's resignation from the directorship of the CIA, in a scandal that originated in a Gmail account, was perhaps simply a twenty-first-century version of the controversies that surrounded Themistocles, Belisarius, and Sherman when they left the battlefield and navigated tumultuous postwar careers. Themistocles and Belisarius, remember, both faced trials on capital charges. Ridgway had a long retirement; and if it was scandal free, it was also marked by serial controversies

Democracy can be unkind to successful military commanders—but especially unkind when the conditions of peace encourage collective amnesia about how close a victorious nation had come to military debacle. America was not only shocked that Curtis LeMay ran as vice president on the George Wallace ticket in 1968, but had forgotten as well LeMay's prior heroic career as a World War II Army Air Force general who shortened the war and saved thousands of American lives. By 2010, David Petraeus was no longer so readily associated with the ever more distant salvation of Iraq in 2007–2008. By 2011, as CIA director, a retired General Petraeus could say little as the Obama administration for whom he worked pulled the last U.S. troops from Iraq. Sherman spent much of his postwar years engaged in constant feuds with former Union comrades and Confederate enemies who repeatedly charged him with preferring warring against civilians rather than soldiers—calling their criticism "bottled piety" possible only after others had secured the peace. When President Dwight Eisenhower pressured Ridgway into retirement in 1955, the public assumed that their heroic president had good reason.

When we are safe, we value consensus and resent troublesome gadflies who claim the enemy is already on the horizon, our strategies wrong and prescriptions for defeat. We do not wish to hear that we are spending too little on defense or that a dangerous complacency has set in among the populace. But when war is upon us, we blame yesterday's timidity. We abruptly borrow what we do not have for war—and in extremis seek out a different sort who can offer us hope of victory when few others dare. In other words, Themistocles no longer seems just a half-Thracian braggart. We call once more out of retirement an aged Belisarius to stop the Huns, take a second look at the despairing William Tecumseh Sherman, send Matthew Ridgway back out to the front from his Pentagon office, or summon a David Petraeus from his classrooms at Fort Leavenworth.

War Is Unchanging

Human nature, even in this sophisticated age of neurology, genetic engineering, improved diet and material circumstances, and advanced brain chemistry, is unchanging. The result is unfortunately threefold in its implications: there will be future wars; history will continue to be a guide to present conflicts; and we will thus often see in many wars initial ebullience, replaced by despair, and then panic as certain defeat looms. That latter fact will be even more true in Western consensual societies, whose affluent and leisured publics will not tolerate wars abroad that do not immediately turn out as they were advertised and in which a demand to cut war's costs rather than to ensure victory will very quickly predominate.

Do not believe that high technology and globalized uniformity have made military leadership, especially eccentric leadership, outdated or even rare. Instead, in the future age of robotic soldiers, fleets of drones, and deadly computer consoles, there will always be commanders waiting in the shadows for their moment, different sorts of people who thrive on chaos and ignore criticism. Whether they will be listened to next time—and whether lost wars are to be saved—hinges on how well we have learned from savior generals of the past.

Acknowledgments

I thank my agents of nearly a quarter century, Glen Hartley and Lynn Chu, who freely offered their valuable advice about the manuscript. My editor, Peter Ginna, at Bloomsbury provided many helpful suggestions, as did Peter Beatty of Bloomsbury as well. Friends Jennifer Heyne and Bruce Thornton of California State University, Fresno, read the entire manuscript and caught a number of errors. I thank Dr. David L. Berkey, a research analyst at the Hoover Institution, for help with editing and preparing the final version of the manuscript. Copy editor Emily DeHuff offered insightful changes. Tom Church, Curtis Eastin, and Ian Hughes aided with the maps and illustrations. Dr. John Raisian, the director of the Hoover Institution at Stanford University, generously provided me with research support, made possible through the kindness of Martin Anderson and his family. I have dedicated this book to my three children, Pauli, Sus, and Bill, in recognition of their constant encouragement and unlimited optimism.

Notes

Chapter One: Athens Is Burning

1. See Plutarch, *Themistocles*, 10.5. In classical literature (much of it reactionary), the older city of Athenian hoplite farmers is associated with virtue—and to be contrasted to the post–Persian War radical democracy of rootless sailors who came into their own after Salamis.

2. On the details of the evacuation of Attica, see Herodotus 8.36–43; Plutarch, *Themistocles*, 8–12. Cf. Strauss, *Salamis*, 73–77, for the evacuees on Salamis itself.

3. On the wall at the Isthmus, cf. Herodotus 8.71.

4. Plutarch, *Themistocles*, 10.2; Herodotus 8.53–57, 60–63. It is rare in military history that the decision how—or even whether—to fight an existential war finally hinged upon an ad hoc, pre-battle shouting match between two rival generals.

5. For a version of the debate, cf. Diodorus, 11.15.2–4; and for Themistocles' sagacity at Artemisium, 11.12.4–7. See Strauss, *Salamis*, 11–30, for a review of the Artemisium campaign. The Persians may have lost over half of their fleet of some 1,300 triremes to storms and in battle; the degree to which those losses were made up by eleventh-hour reinforcements from Ionia, or repairs on the damaged hulls coupled with new crews, is unknown. Yet those earlier losses have great bearing in determining how large the Persian fleet really was a month later at Salamis.

6. See Plutarch, *Themistocles*, 11. Themistocles was not far off the mark, since there were probably at least 180 Athenian triremes in the Greek fleet, and perhaps more. He emphasized the irony that the people without a city were still those with the strongest forces in the Greek coalition.

7. The various ancient accounts of Herodotus, Plutarch, Diodorus, and Nepos concerning the great Greek debate before the battle cannot be quite

reconciled, though Herodotus' version does not show too much rancor between Themistocles and Eurybiades, at least to the point of violence. Rather the chief friction originates between the Corinthians and the Athenians, especially given the now stateless status of Themistocles. Cf. Grote, *Greece*, 5.123; cf. Herodotus 8.58–9.

8. For the campaign and battle, especially the date, strategy, and the numbers of combatants involved, see the controversies reviewed in Lazenby, *Defence of Greece*, 46–64.

9. Agrarian conservatives always claimed exclusive credit for Marathon; see Hanson, *Other Greeks*, 323–27. For the "Marathon fighters," see Aristophanes, *Clouds*, 986.

10. On Themistocles' foresight, see Plutarch, *Themistocles*, 3.3–4. Most Greek generals sought to best use the existing resources their societies put at their disposal; Themistocles, in contrast, ensured that his society would have the wisdom and capability to put the right resources at his disposal.

11. Thucydides, writing perhaps seventy years after the battle, made precisely that point that Persian error as much as Greek skill had led to their failure. He has the Corinthians a half century later argue, in self-serving fashion, that the Persians lost the war—perhaps both at Marathon and later at Salamis and Plataea—largely because of their own mistakes (1.69.5) rather than Athenian genius.

12. On the role between military service and political clout in the Greek city-state, see Aristotle, *Politics*, 4.1297b23–4.

13. On the new silver find at Laurium and the disbursement, Hale, *Lords of the Sea*, 8–14, has a good discussion. Apparently, wealthy private citizens were entrusted with much of the newly minted silver; they, in turn, would use such public funds to oversee the building of a ship. Cartledge, *Thermopylae*, 98–99, explores briefly the decision not to distribute the treasure among the citizenry.

14. Cf. Podlecki, *Life of Themistocles*, 11: "Themistocles' purpose in eliminating his opponents one by one was the realization of a scheme he had cherished at least since his archonship, the transformation of Athens from a second-rate land power to the leading maritime state in Greece."

15. The so-called Naval Bill of Themistocles rests on good ancient authority (cf. Aristotle, *Constitution of Athens*, 22.7; Herodotus 7.143–44; Plutarch, *Themistocles*, 4.1–2; and especially Thucydides 1.14.3). But we are not sure whether 100 ships were built in 482 to augment an existing 70–100, or whether up to fully 200 were ordered newly constructed from the revenues—only that the Athenian fleet that was ready at Salamis two years later numbered some 180–200 triremes. Cf. again Hale, *Lords of the Sea*, 10–15.

16. Herodotus 8.79–82. The nature of these various decrees and their relationship to the texts of Herodotus and Plutarch are under dispute. These earlier resolutions probably concerned general contingency efforts and the recall of exiles, while the famous subsequent "Themistocles' Decree" belonged to late summer 480 and in more precise detail outlined the nature of the evacuation of Attica. We still do not know whether the decree accurately reflects a preemptory and long-planned Athenian decision to leave the city to fight at Salamis *before* the loss of Thermopylae, or was simply a later compilation that drew from several authentic decrees, and thus is at odds with a more accurate Herodotean account that the evacuation of Athens was a somewhat more ad hoc, last-ditch effort *after* Thermopylae was unexpectedly breached. The details of the provisions of the Themistocles decree, and their relationship with the text of Herodotus, were first set out long ago by its discoverer, Michael Jameson. The historical ramifications of the decrees are covered in M. Jameson, "The Provisions for Mobilization in the Decree of Themistocles," *Historia* 12 (1963): 385–404.

17. For discussion of the contradictory numbers in ancient sources, cf. Strauss, *Battle of Salamis*, 42. Hignett, *Xerxes Invasion of Greece*, 345–55, in detailed fashion, reviews the literary evidence, arriving at a low estimate of a Persian army of some 80,000, and a naval force of about 600 ships (that might require some 120,000 seamen).

18. Herodotus (8.25.2) believed that there were 4,000 Greek dead left on the battlefield, which, if true, would mean that almost 60 percent of Leonidas' original force perished at the pass. Apparently that figure would have had to include large numbers of dead on the first two days of battle from the original force of 7,000, together with the vast majority of those (the 400 Thebans, 700 Thespians, 300 Spartans, and some Phocians and helots) left behind with Leonidas.

19. Themistocles at Artemisium, cf. Diodorus 11.12.5–6. There is a good account of the battle and its aftermath in Hale, *Lords of the Sea*, 46–54.

20. Cf. Plutarch, *Themistocles*, 9.3; Herodotus 7.33–4.

21. Cf. Herodotus 49–50. Lenardon, *The Saga of Themistocles*, 64–65, discusses the various interpretations of the famous oracular reply.

22. On Demaratus' advice, see Herodotus 7.235.3. The historian wrote during the initial years of the later Peloponnesian War, and we do not know to what degree, if any, Herodotus put his own ideas about the strategies from a contemporary war into the mouths of his historical characters. For the evacuation and the circumstances around the decree, cf., again, Lenardon, *Saga of Themistocles*, 69–72.

23. For the few who stayed behind either in the Attic countryside or at Athens, see Green, *Graeco-Persian War*, 156–60. A year after Salamis, the Greeks would win a glorious infantry victory at Plataea over Mardonius. But that battle came after careful preparation, was prompted in part by the retreat of King Xerxes and his fleet back to Asia after their defeat at Salamis, and was

waged with near equal numbers on both sides. Fifty years after Salamis, the Athenians were still claiming that the sea victory alone broke the Persians' back (cf. Thucydides 1.73.2–5).

24. On the Greeks' desire to vacate Salamis, see the synopsis in Diodorus 11.15.4–5.

25. Herodotus 8.62; cf. Plutarch, *Themistocles*, 11. We have no reason to doubt this improbable threat, given that it seems to have been accepted by most ancient authorities.

26. Green, *Graeco-Persian War*, 159–60, discusses the operational authority among the Greek generals at Salamis. In general, Grundy over a century ago laid out the main controversies surrounding the numbers, tactics, and topography of the battle; cf. Grundy, *Great Persian War*, 379–95.

27. There were far more ships, and probably far more sailors, than at either the Roman-Carthaginian battle at Ecnomus (256 B.C.) or Lepanto (1571)—two similarly huge "clash of civilizations" sea battles that pitted the proverbial West against the non-West. On the numbers of Greek and Persian ships at both Artemisium and Salamis, see again the review in Hignett, *Xerxes' Invasion of Greece*, 345–50; cf. Green, *Graeco-Persian War*, 162–63, who conjectures an allied fleet of about 311 triremes, corrected for probable losses from the retreat from Artemisium. Herodotus (8.66) implies that the Persian land and sea forces had made up all the prior losses at Thermopylae and Artemisium and were about the same size as when they had crossed into Europe the prior spring. Grote offered the best synopsis of the numbers in various ancient sources; cf. *Greece*, 5.111–12.

28. Herodotus—writing two generations after the battle—believed that the Greek ships were the "heavier." Scholars usually interpret that he meant that they were either water-logged, built of unseasoned, denser timber, or simply larger and less elegant—and thus less maneuverable but sturdier—than the Persians' triremes. Whatever the true case, it was clearly in the Greeks' interest not to go out too far to sea, where they would be both outnumbered and outmaneuvered, but to stay inside the straits where their ramming in heavier ships would have far greater effect. In this regard, we should remember that almost no major Greek battle was ever fought in the open seas far from land.

29. Plutarch, *Themistocles*, 12.3–5; and cf. Diodorus 11.17.2. Many scholars doubt the veracity of the Sicinnus ruse. See the lively account of the trick in Holland, *Persian Fire*, 312–16; but cf. Grote, *Greece*, 5.128. The Persian redeployment of the Egyptian fleet is not found in Herodotus.

30. Aeschylus, *Persians* 371; 412–13; 425–26. Aeschylus, a veteran of the battle, may have meant as well that dozens of Persian ships in the middle of the fleet simply never were able to come into contact at all with the Greeks attacking at the periphery, a sort of naval Cannae in which thousands of combatants were not able to commit to battle for quite some time, if at all. Certainly

the idea that scores of Persian ships could not get at the enemy, or, in turn, fouled one another during battle as the winds and currents increased, seems a key component in the Greek success. On the sounds and confusion of the battle, see Strauss, *Salamis*, 162–73, who has a graphic account of the battle based on ancient literary sources.

31. Aeschylus, *Persians*, 274–76, 282–83. On the losses, see Grundy, *Great Persian War*, 404–5. Herodotus gives no exact figures. Diodorus (11.19.3) says forty Greek ships were lost (i.e., 8,000 men if all the crews were killed) and "more than" 200 Persian ships (in that case perhaps more than 40,000 drowned), not counting those captured. Given the enormous size of the Persian fleet and Herodotus' view of utter destruction, Xerxes' losses were probably far above 40,000, while far less than 8,000 were lost on the Greek side, given their rowers' ability to swim and friendly troops on the shores of the island. As at Lepanto, there is a likelihood that few prisoners were taken, the Greek idea being that any killed in the waters of Salamis would not fight again the next year. See Hanson, *Carnage and Culture*, 46–51, for the motif of *eleutheria* (freedom) that the poet Aeschylus celebrated at Salamis and the role it played in galvanizing the Greeks.

32. On the allied weariness with the overly confident hero of Salamis, cf. Plutarch, *Themistocles*, 22. Of course, we need to remember much of this animosity was elite-driven and did not reflect Themistocles' continued popularity with the Athenian *dêmos* that would continue to invest in his leadership; cf. Aeschylus, *Persians*, 591–94. Aeschylus records (402–5) that the Greeks rowed into battle chanting cries of "Free your children, your wives, the images of your fathers' gods and the tombs of your ancestors."

33. On the virtual disappearance of Themistocles after Salamis, cf. Lazenby, *Defence of Greece*, 209, and especially Grundy, *Great Persian War*, 413–17, who discusses various charges of corruption and Medizing, as well as a general distaste for his imperiousness after Salamis—considerations that eventually led him to either cede or be fired from the allied post-Salamis fleet.

34. The historian Thucydides (1.138) felt that Themistocles died of natural causes, most probably disease, despite the more sensational accounts of suicide alluded to in Aristophanes (*Knights*, 83–84) and stated as fact in the much later account of Plutarch (*Themistocles*, 3.1). We are still unsure why many in the ancient world believed that the rather harmless blood of a bull was lethal to humans; in general, cf. Diodorus 11.58; Nepos, *Themistocles*, 2.10.

35. For the complex itinerary of Themistocles seeking a secure refuge during his exile, see the discussions of Podlecki, *Life of Themistocles*, 71; Lenardon, *Saga of Themistocles*, 108–52; and cf. Diodorus 11.55–58.

36. Plutarch, *Themistocles*, 28.3. The dates of Themistocles' exile and wandering are endlessly under dispute by modern scholars; cf. the review of the problems in Lewis, *Cambridge Ancient History*, vol. V, 66–67.

37. Plutarch, *Themistocles*, 21–22. Ostracism, exile, execution, and confiscation of property were the usual deserts for both politicians and generals throughout the Greek city-states.

38. On the famous Themistoclean ruse of deceiving the Spartans while his countrymen fortified the city, see Thucydides 1.90–91; Diodorus 11.40. While it could take a week to reach Athens and another to return home, it seems incredible that the Spartans had no information concerning Athens's massive wall building while Themistocles conducted his deceptive diplomacy. On Themistocles and Athens's various fortifications, cf. Nepos, *Themistocles*, 2.6–8.

39. For ancient conservative outrage at the nexus between sea power, walls, radical democracy, and evacuation, see the critique of the so-called Old Oligarch, 2.2–14, an anonymous conservative who wrote a near-contemporary treatise on the insidious nature of Athenian democracy.

40. Plato, *Laws*, 4.706; cf. Plutarch, *Themistocles*, 4. To conservatives, Marathon was the last time that Athenian infantrymen fought gloriously in Attica for their own land—in part thanks to scoundrels like Themistocles.

41. Plato, *Laws*, 4.706. Much of Plato's criticism of democracy assumes insidious efforts of lowborn demagogues to emasculate the wellborn militarily, economically, and politically.

42. Plutarch, *Themistocles*, 19.3–4. Almost all extant Greek literature is antidemocratic, in the sense of emphasizing the dangers of allowing a majority of citizens in Athens to set policy by simple majority vote without either constitutional restraints, the checks and balances of parallel but more oligarchial bodies, or the influential presence of senior landowning conservatives.

43. For the bust of Themistocles, see J. Boardman, *Cambridge Ancient History: Plates to volumes V and VI* (Cambridge: Cambridge University Press, 1994), vol. VI, 25, 26a.

44. On the Spartan effort to have the Athenians ostracize Themistocles, see Diodorus 11.55–56.

45. Thucydides 1.138.3; Plutarch, *Themistocles*, 1.1–3, 2.3. "Serpentine": Holland, *Persian Fire*, 165. The ancient notion that Themistocles was as much a political partisan as a patriot makes it hard even today to offer an accurate assessment of his strategic vision in the context of the times.

46. On the "good" battle at Marathon versus the rabble's victory at Salamis, see Plato, *Laws*, 707c; and in general, Hanson, *Stillborn West*, 83–84. For the complicated lineage and status of Themistocles, see the discussion in Davies, *Athenian Propertied Families*, 217–20. Reasons for his exile: cf. Lewis, *Cambridge Ancient History*, vol. V, 66; Diodorus 11.55–56.

47. On the discrediting of Themistocles in the postwar period, cf. Aristotle, *Politics* 5.1304a17–24.

48. Plutarch, *Themistocles*, 2–6.

49. On the assessment of the role of Themistocles, the value of his deceptions, and the tactics at Salamis, cf. Diodorus 11.18–19.

50. Herodotus 8.109–11; Diodorus 11.19. Salamis also ensured that Plataea was an existential battle: Without a fleet to allow a maritime retreat, a defeated Persian army would be trapped deep within Greek territory with the only avenue of escape a march through hundreds of miles of suddenly hostile Greek territory.

51. For ancient generalizations of Themistocles' gifts, see Diodorus 11.59.4, and especially the blanket encomium of Thucydides, 1.138.3–4.

52. Herodotus 60–61. Note that Themistocles himself engaged in "what if" hypotheticals to persuade his fellow generals to accept his strategic plan.

53. Herodotus 8.57. After the battle, there was widespread criticism of the Persians' unexpected disastrous defeat—rich material for the storyteller Herodotus to put into the mouths of sympathetic characters like the ignored advisers Artemesia and Demaratus, who both had supposedly advocated quite different Persian strategies.

54. Aeschylus, *Persians*, 792.

55. Plutarch, *Themistocles*, 18.2.

56. Aeschylus, *Persians*, 242.

57. Diodorus extols Themistocles to such a degree that he concludes by apologizing for his effusive portrait, cf. 11.59.4.

58. Again, see the long assessment of Thucydides (1.138.3–4), which concludes (Crawley translation): "To sum up, whether we consider the extent of his natural powers, or the slightness of his application, this extraordinary man must be allowed to have surpassed all others in the faculty of intuitively meeting an emergency." And for an in-depth modern appreciation of Themistocles as the father of the Athenian navy and the architect of Athenian maritime hegemony, see Hale, *Lords of the Sea*, 3–14.

Chapter Two: Byzantium at the Brink

1. See Robert Graves, *Count Belisarius* (New York: Random House, 1938), 558. The historical version that Graves drew on—that Justinian had Belisarius blinded, reduced to poverty, and turned out in the streets as proof of the ungrateful monarch's treatment of the loyal patriot—had become a favorite topic of the Romantics, among novelists such as Jean-François Marmontel (*Bélisaire*, 1767), and artists such as the neoclassical painter Jacques-Louis David (*Belisarius Begging for Alms*, 1781). For Belisarius in later opera, see Baker, *Justinian and the Later Roman Empire*, 76–77.

2. The trope of Belisarius as blind beggar in ancient accounts is accepted by Stanhope, *Life of Belisarius*, 208–9—a narrative long rejected by most historians, given that the story is attributed to the eleventh-century chronicler Michael Psellus, some five hundred years after the death of Belisarius. The supposed final reduction to indigence probably represents some sort of emblematic encapsulation of the lifelong slights shown the general by the emperor and his wife.

3. On the possibility of the historian Procopius being the same Procopius who supposedly conducted the trial, see Evans, *Age of Justinian*, 257. Cf. Cameron, *Procopius*, 229–30, for the radical change of views of Procopius toward Belisarius, Justinian, and Theodora.

4. On the fascination with Belisarius in later literature and art, especially during the Romantic period, see Cameron, *Procopius*, 261.

5. Even as Justinian rebuilt the city, reconquered Italy and Africa, and codified Roman law, fifth-century-A.D. Christianity was torn apart by schisms between Arianists, Monophysites, Dyrophysites, Donatists, Manicheans, and splits between Eastern and Western Orthodoxy. On the religious turmoil, see Moorhead, *Justinian*, 125–43.

6. Ward-Perkins, *Fall of Rome*, 87–210, discusses "The Disappearance of Comfort" in the years after the collapse in the west.

7. Ward-Perkins, *Fall of Rome*, 59: "The decisive factor that weighed in favor of the East was not the greater power of its armies and their consequent greater success in battle, but a single chance of geography—a thin band of sea (the Bosporus, Sea of Marmara, and Dardanelles), in places less than 700 metres wide, that separates Asia from Europe."

8. G.E.M. de Ste. Croix's classic economic argument for Roman decline (which largely focuses on the east) cites the rise of the Christian bureaucracies, unproductive ecclesiastical ownership of vast estates, and bloated religious orders, e.g., *Class Struggle*, 491–93.

9. "Byzantine," as a pejorative adjective, derives from the hostility of the Western post-Roman period. The term was popularized in modern times through Edward Gibbon's contempt for the empire. Treadgold, *History of Byzantium*, 1–6, discusses the usual prejudices. On the impregnability of Constantinople, see Kaegi, *Byzantine Military Unrest*, 19–20.

10. For the traditional view, largely supported by archaeological evidence, that the fifth-century barbarian invasions marked a radical decline in the standard of living and security of life in the western Roman provinces, again, see, Ward-Perkins, *Fall of Rome*, 182–83.

11. Lee, *Empire at War*, 128–29. There is little evidence that taxes went down, or security increased, when Justinian's occupying generals imposed temporary order in the wake of the Vandalic and Gothic defeats.

12. Procopius, *History of the Wars,* 1.12.20–22. A review of the ancient sources concerning Belisarius' career before the Persian campaign is found in the valuable synopsis in Hughes, *Belisarius,* 45.

13. It was central to Justinian's thinking—again, in the manner that German strategists between the world wars lectured on the need to avoid another two-front conflict—that the east must be quiet before he could pursue his dream of recovering Roman provinces in the west (cf., e.g., Procopius, *History of the Wars,* 3.9.23–10.25).

14. On Justinian's "Persian Problem," see Baker, *Justinian and the Later Roman Empire,* 112–20.

15. Disputed payments and the falling out with the Persians are summarized in Moorhead, *Justinian,* 21–25.

16. The outbreak of fighting did not go particularly well for the Byzantines; see the brief account in Procopius, *History of the Wars,* 1.13.

17. On the Byzantine plan at Dara, see Hughes, *Belisarius,* 57–59, and the vivid account in Procopius, *History of the Wars,* 1.13–15.

18. Battle of Callinicum: Procopius, *History of the Wars,* 1.1.18–20.

19. For a brief assessment of the first Persian campaign, see Moorhead, *Justinian,* 22–24.

20. There is a lively discussion of the nature of the Blue/Green factions in Norwich, *Byzantium,* 184–85, especially the identification of the establishment party of the Blues with religious orthodoxy, the Greens with Monophysite heresy. And cf. Procopius, *Secret History,* 7.8–30; Kaldellis, *Prokopios,* 136–44.

21. According to Procopius—often no fan of Theodora—only the obstinacy and calmness of Theodora convinced her husband to stay, fight, and die if need be as royals (e.g., "Royalty is a good burial shroud," *History of the Wars,* 1.24.38).

22. The apparent fright of the emperor may have convinced some of the rioters to look toward a replacement like Hypatius. If Justinian's temporary loss of confidence turned riots into insurrection, the emperor emerged from the Nika crisis forever suspicious of subordinates. The irony of Belisarius' predicament is that his prompt action saved the emperor, who was convinced never again to be in a position in which a Belisarius might have to intervene to save the head of state. It would later prove to have been a dangerous thing for Belisarius to have seen his emperor once so weak and needy. On the wavering of Justinian at the key moment of the outbreak, see Stanhope, *Life of Belisarius,* 26–27. And again on the role of Theodora: Ure, *Justinian and His Age,* 201–4.

23. Procopius, *History of the Wars,* 1.24.40–41. Procopius' view that Belisarius was the key to the victory over the rioters is discussed in Cameron, *Procopius,* 159. In the ancient world, combat experience mattered far more than

numbers. Belisarius' contingents were in some ways analogous to Julius Caesar's small forces that crossed the Rubicon in 49 B.C. and panicked the much larger, but largely green, legionary armies of Pompey and the Senate. On the vast numbers slaughtered, see Procopius 1.24.54–56.

24. Antonia was the daughter of a lowborn charioteer and actress; see the discussion of her pedigree in Hughes, *Belisarius*, 68–69. In Procopius' view, she was "the most able of all people to achieve the unachievable (*History of the Wars*, 1.25.13). And cf. *Secret History*, 1.12–20; Gibbon, *Decline and Fall*, 4.41 (294); Ure, *Justinian and His Age*, 205–8.

25. For Procopius' review of the origins of the Vandal kingdom in North Africa and prior tragic Byzantine efforts to rout them out, see *History of the Wars*, 3.12–18.

26. The Persians later complained that they had been fooled into signing the supposed "Endless Peace" without realizing that it was an inducement for the Byzantines to increase their power to the west. They soon sent envoys to Constantinople ostensibly for a share in the loot to come from North Africa; cf. Procopius, *History of the Wars*, 1.26.3–4.

27. It is somewhat unclear why the young Belisarius was given the all-important command of confronting the Vandals. Friendship of the emperor and success against the Persians and the Greens may explain the choice, as well as Belisarius' proven ability to win over host populations. His native Latin fluency would come in handy in a western province of the old empire. Cf. Hughes, *Belisarius*, 74–75, for the command and size of the expedition.

28. On the Byzantine landing and plans of Belisarius, cf. Norwich, *Byzantium*, 208–10.

29. Procopius, *History of the Wars*, 3.16.1–2; cf. de Ste. Croix, *Class Struggle*, 482.

30. Stanhope, *Life of Belisarius*, 53, points out that while Belisarius had matched the achievement of Scipio more than 700 years earlier in taking Carthage, unlike his predecessor, he did not inflict a Roman peace, but rather "far surpassed him in clemency and consideration for the vanquished."

31. Procopius, *History of the Wars*, 3.17.6.

32. Procopius, *History of the Wars*, 4.1.15.

33. Rumor of the size of the booty tended to obsess Byzantine occupation troops in Africa for years, cf. Stanhope, *Life of Belisarius*, 57 and 59–60 for the general ebullience at the capital. Many of the original architectural and artistic masterpieces of Rome now made their way to Constantinople, after a century's detour to Vandal-held North Africa.

34. On the origins of the war, see Jacobsen, *Gothic War*, 75–86. The "slavery" of the Italians, cf. Procopius, *History of the Wars*, 5.8.15–20.

35. Procopius, *History of the Wars*, 2.22.1.

36. Procopius gives a vivid description of the carnage and depopulation during these times. In exaggerated fashion, he claimed five million perished in the serial fighting. See Stanhope's review, *Life of Belisarius*, 77–78.

37. It is hard to determine whether Italian natives considered their well-known Gothic overseers or the rather strange, Greek-speaking Byzantines the true foreign occupiers. Neither were native Latin speakers, and the customs of Constantinople were perhaps more foreign than those of an accustomed Gothic-ruled Rome.

38. On the elaborate siege, the numbers of attackers, and the condition of the defenses, see Jacobsen, *Gothic War*, 95–132.

39. Narses, although a sometimes brilliant commander and court insider, was in his sixties and without much recent military experience. He was likely sent to ensure that the now widely popular and extremely rich Belisarius would not return to usurp imperial authority. Accordingly, Narses was sent home when he was assured that Belisarius would not claim the new reclaimed western provinces as his own. On the elaborate siege, see Jacobsen, *Gothic War*, 157–59.

40. On the personal magnetism and heroism of Belisarius, Procopius has much to say: *History of the Wars*, 5.18.10–15.

41. Offers of kingship were made to Belisarius by the Goths: Procopius, *History of the Wars*, 5.18.10–15.

42. Procopius, *History of the Wars*, 2.1.1–3.

43. Procopius, *History of the Wars*, 2.13.23–26. At this point, the vaunted Byzantine strategy of paying bribes to Persians to keep on their side of the border was shown to be somewhat shortsighted, inasmuch as Justinian's western expeditions had made it almost impossible to back any agreement with Chosroes with credible force. For Procopius' additional gossipy view of the second Persian War, see also Kaldellis, *Prokopios*, 12–15.

44. Procopius enumerates the various complaints of the Lazicans in a long, obsequious speech of their envoys to Chosroes (*History of the Wars*, 2.15.14–34).

45. For the terrible outbreak of bubonic plague that reached the capital in spring 542, see Rosen, *Justinian's Flea*, 209–12; Treadgold, *Byzantine State*, 196–217. For at least three months the average rate of death in the plague-infested capital might have soared from a normal twenty to thirty a day to between 2,000 and 3,000. See Luttwak, *Grand Strategy*, 87–94, who, expanding on Treadgold, makes a number of original arguments why the plague has hitherto been underestimated as a factor in stymieing Justinian's strategies.

46. On the plague and an assessment of the second Persian War, see Hughes, *Belisarius*, 199–201; Luttwak, *Grand Strategy*, 87–91; Treadgold, *Byzantine*

State, 192–96. And cf. the relevant passages in Procopius, *History of the Wars*, 2.26–30.

47. Procopius, *History of the Wars*, 2.22–24; cf. *Secret History*, 4.1–8.

48. For the intrigue, see the discussion in Norwich, *Byzantium*, 233–34, who rightly emphasizes that the need for Belisarius' proven talents in the deteriorating provinces alone saved him from court retribution.

49. Procopius did not go back to Italy in 544 (Cameron, *Procopius*, 14).

50. It is likely that the losses to the plague, suspicion of Belisarius, and the toll of over a decade of continual warring all explain the scanty supplies sent to Belisarius, who in his second invasion of Italy was short of both provisions and money. Cf. Baker, *Justinian and the Later Roman Empire*, 160–61.

51. For the mess in Italy in the 540s and the final recall of Belisarius from the west, see Moorhead, *Justinian*, 101–15; and cf. Procopius's charges of incompetence: Kaldellis, *Prokopios*, 21–23.

52. There is a brief assessment of Belisarius' second Italian command and the subsequent role of Narses in Norwich, *Byzantium*, 244–45.

53. Henry Wadsworth Longfellow's poem "Belisarius" ends with the last two stanzas:

Ah! vainest of all things
Is the gratitude of kings.
The plaudits of the crowd
Are but the clatter of feet
At midnight in the street,
Hollow and restless and loud.

But the bitterest disgrace
Is to see forever the face
Of the Monk of Ephesus!
The unconquerable will
This, too, can bear;—I still
Am Belisarius!

In the subhead I have adapted the second to the last line by the addition of "I" ("I can bear").

54. Belisarius found himself called upon to be an emissary between the feuding emperor Justinian and Pope Vigilius in the so-called crisis of the "Three Chapters," in which Orthodox Christians fought the Monophysites over the question of whether Jesus Christ had both a human and divine nature (Orthodox) or was always wholly divine (Monophysite). For the religious wars, see again Ure, *Justinian and His Age*, 121–38.

55. During the career of Belisarius, the emperor expanded its territory by nearly 45 percent, and yet the army did not permanently increase, and, if

anything, due to the plague, perhaps shrank. Agathias (*Histories*, 5.7) claimed that Justinian had allowed imperial forces on all fronts to fall from 645,000 to scarcely 150,000—no doubt in large part because of the devastating outbreak of 542.

56. There is a lengthy account of Zabergan's raid in Agathias' *Histories*, 5.5–27; and cf. the quotes at 5.15.8 and 5.20.5.

57. There is still some disagreement on the actual end of Belisarius. Stanhope long ago made the case that the popular legends about the beggar Belisarius were in fact plausible (Stanhope, *Life of Belisarius*, 208–9).

58. On the accomplishments of Belisarius and what might have been, see Hughes, *Belisarius*, 244–45. "Name can never die," cf. Gibbon, *Decline and Fall*, 4.43 (458). For the role of the plague in derailing traditional Byzantine grand strategy and prompting renewed emphasis on diplomatic initiatives, Luttwak's analyses are excellent and need more dissemination (*Grand Strategy*, 92–94).

59. Cf. Baker, *Justinian and the Later Roman Empire*, 75–76, who cites his only—and perhaps fatal—flaw: "his exceedingly trusting and pliant nature" that ensured that Belisarius was often on the wrong end of court intrigue, much of it instigated by his own wife, Antonia. On the loyalty of Belisarius, see Kaegi, *Byzantine Military Unrest*, 42.

60. Delbrück, *Barbarian Invasions*, 340–41. We are not sure why Procopius praised and then later damned Belisarius. The about-face may have reflected the general's own fortunes at the court in Constantinople, or perhaps Procopius saw originally in Belisarius a sort of magnificent hero who might take on Justinian and Theodora but whose unquestioned loyalty in the end meant to Procopius that the maverick, in fact, was little different from other toadies and intriguers, and bullied by a scoundrel like Antonia. Or, most likely, Procopius proved an encomiast when an ascendant Belisarius was of value to his own career and a critic when he became a liability. Cf. Kaldellis, *Procopius of Caesarea*, 145–47. Roman discipline under Belisarius: Lee, *Empire at War*, 122–23.

61. Procopius, *History of the Wars*, 2.16.7.

62. Liddell Hart, *Way to Win Wars*, 50–56.

63. The multifaceted nature of the Byzantine military is reviewed by Delbrück, *Barbarian Invasions*, 342–45.

64. For the innovative stratagems of Belisarius, see Rosen, *Justinian's Flea*, 153–54. Cf. 82–84.

65. Justinian's propensity both to commemorate himself and the general impermanence of his own megalomania is noted by Stanhope, *Life of Belisarius*, 59–60.

66. For the quotes from Procopius and Gibbon, see Procopius, *History of the War*, 7.1.12–16; Gibbon, *Decline and Fall*, 4.41. On the idea that Justinian's

dream was not improbable, cf. the assessment of Jacobsen, "The recovery of the empire was not to happen, but with Belisarius' military ability, it was—in 540—a distinct possibility. The chance would never come again." (Jacobsen, *Gothic War*, 260.)

Chapter Three: "Atlanta Is Ours and Fairly Won"

1. For a synopsis of Sherman's pre–Civil War life, see variously Hirshson, *White Tecumseh*, 18–70; Kennett, *Sherman*, 23–108. Almost all biographers note both Sherman's failure and his own recognition of such failure—and the importance of it in forming his character and views later on during the war.

2. Hirshson, *White Tecumseh*, 388–89, notes the high incidence of instability in the Sherman family; for Shiloh and Sherman, cf. Hanson, *Ripples of Battle*, 71–94.

3. Hanson, *Soul of Battle*, 214–31, on the Sherman "catharsis" between his leaving the army and Bull Run. Just four years before Shiloh, an unemployed Sherman sighed, "I am doomed to be a vagabond, and shall no longer struggle against my fate." After the March to the Sea, a surprised Sherman said of himself in a letter to his wife, "I look back and wonder if I really did it."

4. For the connection between Sherman's prewar failures and the uncanny knowledge and insight he drew on in Georgia, see again Hanson, *Soul of Battle*, 224–29.

5. Flood, *1864*, 117. Apparently, northerners assumed that Grant could defeat Lee in the manner he had taken Forts Henry and Donaldson, and Vicksburg—without the sort of casualties they had suffered in September 1862 under McClellan, who, it should be remembered, at one point had reached within four miles of Richmond.

6. There is a discrepancy between what McClellan believed and what the Democratic plank on which he eventually was nominated on demanded. As Lincoln put it, a war Democrat was riding into the campaign on a peace horse: The Copperheads had inserted into the Democratic platform a plank calling for an immediate armistice—even as McClellan assured veterans and their families that he would simply not give up the war, but use the carrot and the stick to restore the Union by ignoring slavery. Democratic unity obtained at the convention in late August was doomed to come apart by November, given the seemingly mutually exclusive views of McClellan and the Copperheads—and Sherman's sudden and unexpected military successes. There is a fascinating account of the Democratic convention at Chicago in Waugh, *Reelecting Lincoln*, 276–94. For his speech, Sears, *McClellan*, 595–96.

7. McDonough and Jones, *War So Terrible*, 12–13, review the perfect storm that had hit Lincoln by 1864, from draft riots and higher war taxes to charges that he was either an abolitionist zealot and race mixer, or an appeaser of the Confederacy.

8. See Flood, *1864*, 28–31, on Mary Todd's friends who sought patronage in exchange for enabling her to charge her personal debts as government expenditure. The degree to which Lincoln himself knew of all this is uncertain.

9. For a survey of Lincoln's various personal crises during 1864, see, again, Flood, *1864*, 14, 43–44. The popular anti-Lincoln hysteria that began in earnest before his nomination and then peaked before the November election hinged on Lincoln himself—but not in comparison to any alternative to his policies. For all the furor, no critic had yet explained to the Northern public how in mid-1864 the Union could either sue for peace with an independent Confederacy, bring the South back with slavery, or find a way to crush the rebellion without losing tens of thousands more dead.

10. Waugh, *Reelecting Lincoln*, 132–47. Like any unpopular war, from Korea and Vietnam to Afghanistan and Iraq, unconditional cessation is seen by many as an admission that the previous butcher's bill was all in vain.

11. On the scheming of this talented but ill-assorted bunch, see Waugh, *Reelecting Lincoln*, 32–45. If in 1860, the outsider Lincoln had seemed to be the ideal compromise to bridge the various agendas of eastern politicos, by 1864 he was written off as too unsophisticated and inexperienced to navigate through Washington politics and being devoured by his far more savvy cabinet.

12. Waugh, *Reelecting Lincoln*, 110–20, 273–74. Oddly, the more McClellan posed as Lincoln's replacement, the less he seemed able to explain what he would do instead as commander in chief. The Peninsula campaign had in retrospect looked like a colossal blunder in July 1862; now, by July 1864, McClellan claimed that it did not seem so horrific in comparison with Cold Harbor.

13. For the machinations of Frémont and others, and the general vice-presidency intrigue, see Flood, *1864*, 107–11, 141–43. In general, the fortunes of both Frémont and McClellan were in direct proportion to the news from the front; Union defeat had created their candidacies, and only Union victories would end them.

14. So, too, the midterm elections of 1862 had not gone Lincoln's way, given the so-so performance of Union armies from Bull Run to Antietam. Even amid victories such as Shiloh, there followed disappointment with the Northern inability to translate Southern tactical setback into strategic defeat. Cf. Waugh, *Reelecting Linc*oln, 203; and Castel, *Decision in the West*, 2–5, on the status of the Union army and the Northern cause as 1864 began.

15. Quoted in Waugh, 267; see McClure, *Abraham Lincoln*, 113. Reports, however, of a saddened Lincoln were frequent from nearly the day he entered office to his assassination.

16. Waugh, *Reelecting Lincoln*, 151, 164. There was just as much division in the South as well, among those who wished to rejoin the Union if slavery were kept intact; those who insisted on an independent Confederacy at any cost; and a few who, in exchange for an immediate armistice, were willing to accept a gradual end to slavery and acceptance without penalty back into the Union.

17. Cf. McMurry, *Atlanta 1864*, 12–25. The war would end in Virginia, where the major land battles had started; but Lee's army would more likely surrender before it was destroyed—largely because operations elsewhere to his rear had deprived him of both men and supplies.

18. Grant's ongoing bloodbath in Virginia convinced Sherman that he had to achieve a result that was both spectacular and at seemingly tolerable cost. Cf. Flood, *1864*, 91–116.

19. For the politics of the respective campaigns, see Lewis, *Sherman*, 394–96. Some of the 100-day call-ups of new troops in spring 1864 were apparently predicated on the notion that Grant might win the war within three months of taking over direct command of the Army of the Potomac in Virginia. The distance from Georgia, and the difficult rural terrain in which Sherman operated, made it difficult to fathom the pulse of battle out west between June and September.

20. See Caudill and Ashdown, *Sherman's March*, 5; cf. "Sherman made defeat for the South akin to being beaten by a corporate magnate good at reading balance sheets but indifferent to glory and legacy." For an analysis of the generals on both sides of the Atlanta campaign, see Castel, *Decision in the West*, 28–57. In contrast to General Joe Johnston, who was loathed by Jefferson Davis, the president of the Confederacy, William Tecumseh Sherman enjoyed the confidence of both Lincoln and Grant. Such support gave the latter as much confidence as the former was often unsure of his tenure.

21. There is some controversy over the exact orders given Sherman, and Sherman's own interpretation of what precisely his chief aim was when he left Tennessee—whether to weaken Johnston's army, capture Atlanta, stop reinforcements from joining Lee, occupy Southern territory, or embarrass the Confederacy. Of course, these aims were not mutually exclusive, and in the end Sherman essentially accomplished nearly all of them. See Castel, *Decision in the West*, 90–93, for an excellent discussion of how Sherman opportunistically seemed to emphasize a particular goal at a particular time as he saw fit.

22. Sherman, *Memoirs*, 589; for the Union strategy, see McMurry, *Atlanta 1864*, 12–16, and especially Castel, *Decision in the West*, 563, who makes the salient point that "the most important task was to forestall Johnston from reinforcing Lee." There was an apparent assumption that Lee and the Southern cause were not contingent wholly on their losses in the west; in dire contrast, the viability of the Confederacy in the west hinged in large part how well Lee in saving Virginia and the Confederate capital.

23. Liddell Hart, *Sherman*, 331. Sherman encouraged this notion that a western general, and a largely western army, were superior to easterners, hardier than Southern cavaliers, and would eventually have to save the Union.

24. Bull, *Soldiering*, 99.

25. Sherman, *Memoirs*, 518; Lewis, *Sherman*, 359–60. Cf. a quote from a captured Confederate soldier (360), "Sherman'll never go to hell; he will flank the devil and make heaven in spite of guards." Lewis makes an astute observation (398) that "In practically every section where there was bold Federal action in the summer of 1864, there was a Westerner in command . . . The West was in the saddle." If one argued that three men eventually won the Civil War for the North—Lincoln, Grant, and Sherman—then the idea of western credit for the victory seems logical.

26. Sherman, *Memoirs*, 492; Davis, *Sherman's March*, 4. Residents of Atlanta apparently assumed from the beginning of Sherman's campaign in early May that their own city would be the eventual Northern objective. Cf. Carter, *Siege of Atlanta*, 128–30. On the strategic value of Atlanta, see Liddell Hart, *Sherman*, 233–34.

27. On the relative advantages of each army as the campaign began, see Marszalek, *Sherman*, 260–61. It was true that the majority of Confederate generals were probably more skilled and talented than their Union counterparts, yet the four best (and highest-ranking) Union generals—Grant, Sheridan, Sherman, and Thomas—were perhaps the most talented commanders on either side of the Civil War.

28. For a description of Johnston's army—and the quality of Union forces arrayed against him—see Castel, *Decision in the West*, 110–19. For the quote and discussion, cf., again, Marszalek, *Sherman*, 269. Johnston's aims are discussed at Symonds, *Johnston*, 328–31.

29. There is a good review of how the Confederates had plenty of chances to cut Sherman's rail lines—and why they largely failed—in McMurry, *Atlanta 1864*, 198–203; Sherman as logistician: 26–41, 116–18.

30. For Johnston's inability to fathom the political aspects of his military strategy in Georgia, cf. Symonds, *Johnston*, 384–86.

31. Sherman, *Memoirs*, 500. On the problem of keeping up with Sherman's rapidly changing "thoughts and wishes," see Hirshson, *White Tecumseh*, 220.

32. For the tactical shortcomings of both Sherman and Johnston at Resaca, see Castel, *Decision in the West*, 182–86. Historians critical of generalship

during the Atlanta campaign should remember that the landscape was dense, and the weather often bad, resulting in little accurate intelligence on either side.

33. After the war, Johnston claimed that his primary, though misunderstood, aim all along had been to help the Northern peace party "to carry the presidential election." Cf. Lewis, *Sherman*, 366 and 373–74. For accounts of popular admiration for Uncle Billy and rising morale among Union troops, see Hanson, *Soul of Battle*, 230–31.

34. See Castel, *Decision in the West*, 200–209, for an analysis of the less than stellar generalship of both Sherman and Johnston between May 17 and 20. The problem with criticism of both Sherman's and Johnston's command is clear in hindsight: Hood's later antithetical tactics would soon ruin the Southern effort. And the more Sherman worried about advancing without losses rather than about destroying the enemy army, the more he neared Atlanta with sky-high Union morale. That nothing either Johnston or Hood did stopped Sherman is testament to his tactical and strategic insight.

35. Johnston's strategy is assessed well in Symonds, *Johnston*, 316–18, and especially 358–71.

36. For the campaigning between Cassville and Pickett's Mill and the general ensuing depression in the North, see Castel, *Decision in the West*, 202–54. For a defense of McClellan, cf. Sherman's letter to his wife (Simpson and Berlin, *Sherman's Civil War*, 743).

37. Castel, *Decision in the West*, 293–96. Hood's rashness at Kolb's Farm was a precursor to more to come when he took over from Johnston in July—and explains why Sherman welcomed the enemy change of command.

38. For Sherman's own attitude after Kennesaw Mountain, cf. Marszalek, *Sherman*, 274–75. In short, Sherman defended his frontal charges against dug-in troops—and then never repeated them again.

39. Liddell Hart, *Sherman*, 252; for different analyses of the late June and early July tactics of Sherman, see, again, Castel, *Decision in the West*, 342–47. The more Johnston retreated, the more the Union public was buoyed by Sherman's progress—and the more Sherman was reluctant to risk incurring high casualties.

40. For Hood's life and earlier career, see Miller, *Hood*, 106.

41. Castel, *Decision in the West*, 367; cf, 32, 58. For Union officers rejoicing at the news of Hood's replacement of Johnston, see Carter, *Siege of Atlanta*, 193–94.

42. See Lewis, *Sherman*, 382–83, for the comparative statistics on losses between Lee's and Johnston's records of resistance.

43. Kennett, *Sherman*, 243: "That spring and summer Sherman the commander could be seen at his best in the conventional warfare of his day.

He was now free to direct as he wished the efforts of a hundred thousand men . . . That spring he had just turned forty-four. His keen mind had been further honed by three years of war and he was still possessed of his remarkable stamina. In Georgia he would reach the zenith of his career." For Hood's quotes, Miller, *Hood*, 2007, and see Simpson and Berlin, *Sherman's Civil War*, 694, for the Sherman quote about taking up the dare of war.

44. Castel believes that Union estimates of Confederate casualties at Peachtree Creek and elsewhere were exaggerated and might be reduced by half; cf. *Decision in the West*, 381. Ezra Church: Secrist, *Sherman's Trail*, 53.

45. Sherman, *Memoirs*, 578–79. There was an air of unreality in the South as newspapers and officials clung to the analogy to Napoleon's disaster in Russia a half century earlier—as if Georgia experienced subzero weather, Sherman's lines were thousands of miles long, and Hood's dwindling forces were Cossacks.

46. On the controversial decision to let Hood flee from Atlanta, see Marszalek, *Sherman*, 282–83. On Sherman's fairness about McClellan: Simpson and Berlin, *Sherman's Civil War*, 57.742–43.

47. Sherman, *Memoirs*, 583. For the change of heart and the stunned Southern reaction, see Caudill and Ashdown, *Sherman's March*, 42–44. For all Sherman's hatred of the press—understandable, given its sensational headlines during his depression of early 1862—no Union general was now more worshipped.

48. Castel, *Decision in the West*, 540–47, offers examples from contemporary newspapers and diaries, attesting to the general consensus that Atlanta's fall had ruined the morale of the South, saved the Lincoln candidacy, and doomed McClellan's hopes. Cf. also Bailey, *Chessboard of War*, 8–12; Trudeau, *Southern Storm*, 34–35; Waugh, *Reelecting Lincoln*, 297–99; Hirshson, *White Tecumseh*, 241.

49. Davis, *Lincoln's Men*, 202–7; Lewis, *Sherman*, 409–11.

50. Sherman, *Memoirs*, 583. For most of August, Lincoln despaired that Sherman could not take Atlanta before Grant ground up his army outside Richmond. It was to Grant's credit that he congratulated Sherman even though in some sense his subordinate's success only highlighted his own failure.

51. Simpson and Berlin, *Sherman's Civil War*, 733. Sherman deplored the politics of September 1864 in a letter to his brother, Senator John Sherman. Rumors were rampant that the Midwestern and centrist Sherman might in fact favor McClellan, a fantasy dispelled by Sherman in another letter to his wife, Ellen Ewing Sherman (cf. Simpson and Berlin, *Sherman's Civil War*, 743).

52. Sears, *McClellan*, 604.

53. For the various arguments downplaying the importance of Sherman's capture of Atlanta, see McMurry, *Atlanta 1864*, 204–8, who examines in

depth the argument of Castel that the capture of Atlanta did in fact ensure Lincoln's election. Cf. McDonough and Jones, *War So Terrible*, 319–21; and for some statistics on the vote breakdown, compare Waugh, *Reelecting Lincoln*, 354–55.

54. For a harsh appraisal of Grant's tactics and accompanying losses, see the spirited attack by Liddell Hart, *Sherman*, 274–75 (e.g., "If the commander had not lost hope, his men fought without it."). For Sherman not going after Hood from Atlanta, see Woodworth, *Sherman*, 138–39. On the politics, cf. Liddell Hart, *Sherman*, 275. Grant felt that taking Richmond at any cost might end the war; Sherman believed that nearly destroying his army to capture Atlanta would still lose Lincoln the election. For McClellan's discomfort, see Waugh, *Reelecting Lincoln*, 291–94. Even the Confederacy was confused, as the *Augusta Constitutionalist* wondered, "Are we to take [McClellan] for a peace candidate or a reconstruction war Democrat?" A much quoted declaration from a Union soldier, "It knocks McClellan into pie," summed up the general reaction to McClellan's dilemma; cf. Wortman, *Bonfire*, 322.

55. On Sherman's decision to outsource Hood to Thomas and ignore his movements, cf. Carter, *Siege of Atlanta*, 352–54. In September and October, Sherman variously considered several marching routes before settling on Savannah as his destination; cf. Trudeau, *Southern Storm*, 40–43. On breaking and smashing things, see Sword, *Southern Invincibility*, 308–9.

56. Sherman, *Memoirs*, 589. On "irretrievable ruin," see Bailey, *Chessboard of War*, 9. If Grant had continually promoted Sherman as his own career ascended, Sherman had also saved Grant: talking him out of resigning after accusations of drunkenness at Shiloh, and now taking Atlanta when Grant was stalled outside Richmond.

57. Atlanta was shortly reoccupied by southerners after Sherman left, but the city was in such dire condition that the returnees could hardly turn it into a Confederate asset; cf. Wortman, *Bonfire*, 326–28; Carter, *Siege of Atlanta*, 22–30. On the importance of the reliable Thomas for Sherman's gamble, see Einolf, *George Thomas*, 255–57. For Sherman's letter to Hood, cf. Simpson and Berlin, *Sherman's Civil War*, 711.

58. For complete texts of the exchanges over Atlanta with Hood, cf. Simpson and Berlin, *Sherman's Civil War*, 704–7. Once again, Sherman tried to equate his version of success with a certain moral clarity in war. If Atlanta was truly a city of noncombatants, then it would neither have hosted artillery that fired upon Sherman's columns nor served as a manufacturing center and railhead to supply the army that was killing Sherman's men. In his logic, the city was culpable and much of its population, both for their own protection and his own advantage, would have to be evacuated.

59. Cf. Hanson, *Soul of Battle*, 236–60; Caudill and Ashdown, *Sherman's March*, 6–7. On the continuing controversy over the character of Sherman and the morality of his brand of war, cf. the review in Marszalek, *Sherman's March to the Sea*, 126–29.

60. Simpson and Berlin, *Sherman's Civil War*, 694. Elsewhere in the letter, Sherman dismisses "sickly expedients," the previous half-measures that the Union had embraced, that only prolonged the misery of civil war. In other words, beating back the armies of the Confederacy was not the real solution to healing the wounds of the nation as long as the South believed it had morality and courage on its side; marching into the heart of the Confederacy, daring the enemy to match armies, and punishing the nexus of rebellion in Sherman's mind were essential to both unambiguous victory and lasting peace.

61. Machiavelli, *The Prince*, 17.7. Trudeau, *Southern Storm*, 534. It was not just property, but *landed* property that was so dear to collective Southern mentality, and that Sherman especially targeted. For a summary of the charges against Sherman—anti-Semite, racist, terrorist, womanizer, etc.—see, in general, Michael Fellman's *Citizen Sherman* (New York: Random House, 1995). For the argument that Sherman was a terrorist, see the invective of John B. Walters, *Merchant of Terror: General Sherman and Total War* (New York: Bobbs-Merrill, 1993).

62. See Sword, *Southern Invincibility*, on Sherman's various pronouncements about what was essentially the notion of collective culpability and punishment, 308–10. On a fine appreciation of Sherman's ultimate legacy, cf. Woodworth, *Sherman*, 177–78.

63. Simpson and Berlin, *Sherman's Civil War*, 3. For the full transcript of this famous purported conversation, see Lewis, *Sherman*, 138—taken from Boyd's later written recollections of the conversation on the news of South Carolina's secession.

64. On the respective resources of North and South by 1864, see Carter, *Siege of Atlanta*, 3.

65. Sherman, *Memoirs*, 895; cf. 888–89. Shiloh had a profound effect on Sherman's growing reluctance to engage in a similar bloodbath like that at Pittsburg Landing. Cf. Hanson, *Ripples of Battle*, 87–94.

66. One reason that Sherman was especially critical of the press ("the sickly sycophantic meddling of newspaper men") was that he, better than any Civil War general, grasped the critical interplay between public perceptions of success and continued support for the war—and especially the great damage yellow journalism could do to the Union cause. Cf. Marszalek, *Sherman*, 263, and especially Sherman, *Memoirs*, 889.

67. Fellman, *Citizen Sherman*, 172–75. In a largely unsympathetic treatment of Sherman, Fellman attempts to sort out the many psychological contradictions in Sherman's makeup, though perhaps without much appreciation of his revolutionary views on the art of war. For his desire to be unpopular, cf. Simpson and Berlin, *Sherman's Civil War*, 692.

68. On Sherman's sense of the larger purpose of armies that transcended decisive battle, cf. Marszalek, *Sherman*, 266–68. Cf. Sherman, *Memoirs*, 535, and Liddell Hart, *Sherman*, 34: "He perceived that the resisting power of a modern democracy depends more on the strength of the popular will than on the strength of his armies, and that this will in turn depends largely upon economic and social security."

69. Marszalek, *Sherman*, 262. Battle could be incidental, not always essential, to ultimate victory, in Sherman's view. Modern war, whether the deadlock in Korea or the inconclusive Gulf War I, often bears out Sherman's views.

70. Sherman, *Memoirs*, 594–95. And for the quote about relative courage, see Simpson and Berlin, *Sherman's Civil War*, 688.

71. McDonough and Jones, *War So Terrible*, 23–25, provide a good review of the Sherman genius for capturing in prose his radically new ideas of modern warfare—as a way of exciting public opinion and the attention of superiors and fellow officers.

Chapter Four: One Hundred Days in Korea

1. On the marines' unheralded victories, see Millett, *War for Korea*, 348–49.

2. Bowers, *The Line: Combat in Korea*, 33–34. Americans still had not appreciated that many of the weapons that the Soviet Union had developed on the eastern front against the Wehrmacht—especially tanks and field rockets—were far superior to their own, and were now finding their way into Chinese and North Korean units.

3. B. Cummings, *The Origins of the Korean War*, 746–51; cf. Millett, *War for Korea*, 356–58. MacArthur's idea was to hit Chinese troops as they were grouping and being supplied in Manchuria—although he never quite spelled out why nuclear weapons were felt necessary, given the huge conventional U.S. arsenal of high-explosive and incendiary bombs.

4. Ridgway, *Korean War*, 54. Most rear units assumed they were heading northward as garrison and occupation troops to hold conquered ground where the enemy had fled and the civilian population was friendly.

5. See http://www.gallup.com/poll/7741/gallup-brain-americans-korean-war.aspx; S. Whitfield, *Culture of the Cold War*, 5.

6. Wainstock, *Truman, MacArthur, and the Korean War*, 75–79. Americans still had not fully accustomed themselves to the notion that their former allies, the Russians and Chinese, were now their enemies; their former enemies, the Germans and the Japanese, now their allies.

7. Ridgway, *Soldier*, 199. Yet it was not clear either in Washington or Korea what "victory" actually entailed—a cease-fire at the 38th Parallel, reconquest of the north, or a South Korean state with boundaries somewhat to the north or south of the 38th Parallel. For the nature of the Communist forces, see Millett, *War for Korea*, 380–83.

8. Soffer, *General Matthew Ridgway*, 114. "Criminal neglect," Ridgway termed the inability of the administration to come up with a coherent strategy to thwart both conventional and nuclear enemies.

9. Ridgway apparently did not learn of the actual order of succession, or that he was next up after Walker, until nearly a quarter century later, at a 1975 symposium at the Truman Library in Kansas. On the circumstances and politics of his appointment, see Appleman, *Ridgway Duels for Korea*, 4.

10. Ridgway, *Korean War*, 44. For the Custer references, see Ridgway, *Korean War*, 63, 76–77.

11. Rees, *The Limited War*, 145–46. The Europeans probably went to Korea initially on two premises: that such solidarity was needed to ensure American support in resisting Soviet designs on Europe; and that after the sudden American turnabout, most expeditionary forces would probably be garrison troops sent in after the fighting was over.

12. In fact, MacArthur's audacity in heading north was encouraged from the very beginning by many within the Truman State Department who favored rollback; see Whelan, *Drawing the Line: The Korean War, 1950–1953*, 199–200.

13. Ridgway, *Korean War*, 42. But Ridgway himself, back in Washington, supported the Joint Chiefs' authorization to proceed northward beyond the 38th Parallel.

14. See the discussion in Appleman, *Disaster in Korea*, 56.

15. Ridgway, *Korean War*, 74. Cf. "And how could the Commander in Chief not have realized that his forces were too meager, and too thinly supplied, to have held the line of the Yalu and the Tyumen—even had he reached it—against an enemy known to be concentrated there in great numbers?" (75).

16. On the entire tragic saga surrounding MacArthur's contradictory but shrill communiqués to the Pentagon between October and December 1950, see Whelan, *Drawing the Line*, 250–53.

17. Weintraub, *MacArthur's War*, 297. The degree to which MacArthur was genuinely panicked or sought to convey hopelessness to garner more troops and strategic latitude is still hard to fathom.

18. Ridgway, *Korean War*, 91. To be fair to MacArthur, directions from Secretary of Defense Marshall and others (e.g., "We want you to feel unhampered tactically and strategically to proceed North of the 38th Parallel") seemed to be worded in such a way that final success could be shared, while

unexpected defeat would be MacArthur's alone. Cf. Wainwright, *Truman, MacArthur, and the Korean War*, 60–61.

19. On the postwar politics of the joint-power occupation of Korea, see Stueck, *Rethinking the Korean War*, 11–60.

20. Whelan, *Drawing the Line*, 114–15.

21. See Wainstock, *Truman, MacArthur, and the Korean War*, 10–14; 169–72 on the pathetic status of U.S. forces in the Asian theater following the Second World War.

22. Ridgway, *Korean War*, 11. Nuclear weapons had stopped all conventional fighting against Japan, and in the late 1940s, there was not yet the revisionist criticism against using the bomb on Hiroshima and Nagasaki. In some sense both attacks were seen as humanely precluding bloodbaths like that on Okinawa just a few months earlier.

23. Sandler, *Korean War: No Victors, No Vanquished*, 36–38. No doubt cutting back the army, the navy, and the marines, while investing in strategic nuclear bombers, was seen by Truman as one way of diverting scarce budget dollars to domestic expenditures while preserving U.S. security.

24. For the quotes, see Whelan, *Drawing the Line*, 27; and cf. 50. The effect of Acheson's seemingly inadvertent remark still is vigorously debated. Ridgway in his memoirs both criticizes it as encouraging the enemy, and yet suggests that ipso facto the slip did not trigger the outbreak of the war. Cf. Collins, *War in Peacetime*, 28–29; Blair, *Forgotten War*, 53–55. See also, Stueck, *Rethinking the Korean War*, 80–82.

25. Collins, *War in Peacetime*, 42–43. Stalin's sudden declaration of war against Japan, and rapid entry into Manchuria in August 1945 had reminded Americans of the audacity and capability of the Red Army that had just a few years earlier crushed more than 200 Nazi divisions on the eastern front.

26. See Ridgway, *Korean War*, 12; Wainstock, *Truman, MacArthur, and the Korean War*, 67–69.

27. Ridgway, *Korean War*, 62. Both of Ridgway's memoirs treat MacArthur carefully, given that the latter had both publicly lauded Ridgway but just as often in private criticized him. In any case, there was as much to praise at Inchon as there was to criticize at the Yalu.

28. See the general remarks of Wainstock, *Truman, MacArthur, and the Korean War*, 1–14.

29. See Blair, *Forgotten War*, 97–98. Both apparently thought that the mere possession of nuclear weapons translated into some sort of conventional deterrence—a fallacy that Ridgway appreciated from the very beginning, due to both the general reluctance of the United States to again use such horrific weapons and the growing fear of mutually assured destruction with the appearance of a nuclear Russia.

30. Why did the Chinese cross the Yalu? An entire scholarly industry has explored that question, citing the usual human impulses of Chinese fear, self-interest, and honor. No doubt Mao feared that an American victory would discredit Chinese Communism at home and abroad. He wished to support the North Koreans to whom he owed allegiance. And by November 1950—given the increasing exposure of American troops, lengthening supply lines, and bad weather—Mao felt an intervention would have a very good chance of success. See Stueck, *Rethinking the Korean War*, 108–11. It may be that the Chinese feared American airstrikes into Manchuria rather than the likelihood of a land invasion (e.g. Whelan, *Drawing the Line*, 238–39). For the Communist Chinese perspective, see Li, *Mao's Generals*, 3–60, on the long-term and short-term goals for such an intervention.

31. There were many throughout the Pentagon who wanted to remove MacArthur long before Truman acted; in any case, the Joint Chiefs sent a unanimous recommendation on April 5, 1950, to Secretary of Defense George Marshall to fire the now isolated MacArthur; cf. Collins, *War in Peacetime*, 282–83.

32. Appleman, *Disaster in Korea*, 22. On the poor status of the South Korean army in 1950, see Whelan, *Drawing the Line*, 109–10. For Chinese advantages in airpower at the outset of the war, cf. Roe, *Dragon Strikes*, 322–24.

33. Appleman, *Ridgway Duels for Korea*, 50–52.

34. On Chinese propaganda and battle tactics, cf. Weintraub, *MacArthur's War*, 238–39. For a firsthand description from the Communist side, cf. Li, *Mao's Generals*, 114–18; Roe, *Dragon Strikes*, 432–37.

35. Whelan, *Drawing the Line*, 152–55. There was a larger percentage of allied troops in the American coalition in Iraq (2003–2008) than during the Korean War, albeit the same hardball tactics were once again used to enlist many allies.

36. Rees, *Korea—The Limited War*, 151. There is still controversy over how far MacArthur should have advanced after Inchon, how far the United States later had to retreat, and whether in 1951 a resurgent United Nations force should have recrossed the 38th Parallel—yet almost no argument that in autumn 1950, stopping at the 39th Parallel would have precluded many of the problems and disagreements of the next two years.

37. Soffer, *General Matthew Ridgway*, 118. MacArthur refused Ridgway's request, although he himself had wanted the option to employ nuclear weapons.

38. On Attlee's early December 1950 mission to Washington, see Whelan, *Drawing the Line*, 270–74; and cf. Roe, *Dragon Strikes*, 372–73, and especially Millett, *War for Korea*, 63–65.

39. Wainstock, *Truman, MacArthur, and the Korean War*, 101.

40. Sandler, *The Korean War: No Victors, No Vanquished*, 11–12.

41. Appleman, *Disaster in Korea*, 8, 353. Appleman cites the problems of morale and leadership as the primary culprits in the near American collapse. Cf. Millett, *Korean War*, 291–320; 411–12 on Walker's retreat, and the Chinese growing problems. The horrific losses and problems in supply suffered by the Chinese are also discussed in Li, *Mao's Generals*, especially 124–27.

42. Appleman, *Disaster in Korea*, 384.

43. The record of F-86 pilots against MiGs and their often Russian pilots was quite remarkable, given the near parity in performance per se of the two jets. For the jet war in Korea, cf. Millett, *War for Korea*, 310–11.

44. Appleman, *Ridgway Duels for Korea*, 155.

45. On the American success in destroying Communist forces following Inchon, see Whelan, *Drawing the Line*, 194–95.

46. On the schizophrenic reporting from the front that finally prompted the Joint Chiefs to send General Collins to determine whether MacArthur or Ridgway was deluded, given the vast discrepancy in their memos back to Washington, see Whelan, *Drawing the Line*, 284–85.

47. Ridgway, *Korean War*, 241.

48. On the politics surrounding Ridgway's restoration, see D. Halberstam, *The Coldest Winter*, 594–96. See Cummings, *Origins of the Korean War*, 712–14.

49. Ridgway, *Korean War*, 160; on the turnaround in Pentagon thinking after Ridgway's successes, see Blair, *Forgotten War*, 682–84.

50. Ridgway, *Korean War*, 151.

51. Ridgway, *Korean War*, 86. Korea was the first American war in which soldiers at the front heard media accounts that their efforts might be in vain and the war abandoned without victory.

52. Ridgway, *Korean War*, 97. The fact that Americans were now fighting Communist Koreans and Chinese rather than Japanese, Germans, and Italians made little difference to Ridgway; the challenge was not the enemy per se but the attitude and skill of American forces.

53. Appleman, *Ridgway Duels for Korea*, 9–10.

54. Ridgway, *Korean War*, 87–88.

55. Ridgway, *Korean War*, 100.

56. On Ridgway's removal of division commanders, see Weintraub, *MacArthur's War*, 306–7.

57. Appleman, *Ridgway Duels for Korea*, 145–46.

58. Ridgway, *Korean War*, 90. To validate the MacArthur narrative, American forces would have to do poorly without the sort of leeway that he insisted

was the requisite for recovery; accordingly, Ridgway's victories sometimes served as an embarrassment.

59. Cf. Sandler, *Korean War: No Victors, No Vanquished,* 132–33.

60. For the quotes about Western civilization, see Mitchell, *Ridgway,* 56. And see Soffer, *General Matthew Ridgway,* 122–24, on Ridgway's appeal to the soldier's notion of a liberal American lifestyle imperiled by its enemies in Korea. For Ridgway's role in desegregation, cf. Sandler, *Korean War: No Victors, No Vanquished,* 252–53; and in general, M. J. MacGregor, *Integration of the Armed Forces, 1940–1965* (Washington, D.C.: United States Army Center of Military History Publication, 1981).

61. Halberstam, *Coldest Winter,* 488–89.

62. Ridgway, *Korean War,* 89.

63. Halberstam, *Coldest Winter,* 491. Halberstam assumes that the mostly conscript army was far more representative of American society than contemporary professional soldiers of the post-Vietnam age.

64. On Ridgway's appearance and character, cf. Millett, *War for Korea,* 373–74.

65. For Ridgway's ego, see Millett, *War for Korea,* 373. Cf. Soffer, *General Matthew Ridgway,* 122–24: "he was photogenic, deeply religious, all-American, and was married to a young, beautiful woman. He was one hundred percent Army, individualistic enough to be a family man, yet tough enough to stage Operation RIPPER. The many pictures of Ridgway in popular magazines show a tall man with a craggy, handsome, face and piercing eyes, a ready-made Hollywood war hero." Cf. Appleman, *Ridgway Duels for Korea,* 14–15.

66. "Ancient Stoic": Whelan, *Drawing the Line,* 281.

67. Appleman, *Ridgway Duels for Korea,* 21–23.

68. Ridgway, *Soldiers,* 161–62: "If I had taken the doctors' advice, I'd have retired ten years ago and would have missed all that was to come—the Korean War, Supreme Command in the Far East and Europe, and the two-year period as Chief of Staff, which were among the most interesting, as well as the most arduous, periods of service in my career."

69. Ridgway, *Korean War,* 159: "In the course of this interview, the record of which had been impounded until after General MacArthur's death, the latter, Mr. Lucas reported, rated me at the bottom of his list of field commanders. In the light of all that General MacArthur had said to me in Korea, and of his subsequent statement to Senator Harry P. Cain in Washington, which follows, this presents a puzzle for which I have no satisfactory answer." On criticism of Ridgway by MacArthur, cf. too, Halberstam, *Coldest Winter,* 598–99.

70. Eisenhower and Ridgway: Soffer, *General Matthew Ridgway,* 183.

71. Cf., e.g., Ridgway, *Korean War*, 113: "In General Eisenhower's book, he reports that Seoul was recaptured after General James A. Van Fleet had taken over the Eighth Army. This is untrue." Cf. Appleman, *Ridgway Duels for Korea*, 348: "Could a military man of Eisenhower's long experience, and presumably intense interest in the Korean War at a time when he was running for the president in 1952, display such ignorance of the events?" Cf. Blair, *Forgotten War*, 802–3, on the Ridgway–Van Fleet tension.

72. On integration, see, again, Sandler, *Korean War: No Victors, No Vanquished*, 252–53.

73. Blair, *Forgotten War*, 815–16.

74. Ridgway, *Korean War*, 233. On the bleak developments between 1945 and the outbreak of the Korean War (e.g., Churchill's "Iron Curtain" speech, the Berlin Airlift, the Czech coup, the Soviet detonation of an atomic bomb in 1949, etc.), see Whelan, *Drawing the Line*, 27, 49–74.

75. Jensen, *Reagan at Bergen-Belsen and Bitburg*, 104–6.

76. See Halberstam, *Coldest Winter*, 490–92, for some examples of Ridgway's critical insight in both earlier and later American crises. On Korean War casualties, see Blair, *Forgotten War*, 975.

77. Whelan, *Drawing the Line*, 373–74.

78. On the controversy, and the statements of Van Fleet, again see Whelan, *Drawing the Line*, 319–20.

79. For Yu's analysis of the terrible prices paid by the Chinese, see Li, *Mao's Generals*, 25–27. See the examples of Ridgway encomia collected by Soffer, *General Matthew Ridgway*, 117; cf. 211; cf. also Appleman, *Ridgway Duels for Korea*, 147.

Chapter Five: Iraq Is "Lost"

1. Cf. http://icasualties.org/Iraq/ByMonth.aspx. Petraeus had argued that to quiet Iraq, American troops would have to venture out of their compounds, and assure security to Iraqi supporters. That would lessen casualties in the long run, but surely spike them in the short term. By August and September 2010, two and three Americans had perished, respectively—the lowest fatalities of any months of the seven-year war up to that time.

2. For the hearings and Petraeus's discomfort, cf. Ricks, *Gamble*, 246–47, and especially West, *Strongest Tribe*, 317–23. The full text of General Petraeus's testimony of September 10–11, 2007, can be found at the Department of Defense's online archives (http://www.defense.gov/pubs/pdfs/Petraeus-Testimony20070910.pdf). The remarks of Ambassador Crocker can be retrieved at http://2001-2009.state.gov/p/nea/rls/rm/2007/91941.htm.

3. For the vote and some of the speeches in favor of the war, cf. http://archives.cnn.com/2002/ALLPOLITICS/10/11/iraq.us; http://www.govtrack.us/congress/vote.xpd?vote=s2002-237; http://www.youtube.com/watch?v=4wyCBF5CsCA; http://www.c-span.org/vote2004/kerryspeech.asp. Senator John Kerry had offered an impassioned warning about Saddam Hussein's likely use of WMD: "I have said publicly for years that weapons of mass destruction in the hands of Saddam Hussein pose a real and grave threat to our security and that of our allies in the Persian Gulf region. Saddam Hussein's record bears this out."

4. The disapproval figure is based on a CNN / Research Opinion poll taken between September 7–9, 2007, just hours before the September 10–11 hearings began. For a good review of the monthly approval ratings of the Iraq War between 2006 and 2007, see the data assembled at Pollingreport.com (http://www.pollingreport.com/iraq.htm). More specifically worded polls revealed that at least half the country did not believe the surge was working—and even fewer that the additional cost in blood and treasure was worth it.

5. For Senator Clinton's earlier desire to leave Iraq, see her 2007 interview with Iraq war veterans (e.g., http://www.nationalreview.com/corner/263224/when-vets-freedom-met-hillary-clinton-vincent-g-heintz).

6. For Obama's appraisals of the surge, see an ABC News synopsis at http://blogs.abcnews.com/politicalpunch/2008/07/from-the-fact-c.html, and cf. his remarks in New Hampshire (http://www.nhpr.org/node/13507). For a video of Obama's seven-minute statement at the Petraeus hearings, see http://www.youtube.com/watch?v=cIUej6VJzII. The *Washington Post* reported on his call for combat troops to be out of Iraq by March 31, 2008: http://www.washingtonpost.com/wp-dyn/content/article/2007/01/30/AR2007013001586.html.

7. For Senator Biden's various appraisals of Iraq, see contemporary accounts at http://www.msnbc.msn.com/id/20676775/; http://www.historiae.org/biden.asp; http://www.vanityfair.com/politics/features/2010/05/petraeus-201005. However, on February 10, 2010, then Vice President Biden asserted that an Iraq secured by the surge, and the prior policies of General Petraeus, could soon become one of the Obama administration's "greatest achievements." (http://www.youtube.com/watch?v=rcOv-AbHlCk)

8. http://www.msnbc.msn.com/id/18227928; http://abcnews.go.com/Politics/story?id=3575785&page=1; "happy talk" http://blogs.abcnews.com/politicalradar/2007/09/presidential-ca.html.

9. For a review of the upsurge in violence, see Ricks, *Gamble*, 45–46.

10. The *New York Times* ombudsman found his paper's "General Betray Us" ad troubling—both the matter of the discounted rate, and its personal invective that went against the stated *Times* policy of prohibiting paid attack ads against individuals: http://www.nytimes.com/2007/09/23/opinion/23pubed.html. On the ad, cf. Ricks, *Gamble*, 245–46. Cf. Michael Moore: http://michaelmoore.com

/words/mikes-letter/heads-up-from-michael-moore; Nicholson Baker, *Checkpoint* (New York: Alfred A. Knopf, 2004); on Gabriel Range's 2006 docudrama, *The Death of a President*, see http://www.washingtonpost.com/wp-dyn/content/article/2006/09/01/AR2006090100858.html; Charles Brooker, *The Guardian*, October 24, 2004.

11. On the American losses in Afghanistan, see http://icasualties.org/OEF/index.aspx. On the prebattle confidence of a "cakewalk" in Iraq, see one example from K. Adelman "Cakewalk in Iraq" (*Washington Post*, February 13, 2002): "I believe demolishing Hussein's military power and liberating Iraq would be a cakewalk."

12. What allied governments wished in 2003 and in 2006 were very different things. For a discussion of the role of American allies and the war, see Shawcross, *Allies*, 221–26.

13. The Iraq Liberation Act of 1998: http://thomas.loc.gov/cgi-bin/bdquery/z?d105:HR04655:@@@X (where readers can be directed to the text and vote on the resolution).

14. George Bush admitted later that the flight onto the *Abraham Lincoln* and the carrier's banner were a public relations "mistake" that gave the wrong impression about the status in Iraq, despite qualifiers made evident in his speech. For the president's later remorse, cf. H. Roswenkrantz, "Bush Says He Regrets Use of Iraq 'Mission Accomplished' Banner,"' *Bloomberg News*, Nov. 12, 2008. In fact, the banner may have referred to the completion of the *Abraham Lincoln*'s tour, rather than victory in Iraq.

15. On the problems with the Bremer appointment, see Rumsfeld, *Known and Unknown*, 505–7, 509–16. For the fights over postwar Iraq in 2003–2004, cf. Feith, *War and Decision*, 422–32. For the wish list, see Franks, *American Soldier*, 544–45. For a defense of Jay Garner, see G. Rudd, *Reconstructing Iraq: Regime Change, Jay Garner, and the ORHA Story* (Lawrence, Kansas: University Press of Kansas, 2011).

16. For the general pessimism in and out of the military about the increasing violence of 2003, and the supposed reasons for the American failures, see the review of Gordon and Trainor, *Cobra II*, 498–505. On the problems of the Bremer proconsulship, cf. Feith, *War and Decision*, 448–53.

17. On the controversy over "de-Baathification," disastrous in the short term, perhaps salutary in the long term, see Robinson, *Ends*, 70–71; Rumsfeld, *Known and Unknown*, 515–19; Feith, *War and Decision*, 432–37. Cf. Moyer, *Question of Command*, 216–17. Bremer himself at the time took credit for the move, and yet later argued that he had not made the decision to disband the army. Rumsfeld in retrospect thought that he might have been able to intervene and stop the decision, despite Bremer's direct conduit to the president (Rumsfeld, *Known and Unknown*, 518–19).

18. On the unwise Bush taunt, cf. Wawro, *Quicksand*, 565–68.

19. Strangely, General Sanchez, the ranking officer on the ground in Iraq at the time of Abu Ghraib, in his memoirs called it a "grotesque blessing," criticizing his being unfairly scapegoated for the debacle while in turn blaming the Bush administration for creating a climate of harsh interrogation that was more culpable than his own lax command. See Sanchez, *Wiser*, 375; 456–57. And for a critique of the Sanchez appointment, see Jaffe and Cloud, *Fourth Star*, 127–29.

20. See Ballard, *Fighting for Fallujah*, 12. For the failed first siege, see the analysis of Moyer, *Question of Command*, 229–31.

21. Cf. Ballard on the aftermath and costs of Fallujah, *Fighting for Fallujah*, 95–98. For a different appraisal of the battle, see Holmes, *Fallujah*, 17–21.

22. The Iraqi Coalition casualty count provides a monthly total of U.S. and coalition dead and wounded in both Afghanistan and Iraq at http://icasualties.org.

23. See Robinson, *Ends*, 19–20. Contrast Matthew Ridgway's almost immediate publication of a pamphlet on why Americans were fighting in Korea—"Why Are We Here? What Are We Fighting For?"—as soon as he arrived in Korea.

24. Bush, *Decision Points*, 367.

25. For the Revolt of the Generals, and the various positions of the individual officers, see Ricks, *Gamble*, 37–45.

26. On the bombing of the Golden Mosque and its effects on American strategies, cf. Rumsfeld, *Known and Unknown*, 687–90.

27. Almost no one identified themselves formally with any particular strategy other than the general goal of quelling the violence and withdrawing American troops as quickly as possible. On the bleak scenarios in 2006, see Ricks, *Fiasco*, 430–39; *Gamble*, 3–29; and cf. his *Washington Post* piece on Anbar: *Washington Post*, September 11, 2006.

28. See Rumsfeld, *Known and Unknown*, 508–23. The secretary of defense argued that his commanders in the field did not present proposals for troop increases; the supporters of Generals Casey and Abizaid conceded that that was true, but suggested the generals were given the impression that they were to reflect preexisting Department of Defense wishes for a smaller profile.

29. On the Sanchez tenure, cf. Rumsfeld, *Known and Unknown*, 500–503. For complaints about the failed efforts to train the Iraqi army before the appointment of Petraeus, see Packer, *Assassins' Gate*, 304–9. The bleak assessment is found in Hashim, *Insurgency*, 389.

30. Opposition to a sometimes mentioned huge and counterproductive proposed surge of 100,000 troops was not the same as opposition to a much smaller one of 20,000 to 30,000. For the key distinction, see V. D. Hanson, "Do We Have Enough Troops in Iraq?" (*Commentary*, June 1, 2004). The question was not just whether to surge or not to surge, but how many troops to surge and what sort of mission and tactics were to guide them. http://www.commentarymagazine.com/viewarticle.cfm/nothing-succeeds-like-success-11274?search=1. West, *Strongest Tribe*, 366–67, points out all the additional troops requested would not have been salutary until the Americans found the proper strategy and unity of purpose.

31. See Robinson, *Ends*, 18–22, 27–29. Robinson makes a good attempt to identify at an early stage those officers and civilians identified with the surge and those opposed—contingent upon the realization that all sorts of surges of various sizes were being proposed, and often prominent policymakers, in and out of the military, seemed to hedge their bets, in order to be able to claim support for the surge should it work, or to emphasize their own opposition should it fail. On the politics of the summer of 2006, cf. Rumsfeld, *Known and Unknown*, 692–703.

32. There are various accounts of the principals involved in the surge; all agree that they centered their critiques of the war on promotion for a supreme command under General Petraeus. For the various factions, see West, *Strongest Tribe*, 216–23.

33. Petraeus's April 9, 2004, comprehensive remarks about his experience with the 101st Airborne Division can be accessed at http://washingtoninstitute.org/templateC05.php?CID=1733. See Ricks, *Gamble*, 508–11, on Petraeus's interview with the *Washington Post*, and his growing number of critics: "David tends not to build teams, or think about what happens afterwards. It's the Dave Petraeus Show."

34. For the *Newsweek* cover story, see http://www.prnewswire.com/news-releases/newsweek-cover-can-this-man-save-iraq-75166612.html: "Both the president and Deputy Defense Secretary Paul Wolfowitz met with Petraeus before he was sent back to Iraq with his third star. 'They told me, "whatever you need, you've got it,"' he says." On the training of the Iraq army, see Moyer, *Question of Command*, 226–27. For Sanchez's anger, see *Wiser*, 318.

35. On the Petraeus team, cf. Robinson, *Ends*, 104–13, West, *Strongest Tribe*, 216–20. See Bush, *Decision Points*, 364–65, for his decision to go with the colonels. The advocacy of the surge from the vice president's office is found in Cheney, *In My Time*, especially 446–58. For samples of Powell's pessimism in the interview, see http://www.military.com/NewsContent/0,13319,120754,00.html.

36. A sampling of neoconservative depression on the eve of the surge is the theme of D. Rose's November 2007 essay "Neo Culpa" in *Vanity Fair*, accessed at http://www.vanityfair.com/politics/features/2006/12/neocons200612. P. Galbraith's February 2007 *New York Review of Books* essay "The Surge"

can be accessed at http://www.nybooks.com/articles/archives/2007/mar/15/the-surge/?pagination=false. Galbraith had earlier authored a book arguing for the trisection of Iraq, *The End of Iraq: How American Incompetence Created a War Without End* (New York: Simon and Schuster, 2006), 208–24, and was later involved in controversies over his diplomatic and business interests in Kurdistan.

37. For the formal AEI blueprint for the surge, "Choosing Victory: A Plan for Success in Iraq," chiefly authored by Fred Kagan, with the help of some seventeen other prominent AEI scholars, see http://www.aei.org/files/2009/01/30/20070111_ChoosingVictoryupdated.pdf. See the full quotation on page 45: "It is time to accept reality. The fight in Iraq is difficult. The enemy will work hard to defeat the coalition and the Iraqi government. Things will not go according to plan. The coalition and the Iraqi government may fail. But failure is neither inevitable nor tolerable, and so the United States must redouble its efforts to succeed. America must adopt a new strategy based more firmly on successful counterinsurgency practices, and the nation must provide its commanders with the troops they need to execute that strategy in the face of a thinking enemy. The enemy has been at war with us for nearly four years. The United States has emphasized restraint and caution. It is time for America to go to war and win. And America can."

38. A sampling of Bush's January 2007 poll ratings can be found at http://www.cbsnews.com/stories/2007/01/22/opinion/polls/main2384943.shtml.

39. For the six new principles of securing Iraq, see an accessible version at http://www.savethecolors.com/WordPress/publications/Overview-2007IraqPlans.pdf.

40. For the text of Biden's speech, see http://www.c-span.org/executive/transcript.asp?cat=current&code=bush_admin&year=2006. For a sampling of congressional reaction, see http://www.sourcewatch.org/index.php?title=Congressional_actions_regarding_President_Bush's_2007_proposed_troop_"surge"_in_Iraq.

41. An account of the opposition from Fallon is in Ricks, *Gamble*, 230–37. For the premature political anxiety over the progress of the surge, see Cheney, *In My Time*, 456–64.

42. The change from forward operating bases to small urban billets is discussed in Kagan, *Surge*, 32–34; cf. Robinson, *Ends*, 97–99. And for the headway made in 2007 in Anbar Province, cf. 134–37. I joined an on-the-ground fact-finding mission led by Col. H. R. McMaster in October 2007 through many areas of Anbar Province, the former hotbed of Sunni resistance, and found the area far quieter than on an earlier trip I had made during February 2006 that coincided with the attack against the mosque at Samarra. One radical change was the presence of small numbers of Americans in ground-floor apartments throughout the downtowns of many of the most troubled

Anbar cities. For press accounts of the Reid-Pelosi letter, cf. http://www.breitbart.com/article.php?id=070613203802.7yla5iav. The text of the House resolution is found at http://thomas.loc.gov/cgi-bin/query/z?c110:H.CON.RES.63. For "reckless escalation" and the Obama proposal, see the January 31, 2007, *Chicago Tribune* article, accessed at http://www.popmatters.com/pm/article/democrats-work-to-stop-reckless-escalation-of-war-in-iraq. Cf. Obama's appraisal: "But no amount of American soldiers can solve the political differences at the heart of somebody else's civil war, nor settle the grievances in the hearts of the combatants. The time for waiting in Iraq is over. The days of our open-ended commitment must come to a close. And the need to bring this war to an end is here."

43. For a synopsis of various December assessments of O'Hanlon and Campbell, see their condensed *New York Times* essay "The State of Iraq: An Update" (http://www.nytimes.com/2007/12/22/opinion/22ohanlon.html). O'Hanlon earlier in July (with Kenneth Pollack) had opined, "A War We Just Might Win" in a *New York Times* opinion piece (http://www.nytimes.com/2007/07/30/opinion/30pollack.html?pagewanted=all). And see the reports of the surge's progress, given as a lecture by General Raymond Odierno in March 2008 (http://www.heritage.org/research/lecture/the-surge-in-iraq-one-year-later). West, *Strongest Tribe*, assesses the value of the Anbar Awakening, quite apart from the surge, 365–66.

44. On the Anbar Awakening, see Kagan, *Surge*, 79–81, who argues that the uprising was independent of the surge but quickly and skillfully exploited by Generals Odierno and Petraeus. For the efforts of MacFarland and H. R. MacMaster, cf. Moyer, *Question of Command*, 239–42; cf. 233–34; more on the nature of what worked during the surge, cf. Gericke, *Petraeus*, 149–53.

45. For the changing political positions concerning the surge, as it increasingly seemed to work, review a debate over its success held at the Council on Foreign Relations in May 2008: http://www.cfr.org/iraq/has-surge-put-iraq-path-success/p16185. Steve Simon, "The Price of the Surge" (*Foreign Affairs*, May/June 2008), argued that the surge's short-term success had actually made things worse by encouraging the quasiofficial use of Sunni tribal militias. Well into late 2008, war critics still maintained that the surge had not worked; cf. P. Hart, "Spinning the Surge: Iraq and the Election" (http://www.fair.org/index.php?page=3611).

46. See a review of some of these factors in P. Mansoor, "How the Surge Worked," August 10, 2008 (http://www.washingtonpost.com/wp-dyn/content/article/2008/08/08/AR2008080802918_pf.html), who credits the numbers and strategy of the surge, as well as the leadership of Petraeus, as the catalysts for other positive developments. See, too, his *Sunrise*, concerning Mansoor's pre-surge commands. For a review of the "surge did not work" school of thought, see a synopsis by R. Haddick, "This Week at War: What If

the Surge Didn't Work," *Foreign Policy*, April 15, 2011 (http://www.foreignpolicy.com/articles/2011/04/15/this_week_at_war_what_if_the_surge_didn_t_work).

47. On the notion that counterinsurgency often hinged on killing scores of "irreconcilable" enemy, cf. Moyer, *Question of Command*, 245–46. For the scope of U.S. military operations against the insurgents, see Kagan, *Surge*, 196–204. "Compellence theory": Broadwell and Loeb, *All In*, 101.

48. See Robinson, *How This Ends*, 52–54; Broadwell and Loeb, *All In*, 38–41.

49. On Petraeus's earlier career and attention to both scholarship and fitness, cf. Ricks, *Gamble*, 20–23.

50. Robinson, *How This Ends*, 60–62. For more on Galvin and Petraeus, cf. Broadwell and Loeb, *All In*, 65–69.

51. On the accidental and near fatal shooting of Petraeus, see Robinson, *Ends*, 61–62.

52. On the earlier career of Petraeus in Iraq, and some of the controversy around him at the time of his appointment, cf. Ricks, *Gamble*, 72–73. Mosul: Jaffe and Cloud, *Fourth Star*, 118–22.

53. http://www.washingtonpost.com/wp-dyn/articles/A49283-2004Sep25.html.

54. Mattis: Moyer, *Question of Comm*and, 220–21. On Petraeus at Fort Leavenworth, see Ricks, *Gamble*, 410–11.

55. "Commander's Counterinsurgency Guidance," cf. http://usacac.army.mil/CAC2/MilitaryReview/Archives/English/MilitaryReview_20081031_art004.pdf.

56. See J. Burns, "For Top General in Iraq, Role Is a Mixed Blessing," *New York Times*, August 14, 2007 (http://www.nytimes.com/2007/08/14/world/middleeast/14petraeus.html).

57. See the various Pew polls taken over the Petraeus tenure and phrased in a variety of different formulations: http://pewresearch.org/pubs/770/iraq-war-five-year-anniversary.

58. See J. Burns, "For Top General in Iraq, Role Is a Mixed Blessing," *New York Times*, August 14, 2007 (http://www.nytimes.com/2007/08/14/world/middleeast/14petraeus.html). Robinson, *Ends*, 348–50, credits much of the surge's success to Crocker.

59. For Odierno's key role, see Kagan, *Surge*, 200. The press reacted accordingly as Odierno went from being attacked as an unimaginative punitive commander to praised as a past master of counterinsurgency; best exemplified by the radically different portraits in Ricks's *Fiasco* and his sequel *Gamble*.

60. On the repercussions from the IED threat, cf. Ricks, *Gamble*, 21–23. After the "General Betray Us" ad, most public criticism of Petraeus began to disappear, at least to the extent that he would become a media icon and be appointed CIA director by the most liberal president in a generation.

61. http://www.gallup.com/poll/147038/Gov-Christie-Unknown-Majority-Americans.aspx?utm_source=alert&utm_medium=email&utm_campaign=syndication&utm_content=plaintextlink&utm_term=Politics; for various official praise of Petraeus, see the hagiography in Broadwell and Loeb, *All In*, 6–7; "no way, no how": 55; fifth star: 216. For an assessment of Petraeus, cf. Gericke, *Petraeus*, 184–88.

62. Biden's remarks were aired February 10, 2010, on *Larry King Live*; cf. http://abcnews.go.com/blogs/politics/2010/02/vice-president-biden-iraq-could-be-one-of-the-great-achievements-of-this-administration/.

63. Petraeus and his own rather exalted idea of being a savior general: Broadwell and Loeb, *All In*, 7. Cf. Jaffe and Cloud, *Fourth Star*, 127–29, for Petraeus's earlier acceptance of the nickname "King David" ("I don't know where the King David thing actually came from, but you had to play that role a bit"; Jaffe and Cloud, *Fourth Star*, 130).

64. On Petraeus and his complex relationship with the Obama administration—a saga not fully understood at the time this manuscript went to press: Broadwell and Loeb, *All In*, 120–22.

65. For Petraeus's problems in Afghanistan, see the sympathetic account of Broadwell and Loeb, *All In*, 199–253; and the more critical Woodward quote: 121, "Bush general": http://www.washingtonpost.com/lifestyle/style/gen-david-petraeus-the-troops-cant-quit/2012/01/19/gIQALYlmKQ_story.html.

66. http://www.themonitor.com/articles/petraeus-54289-iraq-cia.html. On rumors of Petraeus's consideration of resignation, see http://www.weeklystandard.com/blogs/report-petraeus-considered-resigning-over-afghan-drawdown_614981.html. Chairman of the Joint Chiefs post: Broadwell and Loeb, *All In*, 147–48.

67. Broadwell and Loeb, *All In*, 202 (reports of exhaustion "irritated Petraeus to no end").

Bibliography

Appleman, R. E. *Disaster in Korea: The Chinese Confront MacArthur.* College Station: Texas A&M University Press, 1989.

——. *Ridgway Duels for Korea.* College Station: Texas A&M University Press, 1989.

Bailey, A. *The Chessboard of War: Sherman and Hood in the Autumn Campaigns of 1864.* Lincoln: University of Nebraska Press, 2000.

Baker, J. *Justinian and the Later Roman Empire.* Madison: University of Wisconsin Press, 1966.

Ballard, J. *Fighting for Fallujah: A New Dawn for Iraq.* New York: Praeger, 2006.

Bauer, J., ed. *Soldiering: The Civil War Diary of Rice C. Bull.* Novato, CA: Presidio, 1977.

Blair, C. *The Forgotten War: America in Korea, 1950–1953.* New York: Times Books, 1987.

Bowers, W. T., ed. *The Line: Combat in Korea, January–February 1951.* Lexington: University Press of Kentucky, 2008.

——. *Striking Back: Combat in Korea, March–April 1951.* Lexington: University Press of Kentucky, 2010.

Broadwell, P., and V. Loeb. *The Education of General David Petraeus.* New York: Penguin, 2012.

Brownworth, L. *Lost to the West: The Forgotten Byzantine Empire That Rescued Western Civilization.* New York: Crown, 2009.

Burn, A. R. *Persia and the Greeks: The Defense of the West.* Stanford: Stanford University Press, 1984.

Cameron, A. *Procopius and the Sixth Century.* Berkeley and Los Angeles: University of California Press, 1985.

Carter, S. *The Siege of Atlanta, 1864.* New York: St. Martin's Press, 1971.

Cartledge, P. *Thermopylae: The Battle That Changed the World.* New York: Woodstock, 2006.

Castel, A. *Decision in the West: The Atlanta Campaign of 1864.* Lawrence: University Press of Kansas, 1992.

Caudill, E., and P. Ashdown. *Sherman's March in Myth and History.* Lanham, MD: Rowan and Littlefield, 2008.

Cheney, R., with L. Cheney. *In My Time.* New York: Threshold, 2011.

Collins, J. L. *War in Peacetime: The History and Lessons of Korea.* New York: Houghton Mifflin, 1969.

Cummings, B. *The Origins of the Korean War*, vol. I: *The Roaring of the Cataract, 1947–1950.* Princeton: Princeton University Press, 1990.

Davies, J. K. *Athenian Propertied Families.* Oxford: Oxford University Press, 1971.

Davis, B. *Sherman's March.* New York: Vintage, 1980.

Davis, W. *Lincoln's Men: How President Lincoln Became Father to an Army and Nation.* New York: Free Press, 1999.

Delbrück, H. *History of the Art of War*, vol. II: *The Barbarian Invasions.* Lincoln: University of Nebraska Press, 1990.

Einolf, C. *George Thomas: Virginian for the Union.* Norman: University of Oklahoma Press, 2007.

Evans, J.A.S. *The Age of Justinian: The Circumstances of Imperial Power.* London: Routledge, 1996.

Feith, D. *War and Decision: Inside the Pentagon at the Dawn of the War on Terrorism.* New York: Harper, 2008.

Fellman, M. *Citizen Sherman: A Life of William Tecumseh Sherman.* New York: Random House, 1995.

Flood, C. B. *1864: Lincoln at the Gates of History.* New York: Simon and Schuster, 2009.

Franks, T., with M. McConnell. *American Soldier: General Tommy Franks.* New York: Regan Books, 2004.

Frost, F. *Plutarch's Themistocles: A Historical Commentary.* Chicago: Ares Publishers, 1998.

Gericke, B. *David Petraeus: A Biography.* Westport, CT: Greenwood Press, 2010.

Gibbon, E. *The Decline and Fall of the Roman Empire.* Edited by J. B. Bury. London: Methuen, 1909.

Glatthar, J. T. *The March to the Sea and Beyond: Sherman's Troops in the Savannah and Carolinas Campaigns.* New York: New York University Press, 1985.

Goodwin, D. K. *Team of Rivals: The Political Genius of Abraham Lincoln.* Simon and Schuster, 2005.

Green, P. *The Greco-Persian Wars.* Berkeley: University of California Press, 1996.

Grote, G. *Greece*, vol. V. New York: Collier, 1899.

Grundy, G. B. *The Great Persian War and Its Preliminaries.* New York: Scribner's Sons, 1901.

Halberstam, D. *The Coldest Winter: America and the Korean War.* New York: Hyperion, 2007.

Hale, J. R. *Lords of the Sea: The Epic Story of the Athenian Navy and the Birth of Democracy.* New York: Viking, 2009.

Hanson, V. D. "A Stillborn West? Themistocles at Salamis, 480 B.C." In P. E. Tetlock, R. N. Lebow, and G. Parker, eds. *Unmaking of the West: Counterfactual Thought Experiments in History.* Ann Arbor: University of Michigan Press, 2006, pp. 47–89.

———. *Ripples of Battle: How the Wars of the Past Still Determine How We Fight, How We Live, and How We Think.* New York: Anchor Books, 2003.

———. *Carnage and Culture: Landmark Battles in the Rise of Western Power.* New York: Anchor Books, 2001.

———. *The Other Greeks: The Family Farm and the Agrarian Roots of Western Civilization.* Berkeley and Los Angeles: University of California Press, 1999.

Hashim, A. *Insurgency and Counter-Insurgency in Iraq.* Ithaca: Cornell University Press, 2006.

Hignett, C. *Xerxes' Invasion of Greece.* Oxford: Clarendon Press, 1963.

Hirshson, S. *The White Tecumseh: A Biography of William Tecumseh Sherman.* New York: John Wiley and Sons, 1997.

Holland, T. *Persian Fire: The First World Empire and the Battle for the West.* New York: Doubleday, 2006.

Holmes, J. *Fallujah: Eyewitness Testimony from Iraq's Besieged City.* London: Constable and Robinson, 2007.

How, W. W., and J. Wells. *A Commentary on Herodotus: With Introduction and Appendixes*, vol. II. Oxford: Clarendon Press, 1928.

Hughes, Ian. *Belisarius: The Last Roman General.* Yardley, PA: Westholme, 2009.

Jacobsen, C. J. *The Gothic War: Rome's Final Conflict in the West.* Yardley, PA: Westholme, 2009.

Jaffe, G., and D. Cloud. *The Fourth Star and the Epic Struggle for the Future of the United States.* New York: Three Rivers Press, 2010.

Jensen, R. J. *Reagan at Bergen-Belsen and Bitburg.* College Station: Texas A&M Press, 2007.

Kaegi, W. E. *Byzantine Military Unrest, 471–843 B.C.: An Interpretation.* Amsterdam: Adolf M. Hakkert, 1981.

Kagan, K. *The Surge: A Military History.* New York: Encounter, 2008.

Kaldellis, A., ed. *Prokopios: The Secret History with Related Texts.* Indianapolis: Hackett, 2010.

———. *Procopius of Caesara: Tyranny, History, and Philosophy at the End of Antiquity.* Philadelphia: University of Pennsylvania Press, 2004.

Kennett, L. *Sherman: A Soldier's Life.* New York: HarperCollins, 2001.

Lazenby, J. *The Defence of Greece, 490–479 B.C.* Warminster, UK: Aris and Philips, 1993.

Lee, A.D. "The Empire at War." In M. Maas, ed., *The Cambridge Companion to the Age of Justinian.* Cambridge: Cambridge University Press, 2005, pp. 113–33.

Lenardon, R. J. *The Saga of Themistocles.* London: Thames and Hudson, 1978.

Lewis, D. M., et al. *The Cambridge Ancient History* (2nd ed.), vol. V: *The Fifth Century B.C.* Cambridge: Cambridge University Press, 1992.

Lewis, L. *Sherman: Fighting Prophet.* New York: Harcourt, Brace and Company, 1932.

Li, X., A. Millett, and B. Yu. *Mao's Generals Remember Korea.* Lawrence: University Press of Kansas, 2001.

Liddell Hart, B. H. *The Way to Win Wars: The Strategy of Indirect Approach.* London: Faber and Faber, 1941.

———. *Sherman: Soldier, Realist, American.* New York: Praeger, 1958.

Macdonough, J. L., and J. P. Jones. *War So Terrible: Sherman and Atlanta.* New York: Norton, 1987.

Mansoor, P. *Baghdad at Sunrise: A Brigade Commander's War in Iraq.* New Haven: Yale University Press, 2009.

Marszalek, J. F. *Sherman: A Soldier's Passion for Order.* New York: Free Press, 1993.

———. *Sherman's March to the Sea.* Abilene, TX: McWhiney Foundation Press, 2005.

Marvel, W. *The Great Task Remaining: The Third Year of Lincoln's War.* Boston and New York: Houghton Mifflin, 2010.

McClure, A. *Abraham Lincoln and Men of War-times: Some Personal Recollections of War and Politics During the Lincoln Administration.* Charleston, SC: Nabu Press, 2010.

McMurry, R. M. *Atlanta 1864.* Lincoln: University of Nebraska Press, 2001.

Miller, B. *John Bell Hood and the Fight for Civil War Memory.* Knoxville: University of Tennessee Press, 2010.

Millett, A. *The Korean War.* Washington: Potomac Books, 2007.

———. *The War for Korea, 1950–51: They Came from the North.* Lawrence: University Press of Kansas, 2010.

Mitchell, G. C. *Matthew B. Ridgway: Soldier, Statesman, Scholar, Citizen.* Harrisburg, PA: Stackpole Books, 1999.

Moorhead, J. *Justinian.* New York and London: Longman, 1994.

Moyer, M. *A Question of Command: Counterinsurgency from the Civil War to Iraq.* New Haven: Yale University Press, 2009.

Norwich, J. L. *Byzantium: The Early Centuries.* New York: Alfred A. Knopf, 1989.

Packer, G. *The Assassins' Gate: America in Iraq.* New York: Farrar, Straus and Giroux, 2005.

Podlecki, A. *The Life of Themistocles: A Critical Survey of the Literary and Archaeological Evidence.* Montreal: McGill-Queen's University Press 1975.

Rees, D. *Korea: The Limited War.* New York: St. Martin's Press, 1964.

Ricks, T. *The Gamble: General Petraeus and the American Military Adventure in Iraq.* New York: Penguin, 2009.

———. *Fiasco: The American Military Adventure in Iraq.* New York: Penguin, 2006.

Ridgway, M. *The Korean War.* New York: Doubleday, 1967.

Robinson, L. *Tell Me How This Ends: General David Petraeus and the Search for a Way Out of Iraq.* New York: Public Affairs, 2008.

Roe, P. *The Dragon Strikes: China and the Korean War, June–December 1950.* Novato, CA: Presidio, 2000.

Rosen, W. *Justinian's Flea: The First Great Plague and the End of the Roman Empire.* New York: Penguin, 2007.

Rumsfeld, D. *Known and Unknown: A Memoir.* New York: Sentinel, 2011.

de Ste. Croix, G.E.M. *The Class Struggle in the Ancient Greek World.* Ithaca, NY: Cornell University Press, 1981.

Sanchez, R., with D. Phillips. *Wiser in Battle: A Soldier's Story.* New York: Harpers, 2008.

Sandler, S. *The Korean War: No Victors, No Vanquished.* Lexington: University of Kentucky Press, 1999.

Sears, S. *The Civil War Papers of George B. McClellan: Selected Correspondence, 1860–1865.* New York: Ticknor and Fields, 1989.

Secrist, P. *Sherman's 1864 Trail of Battle to Atlanta.* Macon, GA: Mercer University Press, 2006.

Shawcross, W. *Allies: The U.S., Britain, Europe, and the War in Iraq.* New York: Public Affairs, 2004.

Sherman, W. T. *Memoirs of W. T. Sherman.* New York: Library of America, 1984.

Simpson, B., and J. V. Berlin, eds. *Sherman's Civil War: Selected Correspondence of William T. Sherman, 1860–1865.* Chapel Hill: University of North Carolina Press, 1999.

Soffer, J. M. *General Matthew B. Ridgway: From Progressivism to Reaganism, 1895–1993.* Westport, CT: Praeger, 1998.

Stanhope, P. *The Life of Belisarius: The Last Great General of Rome.* Yardley, PA: Westholme, 2006.

Strauss, B. *The Battle of Salamis: The Naval Encounter That Saved Greece—and Western Civilization.* New York: Simon and Schuster, 2004.

Stueck, W. *Rethinking the Korean War: A New Diplomatic and Strategic History.* Princeton: Princeton University Press, 2002.

Sword, W. *Southern Invincibility: A History of the Confederate Heart.* New York: St. Martin's Press, 1999.

Symonds, C. *Joseph E. Johnston: A Civil War Biography.* New York: W. W. Norton, 1995.

Tetlock, P. E., R. N. Lebow, and G. Parker, eds. *Unmaking of the West: Counterfactual Thought Experiments in History.* Ann Arbor: University of Michigan Press, 2006.

Treadgold, W. *A Concise History of Byzantium.* New York: Palgrave, 2001.

———. *A History of the Byzantine State and Society.* Stanford: Stanford University Press, 1997.

Trodeau, N. A. *Southern Storm: Sherman's March to the Sea.* New York: HarperCollins, 2008.

Ure, P. N. *Justinian and His Age.* Westport, CT: Greenwood, 1951.

Wainstock, D. D. *Truman, MacArthur, and the Korean War.* Westport, CT: Greenwood Press, 1999.

Ward-Perkins, B. *The Fall of Rome and the End of Civilization.* Oxford: Oxford University Press, 2005.

Wawro, G. *Quicksand: America's Pursuit of Power in the Middle East.* New York: Penguin, 2010.

Weintraub, S. *MacArthur's War.* New York: Free Press, 2000.

West, F. *No True Glory: A Frontline Account of the Battle for Fallujah.* New York: Praeger, 2006.

———. *The Strongest Tribe: War, Politics, and the Endgame in Iraq*. New York: Rantom House, 2009.

Whelan, R. *Drawing the Line: The Korean War, 1950–1953*. Boston: Little, Brown, 1990.

Woodworth, S. *Sherman*. New York: Palgrave, 2009.

Wortman, M. *The Bonfire: The Siege and Burning of Atlanta*. New York: Public Affairs, 2009.

Yon, M. *Moment of Truth in Iraq*. New York: Richard Vigilante, 2008.

Index

A Note on the Author

Victor Davis Hanson is the Martin and Illie Anderson Senior Fellow in Residence in Classics and Military History at the Hoover Institution, Stanford University, and the co-director of the Group in Military History and Contemporary Conflict, a professor of classics emeritus at California State University, Fresno, and a nationally syndicated columnist for Tribune Media Services. He is also the Wayne & Marcia Buske Distinguished Fellow in History at Hillsdale College, where he teaches courses each fall semester in military history and classical culture.